NEWSWORTHY

NEWSWORTHY

THE SUPREME COURT BATTLE
OVER PRIVACY AND PRESS FREEDOM

Samantha Barbas

STANFORD LAW BOOKS
An Imprint of Stanford University Press
Stanford, California

Stanford University Press
Stanford, California

Printed in the United States of America on acid-free, archival-quality paper

Library of Congress Cataloging-in-Publication Data

Names: Barbas, Samantha, author.
Title: Newsworthy : the Supreme Court battle over privacy and press freedom /
Samantha Barbas.
Description: Stanford, California : Stanford Law Books, an imprint of
Stanford University Press, 2016. | Includes bibliographical references and
index. | Description based on print version record and CIP data provided
by publisher; resource not viewed.
Identifiers: LCCN 2016021436 (print) | LCCN 2016018740 (ebook) |
ISBN 9780804797108 (cloth : alk. paper) | ISBN 9781503600836 (ebook)
Subjects: LCSH: Time, inc.—Trials, litigation, etc. | Hill, James,
1908—Trials, litigation, etc. | Privacy, Right of—United States. |
Freedom of the press—United States. | United States. Supreme Court.
Classification: LCC KF228.T549 (print) | LCC KF228.T549 B37 2016 (ebook) |
DDC 342.7308/58—dc23
LC record available at https://lccn.loc.gov/2016021436

Typeset by Bruce Lundquist in 10/15 Adobe Garamond

To the memory of my mother and my father

Contents

NEWSWORTHY

Introduction

Under the law as it currently stands, the press has great latitude to invade the privacy of ordinary citizens. In a series of cases, American courts have held that the press has a legal right—a constitutional right under the First Amendment—to publicize people against their will—to print their photographs, publish their private facts, and thrust them into the public gaze—so long as their affairs are "newsworthy" or "matters of public interest," terms that courts have construed broadly. An authoritative legal treatise, the *Restatement of Torts*, describes privileged "newsworthy" publications as encompassing an array of material, including "publications concerning homicide and other crimes, arrests, police raids, suicides, marriages and divorces, accidents, fires, catastrophes of nature, a death from the use of narcotics, a rare disease, the birth of a child to a twelve-year-old girl, the reappearance of one supposed to have been murdered years ago, a report to the police concerning the escape of a wild animal, and many other similar matters of genuine, even if more or less deplorable popular appeal."[1] It is extremely difficult to win a privacy lawsuit against the news media.[2]

The right to privacy is feeble in the world of print communications and practically moribund in online media. Section 230 of the Communications Decency Act, passed in 1996, exempts publishers of blogs and websites from liability for invasion of privacy. Web hosts are immunized from liability for material posted by third parties, including embarrassing personal facts such as the details of people's sexual affairs, nude photos, and intimate medical information, no matter how much the subjects of unwanted exposure are shamed, threatened, or humiliated.[3]

The United States is an exception in this regard. Europe has a more robust right to privacy that can be invoked against the media. Under circumstances that would be unimaginable in the United States, European courts have subordinated the publishing rights of the press and the public's "right to know" to the individual's right to privacy, defined as a fundamental right of personal dignity. In some

European countries, newspapers or websites can be forbidden from publishing humiliating but ostensibly newsworthy pictures of people or facts in the public record without the subject's authorization.[4] Publications have been prohibited from printing personal information about those who have been convicted of a crime and served their sentences, in the interest of the former criminal's rehabilitation and resocialization.[5] A "right to be forgotten" that requires search engines to remove links to embarrassing or discrediting personal information on demand was approved by the EU's highest court in 2014.[6]

What accounts for this difference? Why are privacy rights relatively weak in the United States, at least when it comes to invasion of privacy by the media? Could we have taken another path?

There is no reason why freedom of the press was destined to trump privacy rights—why the right of the press to publish should be held in higher regard than the individual's right to be let alone. Indeed, there was a point when American law might have gone in a different direction, toward greater protections for privacy and dignity. That moment came in 1967, in the landmark Supreme Court case *Time, Inc. v. Hill.*

~

The events that gave rise to the *Hill* case began fifteen years earlier, in 1952. In September of that year, a family of seven, the James Hill family, was held hostage by escaped convicts in their home in suburban Philadelphia. The family was trapped for nineteen hours by three fugitives who treated them politely, made gracious chitchat with them, took their clothes and car, and left them unharmed. For a few weeks, the Hills were the subjects of international media coverage. Public interest eventually died out, and the Hills went back to their ordinary, obscure lives.

In 1954, an author named Joseph Hayes published *The Desperate Hours*, a "true crime" thriller about a family held hostage in their home by three escaped convicts. *The Desperate Hours* was based loosely on the Hills' real-life story but substantially leavened by Hayes's imagination. The novel was filled with violence and suspense; in the story, the father was beaten, the daughter was sexually threatened, and the family attempted a daring rescue. The book became a best-seller and was made into an award-winning Broadway play, and later a major Hollywood film.

In 1955, three years after the hostage incident, *Life* magazine, the most popular periodical in the country at the time, ran a story on the opening of the play. The

article falsely described the play as a "reenactment" of the Hills' experience, imply-
ing that the family had been abused and the daughters raped. *Life* used the family's
name and a picture of their home to give the piece a "newsy" tie to a "real-life"
crime. The family was devastated by this untrue and embarrassing publicity, which
thrust them into the media spotlight against their will, forced them to relive the
tragedy, and presented them before the public in a false, distorted light. The entire
family suffered; the mother, Elizabeth Hill, entered into a severe depression from
which she never recovered.

The Hills sued Time, Inc., the publishers of *Life*, for invasion of privacy in the
New York courts. They won at trial, and Time, Inc. appealed through the state's
court system, then all the way to the U.S. Supreme Court. Time, Inc. argued that
the judgment for the Hills violated its right to freedom of the press under the First
Amendment. Richard Nixon, who was practicing law at a Wall Street firm in the
years before his presidency, represented the Hills before the Court.

~

Although *Time, Inc. v. Hill* was the first time the Supreme Court addressed
the right to privacy and freedom of the press, the conflict between these two important values was hardly new. The *Hill* case was the culmination of a long and
contentious debate in American law and culture. In the early twentieth century,
in response to the scandalous "yellow" press, states approved a privacy tort, a civil
action for invasion of privacy that allowed individuals to sue over the publication
of embarrassing personal facts, and to recover damages for emotional distress.[7]
With the growth of the publishing and entertainment industries, and increasing
voyeurism and sensationalism in the media, privacy law and litigation expanded
significantly. By the 1950s, plaintiffs whose personal lives were publicized in the
press—their medical histories, personal habits, romantic affairs, and family relationships exposed—were winning judgments for invasion of privacy.[8]

The rise of the tort of invasion of privacy occurred against a backdrop of
widespread concerns with the disappearance of privacy, in all of its meanings
and senses. By the 1960s, personal privacy was seemingly besieged by an array of
forces: not only the media, but governments, employers, researchers, advertisers,
pollsters, and marketers, armed with new electronic surveillance and data collection technologies, including the recently invented digital computer. In 1965,
in the midst of this "privacy panic," the Supreme Court announced its decision

in *Griswold v. Connecticut*. In *Griswold*, the Court declared, for the first time, a broad, albeit vague constitutional "right to privacy," found in "penumbras" and "emanations" of guarantees in the Bill of Rights.[9]

While the invasion of privacy tort was praised for offering protection against an intrusive, exploitative press, publishers decried it as an infringement on their freedoms. Media lawyers described the privacy tort as one of the biggest threats to the publishing industry and the "free marketplace of ideas."[10] A number of courts agreed. While some courts in the mid-twentieth century were expanding liability for invasion of privacy, others went in the opposite direction, limiting the right to privacy in the interest of freedom of the press and the public's right to know the "news."[11] Courts were also increasing protections for the press in the closely related area of libel law. In *New York Times v. Sullivan* (1964), the Supreme Court, altering centuries of established libel doctrine, held that the press had an expansive right under the First Amendment to report on public officials, including a right to publish libelous falsehoods about them, unless the statements were made with "reckless disregard" of the truth. The right of the public and the press to discuss public officials and political affairs, the Court declared, was the "central meaning" of the First Amendment.[12]

∾

It was in this context that *Time, Inc. v. Hill* reached the Supreme Court. The case was decided in 1967 by the Warren Court, at the height of its legendary influence and power. In addition to Earl Warren, civil liberties luminaries Hugo Black, William Brennan, author of the opinion in *New York Times v. Sullivan*, and William Douglas, the author of *Griswold*, occupied the bench. Pitting privacy and freedom of the press against each other, *Time, Inc. v. Hill* forced the Warren Court to navigate between the two constitutional rights it had created and championed.

After arguments by Nixon and Harold R. Medina Jr., a veteran media lawyer representing Time, Inc., the Court initially came down on the side of privacy. A 6–3 majority decided in favor of the Hills, upholding the judgment of the New York courts. The majority opinion, written by Justice Abe Fortas, delivered a scathing critique of Time, Inc. *Life*'s use of the family in the story was not "news," Fortas wrote. It was irresponsible journalism inflicting "needless, heedless, wanton and deliberate injury" on innocent citizens and had no relation to the purpose of the First Amendment.[13]

Expanding the right to privacy established in *Griswold*, Fortas declared that the Hills had a constitutional right to privacy that not only protected them against invasions of privacy by the government but also justified legal protections against an intrusive press. "There is . . . no doubt that a fundamental right of privacy exists, and that it is of constitutional stature," he wrote.

> It is not just the right to a remedy against false accusation. . . . It is not only the right to be secure in one's person, house, papers, and effects. . . . It is more than the specific right to be secure against the Peeping Tom or the intrusion of electronic espionage devices and wiretapping. All of these are aspects of the right to privacy, but privacy reaches beyond any of its specifics. It is, simply stated, the right to be let alone; to live one's life as one chooses, free from assault, intrusion, or invasion except as they can be justified by the clear needs of community living under a government of law. [14]

The constitutional right to privacy was a broad right to personal dignity, and it could, under circumstances, trump freedom of the press. Wrote Fortas: "The deliberate, callous invasion of the Hills' right to be let alone—this appropriation of a family's right not to be molested or to have its name exploited and its quiet existence invaded—cannot be defended on the ground that it is within the purview of a constitutional guarantee designed to protect the free exchange of ideas and opinions."[15]

Had the Fortas opinion come down as law, the Supreme Court would have gestured toward the existence of an expansive right to privacy, one that would have transformed press practices, the scope of the First Amendment, and the tone and content of the news media.

But then it changed its mind.

∿

There was a switch in votes. We need not trouble ourselves with the details right now; they are complex, involving both technicalities in this area of law and internecine politics on the Court—namely, a feud between Fortas and Hugo Black, a First Amendment "absolutist" who believed that the Constitution forbade all restraints on publishing. After discussion and disagreement, the majority that voted for the Hills dissolved; a new 6–3 majority voted in favor of Time, Inc.[16]

William Brennan wrote the majority opinion, issued in January 1967. Invoking the *New York Times v. Sullivan* standard, Brennan held that the Hills could not recover for invasion of privacy unless they could show that *Life*'s story about them was false and that the falsehood was made with reckless disregard of the truth.

The Brennan opinion in *Time, Inc. v. Hill* proclaimed a capacious vision of freedom of the press, one of the broadest in the Supreme Court's history to that time. Human-interest stories, gossip columns, and other less-than-enlightened material—the "vast range of published matter" that appeared in the press, including material that exposed people to unwanted publicity—were protected by the First Amendment, Brennan suggested. If a publication was a matter of "public interest"—if the public was "interested" in it—it was "newsworthy" and constitutionally exempt from liability for invasion of privacy. Brennan dismissed the Hills' privacy argument, claiming that the family had no legitimate expectation of privacy, at least when it came to publicity in the news media: "Exposure of the self to others in varying degrees is a concomitant of life in a civilized community. The risk of this exposure is an essential incident of life in a society which places a primary value on freedom of speech and of press."[17]

Time, Inc. v. Hill dealt the legal action for invasion of privacy a "body blow," in the words of two law professors.[18] What seemed like a possibility in the pro-privacy climate of the 1960s—a strong right to privacy that would permit people like the Hills to recover damages for unauthorized, exploitative media publicity —had been undermined.

～

Time, Inc. v. Hill is a constitutional law classic. It is part of the First Amendment canon and a staple of First Amendment law casebooks. The *Hill* case has been cited in hundreds of cases and over a thousand law review articles. As one of the Warren Court's major First Amendment decisions, and the only case Richard Nixon argued during his time as a practicing lawyer, *Time, Inc. v. Hill* has been the object of a good deal of fascination and curiosity. Despite the significance of the case, there have been no comprehensive, book-length studies of it.[19] Drawing on Richard Nixon's archives and the papers of the justices of the Warren Court, this book is the first to explore the *Hill* case in detail.

Through a narrative of the case, *Newsworthy* presents a portrait of American law, culture, and publishing at a pivotal and transformative moment in the twentieth century. In the postwar era, "privacy"—a right to be let alone, a right to personal autonomy, a right to physical seclusion, and a right to choose–had become a prized value, and its loss portended and greatly feared. The United States was becoming both a privacy-conscious society and a media society, saturated by mass communications produced and disseminated by large media companies. The *Hill* case, pitting an ordinary family against one of the biggest media empires in the country, epitomized what many Americans had come to regard as a pressing issue: the struggle of ordinary citizens to protect their privacy, dignity, and individuality against encroachments by powerful corporations and government institutions.

Newsworthy illuminates two underexplored areas of legal history: the history of libel, privacy, and freedom of the press between 1900 and the 1960s, and the history of American privacy law. There is relatively little scholarship on the history of privacy law, and much of the writing on twentieth-century publishing law and freedom of the press starts with the decision in *New York Times v. Sullivan*.[20] This book traces the development of these areas of law before the 1960s and the many influences that shaped the law, including trends and forces in the publishing industry, in science and technology, and in American culture more broadly. The interplay of law, society, industry, and culture—the intertwined relationship between formal legal doctrines and norms and practices outside the law—is a central theme in the pages that follow.

Part I introduces the Hill family, the *Life* magazine article that gave rise to the lawsuit, and the social context of the case: middle-class America in the 1950s. Part II describes the Hills' lawsuit in the lead-up to the 1962 trial and the unsettled legal terrain on which the battles were fought. Part III details Time, Inc.'s appeal of the verdict for the Hills through the New York courts and then to the U.S. Supreme Court. The 1964 decision in *Sullivan* gave powerful ammunition to Time, Inc.'s claims to an expansive right to freedom of the press that would negate liability for invasion of privacy. The Hills' argument was transformed by *Griswold v. Connecticut*, issued a little over a year later. The appeals in the *Hill* case took place against a backdrop of national concerns with privacy, and the public's sensitivity around privacy issues influenced the course of the case. Part IV describes Nixon's involvement in *Time, Inc. v. Hill,* the proceedings before the Supreme Court, the deliberations that led to the decision, and the impact of the *Hill* decision on politics, privacy, and freedom of the press.

This book is about legal institutions and concepts, and it is also a human story. It is about the personal politics that shape the law and the human sufferings that drive the development of the law and the litigation process. My account of the case focuses on the Hills' experience and the family's efforts over eleven years to use the legal system to restore their dignity, privacy, and reputations. It highlights the insufficiency of the law, in many cases, to redress emotional injuries and those to human dignity and how the legal process can sometimes exacerbate those harms.

Time, Inc. v. Hill is about a choice that the Supreme Court made, and choices that might have been made. It is about possibilities, about paths pursued and those not taken. It is about the intersection of law and culture at a charged moment in the not-too-distant past; it is also about the present, and how we got where we are today. In a world where our privacy is fragile and imperiled, and where the media, armed with new technologies, perhaps more than ever before, threaten our dignity, reputations, and "right to be let alone," the story of the *Hill* case deserves our attention.

PART 1

The Desperate Hours

CHAPTER ONE

The Whitemarsh Incident

On the morning of September 11, 1952, James and Elizabeth Hill got up around six, got dressed, went downstairs, and had breakfast with their five children, as they usually did. The Hills lived in a rented home in the affluent Philadelphia suburb of Whitemarsh Township, in a huge, ivy-covered stone mansion on a 90-acre lot. There were about twenty rooms in the three-story building and a barn in the back that was almost as large as the house. The home was appointed with expensive furniture, and two brand-new Pontiacs sat in the garage.[1]

Through diligence and hard work, James Hill had achieved a comfortable life for his family. Born to a working-class household in Pittsburg, Kansas, in 1908, James had been a star scholar and athlete from elementary school all the way through to the University of Kansas, where he was captain of the baseball team and the basketball team, and was elected to an honor society based on his "character, leadership, scholarship, unselfish service, and breadth of interest."[2] His grades were so high that he got into Harvard Law School; he started in 1929 but dropped out in his second year. After playing basketball for several semiprofessional teams in New England, he enrolled in an executive training program at the Jordan Marsh department store in Boston. During this time he began dating Elizabeth Selfridge, an occupational therapist.[3]

Elizabeth McFie Selfridge, born in 1910, was a Denver native and a graduate of the University of Colorado at Boulder. A psychology major, she had been a member of the Delta Gamma sorority and won a national bathing beauty contest in 1928.[4] After college Elizabeth moved to Boston and took a job at a hospital. In the early 1930s, James and Elizabeth married; their oldest daughter, Susan, was born in 1935, and another daughter, Elizabeth, in 1937. A son, James Jr., came in 1941, and twin sons, Clyde and Robert, in 1948.[5]

James was sales manager at the Dexdale Hosiery Company, which had its mills in Lansdale, about a ten minute drive from Whitemarsh. He organized the company's sales force, coordinated the production of the mills, and worked with major department store clients. Because of job transfers, the family had moved over a dozen times in a decade; they had arrived in Whitemarsh only a year earlier. Whitemarsh was one of Philadelphia's growing suburbs, made possible by rising automobile ownership and low-interest home loans after the war.[6]

In 1952, Elizabeth was a "vivacious housewife," as a local newspaper described her, with a pretty smile and wavy brown hair that was beginning to gray. A full-time mother and wife, she was responsible for all the cooking, cleaning, shopping, chauffeuring, and caregiving for the family. She was a loving and responsible parent, a good friend to many, a member of the PTA, and an efficient home-maker who impressed everyone with her enthusiasm and dedication to her family. Though Elizabeth enjoyed her full life, the burden of her responsibilities weighed on her. The family's moves were especially difficult. Half her time was spent packing, she joked, and the other unpacking.[7]

~

The Hills were symbols and beneficiaries of major social changes that swept the country after World War II. Between 1946 and 1960, America became an affluent society. The gross national product increased about 250 percent, and family incomes almost doubled.[8] White-collar career opportunities multiplied with the expansion of corporations, and in 1956, the number of white-collar jobs outnumbered blue-collar jobs for the first time.[9] Americans went on a shopping spree. Between 1946 and 1950, manufacturers sold 21.4 million automobiles, and by 1960, in a population of fewer than 50 million families, almost 60 million cars were registered.[10] During the 1950s, Americans spent $18 billion annually on recreational pursuits, including books, magazines, and newspapers.[11] Once luxuries, electric appliances and telephones became standard features of the middle-class home.[12]

One of the most stunning consequences of prosperity was the rise of home ownership. Between 1950 and 1960, the number of homeowners in the United States increased by over 9 million, many of them in the suburbs.[13] The rush to build and buy homes was joined by a rush to make families to live in them. Although Americans had long idealized home and family, the 1950s saw a golden age of domesticity. There was a trend toward large families, and a sharp rise in the birthrate, referred to as the "baby boom." The generation born after World War II was the largest in American history. Popular culture centered on family values, as millions spent their evenings watching idealized television families like those portrayed on *Ozzie and Harriet* and *Leave It to Beaver*. After the social upheaval and uncertainties brought about by the war, the home symbolized a secure, comforting private retreat removed from the dangers of the outside world.[14]

Young marriage was the vogue, and for those who could afford it, the wife stayed home and managed family affairs. Domesticity was described as a woman's destiny; *Life*'s 1957 special issue on "The American Woman" featured an essay in which anthropologist Margaret Mead argued that women should not work and that the home was "women's natural habitat."[15] Under the cultural ideal of the "feminine mystique," women were to find fulfillment not in education or paid employment but in their own "femininity"—"sexual passivity, male domination, and nurturing maternal love."[16] The postwar era also marked the creation of the dad — his role as family breadwinner. The idealized middle-class father was an "organization man," a midlevel manager who worked long hours, aspired to advance through the corporate ranks, and was paid handsomely for his efforts.[17]

Though middle-class life was more comfortable than ever before, it was not without burdens, many of them consequences of affluence itself. Wealth created pressures to consume more lavishly than one's neighbors, and many in the corporate world found themselves running what was being described as the "rat race." In his 1955 novel *The Man in the Grey Flannel Suit*, Sloan Wilson wrote of a returning veteran who takes a prestigious public relations job on Wall Street, only to be confronted with crushing emptiness: "All I could see was a lot of bright young men in grey flannel suits rushing around New York in a frantic parade to nowhere."[18] Corporate policy prescribed frequent transfers of personnel, and more families relocated more often in the 1950s than in any previous era—about 33 million Americans moved each year.[19] Noted works of social criticism, from David Riesman's *The Lonely Crowd* to C. Wright Mills's *White Collar*, convincingly demonstrated that Americans were withering spiritually and emotionally despite their material success.[20] Daily life also unfolded against the backdrop of global instabilities and nuclear threats. In 1948 the Soviets blockaded Western access to Berlin; in 1949 they exploded their first atomic bomb. Families built bomb shelters, defense films warned of domestic Communist subversion, and schoolchildren were taught to "duck and cover" in the event of an atomic explosion. The usually optimistic Reverend Norman Vincent Peale spoke of an "epidemic of fear and worry" in the

United States.[21] "Our nation," warned a civil defense pamphlet, is in a "grim struggle for national survival and the preservation of freedom in the world."[22]

Dangers and uncertainties notwithstanding, the national mood remained one of self-congratulatory optimism. "A car was put in every garage, two in many," wrote one commentator at the end of the decade. "TV sets came into almost every home. There was chicken, packaged and frozen, for every pot, with more to spare. Never had so many people, anywhere, been so well off."[23] Observed *Life* magazine in 1952, "We have been watching in the United States something close to a miracle. . . . The once sick American economy has become the wonder of the modern world." "Most of the change has been wrought by a simple but bold economic idea: more of everything for everybody."[24]

American life was becoming "privatized." In the middle-class ethos of the time, success and fulfillment were not to be found in public life and civic engagement, as they once had been, but in the world of the personal, intimate, and domestic—one's family, home, relationships, and material possessions.[25] As people spent more time in their cars and their homes, in their living rooms watching television, immersed in their personal and domestic concerns, private life had become synonymous with the "good life." In 1952—the year when *I Love Lucy* was the most popular television show, when the United States tested its first hydrogen bomb, and when America elected Dwight Eisenhower and Richard Nixon to the nation's two top posts—large, prosperous, suburban families like the Hills, living quiet, insular lives of domestic contentment, were seen as the epitome and embodiment of the American dream.

~

In a federal prison just outside Lewisburg, Pennsylvania, about a hundred miles from Whitemarsh, three men from very different backgrounds were pursuing their own vision of happiness and freedom. On September 10, 1952, Joseph Wayne Nolen, his brother Ballard Nolen, and Elmer Schuer sawed through the window bars of the second-floor cell they shared at the Northeastern Federal Penitentiary. Using a rope made of towels, the Nolens and Schuer lowered themselves to the prison yard, then scaled the walls with a crude metal ladder fashioned out of pipes they'd hidden in the yard.

Joseph Nolen was twenty-six and Ballard twenty-two. Born in mountainous Leslie County, Kentucky, to a coal mining family, the brothers were serving twenty-five-year terms for a bank robbery in 1950. Elmer Schuer, the son of a marble cutter, had been in a gang that robbed several banks in the Chicago area. For his 1950 robbery of the People's Federal Savings and Loan Association, Schuer was serving thirteen years in federal prison. A slender, nervous-looking man who had the word "Lucky" tattooed over a horseshoe on his right arm and "Death or Glory" over a dagger on his left arm, Schuer was just twenty-one.[26]

On the campus of nearby Bucknell University, the fugitives stabbed a campus guard when he refused to drive them away in his car. They walked down the road two miles, broke into a house, got the resident out of the bed and made him drive them to a nearby gun store. They threw the man out of the car, took the automobile, and abandoned it in the woods. Later in the day, they stole another car from outside a farmhouse, drove to West Reading, Pennsylvania, and broke into a sports shop, taking six guns and seven boxes of ammunition. The fugitives went on to Philadelphia, arriving on the morning of September 11. They hoped to find a comfortable suburban home to break into and occupy while they ate, rested, and planned their next move.[27]

~

Around 8:15 on September 11, James Hill left for work in one of the family's brand-new Pontiacs. On the way, he dropped off his daughters, Susan and Betsy, at Norristown High School. Eleven-year-old Jimmy was getting ready to go to school, and he went out the back door to get his bike. Standing before him was a scruffy- looking man with a shotgun pointed at him. "Where are you going?" the man asked. "To school," Jimmy replied. "Not today, get back inside," the man said, as he pushed Jimmy back toward the house.[28]

Joe Nolen knocked at the back door, and Elizabeth answered it. "We're not going to hurt you—we just want your house for a day. If you do what we tell you, nobody will be hurt," he said. As he forced open the back door, Ballard Nolen and Elmer Schuer appeared with shotguns, pointing them at a stunned Mrs. Hill.[29]

The three convicts entered the house and searched it from attic to basement. Joe Nolen, the older brother, was the leader of the gang, and the other two followed his orders. The men said they were hungry, and Elizabeth prepared scrambled eggs, bacon, and coffee. After breakfast, Elizabeth and Jimmy were taken to a second-floor bedroom and locked in with Clyde and Robert, the four-year-old twins.[30]

The men took baths, shaved, and helped themselves to James's expensive toiletries and clothes. According to the *Philadelphia Bulletin*, the executive wore suits that cost around $125.00, $25.00 shoes, and $12.50 monogrammed shirts (around $1,100.00, $220.00, and $110.00 in 2016 dollars, respectively). Joe Nolen picked out a bluish gray suit for himself. When he discovered that the suit didn't fit him, he sat down at an old sewing machine and altered the trousers and sleeves. The thread broke repeatedly, and he asked Elizabeth to help rethread the needle, which she did with shaking fingers. Ballard Nolen was too small to wear James's clothes, so he took one of Jimmy's blue jackets and wore it as a shirt. After the men bathed, shaved, and dressed, Elizabeth recalled, they looked just like "three brisk young men whom you might see in a Chestnut street store waiting on customers."[31]

Around three, Susan and Betsy called from a pay phone to say they had gotten off the school bus and were waiting to be picked up. Elizabeth told them they'd have to walk home. When the daughters returned, Ballard Nolen met them at the door, and the girls thought it was a practical joke.[32] It was only then, when Betsy handed her a newspaper, that Elizabeth realized who her captors were.

The Hills' captivity was the beginning of what would become a weeks-long spree of theft, violence, and murder. The Nolen brothers and Schuer were ruthless, shrewd, experienced criminals, described by the federal judges who sentenced them as "desperate" and "potential murderers." They were also unusually polite. They used no profanity and were courteous and respectful. They offered to play games with the children and teach the boys to shoot. One of the men asked Betsy to join them in a game of poker. Throughout the afternoon and evening, they amused themselves by pointing shotguns at pictures on the wall, telling the boys that they wanted to "improve their aim." They played dance music on the radio. They were so well mannered that they even apologized for interrupting a conversation. They were, in Elizabeth's words, "perfect gentlemen."[33]

⁓

When James got home that evening, he saw Elizabeth standing nervously by the back door. "Please don't do anything that you will be sorry for," she said. "Something terrible has happened to our family." They went inside to find Elmer Schuer and Joe Nolen in the dining room with shotguns. "Mr. Hill, we have taken over your house and we intend to keep it as long as we need it," Nolen said.

"We need shelter. We need clothing. And we are going to stay as long as we need them. If you folks do what you are told, nobody will be hurt."[34]

Nolen invited the Hills to eat dinner, and Elizabeth prepared canned soup, spaghetti, chili con carne, milk, and coffee. The convict sat down at the table, apologized to James for taking over his house, and complimented him on his beautiful children. "That boy has an IQ of 100 already and he's only four," he said, pointing to four-year-old Robert. When Robert asked, "Daddy, what is that man doing wearing your trousers?" James quipped, "That's what I'd like to know," and he and Joe Nolen laughed together.[35]

Night fell. Nolen told the Hills to sleep in one room so he could watch over them. The family trudged upstairs to a third-floor apartment and tried to play a game of hearts. The children dozed off quickly. Elizabeth barely slept, and James sat up all night in a chair at the top of the stairs.[36]

Around midnight, James heard loud noises; the men were rummaging through his closets. Around 3:00 a.m., a car started. About 6:00 a.m., James went downstairs and saw that the men had left. In addition to the car, some luggage and three of his suits were missing. The convicts also took Elizabeth's white rawhide traveling bag, in which they packed extra shirts, socks, and underwear. James waited until 8:00 a.m. before going to a neighbor's house to call the police. Around 8:15, local and state police and the FBI arrived, and the whole family was questioned. The Hills were then besieged by the press.[37]

By noon, representatives from newspapers, television, and radio stations had descended on the Hills' home. Milling around noisily on the porch, they snapped pictures, took notes, smoked, chatted, and yelled at each other.[38] A few reporters pushed their way into the living room. One tore off a screen and crawled in the window. Some tried to question the children.[39]

Unless he made a statement to the press, "the place would practically be torn up," the state police told James.[40] James was at first reluctant, but he agreed. He felt it was important to make clear that no one in the family had been physically harmed. It was especially important to emphasize that the daughters hadn't been sexually assaulted. Premarital virginity was an important value in the culture of the time; if people thought Susan and Betsy had been raped, it would mar their reputations and chances for marriage.[41]

With the police officer and the FBI agent, James wrote out a statement to read to the reporters.[42] Over the din of clicking flashbulbs, he went out on the front porch with the three boys and Betsy. Susan refused to come downstairs, and Elizabeth was so exhausted she had gone to bed.[43] The radio reporters handed James a microphone. In response to questions about whether there had been any violence—"had anybody been struck, how did they act, was there any profanity, did they tear up the house and the furniture"—James explained that the fugitives had been polite and that no one was assaulted. No liquor had been consumed. Elizabeth and the daughters had not been harmed or insulted in any way.[44]

Like so many victims of crime, the Hills were catapulted into the media spotlight. National newspapers—the *New York Times*, *Washington Post*, and *Los Angeles Times*—had front-page articles. The *Chicago Tribune* ran a huge headline: "Escaped Felons Imprison Family Hostage 19 Hours." "Bank Robbers Hold Family in Whitemarsh Prisoners" read the September 12 issue of the *Philadelphia Daily News*. The *Philadelphia Bulletin* announced, "Three Convicts Hold Family Captive 19 Hours In Whitemarsh Home." The major news services—the International News Service, Associated Press, and United Press International—covered it, and the story appeared around the country and the rest of the world. With their morning coffee and doughnuts, Americans from San Diego, California, to Galveston, Texas, to Waukesha, Wisconsin, read not only the details of the hostage incident, but facts about the Hills' personal lives. Articles described the Hills' "palatial" home, the well-dressed family, James's employment at Dexdale, the make and model of the family's cars, and where the children went to school. The location of the house was carefully described; the papers may well have given out the address.

The story needed no embellishment; truth was stranger than fiction. The all-American family, the dramatic prison break, the strange behavior of convicts: the story was at once touching, tragic, and comic, and the press milked it for all it was worth. Accounts emphasized the Hills' calmness and dignity during the ordeal and the fugitives' unexpectedly amiable behavior. "Pardon Me. Convicts Polite to Captive Family" read the story in the Norristown, Pennsylvania *Times-Herald*.[45] *Time* magazine ran a tongue-in-cheek feature on the incident titled "House Party." The article focused on the more light-hearted aspects of the incident, such as the convicts' attempts to befriend the children, Joe Nolen's impeccable tailoring skills, and Ballard Nolen's taste for dance music.[46]

The photographers staged a picture of four of the children sitting in the front yard. The kids, neatly groomed and dressed, appeared stylish, put together, and composed. "Seemingly unruffled by their ordeal during which they were held captive by three escaped convicts . . . are four of the seven members of the Hill family, pictured relaxing on the lawn of their home," read the caption.[47] The photo, a perfect vision of the young, well-off, contented American family, appeared world-wide and became iconic.

~

As the media circus unfolded on the front lawn at Whitemarsh, the fugitives sped north in the Hills' green Pontiac. State and local law enforcement initiated a colossal manhunt. During this time, the Hills were under police protection; all seven members of the Whitemarsh Township Police Department took turns guarding the family.[48]

The trio continued their spree of eating, drinking, driving, stealing, and shooting. Around five in the morning on September 12, two of the men walked into a diner in Hamburg, thirty-five miles north of Harrisburg. They lined up two employees and four patrons, took $135 from the cash drawer, and walked away, telling the six to lie on the floor. Shortly afterward, police manning a roadblock near Allentown saw a two-tone Pontiac sedan go by, and the search went north to that area. Later the fugitives bought chocolate and white milk and a loaf of bread in a country store in Guthsville, two miles north of Allentown. In the tiny eastern Pennsylvania town of Slatedale, a man identified as Joseph Nolen walked into the bar of the Slatedale Hotel and asked what kind of beer they had. When told that the bar served a local beer, he replied, "I never heard of it. Give me one." One of the witnesses said that Nolen drank only part of the beer before leaving. He was "wild-looking and very nervous."[49]

By September 17, when the escapees arrived in New York City, an almost suicidal mania had set in. The Nolen brothers and Schuer held up DeMayo's Gunshop in the Bronx, taking twelve revolvers and automatic pistols and 10,000 rounds of ammunition. They rented a small apartment and went on a three-day drinking spree, gorging on gin, beer, potato chips, sausages, strawberries, and sandwiches. They then proceeded to hold up the Bronx branch of the Manufacturers Trust Company and escaped with $12,680. Two days later, detectives forced their way into the heavily barricaded apartment. Detective Philip LaMonica made his way into the back bedroom and found Joe Nolen standing on the bed, wearing only pants. "I give up," Nolen said, holding out one hand. The other was behind his back. Nolen pulled a gun and began shooting.[50]

In the ensuing battle, the Nolen brothers and LaMonica were fatally shot. Schuer surrendered and was booked on charges of homicide and felonious assault. He later pleaded guilty to robbery and kidnapping charges in a Bronx court and was sentenced to eighty years in prison. Assistant District Attorney Alexander Herman told the magistrate that Schuer was the last survivor of "three mad dogs who set on a path of crime that included kidnapping, robberies, . . . and a homicide."[51]

~

The demise of the convicts, which the Hills heard about over the radio, brought more unwanted attention. Reporters showed up at the Hills' home, demanding photographs, interviews, and statements. Newspapers made reference to the "James Hill family," and several featured pictures of the family and their home. One day Elizabeth and the twins were sitting in the garden, reading a book together. Uninvited, a photographer walked into the yard and snapped a picture without asking.[52] She found it in the newspaper the next day.[53]

Over the next few weeks, James turned down offers from New York and Philadelphia radio stations to broadcast his story. Inez Robb, a nationally syndicated newspaper columnist whose column was carried in 140 newspapers and was a household name in the 1950s, wanted to collaborate with James on an article. He responded flippantly, telling her that he would be glad to give her a story on Dexdale hosiery, the "finest in the world." The Hills were even invited to appear on The Toast of the Town, the popular variety show hosted by Ed Sullivan. Sullivan offered to pay the Hills for an appearance and to "show them the town." James declined; the family was not interested in going on TV, and they'd already seen New York City. While some might have enjoyed the publicity, the Hills wanted nothing more than to be left alone.[54]

The Hills understood that as crime victims, they would attract media attention. Although they were appalled by the conduct of the reporters at their home, the publicity itself did not upset them. What most bothered them was the media's ongoing interest in them. In their view, the "news" had an expiration date. Two or three weeks after the crime, they were no longer newsworthy and had a right to sink back into anonymity. "We wanted to take [the hostage incident] out of our minds just as quickly and as completely as we possibly could," James said. He believed that the family had a "right to be forgotten."[55]

Two months later, the Hills moved from Whitemarsh to Old Greenwich, Connecticut, a forty-five-minute train ride from New York. The center of the hosiery business had always been in New York City, and James convinced the president of his company to take the selling office from the Philadelphia area to New York.[56] The Hills' relocation was reported with great interest by the Philadelphia newspapers. As the *Conshohocken Recorder* reported on November 20, 1952, "The James Hill family will move Monday from their home . . . which plunged them into the nationwide limelight just two months ago. Their removal will write the final chapter in one of the most bizarre incidents ever to take place in Whitemarsh Township police annals."[57] The Sunday *Philadelphia Bulletin* of November 23, 1952, announced, "Captive Family Moving to Connecticut."[58] Shortly before the move, James had been in a minor car accident, and the press seized on that too: "Hill Unhurt. Car Wrecked in Crash," read the headlines. "On the eve of their removal from Whitemarsh Township to Connecticut, fate again singled out the Hill family for a bit of attention. Hill was en route to the plant when his car went out of control, ran up to a bank, was rolled over, and damaged badly." The paper noted that this was a new car the family had purchased, the original one having been impounded by New York police and held as evidence.[59]

By the end of 1952, the family had moved into an expansive 4,000-square-foot home. James had begun work in the New York office of his company, and the children started new schools. Elizabeth threw herself into the community's social life: she joined a sewing group called the PEO, a chapter of the Delta Gamma sorority, and a bridge group. She taught Sunday school at a Congregational church and did cafeteria duty at her children's school. By spring 1953, the media's attention in the family had seemingly died out.[60]

CHAPTER TWO

Fact into Fiction

Many people realized the literary potential of the hostage incident, including Elizabeth Hill. Her experience, she told a local newspaper, seemed like a "stage show or drama in which we were all taking part." "I should write a book—or a least a story on it," she joked.[1] She was not the only one with that thought. In 1954, Joseph Hayes wrote a best-selling novel, *The Desperate Hours*, based loosely on the Hills' ordeal. The novel was adapted into a hit Broadway play and, a year later, a major Hollywood film.

The Desperate Hours turned Joseph Hayes into one of the nation's most sought-after novelists and playwrights. It ignited the career of actor Paul Newman and reinvigorated the fame of an aging Humphrey Bogart. The Hills' misfortunes had launched publishing and entertainment fortunes.

&

In 1953, Joseph Hayes was a struggling thirty-five-year-old novelist and playwright in a frantic search for recognition. Born in 1918 in Indianapolis, the son of a furniture factory worker and the grandson of a former minstrel show performer, Hayes wrote his first play while attending high school in southern Indiana. At Indiana University in the 1930s, he pursued drama and engineering with his wife, Marrijane, an actress and a playwright.[2]

After college Joseph and Marrijane hitchhiked to New York City with $267 to their names. For two years, Joseph worked as an assistant editor for Samuel French, a major theatrical publishing house. When he passed along a check for twelve thousand dollars to an author for only a half-year's royalties, he realized he was on the wrong side of the desk. In 1943, he and Marrijane wrote their first successful play, *And Came the Spring*, a comedy, and Joseph quit his day job. During the next few years, the couple wrote nineteen plays—described as "hilarious hits for the school theater"—published by Samuel French and performed throughout the country.[3]

Hayes's first real notice as a playwright came in 1947, with his melodrama *Leaf and Bough*, which won a prestigious drama prize awarded by the University of Chicago. The noted film and stage director Rouben Mamoulian took on the play, about the son of a dysfunctional family who struggles to win the love of a pure-hearted farm girl. When *Leaf and Bough* debuted on Broadway in January 1949, it was a complete disaster. It closed after three nights, and the production company lost $97,500.[4]

Hayes also wrote scripts for radio and television and freelance articles for national magazines. Wiry, energetic, quick talking, and chain-smoking, Hayes was a disciplined, workmanlike writer who spent most of his waking hours in deep engagement with his typewriter. In 1946, he sold an article to the *Woman's Home Companion* called "The Voice of Yesterday," about a family held hostage by criminals. This marked the beginning of his interest in what he called the "hostage theme."[5]

Every time newspapers reported on a hostage incident, Hayes clipped the story and filed it in a folder. By the early 1950s, the file was quite thick. It included articles on an episode in Nebraska in 1949 in which two brothers named Bistrom and a third criminal escaped from prison and took six people hostage in their car, including a police officer.[6] In 1947, a burglar held a twenty-six-year-old woman hostage after he broke into her home, using her as a shield.[7] A fugitive gunman was shot in a church in Ohio by a state highway patrolman after he held the rector hostage for an hour.[8] In 1951 in Omaha, escaped convicts took a deputy sheriff and an attorney hostage.[9] Three convicts in California went into the home of a family and forced the father, at gunpoint, to go into town and buy a car.[10] In June 1952 in Mahopac, New York, Donald Snyder escaped from the Green Haven State Prison. A day later he appeared at the home of Marvin Arnold, a wealthy executive. Snyder charged into the kitchen, picked up an eight-inch knife from the table, and seized the Arnolds' nine-year-old daughter. The convict stabbed the girl in the stomach, and she died a few hours later.[11]

Hayes lived in Brookfield Center, Connecticut, by the Danbury Federal Penitentiary, and this fueled his interest in the hostage theme. He often stayed up at night wondering what would happen if prisoners escaped and threatened his wife and two young sons. "From the top of our hill in Connecticut it is possible to see, at night, far across a lake, the circle of lights that is the federal correctional institution at Danbury. Bright as a carnival, sinister as a gun, they catch the imagination, hold it in pity, or horror. I have sometimes found myself asking the question, 'What if there were a prison break and one or more of those desperate men escaped in this direction?'" he wrote.[12] The Hills' story in September 1952 captured Hayes's attention, and he put the *New York Times* article on the incident in his clippings folder.

Three months later, the Hayes's eight-year-old son, Jason, contracted pneumonia. He was in the hospital three times, and doctors feared for his life if he spent the winter in the Northeast. In December, the family packed up their belongings and moved for the season to Anna Maria Island, near Bradenton Beach, Florida. Hayes joined a famous writers' colony at Sarasota that included novelist and screenwriter Budd Schulberg and Leslie Charles McFarlane, author of the Hardy Boys mysteries. A dozen authors and journalists met at the same restaurant every week to talk and buy each other drinks based on a game they played using the serial numbers on dollar bills.[13]

Hayes's literary agent had long urged him to write a "suspense mystery" novel. "It seems very important to me that you get a book under your belt," he had written. "Somehow you've got to begin thinking in more secure and stable terms than the magazine field alone."[14] By early 1953, with the family nearly broke, Hayes finally began planning for a novel about a family held hostage by escaped convicts. Using his clipping file for inspiration, Hayes wrote the text of *The Desperate Hours*. He completed the ninety-thousand-word manuscript in six weeks in April and May 1953. It was a "day and night job," he recalled, "done at white heat."[15] The book was published a year later, in March 1954. Within three weeks, it landed on the best-seller list and stayed there for sixteen weeks. It became a Book of the Month, distributed and published by the Literary Guild of America. It was also serialized in *Collier's*, excerpted in the *Reader's Digest*, and published as a paperback by Pocket Books. *The Desperate Hours* sold more than a half a million copies and was lauded as the "hottest literary property" of 1954.[16]

~

The Desperate Hours begins in the early dawn hours outside a federal penitentiary near Terre Haute, Indiana. Three prisoners—Glenn Griffin, his brother Hank, and a third man, Robish—have just broken out of the cell they shared. Running through the woods in the morning fog, the convicts come across a farmhouse, where they attack the farmer and steal his car.

Their plan was to hide out in a suburban home, selected at random, until Glenn's girlfriend could join them with some stolen money. The convicts choose the home of the "Hilliard" family. Dan Hilliard is an undistinguishable but likable personnel manager working in a department store. His wife, Eleanor Hilliard, presides over the home. There are two children, a ten-year-old son and a nineteen-year-old daughter who works but lives with the family. The Hilliards reside in a clean, peaceful, affluent suburb outside Indianapolis.

The fugitives arrive at the Hilliard home at 8:30 a.m. on a late summer day. "The front doorbell rang," Hayes wrote, and "the man who faced [Mrs. Hilliard] on the porch, a very young man with short-cropped but soft-looking and glistening black hair, wore faded blue farmer's overalls and was smiling almost apologetically." The man drew a gun, and "after that, everything happened so fast and with such cool mechanical precision that she was paralyzed, mind and body."[17] The convicts enter the house at gunpoint; the daughter, son, and father return home later in the day to find Mrs. Hilliard in captivity.

The parallels between the Hilliards and the Hills are obvious: an attractive, affluent couple in their early forties, a stay-at-home mother and a father with a respectable white-collar managerial job, a suburban house, a teenage daughter and a younger son, three escaped felons, two of them brothers. In *The Desperate Hours*, as in the Hills' real-life experience, the convicts search the premises for a firearm, point guns at the family, play dance music on the radio, and steal the father's car and fine clothes. The fictional family, like the real family, emerged unharmed; the brothers are killed during their escape in gun battles with the police, and the third convict is captured alive.

But there were also important differences. Most notably, unlike the polite fugitives at Whitemarsh, the convicts in the novel are vulgar, profane, and threatening. "Take it easy lady. You open your mouth, your kid'll come home from school and find your body," Glenn says to Eleanor Hilliard. Though James Hill was unharmed, the father in the story, Dan Hilliard, is beaten into unconsciousness. The convicts put the family "through two days of nightmarish hell," Hayes wrote. The family was "threatened and terrified"; the men "brought violence and the smell of blood and filth" into the home.[18]

The novel is laden with violence and sexual innuendo. Glenn threatens Dan Hilliard menacingly: "You remember Pop I could kill you just for kicks." Robish drunkenly attempts to paw the daughter, Cindy. "Lift your arms baby. I'm gonna search you personal," he says.[19] Glenn and Hank appraise Cindy as a "honey," and Glenn tells Hank that when they leave, they will take the mother and daughter and that Cindy will be "just for" Hank. Advertisements for the book played up this theme. One ad showed a young girl sprawled before the convicts with the text, "a teenage girl at the mercy of escaped killers who haven't seen a woman in years!"[20] Unlike the Hill family, the Hilliards fight back. The son, Ralphie, tries to get a message to the police, and the daughter bites the wrist of one of convicts to get his gun away.

Throughout the story, the fugitives use the mother and son as hostages to make the father and daughter comply with their criminal scheme. Dan is made to go to his office and receive a letter containing large sum of money, which the convicts will use to pay a killer to murder a deputy sheriff whom Glenn despises. Later, Robish shoots a garbage man and demands that Dan participate in the cover-up. When the convicts send Dan out of the house to run errands, he considers going to the police. He hesitates, concluding that it would risk his family, held at gunpoint in the home. In the final scenes, Dan tricks Glenn and gets a hold of his gun. He is tempted to murder the convict but resists. The police learn of the convicts' whereabouts, and they surround the residence. Glenn runs from the house and is shot by the deputy sheriff.

Intentionally or unintentionally, Hayes tapped into powerful cultural themes. Some reviewers looked for—and found—a deeper meaning in the thriller. Only a year before the book's issue, the Korean War had ended. In 1953 the Soviets tested a hydrogen bomb, a year after the first U.S. test in 1952. The House Un-American Activities Committee continued its investigations into alleged Communist infiltration of the government and other prominent institutions. Themes of invasion and violation, especially home invasion—by Russians, criminals, and even space aliens—pervade the popular culture of this time. Writes historian Wini Breines, "literal and figurative boundaries were important in the fifties, a period in which distinctions between them and us flourished."[21]

Rather than react with fear or violence, the Hilliards respond calmly and with dignity. Faced with the opportunity to kill his tormentors, Dan Hilliard hesitates long enough to realize that he is not "one of them." The American way, the book suggests, is to meet violence with nonviolence. As Hayes wrote in the *New York Times*, a major part of the story centers around the father's discovery of "jungle urges of revenge" within himself—even a "passion to murder."[22] That urge is quashed because Hilliard is "civilized"; that is what makes the suburban businessman different from his degraded captors. As the *Washington Post* observed, "In one sense, all of us are as endangered as the Hilliards. And, quite possibly, we too must fight our way against insidious threats to our way of life." [23] "The terror these criminals . . . strike into a normal, sane home will seem almost allegorical to the discerning. How are we to treat the thugs, domestic or international, who threaten our very foundations?" [24] Moralistic gestures notwithstanding, the appeal of the book is largely visceral. Hayes packed the novel with hair-raising close calls and Hollywood-style plot turns that were too fantastic to invite reflection or pause. The book was, for the most part, a mindless page-turner, of the sort one might read to pass the time late at night, on an airplane, or on a day off at the beach.

～

In spring 1954, reviewers throughout the country received copies of *The Desperate Hours* with a strange note attached. "A book came in from Random House the other afternoon with a note tagged to it," wrote the syndicated book reviewer Whitney Bolton. "The note said that Joseph Hayes, back . . . around 1949, had had a play called *The Leaf and the Bough* on Broadway and that most of the critics had taken it apart and this book was being sent along to prove that Hayes was after all a terrific writer. That's a cockeyed way to get a book reviewed." *The Desperate Hours* needed no disclaimer, Bolton wrote: it was "a whale of a story, a big fat whale with tensions, agonies, hopes, and prayers salted deeply into every page." [25] "Turn on your reading lamp above your pillow. Sigh happily. Take a sip of your nightcap and read the first paragraph of *The Desperate Hours*. I bet you will not put this novel of suspense aside until you have reached page 203," commented the reviewer for the *Washington Post*. [26]

In publicity pieces, Hayes described the story as an amalgam of fact and fiction, based on actual hostage incidents but leavened by his own imagination. In an article titled "Fiction Out of Fact" that appeared in the Sunday *New York Times* in January 1955, Hayes explained: "In California, in New York State, in Detroit, in Philadelphia, frightened and dangerous men entered houses [and] held families captive in their own homes." "What of the . . . personal stories involved? What are the thoughts and emotions of the guards and waiting relatives? And what of the inner struggles of the convicts themselves?" *The Desperate Hours* sprang from "conjectures such as these." [27] Referring to both the Snyder incident and the Hill incident, Hayes wrote in the *Literary Guild* magazine, "Over a year ago, the newspapers carried accounts of two [hostage] incidents, both front page stories."

Escapees held a family hostage, "hid there, eating and sleeping, and then left, without violence." "Newspaper readers all over the country breathed relief . . . but an astonishment lingered. How many readers asked themselves *what if?*"[28]

Ads played up the story's "real life" connections. "The . . . distinction of Hayes' novel . . . was that it read like a factual news account," wrote the *Los Angeles Times*.[29] Philadelphia-area reviewers emphasized the link between *The Desperate Hours* and the Hills' experience. "In this tense, compactly built tale of terror Philadelphia readers will recognize a slice of real life out of the fairly recent past," noted the *Philadelphia Inquirer*. "Joseph Hayes has simply drawn to its logical conclusion in a single time sequence what might have happened when three escaped convicts took over the home of a well-known Whitemarsh [family] as a hideout and held members . . . hostages." "The author has transferred his locale to the outskirts of Indianapolis; his convicts are from Terre Haute instead of [Lewisburg] . . . beyond that, he has played out the story that could have developed in Whitemarsh."[30]

After editors at Random House showed galley proofs to Hollywood producers, Hayes was besieged with offers to make *The Desperate Hours* into a movie. Virtually every studio bid on the rights.[31] Humphrey Bogart, who had recently started his own film production company, issued the high bid until he was topped by Paramount Studios. Hayes signed an unprecedented deal with Paramount for $100,000 up front plus a percentage of the gross receipts.[32] The film version of *The Desperate Hours* would be directed by William Wyler, a renowned "master craftsman" of the cinema whose credits included the Academy Award–winning *Mrs. Miniver* and *The Best Years of Our Lives*.[33]

Hayes was also making plans to turn *The Desperate Hours* into a play. In spring 1954, a young actor and theater producer, Howard Erskine, saw proofs of the novel. He read it in one sitting, flew to Florida where Hayes was vacationing, and convinced him that they should turn *The Desperate Hours* into a Broadway production.[34] Hayes and Erskine found backers and created the Desperate Hours Company, a partnership of Erskine, Hayes, and sixty-three "angels," including the composer Stephen Sondheim, novelist Dominick Dunne, and actor John Forsythe. The film actor Robert Montgomery, then hosting an NBC television show, was brought on board to direct. Hayes wrote the stage play and the screenplay in summer 1954, and both the film production and casting for the play started in the fall. The release of the movie was delayed until late 1955 to give the play a chance to succeed.[35]

The play opened in New Haven the first week of January 1955 and in Philadelphia a week later. On February 11, 1955, it debuted at the prestigious Barrymore Theater in New York, where it ran for more than two hundred performances. Critics praised it as "slam bang melodrama," "a lightning-paced thriller,"[36] a "sizzler" in which both the Hilliards and the audience "sweat it out."[37] "Twisting and turning, the play . . . achieves a maximum of melodramatic thrills, if never quite of spine-chilling terror," observed *Time* magazine. Viewers got a sense of "normal life suddenly swimming in nightmare."[38]

Karl Malden, known for his psychologically intense performances, played Dan Hilliard. Malden's acting in *The Desperate Hours* was praised as "majestic," "encompassing a whirlwind of emotions and thoughts."[39] An aspiring twenty-nine-year-old stage and television actor, Paul Newman, was cast as the convict Glenn Griffin, and he gave a "tensely maniacal performance" that was "charged with nervous energy."[40] *The Desperate Hours* launched his career. The production was also celebrated for its "breakfront set," a two-storied, double-decker "cut-out" house that showed several rooms in the Hilliard home. The living room and the kitchen downstairs could be seen at the same time as the master bedroom and the child's bedroom upstairs.[41]

The Desperate Hours won the Tony Award for Best Play and Best Direction in 1955. Hayes received the annual gold medal of the national Theater Club for the best play of the year by an American playwright. The work had an incredible cultural half-life. By 1956, community and school theaters around the country—from the Maxinuckee Playhouse in Kokomo, Indiana, to the Bushkill Theater in East Stroudsburg, Pennsylvania, and the Little Theater in Corpus Christie—were staging productions. In 1967, it was made into an ABC television drama, and the play continues to be performed. The man who had once struggled to keep a roof over the family's head in Florida took his royalties to that state and bought an expansive home. His career as a novelist and playwright spanned the next four decades; successes included a string of crime thrillers and the screenplay for the 1967 Disney movie *Bon Voyage*.[42]

The film version of *The Desperate Hours* opened in October 1955. It was shot in the new, wide-screen Vista Vision format, and in the popular film noir style, with scenes filmed at sharp angles and dramatic lighting that created intense contrasts, heightening the sense of doom. The movie "jabs so shrewdly and sharply at sensibility that the moviegoer's eye might feel that it has not so much been entertained as used for a pincushion," wrote *Time*.[43] Thirty-five years later, the story still had appeal. In 1990, the film was remade, starring Mickey Rourke as the escaped convict and Anthony Hopkins as a modern-day James Hill. Then in his seventies, Hayes collaborated on the screenplay.

Marlon Brando and James Dean, both in their twenties, had been Wyler's first choice for the Glenn Griffin role. Humphrey Bogart, who played a similar role in *The Petrified Forest* twenty years earlier, was ultimately chosen because he had more box office clout.[44] Bogart's escaped convict is humorless, full of rage, and maniacal. He leers murderously at the family, explodes into tantrums, and smashes dishes violently. One reviewer described him as the "epitome of criminal insanity."[45] At the time, Bogart was seriously ill with the cancer that would kill him a few years later, and his haggard, sallow, and sunken-eyed visage heightened the hard-living desperation of the Griffin character. The fifty-eight-year old Academy Award–winner Fredric March, who had come out of retirement for the film, played Dan Hilliard with great poise and gravitas and was lauded for his "impressive dignity as the citizen whose house has suddenly been taken over."[46]

As with the book and the play, the selling point of the film was its real-life foundations. Paramount advertised *The Desperate Hours* as the "Story of a Real Family." "Author John [sic] Hayes based his story on actual facts," wrote one small-town reviewer.[47] According to the critic for the *Saturday Review*, "*The Desperate Hours* gives the impression of having been the result of [the] . . . headline THREE ESCAPED PRISONERS TAKE OVER HOME OF RESPECTABLE FAMILY."[48] A key scene in the film featured a newspaper with a screaming headline that could have come out of the Philadelphia papers in September 1952: "Convict Trio Still at Large." The moviegoer got a sense that he was "witnessing . . . an animated newspaper headline," *Time* observed.[49]

Though the acting was stellar, the real star and hero of The *Desperate Hours* was the hardy, resourceful middle-class American family, said critics. The film opened with a shot of a pristine, placid suburban street on a bright summer morning; the well-dressed, well-groomed, cheerful Hilliard family could have stepped out of the television show *Leave It to Beaver* (the exterior of the house in *The Desperate Hours* was in fact later used on the set of *Leave It to Beaver*).[50] "The Hilliards are people of courage and pride," observed the *New York Times*. "Their home represents to them an ideal of living. Apart from the terror of being threatened with guns, they feel that the privacy of their home has been violated."[51] The *New York*

Post's Richard Watts Jr. described *The Desperate Hours* as "a cheering and credible little tribute to the potential courage of decent average people when pushed too far."[52] "The story that is important is not why do escaped criminals seize a home as a hideout, or how they do it. The story is: what happens inside that home to decent, honest, unpretentious people."[53] Ads for the movie proclaimed, "As long as there are families, *The Desperate Hours* will be remembered."[54] The Hilliard family's devotion to the integrity and privacy of their home may have been the most compelling aspect of the plot in the family-centered culture of the time.

~

One day in April 1954 a friend told Elizabeth Hill that her story had been "written up into a book." Another gave her a copy of *The Desperate Hours* and a newspaper clipping saying that the book had been written based on "an incident that happened to a family living in Whitemarsh." That is "not our story," Elizabeth said angrily. "We have nothing to do with that story."[55] Elizabeth's friends talked constantly about *The Desperate Hours*, and the children were teased and called "gun molls."[56] James was peppered with questions from his clients and colleagues. "They wanted to know which one of the children was this character. They . . . confused parts of the *Desperate Hours* story with my family," James recalled.[57] At parties, he and Elizabeth were cornered by friends who insisted on talking about the book, the play, and the movie.[58]

The family was suddenly confronted with memories they had worked hard to put behind them. They feared people would think they'd collaborated with Hayes on the book, or they'd sold the rights to their story—that they were making money off their tragedy. Every time someone asked him about *The Desperate Hours*, James told them it had nothing to do with his story. "My family was not subjected to any violence. They were not subjected to that type of language . . . not subjected to the possibility of the women being violated."[59] "There had been no molesting of my wife or of my daughters, there had been no profanity, and . . . there had been no harm to any of us."[60] The media circus started again. In April 1954, a freelance writer for *Male* magazine wrote to James asking if he could talk to the family. The editor thought "such an article would help the public to understand how to contend with criminals."[61] "For the best interests of our children we have felt that it was best to avoid any course of action that might remind them of our experience in September 1952," James replied curtly. "Following this policy, we have refused all radio, television, magazine, [and] newspaper offers connected with that experience."[62]

After the book came out, Elizabeth became depressed and withdrawn. She felt as if she was being whispered about wherever she went. She stopped going to social events, and her fashionable clothes didn't please her anymore. The unwanted exposure in *The Desperate Hours* added to the stress she was already experiencing in her life. That summer, she recalled, she had "two girls home from college finding summer jobs, a high school boy playing baseball," and two young sons with free time on their hands. She was trying her hardest to be "a good mother, wife, and citizen," but she felt tired and overwhelmed. A local doctor prescribed hormones and vitamins, to no avail.[63] Her condition worsened in February 1955 when *Life* ran a photoessay describing the Hills—by name—as the family in *The Desperate Hours*.

CHAPTER THREE

The Article

In the 1950s, *Life* was America's most popular magazine. With its bold, oversized images, the weekly publication was the common denominator of American culture, enjoyed by millions. Half of the population over the age of ten looked at *Life* regularly.[1] In 1954, the magazine sold a hundred million dollars of advertising, the largest of any publication to that time.[2] The average issue used four thousand tons of paper and one hundred tons of ink, and it filled ninety freight cars.[3] The writer Russell Baker, working for the post office in Baltimore, dreaded the weekly arrival of the weighty tome. "The great backbreaker was *Life* magazine," he wrote. "Every Baltimorean with a mailbox seemed to subscribe."[4] *Life* was a trendsetter and tastemaker, and a creator and mirror of American culture. Its mission was to educate and amuse by providing a vivid chronicle of real life—showing people and the world as they really were, in all their splendor, curiosity, and horror.

Life was the jewel of Time, Inc., the most prestigious publishing company in the nation. The empire had begun back in the 1920s when two Yale graduates, Henry Luce and Briton Hadden, came up with the idea for a weekly newsmagazine. Aimed at the modern professional who wanted to be informed but had little time to read, *Time* would be a readers' digest, a breezy summation of articles taken from other sources. In its first issue in March 1923, the week's news was lifted almost entirely from the *New York Times* and rewritten in the magazine's famously snarky style. (The double epithet—"snaggle-toothed, weed-whiskered"—and the inverted sentence—"backwards flows the sentence in *Time*"—were among "Timespeak's" most notorious elements).[5]

Punchy, pithy, and arrogant, *Time* was a runaway success, and it spurred the creation of a business monthly, *Fortune*, in 1930. In 1935, a weekly newsreel based on *Time* stories, the "March of Time," debuted, and it was viewed by more than 20 million moviegoers each week.[6] A year later, Luce, who assumed control of the empire after Hadden's death, came up with the idea for *Life*. The concept was brilliantly forward looking: a general interest magazine that would report the news almost entirely through photographs.[7] All 200,000 newsstand copies sold out the first day.[8] By its seventh issue, *Life*'s circulation reached 760,000, making it the most popular new magazine in history.[9]

Like *Time*, *Life* bore the unmistakable imprint of its creator. Henry Luce—the son of Presbyterian missionaries, raised in China, and a 1920 graduate of Yale—became infamous in his long publishing career for his grandiosity, pro-business conservatism, rabid anticommunism, and messianic zeal. A complex, mercurial personality, a man of great cruelty, energy, and ambition, Luce was a pioneer of modern journalism with an uncanny ability to gauge the needs, anxieties, and sensibilities of his time.[10] He was widely regarded as a genius, a prodigious intellect who wrote dense, excitable prose at phenomenal speed, ranging from vigorous treatises on foreign policy to irritated directives to his staff. He was the stereotypical media titan, "responsible to his balance sheet and conscience alone, thumbing his nose at advertisers, politicians, correspondents, critics, anyone who stood between him and the view of reality he expected his magazines to deliver," wrote Time, Inc. journalist Theodore White.[11] His most passionate concerns were "individualism, God, the United States, and Time, Inc.—probably in reverse order."[12]

As with all his other magazines, Luce had great hopes for *Life* beyond just making a profit. *Life* would serve as an agent of education, civilization, and uplift, offering readers a record of current history, revealing "the nature of the dynamic social world in which we live."[13] The magazine's initial title was *The Show-Book of the World*.[14] Luce vowed that *Life* would never pander to its readers. Most Americans, Luce said, would rather be enlightened than titillated; self-education was a national passion, and people wanted to learn about "science, deep philosophy, and world situations." Luce attacked what he described as the "give the public what it wants" theory of journalism. In it lay "the danger of sensationalism and the danger of mediocrity," and "another and greater danger: the danger that such a press will not give the people what they must have"—the news that they "will perish without."[15] Luce believed that the press had a constitutional duty, "under the clause of the Bill of Rights which guarantees freedom of the press," to report "the news." "Whatever other duties the press may have, it has no more vitally important duty than to tell the people what the situation *is*."[16]

By 1940, *Life* had earned a reputation as a serious source of information on public affairs, albeit with a distinctive slant. The magazine was pure Americana, serving up Luce's ideal of nationalism, capitalism, classlessness, and a democratic people devoted to the values of community, family, and independence. *Life* was celebrated for its patriotic coverage of the battlefield and the home front and was instrumental in swaying public opinion in favor of U.S. involvement in the war. In the magazine's pages, home front frivolity and shocking images of tragedy existed side by side: pictures of bombed ruins, brave soldiers, and invaded cities were juxtaposed with views of movie star Betty Grable in a bathing suit, high school proms, and kids frolicking at county fairs. In what had become its classic formula, the magazine blended news, ideology, and show business.[17]

The 1950s were *Life*'s glory years. Although Luce had always championed American progress and prosperity, the nation's postwar affluence became a near-obsession for the publisher. Luce and his wife, the ambassador, playwright, and former congresswoman Clare Boothe Luce, were staunch conservatives and influential in the Republican Party. *Life* promoted the Eisenhower administration and the dominant "consensus" thinking of the time: the belief that America was the most successful and democratic nation in the world, reaching toward even greater wealth and freedom.[18] Americans were "putting their minds and energies to work" and enjoying "football games, automobile trips, family reunions, and all the pleasant trivia of the American way of life," it reported.[19] The country was "embroiled in no war, impeded by no major strikes, blessed with almost full employment" and "delighted with itself."[20]

Editors tried to boost *Life*'s cachet by publishing work from political and literary notables. In 1952, the magazine ran the entirety of Hemingway's *Old Man and the Sea*, and in 1953, recently retired President Truman sold *Life* the rights to his memoirs. There were more ambitious educational features and projects, such as a twelve-part series, "The World We Live In," which involved the efforts of *Life*'s best photographers, 10 specially commissioned artists, and 255 consultants.[21] Postwar *Life* also increased its coverage of the news. Major stories of the decade included the McCarthy hearings, the civil rights movement, the Korean War, and other traditionally newsworthy events such as earthquakes, assassinations, and plane crashes.[22] A promotional pamphlet, "How *Life* Gets the Story," celebrated the magazine's winning journalistic formula: its "ability to use camera equipment, reportorial skills, and every imaginable production device" to serve the "American right to know what is going on."[23]

"News" and culture notwithstanding, *Life*'s pictures and breezy, lightweight features were responsible for its tremendous appeal. *Life*'s managing editor had a budget of around $10 million a year, the highest of any other magazine, and much of it went to high-quality images.[24] The typical issue in the 1950s was a grab bag of substance and ephemera. Photoessays on the 1956 coup in Hungary, thought-provoking reports on small-town America, features on the Hollywood glitterati, and pictures of young women on the beach appeared seriatim. The magazine's huge, lavish photos, taken by some of the most renowned photographers of the day, depicted both major world events and the minor curiosities of everyday life, with a healthy dose of celebrity and cheesecake thrown in—actresses and sports figures were popular cover icons. In many ways, the magazine, with its big, bold illustrations, had the same expansive, showy visual feel as two other media of critical importance in that era: movies and television.

To Luce, the most poignant symbol of America in the new "age of abundance" was the middle-class home and family. Because "people are interested in people," as Luce often said, *Life* used stories about average families to represent the successes of postwar society.[25] A story and picture of a real family of five was used as the lead for the January 5, 1953, cover story, "The American and His Economy."[26] For one series on the daily life of a typical family, reporters rented a nearby house, and over the course of a year, they took twelve thousand pictures of them. Features depicted parents and their children engaged in routines such as fixing a car, planting a garden, playing games, and grocery shopping—prosaic acts, to be sure, but testaments to the peace and prosperity that made them possible. "*Life*'s special gift," writes critic Wendy Kozol, "was to . . . [locate] the tensions of an unfamiliar world within the seemingly familiar and nonthreatening orbit of the happy nuclear family."[27]

Like owning a car, a television, and a home in the suburbs, a subscription to *Life* became part of the middle-class lifestyle. In 1950, *Life*'s primary audience was young men and women living in northeastern cities who had a new car, a television, and at least one year of college. Ninety-five percent of professional and semiprofessional households subscribed. In an era when magazine readership was at an all-time high, *Life* was the leader of the pack, far ahead of its closest competitors *Collier's*, *Look*, and the *Saturday Evening Post*. Its circulation was almost twice that of the *Post* and almost three times that of the *Ladies' Home Journal*; its audience surpassed the popular Jack Benny radio show and television's *Colgate Comedy Hour*. At its peak in 1956, the magazine sold 8 million copies a week in the

United States and Canada and almost another 1 million abroad. When managing editor Ed Thompson was asked for *Life*'s primary competitor, he quipped, "the neighborhood bowling alley."[28]

~

Life was headquartered on the thirty-first floor of the Time-Life Building at 9 Rockefeller Center, directly above *Time*. In contrast to the floor below, where a soothing, genteel reception area with plush carpeting, velvet sofas, and irides-cent curtains beckoned visitors into the world of Time, Inc., *Life*'s office was a frenzied hive of activity, cluttered with long wooden layout tables, light boxes, paper-strewn desks, and overflowing ashtrays.[29] As many as 150,000 words were generated for a single issue of *Life*, and only a fraction made it into print.[30] An ed-itor saw about thirty-five pictures for every one used in the magazine, and photo-graphs were littered across desks, countertops, and floors.[31] The managing editor juggled the contents of as many as six issues at a time. Saturday nights, when the last sixteen pages of an issue went to press, saw the beginnings of a grueling work shift that sometimes continued into Sunday morning.[32]

Tom Prideaux was the chief editor of the entertainment department, in charge of *Life*'s reporting on movies, television, theater, and nightclubs. His job con-sisted, in his words, of deciding "what stories to shoot, what stories were suitable, what stories were newsworthy, requesting that photographers be assigned to these stories . . . , making the arrangement to have the stories photographed . . . [and] making layouts.[33] He was also a respected theater critic, known as *Life*'s "one-man theatre editorialist."[34]

Like so many in Time, Inc.'s top echelons, Prideaux was a product of the Ivy League.[35] A forty-seven-year-old native of Hillsdale, Michigan, born to a wealthy business family, he had been a literary wunderkind at Yale in the 1920s: the Class Poet; chief editor of the literary magazine; a member of the Elizabethan Club, dedicated to "tea, the art of the book, and literature"; and Chi Delta Theta, a secret literary society. For a time, Prideaux was Yale's "leading literary man." After college, he taught English for five years at the private, experimental Lincoln School in New York, authored plays, and wrote a book on prehistoric Egypt. Prideaux started at *Life* as a reporter in 1938 and worked his way up to a senior editorial posi-tion. Under his leadership, *Life*'s entertainment section gained a reputation as one of the most sophisticated outlets for theatrical reporting in magazine journalism.[36]

Prideaux was cocky, headstrong, and eccentric.[37] His speech was packed with puns, allusions, trivia, and poetry, and he was famous for his total recall of pop song lyrics. A lifelong bachelor, Prideaux lived for twenty-six years in the same Manhattan apartment, filled with ancient Greek sculptures, plexiglass tables, reproductions of Rubens paintings, modern art, Beethoven recordings, and rock and roll records. Most of the time he looked rumpled, confused, and slightly distressed; his most distinguishing physical feature was a set of huge, uncontrolled eyebrows, which accentuated an already stern gaze.[38] He wore a bow tie and was crotchety when writing. He was famous at *Life* for launching a campaign—not in jest—against the use of canned music in company elevators.[39] It was Prideaux who was responsible for the Hills' appearance in *Life*.

In late 1954, Bradley Smith, a freelance photographer who did work for *Time* and *Life*, was riding home to Connecticut from New York with his friend Joseph Hayes.[40] Hayes and Smith were scheming about how *The Desperate Hours*, which was about to open in Philadelphia, might be sold to the press.[41] Hayes told Smith that one of the hostage incidents that inspired *The Desperate Hours* had taken place in Philadelphia, and Smith saw the publicity potential of this connection. Shortly after, Smith ran into Prideaux in the halls of the *Life* office,[42] and he asked Prideaux if he'd heard about *The Desperate Hours*. Prideaux said he'd read about it in the papers. Smith suggested that *Life* run a photoessay on the play's opening in Philadelphia, connecting it to the Hills' captivity in 1952.[43] Prideaux was running to make a deadline; he acknowledged Smith and went back to his office.

A few days later, Prideaux called Hayes, who was in Philadelphia, and asked him if he was interested in having *Life* come down to take pictures of the cast doing scenes in the Hills' former home.[44] A photoessay tying the opening of the play to the Hills' saga would resonate with one of *Life*'s most prominent themes, Prideaux said: the dignity of the ordinary, middle-class American family. Connecting the play to a real-life hostage incident would be a great hook for the article—in Prideaux's words, an "interesting gimmick" to make the story dramatic, compelling, and "newsy."[45]

≈

In the middle of January 1955, Prideaux took the train to Philadelphia to meet with Hayes and theatrical producer Howard Erskine. With him was Laura Ecker, a short-haired, bespectacled Vassar graduate who was a researcher for the theater department.[46] Each department at *Life* consisted of at least one male writer and one researcher, usually a young, unmarried woman with a degree from an elite college. The researcher's job was to fact-check copy and do the legwork for the stories assigned to her.[47] The stated rationale for this division of labor was that men were "dreamier and more creative," while women were more "down-to-earth and practical."[48] The real reason was sexism: Time, Inc. was a man's world, run by an "all-male aristocracy" of executives and editors.[49]

Prideaux and Ecker met Hayes and Erskine at a downtown hotel, and they took a cab out to Whitemarsh. The big mansion looked just as it had in the news photos, except that the yard was now covered with snow. With permission of the current residents, Hayes and Prideaux walked through the house. Hayes told Prideaux that the house adequately represented his vision of the Hilliard home, and he agreed to do the story.[50] Prideaux assured Hayes that *Life* would capture the spirit of *The Desperate Hours*; it was a "moving story" about an American family, their courage and devotion, their "level-headedness, stamina, [and] sticking together."[51]

That evening, Prideaux and Ecker attended a performance of the play. A few weeks later, Prideaux, a researcher named Virginia Shevlin, and *Life* photographer Cornell Capa went back to Philadelphia to photograph the cast doing scenes in the Whitemarsh home. Back at the *Life* office, film editor Peggy Sargent reviewed Capa's photographs, printed on a contact sheet, and selected several to be enlarged. The blown-up prints were sent to Laura Ecker, who laid them out in a grid format and mounted them on cardboard. Prideaux took the photo layout to managing editor Ed Thompson to get the go-ahead to write the text of the story.[52]

A fifty-year-old former newspaper reporter from North Dakota, regarded as *Life*'s finest managing editor, Thompson was responsible for virtually everything that appeared in every issue.[53] Although Luce was involved in shaping *Life*'s overall vision, he trusted day-to-day oversight of the magazine to Thompson.[54] Like Luce, Thompson believed that *Life* had a duty to report the news, and the more dramatic the better—he loved "catastrophe, heroism, crime, politics, conspiracy, [and] heartbreak."[55] The key to *Life*'s success, he believed, was "good solid sensations."[56] "The bulk of our circulation is attracted by the kind of sensational reporting that only *Life* produces," he wrote in a memo to Luce.[57] He was notorious for his "hard news instinct" and his "slam-bang, beat the opposition approach" to journalism.[58]

Thompson approved Prideaux's idea for *The Desperate Hours* story, with its interesting "real-life" connection. To play up the "newsy" angle, he asked Prideaux to include in the photoessay a *Philadelphia Bulletin* headline from September 12,

1952, "Bank Robbers Hold Family in Whitemarsh Prisoners," as well as a photo of the Hills' former home.[59]

Prideaux sat down to write the captions and the text block, the short article that would introduce the photos.[60] Text blocks were usually based on preexisting news sources, such as wire service reports and published newspaper articles. Laura Ecker went to Time, Inc.'s reference library, known as the morgue, a large room filled with manila envelopes stuffed with news clippings, and found reviews of the play from the *New York Times*, *Variety*, and other publications, which she put in a green envelope and gave to Prideaux. Also in the "story file" were the 1952 *New York Times* story on the hostage incident and the January 30, 1955, *Times* article by Joseph Hayes, "Fiction Out of Fact," in which Hayes explained his inspiration for *The Desperate Hours*.[61]

The first draft of the article connected *The Desperate Hours* to the Hill incident but suggested that the play and novel were not an exact account of the family's experience. *The Desperate Hours* was "somewhat fictionalized":

> In 1952, a young Indianapolis author, Joseph Hayes, read a hair-raising report of a suburban Philadelphia family held prisoner in their home by three escaped convicts. This true story sparked off Hayes to write a novel, *The Desperate Hours*, which he later did as a screenplay. While it was being filmed, a New York producer persuaded Hayes to turn his novel into a Broadway play. The movie producers agreed not to release the film for a year in order to give the play a chance to pay off. Now that *Desperate Hours* is a Broadway hit, and two more companies are rushing into production, Hayes stands to make a half million dollars on his Philadelphia horror story. Directed by Robert Montgomery and expertly acted, Hayes' play is a somewhat fictionalized but heart-stopping account of how one family rose to heroism in a crisis. *Life* photographed this play at its Philadelphia tryout and transported some of the actors to the actual house where the family, who no longer live there, were besieged. On the next page scenes from the play are reenacted on the original site of the crime.[62]

Prideaux typed up his work, carbon copies were made, and it was sent around the office for fact checking and editing.

∾

Every article that appeared in *Time* and *Life* was a product of "group journalism": writers wrote text, researchers checked it, copy editors refined it, a series of senior editors distilled it, and it emerged in final form in the magazine. Luce believed that this group technique produced a consistent tone and viewpoint by bleaching all material of authorial idiosyncrasies. He also thought that the group approach yielded greater accuracy than having a single author responsible for a story. "Not since the Vatican Council of 1870," joked one *Time* writer, "has the world witnessed such a heroic effort" to arrive at accuracy "through the impersonal collaboration of many minds." "After such triple-distilling the indescribably pure product is ready for the printer—who presumably wears antiseptic rubber gloves."[63]

Luce never claimed that his magazines were objective. "I am biased in favor of God, the Republican Party, and free enterprise. . . . Our readers know where we stand," he once said.[64] To "hell with objectivity." Luce believed it was impossible "to select, recognize, and reorganize facts without using value judgments."[65] Since there was "no such thing as objectivity," Time, Inc.'s goal was simply to be "fair."[66] At the same time that Luce rejected objectivity, he aspired to accuracy. The basic facts of an article—the "who, what, where"—should be error free, but the interpretation of the story—the how and why—was apparently a matter of discretion.[67] Luce claimed to be obsessed with "facts" and the "truth." "The whole editorial staff" of Time, Inc., Luce declared, was "joined together in the search for Truth."[68]

For over a century, accuracy had been a paramount ideal in journalism. In the early twentieth century, in an attempt to distance themselves from the disreputable practices of nineteenth-century publishers, including outright faking of the news, the American Society of Newspaper Editors adopted accurate reporting as a mandate of the profession. Its code of ethics, from 1923, directed that "by every consideration of good faith a newspaper is constrained to be truthful" and that it was "the privilege, as it was . . . the duty . . . to make prompt and complete correction of . . . serious mistakes of fact or opinion, whatever their origin."[69] In 1947, the Hutchins Commission on Freedom of the Press, a prestigious academic commission devoted to studying press affairs—and funded by none other than Luce—announced that the "first requirement" of a "free and responsible press" was "that the media should be accurate. They should not lie."[70] The public had a right to know the "truth," as fairly and precisely as could be told. Another reason factual accuracy was held in high regard was the threat of lawsuits, particularly suits for libel.

Time, Inc. was at the forefront of this accuracy movement in mass publishing. In the 1920s, *Time* had created its pioneering research department, dubbed the "headquarters against errors of fact." Researchers were given a copy of every article that was to be published and instructed to check every word. The researcher was responsible for vouching that each word was spelled correctly, used correctly, and factually correct. To make sure she actually saw each word, the researcher was to put a dot over every word she verified. This "dotting function" was seen as "sacrosanct."[71] During the magazine's heyday in the 1950s, the chief of research, Marian McPhail, known as *Life's* "dean of women," supervised the research department.[72]

Despite this elaborate process, major errors of fact pervaded all the Time, Inc. publications. One day a freelance writer spotted in *Life* a page lifted from his book. The researcher had failed to put quotation marks around the statement, and *Life* used it without alteration.[73] The author, George Horace Lorimer, discovered fourteen important factual errors in *Time's* short article about his career.[74] In one article, icosahedrons were described as "two-sided solid figures" (they have twenty sides). The New York Hilton Hotel was said to provide its guests with "free parking" (in reality, it charged $4.75 per day). Amy Vanderbilt was described as the "official etiquette consultant for the U.S. State Department." No such position existed.[75] In the opinion of many journalists, the Time, Inc. magazines, despite being weekly publications with long story lead times, had more errors than most newspapers and were the worst on accuracy of all the newsmagazines. When the Washington press corps in 1962 was asked to rank all the magazines in the country for their reliability, *Time* got only nine votes, compared to seventy-five for *Newsweek* and sixty-six for *U.S. News and World Report.*[76]

One reason for the profusion of mistakes was the exhaustion of the researchers. Researchers often dotted words they couldn't verify because they were burned out, tired, and frustrated. One researcher was assigned to check an article on a rare Los Angeles snowstorm. The writer claimed that it was so cold that the oranges froze and dropped from the trees. The researcher searched for confirmation but couldn't find it; disgusted, the researcher marked the black dots anyway.[77] Sometimes senior editors would simply ignore the researchers' dots if they felt they got in the way of the story they wanted to tell. Luce's reporters gathered facts, but in Time, Inc.'s editorial offices, "those facts were assembled by his editors to his design," observed

Theodore White. "Freedom of the press, [Luce] held, ran two ways: his reporters were free to report what they wished, but he was free to reject what they reported, or have it rewritten as he wished."[78]

The Luce publications were notorious for "gimmicking" the news—distorting facts to make them seem more dramatic and sensational than they really were. Reporters in New York, Washington, and elsewhere saw the daily news come in over the wires and deplored how *Time* and *Life* spun it. The distortion was said to be even worse on *Life*; in *Time*, points were "buried in words," but in *Life*, "it was given a headline and . . . a perhaps factitious reality by the massive impact of pictures," observed one editor.[79] College journalism classes studied *Time* as an example of the egregious "distortion and coloration of news."[80] According to Luce biographer William Swanberg, the Time, Inc. publications made few typos but "oozed with the inaccurate or misleading . . . because of the constant effort to improve on fact and make a 'good story.'"[81] "News manipulation was sheer policy . . . performed as a matter of office routine. It often resulted in entertaining trivia chiefly in its corruption of gimmick-seeking editors and writers and its general and pervasive debasing of the truth."[82]

∾

A week before *The Desperate Hours* article was scheduled to run, Laura Ecker fact-checked it using newspaper clippings, reference books, and other sources.[83] She put a dot over every word she verified and marked incorrect or unclear statements with a question mark.[84] Ecker put a question mark over the phrase "somewhat fictionalized"; it was unclear to her whether *The Desperate Hours* was a true, fictionalized, or "somewhat fictionalized" depiction of the Hills' experience.[85]

The marked-up article was sent to senior editor Joseph Kastner, responsible for checking every article before it went back to Thompson for final approval.[86] A burly man with pale red hair and a disarming smile, noted for his terse prose, Kastner sat in a small office next to Thompson's with a jar of number two pencils on the desk.[87] He edited viciously; staffers joked that "if you put a hamburger in front of Joe, he would edit it." Kastner was considered the second most important figure at *Life* other than Thompson, who reported directly to Luce.[88]

If Kastner's complaints with an article were minor, he and the writer would work out the problems on the spot. Kastner would then "put the story through" to Thompson for the final editing.[89] If there were major problems, he would send the writer back to his typewriter for another try. Kastner believed that "if I didn't trouble the writers, I wasn't doing my job."[90]

Like Thompson, Kastner was preoccupied with "news" and "facts." The more facts in a story, the better. He believed that artful phrases and literary subleties had to be eliminated in order to "cram facts in and get to the heart of the story."[91] Kastner was particularly fussy about the opening sentence of the text blocks, crucial to getting readers "into the tent."[92] Kastner thought that the first draft of Prideaux's article, which led with a reference to Joseph Hayes, obscured the "newsy," real-life connection to the Hill family.[93] He told Prideaux to change the first sentence to focus on the Hills' experience and to include the family's name. The new opening sentence read, "Three years ago Americans all over the country read about the desperate ordeal of the James Hill family, who were held prisoners in their home outside Philadelphia by three escaped convicts."[94]

Kastner also told Prideaux to take out the phrase "somewhat fictionalized," so that the sentence read, "directed by Robert Montgomery and expertly acted, Hayes' play is a heart-stopping account of how one family rose to heroism in a crisis."[95] Prideaux had initially written that the Hill incident "sparked off" the book. In the new version, the novel was "inspired" by it. The revised version also said that the Hills' story was "re-enacted" in the play.[96]

In the second paragraph, the Hill name was substituted for a vague reference to "the family."[97] The initial draft's statement that the Hills "no longer live" in the Whitemarsh house was struck out. The result of Kastner's edits was to depict *The Desperate Hours* as a near-faithful portrayal of the Hills' experience.

This version went back to Ecker for fact checking. Working quickly to meet the publication deadline, Ecker dotted every statement, including that the novel had been "inspired by the family's experience" and that the Hills' hostage saga was "re-enacted" in the play. She based this conclusion on conversations with Prideaux, who asserted that there was a "close relationship" between the play and the Hills' experience.[98] The piece went to Thompson for final approval. Reviewing the piece quickly, he scrawled his initials on it, and the article was prepared for publication.[99]

～

The three-page photoessay, "True Crime Inspires Tense Play," with the subtitle, "The Ordeal of a Family Trapped by Convicts Gives Broadway a New Thriller, 'The Desperate Hours,'" ran in the *Life* issue dated February 28, 1955, which appeared on newsstands on Monday, February 21. The piece consisted of nine large, dramatic black-and-white photos, spread out over three pages, surrounded by minimal text: two short paragraphs and nine captions.

> Three years ago Americans all over the country read about the desperate ordeal of the James Hill family, who were held prisoners in their home outside Philadelphia by three escaped convicts. Later they read about it in Joseph Hayes's novel, *The Desperate Hours*, inspired by the family's experience. Now they can see the story re-enacted in Hayes's Broadway play based on the book, and next year will see it in his movie, which has been filmed but is being held up until the play has a chance to pay off.

> The play, directed by Robert Montgomery and expertly acted, is a heart-stopping account of how a family rose to heroism in a crisis. LIFE photographed the play during its Philadelphia tryout, transported some of the actors to the actual house where the Hills were besieged. On the next page scenes from the play are re-enacted on the site of the crime.[100]

At the top of the first page appeared a photograph of the Hills' former home and the September 12, 1952, *Philadelphia Daily News* headline, underscored by the caption, "Actual event, as reported in newspaper, took place in isolated house about 10 miles from Philadelphia. The three convicts from Lewisburg penitentiary held family of James Hill as prisoners while they hid from manhunt. All three convicts were later captured."[101]

The bottom of the first page showed a large photo of actors in the stage set with the caption, "Two convicts in living room harangue the daughter while the mother (Nancy Coleman) watches helplessly. In bedroom . . . the father tries to comfort his son, as a third convict listens in on telephone calls in the upstairs hallway."[102]

On the second page, under the bold, all-caps headline "THREE CRISES AT A BACK DOOR," ran three photographs of scenes from the play taken at the Whitemarsh home: "At real house where family was trapped, actors do scenes from the play. Here daughter Cindy stalls off her beau from entering the beleaguered home." Another photo showed an angry Karl Malden tossing a gun out of the house, under the caption "BRAVE TRY to save family fails when father (Karl Malden) has to toss out gun because son is held as hostage."[103]

The third page of the article contained three more photographs of violent scenes from the play with captions describing the actions of the "Brutish Convict" who "roughs up the young son Ralphie . . . who shows his spunk by talking up to the criminals." Another photo, titled "Daring Daughter," showed the Hilliard daughter biting the hand of the youngest convict to make him drop his gun, and a picture marked as "Feverish Father" depicted Dan Hilliard's efforts to "cleverly [foist] off [an] unloaded gun on the leader" of the gang, and in so doing "[save] his son and family."[104]

"True Crime Inspires Tense Play" appeared on pages 75 to 78, at the back of the magazine. Despite its bold photos and headlines, the article was almost indistinguishable from the sea of advertisements around it. An ad for Barbasol shave cream filled half of the article's second page. In between the second and third page ran a full-page ad for Walkers DeLuxe Bourbon. On the third page of the piece were ads for a folding aluminum armchair, Hilton's Oyster Stew, and A-1 Sauce. The pages immediately following the piece distracted readers with shockingly bright, bold images of Chevrolet cars, prefabricated homes, and steaming bowls of Chef Boyardee spaghetti.

～

It wasn't false to say there was a connection between the Hills and the play and that the Hills' story had "inspired" *The Desperate Hours*. But describing *The Desperate Hours* as a "re-enactment" of what happened to the Hills was a serious exaggeration, even an outright lie. Certainly there were similarities between Hayes's work and the Whitemarsh incident. And given the publicity for *The Desperate Hours*, it's not hard to see how *Life* could have assumed the play was based on real life. But even a cursory reading of *The Desperate Hours*, the news articles from September 1952, and Hayes's published musings on his creative process would have revealed that the play didn't reenact the Hills' experience. *Life* had, willingly or negligently, distorted the relationship between the Hills and *The Desperate Hours*. The use of the picture of the Hills' former home, the newspaper headline, and the family's name was perhaps *Life*'s greatest sin. The opening of *The Desperate Hours* could have been reported without any mention of the Hills whatsoever. The exaggeration of the connection between the Hills and the play and the inclusion of the family's identity for "newsy" effect were classic *Life* "gimmicks."

The Hills received the issue in their mailbox on Friday, February 25, 1955. Stunned, they spent the weekend looking at the article over and over, getting angrier every time. "We couldn't understand how [*Life*] could do that just for the sake of some free publicity," James recalled. "We certainly couldn't understand how *Life* could publish an article such as this without first checking the newspapers or at least picking up a telephone to find out whether this was the truth or how we felt about it. It was just like we didn't exist, like we were dirt, like they didn't care."[105]

It wasn't just about *Life*. It was about the reporters who burst into their house back in September 1952; it was about the hounding for statements and interviews in the weeks afterward; it was about Hayes and Erskine and William Wyler and Random House and Paramount and everyone who exploited them for their own gain, whether for money or recognition. James knew that this would be the beginning of more unwanted publicity for the family, and he worried about Elizabeth's mental health. "I just wanted to get my hands on Joseph Hayes and on the *Life* crew that had pulled this stunt," he said. He wanted to "throttle" Hayes and the editors of *Life*. Instead, he picked up the phone and called a lawyer.[106]

PART II

Hill v. Hayes

CHAPTER FOUR

The Lawsuit

A week after the *Life* article appeared, James Hill met with Bob Guthrie, his old roommate from Harvard Law School. Guthrie was a high-ranking partner at a Wall Street law firm, Mudge, Stern, Baldwin, and Todd. James announced to his friend that he wanted to file suit against everyone involved with the novel, the play, and the film *The Desperate Hours*. Above all, he wanted to sue the hell out of *Life*. *Life* put his family in a "goldfish bowl" and hawked them to the public as "strange and unusual specimens," he said. The magazine behaved with "utter disregard for my family's rights."[1]

James's decision to reach out to a lawyer was fairly unusual. Injury victims, whether the harms they experience are physical or emotional, tend to endure their sufferings passively rather than file legal claims. "Most injury victims, even those who could bring legitimate tort actions, do not assert a claim of any kind against their injurer," writes legal scholar David Engel. "Instead, they absorb their losses. . . . Litigation proves to be a rare event even in most personal injury cases."[2] Some potential plaintiffs are put off by their unfamiliarity with the legal system. Others face difficulties finding a lawyer. Some fear being marked as troublemakers or litigious, or feel that their injuries aren't serious enough for a lawsuit. Others conclude that the costs of litigation, including stress and anguish, outweigh possible benefits. Taking on the press in the courtroom was a daunting prospect, not for the faint of heart. Publishers were known to be vindictive; some were famous for digging up dirt about plaintiffs and smearing them in print. "It is a rare citizen who can stand the limelight on all of his private affairs," warned one media lawyer in the 1940s. "Newspapers are powerful. . . . Be careful about fighting them."[3]

To be clear: James was not suing for money. He did not see a lawsuit as a potential jackpot. Like many who sue the press, one of his main goals was reputational: he wanted to let the public know that *Life* had gotten it wrong, that his family was not the Hilliards of *The Desperate Hours,* and that his daughters had not been raped, as Hayes had suggested. Like many plaintiffs against the press, James also wanted to punish Hayes and Time, Inc.[4] He wanted to get back at them by forcing them to deal with the burdens of litigation: negative publicity, stress, headaches, time, and attorneys' fees.

~

Under usual circumstances, a lawsuit like that of the Hill family would have been handled by an attorney dealing in personal injury claims, a growing legal specialty in the 1950s.[5] The lawyers of Mudge, Stern, Baldwin, and Todd were, by contrast, high-profile corporate lawyers: "legal strategists for high finance and its profitable reorganizations, handling the affairs of a cluster of banks and companies in their sphere in the cheapest way possible," in the words of sociologist C. Wright Mills.[6] Staffed by graduates of the nation's top law schools, partners commanded associates from "Harvard, Yale, and Columbia" and had a squadron of "clerks, secretaries, and investigators to assist" them.[7] The office, occupying the top floors of a twenty-seven-story building at 20 Broad Street, which hugged the New York Stock Exchange, was equipped, as many other Wall Street firms of that time were, with an internal elevator, lavish conference rooms, oriental rugs, antique desks, paneled walls, and a huge library with leather chairs, costs passed on to clients and accounting for as much as 30 percent of the fees charged.[8]

Although the firm was highly regarded, it was not what it had once been. Founded in 1869, Mudge reached its prime in the 1920s. Its main client had been the Chase Manhattan Bank. With the financial crash of 1929, the bank's fortunes plummeted, and with it, the firm's. By the 1940s, the firm, then known as Mudge, Stern, Williams, and Tucker, had become a "legal backwater."[9] It had "good clients, good lawyers, and interesting business, but not quite enough of each," recalled one former partner. It was a "Wall Street wallflower, solid and respectable, but somewhat staid and old-fashioned."[10] Cynics called it "Mudge, Sludge, Fudge, and Won't Budge."[11] In 1955, the firm merged with another respected firm, Baldwin, Todd, Herold Rose & Cooper, to become Mudge, Stern, Baldwin, and Todd.[12] The merged organization was the eighteenth largest law firm in New York at the time, with nineteen partners and thirty-six associates.[13]

In the mid-1950s Bob Guthrie led a slight resurgence at the firm.[14] A South

Carolinian graduate of Harvard, Guthrie had crinkly eyes and a round, cherubic face that belied a powerful intellect, restless mind, and "endless commercial cunning." Guthrie's great passions in life were said to be pursuing clients, charging large fees, and turning Mudge into a prosperous institution. His trademark phrase was, "You know, we have a lot of fun"[15]—as in, "Boy, we're going to be the biggest and best goddamn law firm in America, make the most goddamn money, drink the most goddamn martinis, have the most goddamn fun."[16] By the end of the decade, thanks to Guthrie's efforts, the firm could count among its clients the Warner Lambert Pharmaceutical Company, Consolidated Textile, Chase Bank, the Hat Corporation of America, General Cigar, and Studebaker Packard.[17]

Although Mudge generally didn't take personal injury cases, Guthrie made an exception for James Hill, whom he agreed to represent on a contingent fee basis. Guthrie assigned the case to a thirty-one-year-old associate, Leonard Garment, one of the firm's rising stars. Garment was Guthrie's protégé, highly respected for his razor-sharp intellect, passionate personality, and extraordinary capacity to work long hours and rack up huge quantities of billable time. His excitable, talkative, irreverent demeanor was magnetic: friends described him as "jovial . . . cultured, and interested in everything," a "hip . . . gadfly."[18] The Hills' lawsuit became for Garment a "fascinating diversion"—in his words, "a kind of adventure in lawyering" outside the staid, conventional commercial practice he was used to.[19]

❧

Born in 1924 on a kitchen table in a Brooklyn apartment, Leonard Garment was an outsider to the elite world of Wall Street law. His father, who owned a dress factory in Queens, was a Lithuanian Jewish immigrant, and his mother had come from Poland. Garment's 1997 autobiography, *Crazy Rhythm*, describes a childhood of wit and learning, tinged with longing, aspiration, and the emotional burdens of hardscrabble poverty. At Samuel J. Tilden High School, "filled with hundreds of first generation Jews, bright, ambitious, intensely competitive," Garment won writing prizes and became student body president and a member of the honor society. At the same time his academic star was rising, he was being seduced by the jazz lifestyle. Garment took up the clarinet and saxophone as a child and by high school was playing jazz professionally. "I loved everything about the jazz culture—practicing, listening, searching for the perfect reed, walking Brooklyn streets with musician friends singing the recorded jazz solos we knew by heart," he recalled. He played gigs from Manhattan to the Catskills, and for a time led his own nine-piece band, enjoying an enchanted life that offered an escape from what he saw as the "dreary confines of Brooklyn."[20]

During his first year at Brooklyn College, Garment attended class in the mornings and immersed himself in the music scene at nights. After he was hired to play saxophone in Henry Jerome's dance band, his grades plummeted and he dropped out of school. A short stint in the service during World War II resulted in an honorable discharge for anxiety and stomach ulcers. Garment returned to Brooklyn College, determined to turn himself around. An encouraging political science professor led him to a new sense of academic purpose; his grades improved, and he decided to attend law school.[21]

In 1946, Garment started Brooklyn Law School, where he had a stellar career. He achieved almost every award available to a law student: summa cum laude, the highest GPA in the class, editor of the law review, winner of a prize for "the student who . . . evinces the highest degree of legal capacity," and captain of the moot court team.[22] At a moot court round in his senior year, he was "discovered" by Joseph V. Kline, a recruiting partner of Mudge, Stern, Williams, and Tucker. He landed on Wall Street in 1950, "cast in the role of ethnic icebreaker." Historically the big law firms had confined hiring to white Christian males, but during World War II, that policy began to break down, albeit slightly.[23] During the war, there was such a shortage of lawyers that even women were temporarily hired by Wall Street firms.[24] Because law school enrollments had plummeted during the war, there remained a dearth of top lawyers for several years, enough that the "law factories" took on Jewish associates, with the number often circumscribed by quota.[25] When Garment first met partner Henry Root Stern, Stern cautioned him that as a Jew and a Brooklyn Law School graduate, he carried "special burdens and responsibilities— not unlike Jackie Robinson's."[26]

Garment's specialty was commercial law; he tried "shareholder suits, takeover contests [and] represented clients before regulatory commissions," in his words.[27] Garment represented Warner Lambert in contract cases and defended Carter Products, the makers of Arrid deodorant, in a case brought by a couple who contracted a serious rash in both armpits from using the deodorant.[28] He found the work exciting and intellectually challenging; it was "great fun," he recalled. Garment became a renowned, highly successful trial lawyer, noted for his meticulous preparation, "remarkable intellect, gift for language, and contagious enthusiasms," according to one colleague.[29]

During his early years at the firm, Garment married Grace Hicks, a secretary at a nearby advertising agency. Grace was witty, intelligent, and gifted, and wracked by a seemingly bottomless depression. Leonard Garment too struggled with depression, though he never saw the depths that Grace endured. Grace tried to deal with her problems through psychiatry. Garment threw himself into a frenetic work routine, putting in long hours for six or seven days a week. The couple had two children; they spent Garment's salary freely and tried to avoid their demons. "The fifties passed this way. I tried cases, traveled on business, rose in the firm, and made more money. . . . We lived a yuppie life long before the term was coined." Referring to the depression that both bonded and burdened them, Garment wrote, "We had good times, ran around and laughed a lot, played charades for fun and for real, but at the end of the day, so to speak, we always returned to find the same gloomy houseguests waiting for us."[30]

Garment was drawn to the *Hill* case. The lawsuit's intellectual puzzles intrigued him, and he handled the legal issues with the highest level of professionalism and skill. Garment also became emotionally attached to the Hills, whom he got to know well during the eleven years of litigation. The *Hill* case became for Garment a personal, even moral crusade.

⁓

The Hills' action against Time, Inc. and the creators of *The Desperate Hours* started like many lawsuits against the press did, with an angry letter attempting to avert a lawsuit. In April 1955, Garment sent a letter to *Life* demanding a retraction.[31] He sought a notice, printed in a subsequent issue, saying that it had erred in connecting the Hills to *The Desperate Hours* and that the Hilliards were fictional, a figment of Hayes's imagination.

Most newspapers and magazines had a policy of retracting when confronted with errors.[32] When caught publishing an undisputed falsehood, "almost any newspaper will publish a satisfactory retraction," observed a newspaper lawyer in the *American Bar Association Journal* in 1955.[33] "The best rule for the editor is to preach accuracy, fair play, and respect for privacy. . . . And if a slip does occur, he [should] be willing to rectify the error as prominently as it was made," noted a top editor at a major newspaper chain.[34] There were legal incentives to retracting:

a retraction could mitigate compensatory damages, and several states had statutes that prohibited plaintiffs in libel cases from recovering punitive damages after a retraction was published.[35]

Nevertheless, editors were not eager to retract, as it tarnished their credibility and reputation. Retraction, described by one writer as the "ultimate disgrace in journalism," had a "dirty word" character in publishing.[36] Recalled one Time, Inc. editor, journalists are "surrounded by critics. . . . As a result of torrents of complaints that have little or no validity, journalists develop a reflex of suspicion and defensiveness, which is automatically activated whenever their work is challenged. They would rather fight on a marginal issue to seem right rather than retract in public and admit they were, or might be, wrong."[37] The legal department of the *New York Times* responded firmly to such requests: "Although the *New York Times* is always ready to correct any error in its columns which is called to its attention, we must advise you that our attorneys have informed us that the article of which you complain was a true, correct, and fair report . . . and that . . . there is nothing for us to do other than to await the presentation of your attorneys."[38] Wrote one editor, "the first rule" in dealing with such complaints was to tell the complainant "to go to hell."[39]

Time, Inc. rarely published retractions. Out of every hundred requested retractions, *Life* printed only about three, which appeared in the letters to the editor section near the front of the magazine.[40] Some of them seemed truly sincere. In 1946, a Mrs. Hewitt Griggs Robertson wrote in complaining about an uncomplimentary photo with a caption describing her as a "heckler." "I resent being . . . held up to ridicule. . . . It seems to me that there should be a retraction for such improper and erroneous words as used by your magazine," she wrote. *Life* printed the letter with a comment: "*Life's* apologies to Mrs. Robertson—ED."[41] A priest who had been labeled as "Hague's priest"—a reference to the infamous, antilabor New Jersey mayor Frank Hague—wrote in saying that the caption was "derogatory to the Catholic priesthood in New Jersey and insulting to our Church." *Life* responded: "*Life* knows that the Catholic Church and its representatives have an allegiance superior to any individual or group, deeply regrets an unintentional inference that Mayor Frank Hague did or could own and control any priest."[42]

More often than not, retractions became an opportunity for the magazine to exact a kind of coy revenge on the complainant. In 1940, *Life* ran a story about presidential candidate Wendell Willkie's hometown of Elwood, Indiana. An irate citizen sent a letter: "I notice you say: `young girls drink Coca Cola chasers with their whisky while planning to attend Baptist Sunday School next morning.' I happen to be the teacher of a class of young girls in our Baptist Church and no one, not even the editors of *Life*, can say things about my girls without my fighting back. They aren't that type of girl." *Life* replied: "A public apology is due the citizens for your misrepresentation of Elwood in *Life*." "The facts for the Elwood story were gathered by a *Life* reporter who personally observed the Sunday School girls. . . . [*Life*] had no intention to imply that this incident was typical of all Elwood Sunday School pupils and is glad to record the feelings of Elwood citizens who think *Life* painted too dark a picture of their city." The magazine, of course, got the last word.[43]

Predictably, *Life*'s editors refused Garment's demand, saying they had done nothing wrong and citing "freedom of the press." They refused to retract because it was "impossible to retract the truth." *Life*'s flippant response outraged the Hills, and Garment pushed ahead with legal proceedings.[44]

~

At the outset of the case, Garment thought the family had a good claim for libel. Libel is an ancient legal action dating back to the earliest history of the English common law.[45] The libel tort applies to defamatory material in print, and slander, spoken defamation. Libel and slander are civil actions between private parties for money damages. Although "malicious libel," a libel directed against an individual with an intent to "breach the peace," was a crime in most states in the nineteenth century, prosecutions for criminal libel were rare.[46] Libel and slander were transplanted to the United States with the rest of the common law and had a rich life in early American political culture. Libel suits had been typically brought by public officials over criticism in the press, while slander cases policed the excesses of gossip in small communities—chatter about people's crimes, misdeeds, and sexual affairs.[47]

To be actionable as a libel, a statement had to be both false and defamatory. The guiding premise of libel law is that there is no social value in a false fact, especially one that seriously harms a person's reputation. A defamatory statement injures a person's good name in his or her community and seriously lowers that person's esteem in the eyes of others. It typically has a moral dimension; the quintessential defamatory statement is an attack on one's character. Accusations of having committed a crime, engaging in professional incompetence, having a promiscuous tendency, or a "loathsome" illness—a venereal disease—were considered so damaging as to be defamatory per se.[48]

Until the latter part of the twentieth century, American libel law was fairly unfriendly to the press. In most states, the plaintiff in a libel case did not have to prove that the statement in question was false or that his or her reputation had actually been harmed in order to win damages for injury to reputation. The plaintiff needed only to present the derogatory statement and demonstrate that it could *potentially* hurt his or her reputation. The falsity of the statement was presumed; the publisher could exonerate itself by proving its truth. The rationale was that a person's reputation was a very serious matter, critical to social standing and employment, and that saddling the plaintiff with the burden of proving falsity would result in undeserved victories for the press. As one law journal explained, media publications created a substantial risk of injury to reputation; as such, they were "dangerous instrumentalities" like toxic chemicals or automobiles "whose owners should be insurers against the harm necessarily resulting from their business operations."[49]

For this reason, libel was a strict liability tort: the publisher was responsible for his statements regardless of whether he published them innocently or maliciously. To hold publishers liable only when they intended to defame or were negligent in publishing would probably result in no liability in many cases, and "such relief from liability seems unjustified in view of the enormous risk of harm inherent in these media," noted the *Harvard Law Review* in 1956.[50] Punitive damages could be awarded for defamatory statements made with malice—hatred or ill will toward the plaintiff. The only deviation from these stringent rules involved statements about public officials and public issues. In all the states, there was a "fair comment" privilege that permitted publishers to make defamatory statements of opinion about public officials in their official capacity and "matters of public concern," provided they were issued fairly and with "an honest purpose."[51]

Before the 1960s, libel posed a substantial threat to press operations. Editors and publishers described the "nightmare" of libel litigation.[52] Some newspapers and magazines had gone out of business as a result of libel suits, bankrupted by large judgments. Even when libel cases were settled or dismissed, the burden on a publisher could be formidable. "Once a libel suit has been started, it must thereby be regarded as a loss to the newspaper, whether it be withdrawn, settled, or tried," observed *Editor and Publisher*.[53] "The expense of investigation, of retainers and trial fees is considerable and even a suit which goes no further than the service of a summons involves expense."[54]

~

While a claim for libel seemed promising at first, it didn't take long for Garment to realize that it would go nowhere. *The Desperate Hours* and the *Life* article may have upset the family, but they didn't defame them. Defamatory words exposed a person to "hatred" or "contempt," and "cause[d] him to be shunned or avoided by his neighbors."[55] Nothing in the novel, the play, the movie, or the *Life* article accused the Hills of anything loathsome, illicit, or immoral.

To the contrary, the article, the novel, the play, and the movie presented the Hills in a positive, flattering light—as noble and heroic. Garment then investigated the possibility of a claim for invasion of privacy. Under the invasion of privacy tort, people could sue and recover damages when they were depicted in the media in an embarrassing, invasive, distressing manner, regardless of whether the publication was negative, critical, or defamatory. The interest protected by the tort was the individual's dignity, autonomy, and sense of self—the ability to avoid unwanted publicity and control how he or she appeared in the public eye.

CHAPTER FIVE

Privacy

Only a few years before the Hills brought their case, a young girl won a major privacy suit against the *Saturday Evening Post*. The magazine had run a photograph of her as she lay in the street after being hit by a car. The photo was graphic and gruesome; it depicted her face distorted in pain, her hair and clothing in disarray, and her legs exposed to her hips. The picture ran in conjunction with an article titled "They Ask to Be Killed," about pedestrian carelessness that led to traffic accidents. In fact, the girl had not been careless at all. She sued for invasion of privacy, and a jury awarded damages.

The court noted, "Where a magazine chooses to publish, without permission, a picture of a private individual in a humiliating situation, for the sole purpose of attracting attention to the leading article, it takes a risk that a jury will find, as the jury in this case did, that the publisher should have realized that the publication would be offensive to a person of ordinary sensibilities and unreasonably interfere with her right to privacy."[1] By the 1950s, the tort action for invasion of privacy had been recognized in most states, and it was a growing and highly contested area of the law.

∽

To understand what happened next in the *Hill* case, we need to make an excursion back in time, to the origins of privacy law. The law of privacy was a response to the rise of mass publishing and the human injuries caused by mass publishing.

The last quarter of the nineteenth century saw a publishing explosion in the United States. Advances in printing technology, rising literacy rates, and expanding urban populations led to an outpouring of printed material. Newspaper readership increased 400 percent, and the number of newspapers doubled.[2] General-interest magazines such as the *Ladies' Home Journal* debuted and became popular.[3] Major news publishing chains developed, including the Hearst, Scripps, and Pulitzer empires.[4]

Once a source of news about politics aimed at an audience of educated men, newspapers became a mass medium. Seeking to cater to a popular readership, papers began to feature entertaining, salacious, titillating material—gossip columns, celebrity trivia, and "human interest" stories. Publishers courted urban workers by fashioning the newspaper as a form of cheap entertainment and featuring stories that "contain[ed] the thrill of sensation loved by the man on the street and the woman in the kitchen," in the words of media titan William Randolph Hearst.[5] In the 1890s, this reached new heights with sensationalistic yellow journalism, rife with prominent illustrations, large type, and detailed and dramatic coverage of murders and sexual affairs.

Presaging the gossip magazines and tabloids of our time, there was a media frenzy around personal life. Socialites, celebrities, and politicians were endlessly scrutinized. When President Grover Cleveland married while in office in the 1880s, reporters pursued the honeymooning couple, standing in the trees and shrubbery outside their residence and "distend[ing] their ears to catch every scrap of conversation."[6] Ordinary people's private lives were also exposed, sometimes cruelly. Crimes, love affairs, divorces, holidays, social outings, illnesses, births, deaths—matters of ordinary existence were dredged up by aggressive roving reporters and fed to a curious public. "It is scarcely possible to take up a newspaper without finding in it invasions of the sacred right to privacy," lamented a critic in 1891. "Not only the private affairs of persons holding public relations are pried into, but those of persons who have no public functions whatsoever."[7] In pursuit of news and gossip, reporters climbed through open windows, eavesdropped, and assumed disguises. Armed with the newly invented Kodak camera, photographers stood in the street and took random pictures of people that were often published without the consent of the subjects. The news value of such photos was not so much "that the photographs [were] of notabilities" but that they were unposed and revealing, often "taken by stealth when the subjects were unconscious of the purpose of the person manipulating the camera."[8]

With its candid photos and dramatic stories about the secretly sensational lives of average people, the press tapped into a rich vein of popular interest. The late 1800s was an era of rapid urbanization in the United States. In cities, where people lived behind closed doors and were often strangers to each other, readers were interested in knowing what their neighbors did and how the other classes lived. Information about the way people dressed, ate, worked, loved, and spent their leisure time offered migrants to the city critical information about the lifestyles and cultures of their new social environment. The function of popular journalism was to provide a mirror on an expanding, diversifying, increasingly cosmopolitan world that was becoming too vast and complex for readers to take in on their own.

While the focus on "real people" and "private lives" interested and amused readers, it often devastated the victims of unwanted publicity. When a newspaper reported the youthful crimes of a man who had reformed his ways and become a respectable member of his community, the man became distraught and died from the stress.[9] In one notorious incident, a young woman whose only claim to fame was that her fiancé committed suicide was publicized in all the major papers, causing her extreme distress.[10] "The sheer, unmitigated brutality" of media invasions of privacy, wrote one critic, "is so constantly illustrated in the columns of many newspapers that a large part of the American people have come to acquiesce in it as one of the fixed conditions of modern life."[11]

Under the law as it then stood, the victims of these invasions of privacy had no recourse whatsoever. Unless the publication was false and defamatory, a suit for damages was foreclosed. "Some merely curious incident in a man's life may be seized upon by a reporter with the result that for the time being, he is the most conspicuous person in the country," observed lawyer Elbridge Adams. "Yet according to our present notions of the law of libel no cause of action would accrue to him unless his character had been defamed."[12] This gap in the law disturbed two young Boston lawyers, and it led them to write a groundbreaking proposal.

~

Samuel Warren was a member of the Boston social elite. In 1878, he graduated from Harvard Law School along with his friend Louis Brandeis, a brilliant student from a Jewish merchant family in Louisville, Kentucky. After graduation, Warren and Brandeis founded their own law firm.[13]

In 1883, Warren married the daughter of Senator Thomas Francis Bayard. The new couple held social events at their home, which were written up breathlessly in the society columns of newspapers such as the *New York Times* and the *Boston Globe*.[14] Outraged by this intrusion into his family's affairs, Warren turned to his more intellectual friend, who helped him channel his anger at the press into an article titled "The Right to Privacy." The piece, published in the *Harvard Law Review* in 1890, became the foundational text of American privacy law.[15]

"The press," Warren and Brandeis wrote, "is overstepping in every direction the obvious bounds of propriety and decency." "Gossip is no longer the resource of the idle and of the vicious, but has become a trade, which is pursued with industry as well as effrontery." "Persons with whose affairs the community has no legitimate concerns" were "being dragged into an undesirable and undesired publicity."[16] Having one's personal details publicized in a newspaper caused embarrassment and "mental pain and distress" "far greater than could be inflicted by mere bodily injury."[17] Warren and Brandeis proposed a "right to privacy," a cause of action under the common law that would allow individuals to sue the press for unconsented, invasive, injurious publicity and recover damages for humiliation and emotional distress.

Warren and Brandeis distinguished between the interests in privacy and reputation. Reputation, one's good name and the material and social benefits that flowed from it, was a matter of "substance," something that was measurable and potentially calculable in terms of dollars and cents. The interest in privacy, by contrast, was ethereal and intangible; it lay not in the opinions of others but in one's sense of self and personal dignity. Dignity, a belief in the intrinsic value of every individual, was an important cultural value at this time, particularly in the northern states.[18] Yet for the most part, the common law did not recognize the interest in dignity; the law's focus was tangible harms, injuries to the body or to property.[19] In arguing that individual dignity, feelings, and personhood were worthy of legal protection, "The Right to Privacy," in the words of Harvard Law dean Roscoe Pound, "did nothing less than add a chapter to our law."[20]

At the time Warren and Brandeis wrote, the idea of a legal right to privacy was not entirely novel. Protections for various kinds of privacy existed in several different areas of the law. The common law tort of trespass protected domestic privacy—the "inviolability of one's house" and the householder's right to "quiet and peaceable possession." Under the common law of nuisance, courts prevented unreasonable noises or smells that interfered with the "quiet enjoyment" of property by its owners.[21] The privacy of one's body—a right to be free from unwanted touching—was shielded under the law of assault and battery. Federal and state statutes protected the privacy of personal communications by making it a crime to tamper with the mails, and more than half the states had laws that prohibited the disclosure of telegraph messages by telegraph company employees.[22] Eavesdropping and wiretapping were regularly prosecuted on the ground that "no man has a right . . . to pry into your secrecy in your own house."[23] In 1891, the U.S. Supreme Court held that a person bringing an action for personal injuries against a railroad could not be forced to submit to a surgical examination as part of the "right to one's person to be . . . let alone," a phrase coined by the Michigan Supreme Court judge Thomas Cooley in his influential 1880 treatise on torts.[24]

Although the term privacy appears nowhere in the Constitution, various provisions in the Bill of Rights implied protections for aspects of privacy. The constitutional prohibition against unreasonable search and seizure under the Fourth Amendment was said to protect the "sanctities of a man's home and the privacies of life," the Supreme Court declared in 1886.[25] The Fifth Amendment gave individuals the right not to be compelled to give evidence that could be used against them in criminal proceedings.[26] The First Amendment rights of freedom of speech and religion shielded privacy in that they permitted a person to possess and control his or her thoughts free from government dictate; that amendment also protected citizens from being compelled to disclose their political affiliations.[27] Joseph Story, a U.S. Supreme Court justice and leading legal scholar of the early national period, wrote in 1833 that First Amendment freedoms were envisioned by the framers to protect "private sentiment" and "private judgment."[28]

Though privacy already existed as a legal concept, the *Harvard Law Review* article marked the first call for a freestanding right to privacy under the common law, and it became a legal landmark. At a time of great anxiety around the new media of mass communications, "The Right to Privacy" was discussed, analyzed, and praised in both legal journals and the popular press—remarkable for a law review article. "If a man may appear in public, or seclude himself, as he sees fit, there is no sound reason why he should not determine the circumstances under which his face shall be exhibited in the newspapers," opined Supreme Court justice Henry Billings Brown.[29] "Does not the license of yellow [journalism] suggest the absolute need of and establish the principle and righteousness of privacy?" asked a writer in the *Green Bag* in 1903.[30] By reasoning of their "thorough research" and the "bold application of principles so established, to a new order of things," the Warren and Brandeis article made a major contribution to the problem of the "generally recognized abuses of the press," a major issue for the "people at large."[31] By the early twentieth century, several states had recognized some version of the privacy tort, awarding damages to plaintiffs who had been injured by publications that were invasive, humiliating, and offensive, as determined by the courts.

◇

A little over ten years after the Warren and Brandeis article, New York passed a privacy statute, a law against unwanted and injurious publicity. In April 1903 the state legislature approved a law that penalized the use, without consent, of a person's "name, portrait, or picture" for "advertising" or "trade" purposes. Section 50 of the Act to Prevent the Unauthorized Use of the Name or Picture of Any Person for the Purposes of Trade made the violation a misdemeanor. Section 51 granted the right to sue for an injunction and damages for shame, indignity, and emotional distress.[32]

The law originated from the angst of a teenage girl named Abigail Roberson. In 1900, Roberson's likeness was used without her consent in an ad for Franklin Mills Flour. When Roberson saw herself in the ad, she was shamed and "mortified," and she became so ill that she had to take to her bed and be treated by a doctor. She brought suit against the advertiser, the Rochester Folding Box Company. Citing the Warren and Brandeis article, Roberson's lawyer argued that the advertisement invaded her privacy by exploiting her image and exposing her to the public gaze in an undignified and humiliating manner. She won at trial, but the highest court in New York reversed the decision. It refused to recognize a right to privacy, suggesting that to do so would unleash a "floodgate of litigation."[33]

The decision spurred massive protest. Publications were deluged with letters and articles attacking it. One writer expressed the prevailing mood when he observed that it was "outrageous that modest women who in no way put themselves before the public" could "be dragged into notoriety by any adventurer who thinks he can fill his pockets by exploiting them."[34] In response to the outcry, the state legislature enacted the "right to privacy" law.

The New York privacy law was originally aimed at the unauthorized use of people's images in advertisements. As one judge described the law's purpose, legal recovery could be had for the indignities caused when an advertiser "ma[d]e use of a portrait of a beautiful woman to attract attention to some article of trade"[35]— when one's picture "was unauthorizedly published or used . . . in connection with the advertisement of some patent medicine or some other commodity which the advertiser was interested in selling."[36] At a time when advertising was held in low regard, viewed as crass and even immoral, using a person's picture in an ad—

commercially exploiting someone's identity—was regarded as a great indignity and personal affront.[37]

Immediately after the law's passage, plaintiffs brought lawsuits over the unauthorized use of their photographs and likenesses in commercial endorsements for products ranging from soaps to books to cold remedies. Eventually people began bringing claims not only over advertisements but all sorts of undesirable media representations—the reproduction of their images, names, and likenesses in newspaper and magazine articles, books, and films, which they described as unauthorized commercial or "trade" uses of their identities. It was the New York privacy law that Leonard Garment would invoke in the Hills' case.

~

By the mid-twentieth century, the tort of invasion of privacy was well established.[38] The American Law Institute included it in its 1939 summary of legal doctrines, the *Restatement of Torts*: "a person who unreasonably and seriously interferes with another's interest in not having his affairs known to others or his likeness exhibited to the public" could be liable for invasion of privacy, according to the *Restatement*.[39] The notion that the law should focus only on tangible, material injuries had by this time been largely discredited. Earlier hesitance about the propriety of awarding damages for emotional distress had dissipated in a culture, influenced by the emerging discipline of psychology, where emotional harms were seen as legitimate and "real." "Although invasion of the right of privacy is less frequently litigated than its closest tort companions, libel and slander, the number of cases which have recently appeared in courts of last resort indicate that the action is continuing to grow as a major remedy for tortious publications," noted the *University of Chicago Law Review* in 1948.[40] By the end of the 1940s, eighteen states recognized the tort, and over thirty states acknowledged it a decade later.[41]

There was an upsurge of privacy litigation in the 1930s and 1940s, and it tracked the growth and proliferation of the mass media. By 1940, 90 percent of Americans were estimated to be newspaper readers.[42] At the beginning of the 1950s, there were 1,773 daily newspapers, 543 Sunday newspapers, 9,591 weekly newspapers, 1,421 weekly periodicals, 221 semimonthly periodicals, 3,643 monthly periodicals, and 625 quarterly periodicals in the United States.[43] Over 90 million Americans went to the movies each week, and half the homes in the United States contained at least two radios, which were on for about five hours a day.[44]

By this time, most publications had come to rely on advertising as their major source of income. Many advertisers would buy space only in major magazines or the largest newspapers in a community, leading to brutal "circulation wars." Seeking to expand their audience base, publishers sensationalized copy and blurred news and entertainment. Whether practiced by tabloids like the *New York Daily Mirror* or more staid outlets like the *New York Times*, reporting the news involved personalization—highlighting the individuals involved and their personal details. If someone assumed office or "built a better mousetrap than his neighbor," the press "will make newsreels of him and his wife in beach pajamas, it will discuss his diet and his health . . . it will publicize him, analyze him, photograph him, and make his life thoroughly miserable by feeding to the public [personal] details," the *American Mercury* noted in 1935.[45] As the *North American Review* observed in 1937, there was tremendous popular demand for "detailed, intimate information" about "who [people] are, . . . what they do," and especially "what they look like."[46]

Hand-held Kodak cameras had been in use since the late nineteenth century, but in 1928, the "candid camera," with a super-fast lens and flash bulb, was invented. The candid camera gave rise to a formidable paparazzi,[47] notorious for its "spying, bribing, stealing, [and] camera clicking."[48] During the notorious press coverage of famous aviator Charles Lindbergh in the early 1930s, reporters "descended upon [his] household, prying, spying, and trespassing in a ruthless stampede for news."[49] It was not only celebrities who were hounded. Newspaper and newsreel cameramen patrolled the city seeking curiosities and spectacles: accidents, unusual faces, pretty women, dogfights.[50] "No longer is it necessary to be spectacular . . . in order to face the camera," observed the *New York Times*. "Now the newsreel companies search out their own material, and youth, going for a stroll in the park, may suddenly find himself as part of a human interest sequence called 'Under a Lovers' Moon.'"[51] One's "home is still his castle—in theory at least," lamented one lawyer in 1948. At home, a person didn't "have to answer the doorbell or telephone; he can pull down the shades; he can hide like a grub under a stone. But when he ventures out he is clearly off base and fair game for any snooper who thinks him 'newsworthy.'"[52]

～

The public reacted to these invasions of privacy with both fascination and disgust. Audiences eagerly consumed them, yet at the same time claimed to be outraged and offended.[53] Surveys from the 1930s and 1940s indicated that the majority of Americans thought press content was too lurid, invasive, and salacious. A 1935 study reported that 73 percent of adult men and 93 percent of adult women thought that newspapers indulged in sensationalism, and "it is the popular belief that the press is venal, biased, and inaccurate."[54] In a 1949 survey, 36 percent agreed with the statement that newspapers devoted too much space to "trivialities, scandals, sensations, divorces."[55]

When editor Marlin Pew appeared before a group of teachers in 1935, he was peppered with "indignant inquiries concerning indefensible practices in certain metropolitan newspaper offices." They wanted to know "whether the right to privacy [was] a dead issue, and if so, what could be done about it." One woman said that the virtues of a free press had been "so completely discounted by licentious editorial practices, . . . that she would welcome censorship regardless of what the forfeiture of civil liberty would entail." Said another: "I despise . . . newspapers . . . because their gossip is degrading, unfair, a vile intrusion on sacred family life . . . the government should stop it."[56] A superior court judge in Baltimore observed in 1932 that there was growing interest in privacy law "because of the flagrant abuses of the tabloid and other press, and their old assertion of a right to [invade privacy] under the constitutional guarantee of freedom of the press." The "abuse of human rights" by the media had become a matter of serious public discussion, and the trend of popular sentiment was undeniably in "the direction of the recognition of the right of privacy."[57]

∽

By the middle of the twentieth century, authors, newspaper and magazine publishers, publishing houses, radio broadcasters, photographers, and film companies faced a barrage of privacy lawsuits brought by plaintiffs from all walks of life.

In 1926, woman named Louise Peed was found unconscious in the apartment of a man who was not her husband, asphyxiated by a "carelessly closed gas jet." The *Washington Times* published a picture of Peed with a story about the incident. Humiliated, she sued the newspaper for invasion of privacy, and the defendant's motion to dismiss was rejected. The court mocked the newspaper's efforts to invoke freedom of the press: that liberty did not carry with it the "privilege of invading any . . . right of the citizen," including one's right to keep one's embarrassing misfortunes out of the papers.[58]

In *Melvin v. Reid*, from 1931, the plaintiff was a former prostitute who had been tried for murder and acquitted, but who rehabilitated, married, and achieved a place in respectable society. A Hollywood movie was produced based on the true story of her life, using her true maiden name. Outraged that her disreputable past had been revealed to a national audience, she sued the producer and recovered damages for invasion of privacy.[59]

In 1948, the *Saturday Evening Post* ran a critique of taxicab drivers titled "Never Give a Passenger a Break." The piece attacked the "haughty" cabbies of Washington, DC, and accused them of cheating their customers. Several photographs ran with the article. One depicted a woman, a smiling, well-dressed "lady cabby," talking to the article's author on the street.[60] The woman had consented to the photograph but did not know that it would be used in an article on cheating cabbies. Upset by the unconsented, distorted use of her image, she sued for invasion of privacy. A federal district court held that she had a valid claim. Innocent people needed the law's protection against the media and its "undue and undesirable publicity," the court determined. The publication of a photograph of a "private person without his sanction" violated his right to privacy.[61]

≈

The publishing world viewed these developments with alarm. The American Society of Newspaper Editors was so concerned by privacy lawsuits that it went on a public relations campaign, reminding readers that the profession, in its 1923 Code of Ethics, had pledged not to "invade private rights or feelings without sure warrant of public right as distinguished from public curiosity."[62] "How can rotten government be exposed, or dirty business methods brought to light, without unfettered expression?" asked one editor.[63] "If some innocent person gets hurt in the process, it is still for the public good."[64] Invasions of privacy were not the fault of editors and reporters, but "the circumstances which have made the private affairs of certain persons a matter of public interest, and the insistence of the public that its interest be satisfied," a 1930 newspaper manual explained. The "paper never prints anything for the general public that is worse than what the general public wants."[65]

In a 1936 lecture to the American Society of Newspaper Editors, the editor of the *Detroit Daily News* warned of the threats posed by privacy litigation: the difficulty and costs of legal defenses, "the aggravations, annoyances, harassments, of actions that may be begun by the vengeful, the avaricious and the psychopathic reader, the strain of endeavoring to produce a newspaper under repressive influences." In their approval of a right to privacy, the "bench, bar and legislature" had "gone sufficiently far to suggest the possibility of a complete reordering of the processes of newspaper editing and publishing." "If the press is worth continuance," he argued, "it must have more freedom of action than the extension of the principle of privacy would seem to promise."[66] Publishers argued that privacy law, as it was being interpreted by the courts, constituted an abridgment of freedom of the press.

CHAPTER SIX

Freedom of the Press

Although the legal action for invasion of privacy was praised for its protection against an invasive, intrusive press, it raised doubts and criticisms from the start. Insofar as it restricted what could and could not be published, it had potentially significant implications for freedom of the press. By the 1950s, the right to privacy and freedom of the press were on a collision course, and the Hills' case would be at their juncture.

∽

Under the First Amendment to the U.S. Constitution, "Congress shall make no law . . . abridging the freedom of speech, and of the press."[1] Like "privacy," "freedom of press" was an elusive and vague concept in the law. No specific definitions of "freedom" were offered by the First Amendment's architect, James Madison, or in the congressional consideration, or by the state legislators who voted to ratify the Bill of Rights.[2] As First Amendment scholar Zechariah Chafee aptly summarized, "The truth is that the framers had no very clear idea as to what they meant by the 'freedom of speech or of the press.'"[3] The legal community has long debated whether the original meaning of "freedom of the press" meant only that publishers had a right to publish without prior restraints—free from government censorship or licensing—or whether the First Amendment also protected the press from being punished for its utterances, after the fact. This dispute goes on, and it remains inconclusive.[4] One thing seems fairly clear: although the press was singled out for special mention in the Constitution, it enjoys no greater protection under the law than any other speaker. The framers saw "freedom of speech" and "freedom of the press" as equivalent, and to this day there is no special "press clause jurisprudence."[5]

At the time Warren and Brandeis wrote, the prevailing judicial interpretation of freedom of the press was narrow and restrictive by today's standards. The First

Amendment prohibited prior restraints, the suppression of material before publication, but did not protect people from being punished for their words. One
could speak, write, and publish as one pleased, subject to punishment for being
too offensive—for uttering speech with a "bad tendency."[6] State and local governments could employ their police power for protection of their communities,
passing laws to promote "public convenience, general welfare, prosperity, and an
orderly state of society."[7] The state had an interest in self-preservation that could,
under circumstances, trump individuals' free expression rights.

Under the "bad tendency" rule, publishers were fined and imprisoned under
state laws that prohibited the publication of descriptions of "bloodshed, lust, and
crime."[8] A newspaper publisher who truthfully described an execution was convicted on the basis that such material "naturally tends to excite the public mind
and thus. . . . affect[s] the public good."[9] Socialist and anarchist journals were tar-
gets of criminal laws punishing material that threatened to "breach the peace."[10]
The bad tendency doctrine lasted into the early twentieth century. In *Patterson v.
Colorado* (1907), the U.S. Supreme Court approved the power of a state court to
hold newspapers in contempt for printing editorials accusing the state court of
corruption. Statements deemed "contrary to the public welfare" could be punished whether true or false, the Court declared.[11] In 1915, in *Fox v. Washington*,
the Supreme Court upheld a man's conviction under a Washington State statute
for publishing a salacious newspaper. The paper's offense was that it encouraged
readers to go out in the nude.[12]

Insofar as they injured people and lowered society's moral tone, sensationalistic gossip and other exposés of private life had a "bad tendency" and could be subject to liability. As the *Virginia Law Register* noted in 1906, freedom of the press
was not a license for newspapers to invade the rights of individuals, including the
"right to be let alone."[13] "The press never had any real right to invade proper privacy, so a law defining what privacy is and fixing a penalty for its invasion would
not be any abridgment of the right of publication, for the right of improper publication never existed," according to one lawyer. Freedom of the press, it was often
said, was not a "license for its abuse."[14]

Yet in the views of some forward-looking commentators, the legal action for
invasion of privacy did in fact impair free speech and freedom of the press. Under
the privacy tort, newspapers could be made to pay damages for innocently and
unwittingly publishing embarrassing pictures of people. Politicians and public

officials could use their "right to privacy" to quash criticism or suppress reports of misdeeds or corruption. Not knowing what a person might see as humiliating or invasive, publishers could self-censor truthful material, inhibiting the dissemination of important news.[15] In *Corliss v. Walker* (1893), the wife of a famous deceased inventor brought suit against the publisher of an unauthorized biography of her late husband, claiming an invasion of privacy.[16] The court rejected the claim, concluding that the imposition of liability for the publication of the life story of a public figure would be a "remarkable exception to the liberty of the press."[17]

∽

These concerns with the free speech implications of the privacy tort intensified in the 1930s and 1940s, an era that saw the transformation and liberalization of free speech law. In the words of First Amendment scholar Harry Kalven Jr., this was the era when "speech starts to win."[18] There was a "tendency on the part of . . . [the] courts to grant the press an ever increasing freedom to print and publish," noted one scholar in 1942.[19] This movement was led by the U.S. Supreme Court, which became the nation's leading court protecting civil rights and civil liberties.

Prior to 1925, the First Amendment did not apply to the states, although most state constitutions had free speech provisions that paralleled the federal constitutional guarantee. In *Gitlow v. New York* (1925), the Supreme Court "incorporated" the First Amendment through the due process clause of the Fourteenth Amendment, making it enforceable against state governments.[20] The Court also rejected the "bad tendency" test. In 1919, Justice Oliver Wendell Holmes proposed a "clear and present danger" test in free speech cases. The mere "tendency" to create harm was no longer enough to justify liability; courts now had to ask "whether the words used are used in such circumstances and are of such a nature as to create a clear and present danger that they will bring about the substantive evil that Congress has a right to prevent."[21] Influenced by the government repression of political dissenters during World War I and the writings of Progressive-era social theorists, who regarded freedom of expression as essential to political participation, Holmes linked freedom of speech to the concept of the "marketplace of ideas," in which all ideas would be expressed and the best would win out.[22] In *Whitney v. California* (1927), about the conviction of a member of the Communist Party under a California criminal syndicalism act, Louis Brandeis, now a Supreme Court justice, wrote a concurrence in which he argued for the adoption of "clear and present danger." Robust protections for freedom of speech would safeguard the citizen's right to participate in "public discussion" of public affairs, a fundamental duty of every individual in a democratic society.[23]

In the 1930s and 1940s, "clear and present danger" became the majority doctrine on the Court.[24] In a series of cases, the Supreme Court invalidated the convictions of religious minorities, socialists, Communists, and labor activists under state laws restricting various forms of speech that did not pose an immediate threat to public safety. Since free expression was the essence of democracy—"the matrix, the indispensable condition, of nearly every . . . form of freedom"— the Court would view claims involving First Amendment rights with heightened judicial scrutiny, with a "thumb on the scale" for speech.[25] State actions restricting speech could not stand unless justified by a compelling government interest beyond mere disagreement with the views espoused.[26] In the 1940s, the Court's liberal bloc—Hugo Black, Frank Murphy, William O. Douglas, Wiley Rutledge, and Robert Jackson—announced a "preferred position" doctrine, an expansive vision of free speech that, in the words of one historian, "elevated First Amendment freedoms to heights of importance almost above every other societal interest coming into conflict with them."[27]

The Court's free speech jurisprudence reflected emerging ideals of pluralist democracy—the notion of democracy as a participatory enterprise built on discussion involving all members of society. Democracy depended on vigorous debates on "matters of public concern," "all issues about which information is needed or appropriate to enable the members of society to cope with the exigencies of their period."[28] The Court recognized the critical role of the press in democratic "public discussion." In *Grosjean v. American Press Co.* (1936), which invalidated a state income tax levied on newspapers with large circulations, Justice George Sutherland observed the value of a free press in enabling the public to unite for its "common good" as "members of an organized society." "The newspapers, magazines, and other journals of the country, it is safe to say, have shed and continue to shed more light on the public and business affairs of the nation than any other instrumentality of publicity." The predominant purpose of freedom of the press was "to preserve an untrammeled press as a vital source of public information." "Since informed public opinion is the most potent of all restraints upon misgovernment, the suppression or abridgement of the publicity afforded by a free press cannot be regarded otherwise than with grave concern. A free press stands as one of the great interpreters between the government and the people. To allow it to be fettered is to fetter ourselves."[29]

Between the 1920s and the 1940s, the Supreme Court heard more cases dealing with freedom of the press than in all of its previous history.[30] The growing centrality of the media to American life demanded that it take seriously the social and political implications of legal restraints on publishing. The destruction of a free press in fascist nations brought attention to the significance of an independent press to democratic societies. Perhaps the most significant reason the Court began to address press issues was that the press and its lawyers were asking it to. The interwar period saw the emergence of the press as a strategic litigator in the area of First Amendment rights.[31] Major publishers retained lawyers specializing in legal issues involving the media, trade organizations such as the American Newspaper Publishers Association formed litigation branches, and the era saw the beginnings of an organized media bar.[32] The American Civil Liberties Union, a nonprofit civil rights and civil liberties organization that had been active in free speech litigation since the 1920s, also took up the cause of freedom of the press, and it worked with publishing industry lawyers on cases defending press rights, including several cases before the Supreme Court.[33]

In *Near v. Minnesota* (1931), litigated by the American Newspaper Publishers Association and the law firm Kirkland and Ellis, employed by the *Chicago Tribune*, the Court struck down a Minnesota "nuisance law" that prohibited the publication of a "malicious, scandalous, and defamatory newspaper, magazine, or other periodical." The statute was aimed at the distribution of matter "detrimental to public morals and to the general welfare," "tending to disturb the peace of the community" and provoke "assaults and the commission of crime." Under the law, the state had shut down a "scandal sheet," the *Saturday Press*, an anti-Semitic tabloid. The majority in *Near* characterized the law as a prior restraint—"the essence of censorship"—and noted the importance of a "vigilant and courageous press" that would expose the abuses of corrupt governments and "unfaithful officials." "The fact that the liberty of the press may be abused by miscreant purveyors of scandal does not make any the less necessary the immunity of the press from previous restraint in dealing with official misconduct," it observed.[34] One legal expert at the time called *Near* "the most important decision rendered since the adoption of the First Amendment."[35]

Near v. Minnesota placed a constitutional blessing on the Blackstonian position of no prior restraints. In cases in the 1940s, the Court also suggested that it would carefully scrutinize subsequent punishments—civil or criminal liability imposed on the basis of disfavored content. In *Bridges v. California* (1946), the Court reversed the conviction of the *Los Angeles Times Mirror*, which had been fined for contempt of court for critical comments pertaining to pending litigation. A majority led by Justice Hugo Black concluded that the article did not rise to the level of a "clear and present danger" and that the conviction violated the First Amendment. That amendment, he wrote, "does not speak equivocally. It prohibits any law 'abridging the freedom of speech, or of the press.' No suggestion can be found in the Constitution that the freedom there guaranteed for speech and the press bears an inverse relation to the timeliness and importance of the ideas seeking expression."[36]

In the 1940s, the liberals on the Court applied these free press concepts not only to news publications but also to commercial entertainment, traditionally considered outside the scope of freedom of the press. In *Winters v. New York* (1948), the Court overturned the conviction of a bookseller who violated a New York law prohibiting material containing descriptions of "bloodshed, lust and crime." "The line between the informing and the entertaining is too elusive for the protection of that basic right. . . . What is one man's amusement, teaches another's doctrine. Though we can see nothing of any possible value to society in these magazines, they are as much entitled to the protection of free speech as the best of literature," the majority noted.[37]

At the same time, the Court was not willing to completely jettison the state's ability to restrict speech in the name of important public interests. In the 1940s and 1950s, a majority believed that certain kinds of speech, "low value speech," were not protected at all under the First Amendment.[38] *Chaplinsky v. New Hampshire* (1942) involved a man convicted of violating a state statute that prohibited addressing any "offensive, derisive or annoying word to any other person who is lawfully in any street or other public place, or calling him by any offensive or derisive name." The Court upheld the conviction, noting that "it is well understood that the right of free speech is not absolute at all times and under all circumstances. There are certain well-defined and narrowly limited classes of speech, the prevention and punishment of which has never been thought to raise any Constitutional problem. These include the lewd and obscene, the profane, the libelous, and the insulting or 'fighting' words. . . . It has been well observed that such utterances are no essential part of the exposition of ideas, and are of such slight social value as a step to truth that the benefit that may be derived from them is clearly outweighed by the social interest in order and morality."[39] The Court left open the possibility that the press could be subjected to liability for invasions of privacy, like libel, without infringing on its constitutional liberties. But this was an issue that it would not address squarely until over a decade later.

~

These emerging liberal free speech trends were reflected in state laws regulating the press. In the 1930s and 1940s, liability for invasion of privacy was expanding, as we've seen. Yet at the same time, some courts were going the other way, limiting the right to privacy in the interest of freedom of speech and press and the public's "right to know" about "matters of public interest."

Warren and Brandeis, writing in 1890, were aware of privacy law's implications for freedom of publishing, and they built limited protections for the press into their privacy proposal. The publication of "matters of public concern" would be exempt from liability for invasion of privacy, they had written. Their definition of "matters of public concern" was narrow: topics that served the "public interest" in the sense of the public welfare or common good, such as serious news about politics and public affairs. Mere trivia and gossip, though perhaps "interesting," were not "matters of public interest."[40]

Beginning in the 1930s, some courts began to expand the privilege for "matters of public interest" or "matters of public concern." The Warren and Brandeis view of "public interest" had been a normative one: what was a matter of public concern or public interest was not what actually interested the public but, rather, what judges believed that the public should know, in its own best interest. In the new model, "matters of public interest" became a descriptive term: if material attracted the public's attention or interest, it was a legitimate "matter of public interest" or, in the parlance of some courts, "newsworthy." The objective of the broad "public interest" or "newsworthiness" standard was to get courts out of the business of judging content, of making value judgments about the worth of publications.

Because there was great curiosity in the private lives of public figures like celebrities and politicians, information about their personal affairs, including gossip, was a privileged "matter of public interest," according to some courts. Public figures were said to have waived their right to privacy over their personal affairs when they assumed a public position. The public figure must "pay the price of even unwelcome publicity through reports upon his private life and photographic reproductions of himself and his family," noted the *Restatement of Torts*.[41] When NBC broadcast a conversation between Charlie Chaplin and a radio commentator that had been obtained by wiretapping, Chaplin sued for invasion of privacy. The court held that Chaplin had waived his right of privacy over the phone conversation because he was a "prominent public figure whose activities are of general public interest."[42] The public figure's waiver was apparently permanent. In a 1949 case from California, a former professional boxer who went under the name Canvasback Cohen had retired from the ring, but ten years later, an announcer mentioned his name in a radio broadcast, and Cohen sued for invasion of privacy. The court held that no matter how much he wished to retreat from the public eye, he could not "draw himself like a snail into his shell" and retreat from public view "at his will and whim."[43]

"Private figures"—ordinary citizens—had a stronger right to privacy than public figures, but according to some courts, even they waived their right to privacy when they were involved in "matters of public interest," whether intentionally or unintentionally. "One who is not a recluse," according to the *Restatement*, must expect commentary on "the ordinary incidents of community life of which he is a part. These include comment upon his conduct, the more or less casual observation of his neighbors as to what he does upon his own land and the possibility that he may be photographed as a part of a street scene or a group of persons."[44] Insofar as they generated public interest or curiosity, there was "no invasion of a right of privacy in the description of the ordinary goings and comings of a person or of weddings, even though intended to be entirely private."[45] In a 1929 case, *Jones v. Herald Post*, a woman named Lillian Jones witnessed her husband assaulted and stabbed to death on the street, and she tried to fight back against the attackers. She sued for invasion of privacy when the *Louisville Herald Post* published her picture with a truthful account of her heroic efforts. The court concluded that the woman had, albeit unwillingly, become an "innocent actor in a great tragedy in which the public had a deep concern," and as such, it was not an invasion of privacy to publish her photograph.[46]

Technically the privacy tort did not raise a formal First Amendment issue; tort liability was not considered state action at that time.[47] Courts nonetheless described the broad public interest privilege as important protection for freedom of the press. As a New York trial court noted in 1937, a right of privacy that imposed liability for "news items and articles of general public interest, educational and informative in character," implicated the rights of a "free press."[48] Stories about a politician's home and family life, a sensationalistic article about a homicide in *Official Detective Stories* magazine, news about the embarrassing personal habits of celebrities and former celebrities—however crass, invasive, or trivial, they served the "public's right to be informed" about "matters of public interest."[49]

~

The courts of New York, the center of the publishing industry, were among the most protective of the press in the country. Recall that the state's 1903 privacy statute penalized the use, without consent, of a person's "name, portrait, or picture" for "advertising" or "trade" purposes. Almost immediately after the passage of the law, the state's courts made clear that in the interest of a free press, the use of names, portraits, and likenesses for the purposes of disseminating the news did not fall under the prohibition of "trade" uses.[50]

Although the New York courts would never specifically define "the news," they suggested that it extended beyond straight factual reporting on public affairs to gossip and sensationalistic, lowbrow journalism. In the 1914 case *Colyer v. Fox,* the plaintiff was a professional high diver who had her photograph taken in costume. A copy came into the possession of the *National Police Gazette,* a disreputable, bawdy men's publication. The woman claimed that the *Gazette* was not a serious news publication and therefore publishing her photograph was a "trade" use. The court rejected the argument. Given that many newspapers were entertaining and mildly salacious, "applied as the appellant would desire, [the statute] would cover nearly every issue of our newspapers, and especially our great number of monthly magazines."[51] "Newsworthy" material included "all events and occurrences which have that indefinable quality of interest, which attracts public attention," a federal district court announced in 1936. "Such articles include, among others, travel stories, stories of distant places, tales of historic personages, and events, the reproduction of items of past news, and surveys of social conditions."[52]

This broad definition of newsworthiness did not mean that publications had free rein to use people's pictures, names, and life stories, however. According to the New York courts, false and "fictionalized" material was, by definition, not newsworthy. This rule was first announced in a 1913 case, *D'Altomonte v. New*

York Herald. The plaintiff was a member of the Italian nobility, "a professional newspaper correspondent, traveler, writer, and lecturer of recognized ability." The *New York Herald* published an article under D'Altomonte's name, but he did not write it. The article, he alleged, was falsified and made him look foolish and un-educated. He sued under the privacy statute. The court agreed that the article was not news because it was false, and could therefore be subject to liability as an unauthorized trade use of his identity. The falsity of the material indicated that it was principally for commercial or profit-generating purposes rather than for dis-seminating news, and therefore fell under the statute's proscriptions.[53] There was value in true information, and the press must be protected in delivering it, but there was no value in intentional falsehoods.

The most contested cases under the New York privacy law involved sensa-tionalistic articles in which facts were highly dramatized although not completely false. In *Sutton v. Hearst,* from 1950, a newspaper ran a story of a soldier who had made a strange bequest before his death. He had asked that his money be used to purchase one rose a week for a female coworker he knew only casually. Although the events described in the story had in fact occurred, embellishments in the story suggested that the woman and the man had been involved in a romance. The woman was married, and she was outraged by this implication. The trial court rejected the newspaper's motion to dismiss the privacy claim, alleging that the distortions rose to the level of falsification, and the decision was upheld on ap-peal.[54] Two appellate justices wrote a strong dissent: "The fact that some of the statements in the article may not be strictly factual does not destroy a press priv-ilege which otherwise exists." There was a line to be drawn between falsehoods and innocent exaggerations, between lies and mere "literary license."[55] To hold the press to a standard of perfect accuracy would infringe on freedom of the press.

By 1950, privacy law was in a state of disarray. Courts found invasions of privacy in all manner of depictions that plaintiffs considered to be embarrass-ing, offensive, or otherwise injurious to their sense of self. Yet other courts were interpreting the "newsworthiness" and "matters of public interest" privileges ex-pansively, in the interest of a free press and the "public's right to know." State laws varied considerably, and there were no clear definitions as to what was news-worthy, false, or a matter of public concern. A federal judge, writing in 1956, described privacy law as a "haystack in a hurricane."[56]

This was the legal maelstrom in which the Hills brought their case.

~

In October 1955, Leonard Garment filed a complaint under the New York privacy statute against every party involved in the creation, publication, and dissemination of the book, play, and movie *The Desperate Hours*, as well as the *Life* article: Joseph Hayes, Marrijane Hayes, Howard Erskine, The Desperate Hours Company, Time, Inc., Paramount Pictures, Random House, the Literary Guild, Crowell Collier Book Publishing, Pocket Books, and the Reader's Digest Association. The suit was brought in the name of the entire family: James Hill, Elizabeth Hill, and their five children. Connecticut, where the Hills resided, had not recognized the privacy tort, and James's employment in New York City was sufficient to establish jurisdiction under New York law.[57] On March 7, 1956, the Hills served an amended complaint in which the children were dropped as plaintiffs. James and Elizabeth decided that it would be too traumatic to expose the kids to the litigation.[58]

The complaint characterized the novel, the play, the film, and the *Life* article as unauthorized "commercial" or "trade" uses of the Hills' identities, and thus "invasions of privacy" under New York law. The Hills had been connected to *The Desperate Hours* as a "promotional scheme" to "increase the dramatic impact of the novel, play, and motion picture and greatly increas[e] the commercial value thereof." "The writing, publication, distribution, and sale of the . . . *The Desperate Hours* . . . were not intended as a fair and accurate report of news whether past or current, but were solely for the purposes of entertainment, advertisement, and trade."[59] Garment argued that Hayes, the producers of the play and the movie *The Desperate Hours*, and the *Life* editors had presented the Hills in a manner that was commercialized, distorted, and fictionalized, and thus "non-newsworthy." "In truth and in fact, said novel was based upon the actual occurrences of September 1952 in which plaintiffs Hill were involved . . . with certain modifications of the actual facts, including the partial modification of the name of the family involved from Hill to Hilliard, the reduction of the size of the besieged family, the creation of numerous melodramatic and violent incidents which did not in fact occur, the insinuation of sexual approaches by one of the convicts to the hostage daughter, and with numerous other fictional embellishments in the characterization of the personalities, relationships, attitudes, and acts of the members of the besieged family."[60]

Garment alleged that all of the defendants were complicit in the *Life* article. Joseph Hayes, Howard Erskine, the Desperate Hours Company, Random House,

Pocket Books, Paramount Pictures, and the magazines that serialized *The Desperate Hours*—*Collier's* and the *Reader's Digest*—allegedly collaborated on the *Life* piece as part of an "advertising scheme." The complaint continued:

> On or about February 1, 1955, and as part of said promotional and advertising campaign, defendants Hayes, Erskine, and *The Desperate Hours* company made arrangements with Defendant Time, Inc. to publish a special photographic layout in *Life* which would disclose the true identity of the purportedly fictional Hilliard family . . . thereby enhancing the dramatic interest of the play, novel, and motion picture . . . and advertising its true-life origin to the millions of persons who read *Life* magazine, while simultaneously creating a sufficiently unique and imaginative human interest story to justify the allocation thereto of substantial space by a magazine with the vast national and international circulation of *Life* magazine.[61]

The *Life* article was devoid of "news" value, Garment claimed; it was a "promotional and advertising scheme, pure and simple."[62] There was no legitimate reason "as a matter of news dissemination or otherwise, to identify the plaintiffs Hill with the Hilliard family, to reprint newspaper headlines of September 1952, or to photograph the members of the cast of *The Desperate Hours* in the former home."[63] As a result of the book, the play, the film, and especially the *Life* article, the Hills suffered "emotional distress and embarrassment, have been subjected to extensive and undesirable publicity and comment, [and] have sustained serious impairments of their ordinary business, social, and educational relationships." The family sought what was then the extraordinary sum of $350,000 in damages.[64]

CHAPTER SEVEN

Suing the Press

Time, Inc.'s lawyers were unfazed. Every year in the 1950s and 1960s, about two to three hundred readers threatened to sue Time, Inc. for libel or invasion of privacy. Many didn't follow through, convinced by the company's lawyers or their own lawyers that they had no case.[1] Most who sued didn't win.

Like most other major publications, Time, Inc. had an in-house legal department. Its head was John Dowd, "a tall, unflappable Irishman" regarded as one of the best journalism lawyers in the country.[2] A Harvard Law School graduate, Dowd was chief editorial counsel for Time, Inc. from 1944 to 1973.[3] He started his legal career at the Wall Street law firm Cravath, Swaine, and Moore, which did legal work for Time, Inc. His assistant was a former Cravath associate, Gabriel Perle, who went on to become Time, Inc.'s general counsel.[4] Under Dowd, Time, Inc. developed an efficient, small department—at times, only three or four lawyers—with expertise in publishing issues such as copyright, trademark, privacy, and libel.[5]

One of Dowd's jobs was advising reporters and editors on the legal implications of their articles. Journalist Charles Champlin remembered an incident in the 1940s when a *Time* reporter wrote that unscrupulous landlords near Fort Dix, New Jersey, were "gouging young married GIs living off the base." Champlin was assigned to take pictures for the story.[6] "We got a memorable photograph of a young couple living in what had been a chicken coop, lit by one bare bulb," he recalled. "But we were also chased off another property by a landlord with a shotgun, and were threatened with lawsuits by other landlords, charging invasion of privacy." This scared him, and he reported the incident to Dowd. Dowd advised him, "The woman can't sue us in New Jersey; we don't do business there. We'll send thirty photographers over to her place and take pictures of every piece of chicken shit in sight. Then we'll get her in front of a . . . judge here in New York, and she'll be lucky if she doesn't go to jail herself." "After the story ran, there wasn't a peep from the woman or any of the other landlords," Champlin recalled.[7]

One of the legal department's most important functions was reviewing articles for potential libel or privacy lawsuits. This practice of "self-censorship" was routine at most major news outlets by the 1950s. In 1937, a trade journal noted that half of the major New York newspapers used lawyers as "censors." "Legal censorship," if "intelligently used," can result in "considerable saving to any newspaper of large circulation," observed *Editor and Publisher*.[8] In addition to proofreading and fact checking, most publishers had "every manuscript read by a libel expert before it is passed for manufacture," noted the *Saturday Review of Literature* in 1950. "Readings often disclose a statement which needs proof before it can be retained, or some phrasing which needs correction because it is obviously dangerous."[9] Self-censorship was time-consuming and costly; every single word in every article had to be read and passed on.

Time Inc.'s lawyers read every issue of *Time*, *Life*, and *Sports Illustrated* (launched by Time, Inc. in 1956) and warned editors about articles or statements that could be legally actionable. It was assisted in this process by two lawyers from Cravath, Harold Medina Jr. and Alan Hruska. The "libel checks" were usually done on Saturday mornings, before the magazine went to the printer on Saturday afternoons.[10] When the lawyers found something dangerous, they alerted the editors. Sometimes the editors took the advice and eliminated the statement. If the editors insisted on running it, Dowd usually gave in, warning them that the publication could be costly. Lawyers at Time, Inc. "played second or third fiddle to editors," recalled one Time, Inc. editor. "As a matter of policy, they never advised editors what to print or what not to. They simply pointed out what was actionable in law and what Time's exposure would be. Editors made all the decisions."[11] *Life*'s managing editor in the 1950s, Ed Thompson, said that Dowd was a "joy to work with because he really wanted to let us say what we wanted, with a realistic appreciation of the risks involved."[12]

It was well-established policy at Time, Inc. to never settle a libel or privacy claim. When Thompson thought *Life* was right about something, he urged the lawyers to resist settling, even though it may have been financially savvy to do so. The point of the policy was to discourage so-called nuisance litigation. It was thought that a reputation for easy settlement would invite frivolous lawsuits.[13] Other major publications had a similar practice. Wrote *New York Times* publisher Adolph Ochs to his paper's lawyers, "You know my views about settling libel suits.

. . . I would never settle a libel suit to save a little money. . . . If we have damaged a person we are prepared to pay . . . and we accept the decision as part of the exigencies of our business."[14] In response to threatened libel suits, the *New Yorker*'s in-house counsel developed a standard procedure: notifying the complainant that the magazine had not libeled him and using "explanation or persuasion" to convince him to give up his claim.[15] Through its policy of refusing to settle, the lawyers claimed, the magazine had established a "reputation for not being a sucker" and had allegedly been "less plagued" by libel and privacy complaints than other periodicals.[16]

When Time, Inc. faced an undeniable mistake and a persistent plaintiff, it did settle, albeit infrequently. One case that ended in settlement involved a photograph of a woman wearing a bikini in a 1949 issue of *Life*. The writer thought he detected an operation scar on the woman's stomach. He wrote a caption saying that girls who wear bikinis should not have stomachs looking like golf balls. The flaw turned out to be in the photograph, not on the woman. Dowd resolved the case out of court.[17]

Another nightmare case was the so-called case of the non-Italian. It began when a *Life* photographer stationed in Europe decided that there was a "special brand of highly pictorial machismo in Italian men," according to former researcher Jeanne Hamblin. The photographer took pictures of Italian men arguing in traffic jams, "mooning at pretty girls, [and] admiring themselves in restaurant mirrors." The photos were laid out on several pages in *Life*, and a writer was assigned to create captions. One described a photo of a "tall, curly haired Mr. Universe type happily flexing his muscles." A few days after the story was published, Dowd found out that the man was not an Italian but rather an American professional, and the photographer had caught him during his vacation. The man threatened to sue. Dowd took the man to lunch, offered apologies, and assured him it would never happen again. But it did. The picture was later used in another article, on Italian men not being good lovers. Dowd arranged an out-of-court settlement for $7,500.[18]

≈

When cases were litigated, Time, Inc. was represented by Cravath. Luce brought his legal problems to Cravath when his sister married Cravath partner M. T. Moore in 1926.[19] As publishing became a large-scale business enterprise, publishers could afford to hire the most skilled and costly legal advocates. In the early to mid-twentieth century, a number of large, elite law firms, including some of the biggest Wall Street firms, took on major publishing companies as clients. Among others, Kirkland and Ellis represented the *Chicago Tribune*; Weil, Gotshal and Manges represented Scribner's and Fawcett Publishing; Simpson, Thatcher and Bartlett represented Doubleday; and Lord, Day & Lord handled the legal affairs of the *New York Times*.[20] There were also a number of midsize and smaller firms specializing in media law, as well as prominent solo practitioners. The New York–based Greenbaum, Wolff, and Ernst was noted for its work against literary censorship and its acclaimed lawyers, including Alexander Lindey, Harriet Pilpel, and Morris Ernst, all key figures in the American Civil Liberties Union (ACLU).[21] Ephraim London, who argued several cases before the Supreme Court, represented Simon and Schuster, Grove Press, and other book publishing houses in the 1940s and 1950s.[22] The media bar also included in-house legal departments at publishing companies, members of the national ACLU and its state chapters, as well as publishing industry organizations, such as the American Newspaper Publishing Association and the Authors' League of America, which contributed amicus briefs in Supreme Court cases involving the press.[23]

One of the most prestigious of the Wall Street "law factories," Cravath was famed for its "Cravath system" of hiring and promotion. Cravath claimed to hire the "best of the best"—most of its lawyers were top graduates from Harvard, Columbia, or Yale. Cravath was one of the first firms to hire incoming lawyers on a salaried basis. Associates who were not promotable to partnership were asked to leave in an "up-or-out" policy. The lawyers worked hard, under tremendous stress. As the firm's official history explained, in order to succeed, an associate needed to be more than a "bookworm." He also had to have "warmth and force of personality and physical stamina adequate to the pressure to which they [are] subject because of the rugged character of the work."[24] The firm was located near Mudge, Stern, Baldwin, and Todd, at 15 Broad Street, directly opposite the New York Stock Exchange. The atmosphere was stern. As one associate from that era recalled, "No women lawyers, no women secretaries or stenographers, no women in any capacity at all were allowed in the hallways of Cravath, Swaine, and Moore." Ladies would be a "distraction." "Even the messengers, who carried documents from one office to another and sharpened our stacks of pencils every morning, were elderly men in grey office jackets."[25]

Cravath handled the legal affairs of industrial powerhouses, including Ford, Westinghouse Electric, Bank of America, Bethlehem Steel, Dupont, Studebaker, and Squibb Pharmaceuticals. It also represented media giants: the Curtis company, the publishers of the *Saturday Evening Post*; the *Philadelphia Inquirer*; *Look* magazine; *Esquire*; and the *Washington Post*. Time, Inc. was Cravath's most prominent publishing client.[26] Cravath assisted Time, Inc. with a variety of issues related to its business and printing operations, as well as problems stemming from its publications. As the firm's history noted, "The lively, breezy style of all the Time Inc. publications has naturally led to many scores of suits and threatened suits for alleged libel and invasion of the right of privacy." "There have been those who objected to the publication of their pictures on Time's front cover; Huey Long did not like the treatment given him in the March of Time, and even a number of Cravath clients have not been entirely pleased with their write-ups in *Fortune*."[27] In the 1950s and 1960s, Jack Dempsey, Louisiana governor Earl Long, and Bob Hope, among other notables, sued Time, Inc. for libel, seeking multimillion-dollar damage awards.[28]

Many libel cases were defeated at the pretrial motion stage, usually on the grounds that the person hadn't been defamed.[29] In 1962, Time, Inc. was sued over a photo-essay, "Some Idiots Afloat." The article consisted of eight pictures of people in boats, commentary about each of the pictures, and a statement about the carelessness of many boaters. "The same reckless drivers that cause a disproportionate number of highway accidents now infest the once tranquil U.S. waterways. As seen through a telephoto lens, their antics seem lethal. And sometimes they are." Although no names were used in the article, the plaintiff claimed he was the person depicted at the tiller of a small boat in which there were four other passengers. The caption read "rub-a-dub-dub, too many in a tub."[30] Henry Luce, *Life* editors Ed Thompson and Joe Kastner, and head researcher Marian McPhail were the named defendants. The court concluded that the man had not been libeled because the publication was "not 'reasonably susceptible of any defamatory meaning.'" As the judge opined, "exaggeration, slight irony, or wit, or [other] delightful touches of style" did not change the essential meaning of the text, which was that the plaintiff was a careless boater. This accusation may have been insulting, but it wasn't enough to make the article libelous.[31]

Another tactic Cravath used in libel cases was to deploy private investigators to uncover facts about the plaintiff. The gist of a libel claim is injury to reputation. If the plaintiff's reputation was already bad, there could be no action for libel. Press attorneys were "almost always assisted by hired investigators who dig up all the misfortune in the plaintiff's past," noted one prominent libel lawyer in 1950. "It is surprising how many skeletons there are in how many closets and how easily they are opened."[32] In some cases, Time's lawyers would present a file of negative reputation evidence to the plaintiff's lawyer, and the lawsuit would end right there. Sometimes the plaintiff backed down when he found out he was under investigation. As one lawyer for the *New York Times* recalled, "It is said that when a person begins a suit for libel he is inviting an investigation into his past life beginning with his birth. Much has been spent for such investigations. We think they pay off, for sometimes the knowledge of someone's asking questions about him is enough for him to call it quits."[33]

The Cravath lawyers' track record for Time, Inc. was pretty good. Of the libel cases Time, Inc. tried between the 1920s and the 1970s, it lost only nine. Luce himself was never called on to testify. To a man whom *Time* falsely described as a "racketeer" it paid $5,000 in damages.[34] The biggest judgment, awarded in 1948 to a defamed clothing manufacturer, was $40,000.[35]

One costly lawsuit involved a 1955 *Life* article titled "Savagery on Sunday."[36] The article claimed that there was "dirty play" in the National Football League and identified Philadelphia Eagles middle guard Bucko Kilroy and linebacker Wayne Robinson as the worst offenders. The article called Kilroy the toughest of the league's "bad men" and claimed that he deliberately injured other players. The players sued for $250,000 each, claiming that the piece subjected them to "scorn, contempt, and ridicule." The case went to trial in federal court, and the jury found in favor of the players. *Life* paid them each $11,600 in general and punitive damages. The costs of that case were especially high because of the professional football players *Life* hired as witnesses.[37]

In spite of being most involved with libel cases, Time, Inc.'s lawyers were more concerned with privacy lawsuits. Although there were only five or ten privacy suits for every one hundred libel suits, the law of privacy was far less developed than libel law, which had a set of elaborate and well-defined privileges and defenses that protected the press, such as the "fair comment" and fair report privileges, the defense of truth, and the baseline requirement that the publication be defamatory. Privacy law had no such protections. As the law of privacy stood in most states, a plaintiff could potentially recover for a true, nondefamatory statement if a court deemed the material to be "offensive" and not "newsworthy" or a "matter of public concern," vague and ill-defined standards. While libel law required plaintiffs to prove that their reputations had been seriously damaged, privacy law asked the plaintiff only to show that he or she had been humiliated, upset, or insulted. In New York, the courts did not specify how embellished an article had to be in order to be considered false or "fictionalized" and thus fall under the privacy law's purview. Plaintiffs who were offended by publications could circumvent libel and recover under the less stringent rules of privacy—and many were doing exactly that.

~

Time, Inc.'s lawyers were adept at working with privacy and libel law and also the doctrine and rhetoric of "freedom of the press." "Freedom of the press" had long been the primary defense of American publishers, mobilized by press attorneys in cases across the legal spectrum. It had become a talisman of sorts, dangled by media lawyers to ward off a variety of legal burdens ranging from economic regulations such as taxes and postal regulations to liability based on the content of publications, such as libel, privacy, and contempt of court. In the nineteenth century, publishers drew on the idea of freedom of the press in their attempts to fashion special protections for newspapers in the common law of libel. Free press arguments were the forte of the American Newspaper Publishers Association, founded in 1887 as a trade organization. In the late nineteenth and early twentieth centuries, it engaged in numerous state and federal campaigns to liberalize press laws, under the rallying cry of "freedom of the press."[38]

In the 1930s, with the federal government's efforts under the New Deal to tax and regulate the publishing industry, "free press" arguments reached new levels of intensity. Waving the banner of "freedom of the press," publishers fought against the application of economic regulations, such as federal social welfare and labor laws, to press operations. Major publishing associations brought First Amendment challenges before the Supreme Court against the National Labor Relations Act and the Fair Labor Standards Act.[39] The American Newspaper Publishers Association claimed that the First Amendment exempted all of a newspaper's activities from government regulation.[40] These arguments were unsuccessful. In a noted Supreme Court case from 1945, the Associated Press news syndicate attempted to use "freedom of the press" to defend its actions blocking rivals from the news market. Justice Black could find nothing in the Bill of Rights that would exempt the press from the nation's antitrust laws.[41]

Freedom of the press was more successfully deployed as a defense to claims brought over the content of publications. Sometimes lawyers argued freedom of the press as a formal constitutional matter; since the First Amendment did not reach many state laws affecting the press before the 1960s, freedom of the press was more often raised as a policy consideration, one that courts were advised to heed in cases involving the press and publishing prerogatives. We often think of "freedom of speech" and "freedom of the press" as judge-made doctrines, yet the law of freedom of speech was created as much by the publishing industry as it was by courts. Judges rely on parties' briefs and arguments when formulating their decisions. Between plaintiffs' lawyers, typically untrained in media issues, and the media's elite, specialized attorneys, the latter most often presented stronger, more persuasive arguments. As the media bar coalesced and gained strength, press lawyers exerted significant influence over the shape of modern free speech law.

In the mid-twentieth century, Time, Inc. was involved in several key cases that expanded doctrines and concepts of freedom of the press within state law. Perhaps because of its founder's views, Time, Inc. aggressively forwarded free press arguments, arguably more than any other major publisher of that time. Freedom of the press had long been one of Henry Luce's pet concerns. It was Luce's belief in freedom of the press—in the sense of freedom from government involvement in publishing—that led him in the early 1940s to create and fund the Hutchins Commission on Freedom of the Press, a committee of prestigious academics charged with investigating the legal and social status of the press, with the aim of deterring federal regulation of the publishing industry.[42] In the 1950s, Luce wrote essays and went on lecture tours in which he argued the importance of freedom of the press—meaning liberty to publish his conservative views—for democracy and freedom.[43]

One case in which Time, Inc.'s lawyers used freedom of the press to its advantage involved *Life*'s controversial coverage of a public health film, *The Birth of a Baby,* which featured images of a live childbirth, stunning and shocking to the public in 1938. This forward-looking quasi-documentary had been produced under the auspices of several medical organizations, including the American Association of Obstetricians, Gynecologists, and Abdominal Surgeons, and the Children's Bureau of the U.S. Department of Labor. An issue of *Life* was banned across the country for publishing still photographs from the film. Several states and municipalities declared the movie and *Life*'s pictures of it to be obscene. In Bronx County, the district attorney confiscated the magazines and threatened to bring charges against newsdealers who sold it. The ACLU's Morris Ernst helped to arrange an obscenity prosecution of *Life* publisher Roy Larsen. Larsen went to the office of the district attorney, sold a copy of *Life* to a detective waiting there, and was charged with selling an obscene publication.[44]

In the ensuing trial, the court overturned the conviction. Larsen was defended by Cravath lawyers Maurice Moore and John Harding, and Morris Ernst and Alexander Lindey of the ACLU, who argued that the material was not obscene and that banning it violated freedom of the press. Defense witnesses—public health authorities, welfare workers, and educators—attested to the "sincerity, honest and educational value of the picture story complained of."[45] It was the judge's own opinion that "the picture story, because of the manner in which it was presented, does not fall within the forbidden class. The picture story was directly based on a film produced under the auspices of a responsible medical group. There is no nudity or unnecessary disclosure. The subject has been treated with delicacy."[46] The court concluded, "Conceptions of what is decent or indecent are not constant. . . . Recent cases illustrate the caution with which courts have proceeded in this branch of the law to avoid interference with a justifiable freedom of expression."[47]

It was a victory for freedom of expression. It was also a big victory for *Life*. All available copies of the issue were sold, and there was a spike in subscription requests. Writers, intellectuals, politicians, and celebrities sent comments to the magazine congratulating it on its bold defense of freedom of the press. "It was an absolutely ideal situation for *Life*—the magazine was courageously fighting the forces of censorship to bring its readers information that would only make their lives better," recalled editor Loudon Wainwright.[48] *The Birth of a Baby* case was both important precedent and a great "gimmick," one of the magazine's brilliant publicity stunts.

~

Perhaps more than any other area of the law, battles over freedom of the press were fought in the realm of libel. In the 1940s and 1950s, publishers and their attorneys argued that the common law of libel, with its stringent, antiquated rules of liability, constituted a serious burden on freedom of the press. Under the law of libel in most states, it will be recalled, the falsity of the allegedly libelous statement was presumed; the publisher could exonerate itself only by proving its truth. The plaintiff did not have to prove that his reputation had actually been harmed by the statement; he needed only to demonstrate that it could potentially hurt his reputation. Libel was a strict liability tort: the publisher was responsible for his statements regardless of whether he published them innocently or maliciously. Even a careless error, if it resulted in a false and defamatory statement, could subject a publisher to an unfavorable judgment.

For several decades prior to the 1960s, press lawyers had tried to obtain a decision from the U.S. Supreme Court declaring that libel presented a First Amendment issue and that liability for libel must be restricted on constitutional grounds. Publishers appealed unfavorable libel judgments to the Supreme Court, hoping to obtain such a ruling. As the Crowell-Collier Publishing Company argued in its petition to the Supreme Court in 1947, in a case involving an alleged libel on the governor of Florida, protection for erroneous statements of fact in political criticism was necessary "if the press and others are to function as critical agencies in our democracy." "One of the prerogatives of American citizenship is the right to criticize public men and measures—and that means not only informed and responsible criticism but the freedom to speak foolishly and without moderation."[49] When the Second Circuit Court of Appeals reversed a federal district court's order dismissing a libel claim against the *Reader's Digest* for having called a man a "Communist," the publisher appealed to the U.S. Supreme Court, arguing that the decision had "the effect of circumscribing the rights of freedom of speech and freedom of the press" and "unduly restricts free discussion of political matters of vital public concern." If labeling someone a Communist was libelous per se, "constitutional freedom of speech and freedom of the press" became, "for all practical purposes, uncertain and illusory guarantees."[50] The Court rejected these petitions. One of the only libel cases the Supreme Court took before the 1960s was *Schenectady Union Publishing v. Sweeney*, from 1942, involving a political columnist's attack on the controversial Senator Martin Sweeney, accused of opposing a judicial appointment in Cleveland on the basis of anti-Semitism. An evenly divided Court affirmed the lower court's judgment in favor of the plaintiff without addressing the First Amendment issue.[51]

Although the press never obtained a constitutional ruling on libel before the 1964 decision in *New York Times v. Sullivan*, its lawyers, using free press arguments, did succeed in expanding privileges within the common law of libel. On the urgings of the press, a few states adopted a privilege that exempted false and defamatory statements of fact about public officials unless the plaintiff could show that the publication was false and the falsity was made with malice, or reckless disregard of the truth. Under the privilege, the burden of proof shifted; the burden was on the plaintiff to prove falsity and malice rather than on the defendant to prove the truth, traditionally the rule under the common law. The idea was that the press should have latitude to make some mistakes in reporting on public officials and public affairs; it was impossible to ensure the accuracy of every statement, and to penalize the press for innocent or negligent errors would impair its ability to report the news.[52] As the Kansas Supreme Court noted in its decision in *Coleman v. Mac-Lennan* recognizing the privilege, "It is of the utmost consequence that the people should discuss the character and qualifications of candidates for their suffrages. The importance to the state and to society of such discussions is so vast and the advantages derived so great that they more than counterbalance . . . injury to the reputations of individuals."[53] Time, Inc.'s attorneys aggressively mobilized the privilege in libel cases involving public officials.[54]

Time, Inc.'s lawyers used free press arguments in their efforts to dismantle several other restrictive aspects of libel law. The noted case *Hartmann v. Time, Inc.* involved a 1944 *Life* article that included a picture of a Columbia University professor of psychology, Gregory Hartmann, at a rally for the Peace Now Movement, which was "in favor of an immediate armistice and a negotiated peace with generous terms to Germany and Japan."[55] The article reported that Hartmann had been indicted by the United States as a "fascist." This turned out to be false.[56] *Life*, in a published correction, admitted that Hartmann had not been indicted as a fascist but insisted that he was the leader of a "subversive movement" dangerous to U.S. war efforts. Hartmann sued, alleging that the *Life* article cost him his position at Columbia, damaged his earning power, and led him to "suffer a nervous collapse."[57]

Four million copies of the *Life* issue were circulated throughout the world. The actual printing of the magazine took place in Illinois and Pennsylvania. Hartmann sued for libel in both states. Under the laws in Illinois and Pennsylvania, every copy of the magazine could be actionable as a libel. Other states, however, used a "single publication" rule, in which each issue of a magazine or newspaper, rather than every single copy, constituted the basis of a libel action. Time, Inc. argued that the single-publication rule was mandated by freedom of the press.[58] The

Third Circuit Court of Appeals agreed. "We think that the . . . single publication rule is the preferable one and is recommended both by logic and public policy. Public policy must regard freedom of the press and while the law must exact penalties for libel the instruments of free and effective expression, newspapers and magazines which are published on a nationwide basis should not be subjected to the harassment of repeated lawsuits."[59]

Publishing industry lawyers were also mobilizing "freedom of the press" in privacy law, in their claims for a broad definition of the "newsworthiness" or "matters of public interest" privilege. They argued that anything that was "of interest" to the public, including gossip, sensationalism, and trivia, should be considered a "matter of public interest" or "newsworthy," and therefore exempt from liability. In effect, media lawyers asked the courts to adopt journalism's definition of "the news." As the United Press Association's manual put it, "Anything and everything interesting about life and materials in all their manifestations" was "news."[60] In the words of a 1940 journalism textbook, "News is . . . information that is interesting, that is to say, information that the ordinary human being derives satisfaction or stimulation from reading."[61]

Time, Inc. was involved in a major privacy suit in the 1940s, but its "freedom of the press" argument failed badly in that case. In 1939, *Time* had published an article titled "Starving Glutton," about a woman who had a metabolic disorder that led her to eat huge quantities without gaining weight. "Starving Glutton: One night last week pretty Mrs. Dorothy Barber of Kansas City grabbed a candy bar, packed up some clothes, and walked to General Hospital. 'I want to stay here,' she said between bites. 'I want to eat all the time. I can finish a normal meal and be back in the kitchen in ten minutes eating again.'" The doctor found that although the woman had "eaten enough in the past year to feed a family of ten," she had lost 25 pounds. A picture published with the article, taken by a reporter over the woman's protests, showed Dorothy Barber in bed in a long-sleeved hospital gown. It was a close-up picture showing only her face, head, and arms, with bedclothes over her chest. Captions under the picture read, "Insatiable Eater Barber, She Eats for Ten."[62]

The woman sued for invasion of privacy in the Missouri courts, and a jury awarded damages. Time, Inc. appealed to the state's supreme court. As it argued in its brief, "Articles of current news or immediate public interest, as well as educational articles do not infringe any right of privacy." The story about Mrs. Barber was "newsworthy," and the article was presented "in a factual and reportorial manner as an item of news with educational and informative aspects in a magazine devoted exclusively to the publication of the news. To hold such a publication an invasion of the right of privacy would impose an unreasonable burden on the newspapers and magazines of this state," infringing its right to publish "under constitutional guarantees of freedom of speech and the press."[63]

Barber's lawyers argued that the case was a perfect example of the importance of a strong right to privacy against the press. "It is easy to understand why the great majority of states, and increasing numbers of decisions under modern conditions" were using privacy law to limit the press. "Here the appellant, pandering to the greed of a certain type of mind and morbid curiosity for salacious or private news concerning someone else, takes an unimportant and slight, everyday occurrence . . . [and] builds up its own so-called public interest story, entirely falsely, and then, when called to account, tries to raise the shield of freedom of the press to protect it in a vicious fabrication."[64]

The Missouri Supreme Court agreed with Barber and upheld the $3,000 judgment. "While plaintiff's ailment may have been a matter of some public interest because unusual, certainly the identity of the person who suffered this ailment was not. Whatever the limits of the right of privacy may be, it seems clear that it must include the right to have information given to or gained by a physician in the treatment of an individual's personal ailment kept from publication. . . . Likewise, whatever may be the right of the press, tabloids or news reel companies to take and use pictures of persons in public places, certainly any right of privacy ought to protect a person from publication of a picture taken without consent while ill or in bed for treatment and recuperation." "Freedom of the press was not created merely for the benefit of the press, but because it is essential to the . . . progress of civilization. . . . Therefore, the press, like individual citizens, must not abuse its constitutional rights or overlook its obligations to others."[65]

"Establishing conditions of liability for invasion of the right of privacy is a matter of harmonizing individual rights with community and social interests," the court concluded. "We think they can be harmonized on a reasonable basis, recognizing the right of privacy without abridging freedom of the press."[66]

CHAPTER EIGHT

Maneuvers

The Hills' lives had been thrown into chaos. Like many other victims of unwanted and distorted media publicity, the family suffered deeply. After the magazine came out, people linked the Hills not only to the *Life* article, but "they tied us into the book, they tied us into the play, they revived the incident," James recalled. "We had partially succeeded in burying the [hostage incident]," and the *Life* article "immediately fanned it." The *Life* piece brought back horrible "insinuations"—"the violation of my daughters, and of my wife."[1]

The children were teased by classmates, who laughed at them and called them the "Hilliards."[2] Their friends brought up incidents from *The Desperate Hours* and confused them with the characters in the novel. All of their children were "deeply disturbed" by the *Life* article, according to James. The sudden reappearance of the hostage incident in their lives traumatized them by forcing them to relive it, remember it, and think about it.[3]

James became an object of spectacle and curiosity. Everywhere he went, he was besieged with comments and questions. As a sales manager for a major hosiery company, he traveled extensively on business; within the course of three weeks, he would go from department store to department store in a sweep of the Midwest, from Columbus to Detroit to Chicago to Milwaukee to Minneapolis to Des Moines to Omaha to Kansas City. Whenever he met new clients, "all they wanted to do was to talk about *The Desperate Hours*," James remembered. They "knew my name was James J. Hill. They also knew that I [had] lived in Whitemarsh Township . . . and they knew that I [had] lived in a big old Dutch house. . . . And many of them who had never associated me before with the incident immediately recognized it." In the midst of sales pitches, potential clients would divert his presentation with comments about *The Desperate Hours*, asking whether the family had sold their story to Hayes and if they were making money off of it.[4]

One day when James took the merchandise manager at a major department store to lunch, the entire hour and a half was taken up with a discussion of *The Desperate Hours*. He tried six different times, in vain, to get the manager's attention back to the products he was trying to sell. In another incident, in Dallas, a merchandiser converted James's entire sales pitch into a *"Desperate Hours* situation." "When you have questions [each day] as to 'are you so and so,' or 'which one are you,' or 'did this happen to your wife,' 'are they all right,' 'what was the incident,' or 'did anybody get hurt,' 'what are you working in hosiery for you ought to be living off the royalties.'. . . I have always felt that the salesman has so many hours, so many minutes in which to write orders, and he doesn't have any spare time to be giving a one act play around the country."[5]

Elizabeth's mental state plummeted. After the *Life* article came out, she withdrew from her friends and responsibilities. A feeling of dread, small at first, grew and grew, becoming full-blown, severe depression by the end of 1955. Eventually she was unable to take care of her home, and the family had to hire a full-time housekeeper. Her community activities withered. She stopped going to the PEO, a social organization in which she'd been actively involved, as well as the Delta Gamma sorority, and her local sewing club. She withdrew from cafeteria duty at her children's school and dropped out of the PTA. In 1954, before the *Life* article came out, she had spent several hours each week baking cookies and chaperoning school field trips. She was also a regular Sunday school teacher. All of that went away. Her appearance became disheveled and disarrayed. She often wore the same dress day after day, and her hair was matted and uncombed. She would lay on her bed for hours at a time, too lifeless and despondent to get up.[6]

According to the psychiatrist she consulted, Elizabeth was "a picture of extreme depression and gloom. She appeared haggard. Her facial expression was one of intense sadness. She cried almost continuously. She spoke in a low, barely audible voice. She expressed feelings of abject hopelessness, feelings of uselessness. She felt that she had nothing to live for. She kept repeating over and over again, 'I'm licked.'" At times, she contemplated suicide. "Her thoughts centered chiefly [on] the invasion of privacy of herself and her family as a result of the book, magazine article, stage play, and movie, and she traced the onset of her symptoms directly to those events." A personality test revealed an "abnormal degree of melancholia and obsessive-compulsive-phobic features." The doctor diagnosed her with "severe reactive depression of psychotic proportions" caused by the publicity in *Life* and *The Desperate Hours*.[7]

By 1956, the darkness had her deep in its clutches.[8] She was consumed by "fearful feelings, feelings of anxiety, . . . a very strange, fearful and apprehensive feeling," in her words.[9] Her eyes had a "lost and . . . discouraged" look, according to a friend. Her face was drained of its usual vibrant expression. "Her hair was unmanageable. She didn't have the same joy and enjoyment in her pretty clothes and she was an entirely different person. She had to force herself to see her friends and avoided it when she could." She could be on the upswing for month or two, perhaps three, but would inevitably sink back into despair. Her depression came in waves, with downs that grew deeper and more tenacious as time went on. She took long walks alone on beaches, her eyes and mind distant, lost in another time and place.[10]

Elizabeth's fear that she had been permanently associated with *The Desperate Hours* was not unfounded. Newspapers continued to refer to the Hills in their reports on the play, which was being performed at small theaters throughout the country. In 1956, a newspaper in Amarillo, Texas, reporting on the opening of the play at West Texas College, noted that Hayes "got his idea from a real-life situation which shocked the nation a few years back. This was in 1952 when the James Hill family were held prisoners in their home in Whitemarsh, outside Philadelphia, by three escaped convicts. This true drama made newspaper headlines for nearly two weeks."[11]

In summer 1956, Elizabeth's psychiatrist, Stanley Dean, became alarmed by her worsening mood. Concluding that her mental condition was so dire that it constituted a psychiatric emergency and that "no time was to be lost," he prescribed a course of electric shock treatments. Elizabeth was given six shock treatments in less than two weeks. She improved a little, and Dean put her on a schedule of medications—"a blue, hard-shaped pill . . . a little round orange pill . . . a blue and white capsule," in Elizabeth's words.[12] This rainbow regime did little. According to Dean, Elizabeth was "quite resistant to treatment in general." "It became apparent to me as time went on that I was dealing with a chronic, recurrent, persistent illness."[13]

∾

Around this time, the lawyers for Random House and Pocket Books moved to dismiss the Hills' claim based on *The Desperate Hours* on the ground that a "novel based upon real life incidents and characters" did not violate the New York privacy law where the novel "nowhere uses or contains the name, portrait, or picture of the plaintiffs." The court agreed that the plaintiff's name and image had to be directly invoked in the work to constitute an invasion of privacy under the New

York statute, and it granted the motion. The law "does not prohibit the portrayal of acts and events concerning a person designated fictitiously in a novel or play merely because the actual experiences of the living person had been similar to the acts and events so narrated," the court concluded.[14] Since the Hills were never mentioned in the book, the play, or the movie, the court's decision effectively invalidated any claims brought over *The Desperate Hours*. The only publication that was now at issue in the lawsuit was the *Life* article.

Concurrently, the lawyers on both sides were engaging in discovery, deposing witnesses and obtaining key documents from their opponents. The Cravath lawyer representing Time, Inc. was Oliver Caldwell Biddle, an advanced-level associate at the firm.[15] Joseph Hayes and Howard Erskine were represented by Abe Berman, a well-known theatrical lawyer, and Jerome Malino of Gilbert and Gilbert, a prominent entertainment law firm. The composer Irving Berlin was one of Malino's most notable clients.[16]

James Hill was examined at the Mudge office in October 1956. In the day-long interrogation, Time, Inc. and Hayes's lawyers tried to get James to confess that he had willingly sought publicity after the hostage incident and thus "waived" his right to privacy. James admitted that he had voluntarily spoken to reporters and posed for press photographs. "He tried to explain away the notoriety and publicity given at the time of the incident. He admitted having given a statement to reporters and over the radio," Malino wrote to Hayes.[17]

Biddle and Malino implied that the Hills' claim was specious and that the family had not really been injured. "Am I correct in saying that since 1954 neither you nor any member of your family has lost any money because of failure to get employment, or failure to get proper employment, due, in your opinion, to the publication of the novel *The Desperate Hours*, or the play or motion picture of the same name?" Malino asked James.[18] Malino believed that the Hills were suing for the money—that James "showed an interest in securing commercial advantage out of the *Life* magazine article through a lawsuit."[19]

"We think that we succeeded in having Hill testify negatively and positively to the many facts that will militate against him at the trial," Malino wrote to Hayes. He worried, however, that James's clean-cut "family man" image would go a long way with a jury that would likely be sympathetic to the family. "I regret to say that Hill made an excellent impression and testified readily and with credibility," Malino wrote.[20]

In July 1957, Joseph Hayes was questioned by attorneys for both sides. He was clearly annoyed by the lawsuit, and he resented having to come up to New York from Florida. His career was flourishing—he had just finished his novel *Bon Voyage*, which would later be made into a Disney film—and the litigation was taking up important writing time.

Hayes insisted that he had nothing to do with the planning or creation of the *Life* article. His efforts to track down the Whitemarsh home, arrange for the use of the home, and bring the actors to the house for the photo shoot were not collaboration, he argued. Hayes denied that the *Life* piece was an advertisement for the play and maintained that he had neither come up with the idea for the article nor profited from it.[21]

As Garment questioned Hayes, it became clear to him that *The Desperate Hours* was not really based on the Hills' experience at all—that the Hills' story was one of many sources for the novel and play. Garment had gotten the *New York Times* article, "Fiction Out of Fact," in which Hayes had explained that *The Desperate Hours* was inspired by several hostage incidents and that the novel was largely a product of his imagination. "Would it be correct to summarize all of this, Mr. Hayes, to say that *The Desperate Hours* was no more based upon or inspired by the Hill episode than it was based upon or inspired by . . . several other real life incidents?" Garment asked. "I think that would be correct," Hayes replied.[22] Garment concluded that *Life*'s description of the play as a reenactment of the Hill incident was totally false and an invasion of privacy under New York law.

Tom Prideaux's testimony was especially damning to *Life*'s case. Surly and defensive, the editor's answers to Garment's questions oozed with arrogance, hostility, and condescension. Prideaux admitted that he never asked Hayes whether *The Desperate Hours* was about the Hills. "Was there any discussion [with Hayes] about the location of the real life incidents or the relationship between the [Whitemarsh] incidents and the incidents in the play?" Garment asked. "No, because we were not attempting to recreate the real life incident," Prideaux replied. "We were trying to recreate the play. . . . We had practically abandoned our interest in the real life incident."[23]

> Garment: Did you at any time, in the course of preparing this descriptive material, and of course before the article was published, make any specific inquiry as to whether the incidents depicted in the photographs used in

Life magazine were also incidents which had occurred in connection with
the real life incident?

Prideaux: That, I honestly don't recall.

Garment: You have no recollection of that?

Prideaux: No.[24]

Life researcher Laura Ecker testified that Prideaux never asked Hayes about
the relationship between *The Desperate Hours* and the Hills; he simply assumed a
connection. The *New York Times* article describing the hostage incident was in the
clipping file that she gave Prideaux, but the editor never looked at it or completely
disregarded it while writing the *Life* piece.[25] Researcher Virginia Shevlin admitted
that Prideaux told her that using the Hills' home in conjunction with the article
would be a good "gimmick."[26]

Garment obtained various drafts of the *Life* article that revealed that the relationship between the Hills' experience and the play had been tightened in subsequent versions of the article. Prideaux admitted that editor Joe Kastner changed
Prideaux's first draft of the story to focus on the Hills—to depict *The Desperate
Hours* as a "reenactment"—because he thought Prideaux's initial version was not
"newsy" enough.[27] Garment concluded that the *Life* editors had not merely distorted the connection between the Hills and the play, but had done so deliberately, even maliciously, which opened the door to punitive damages.

~

In March 1958, Garment issued an amended complaint that alleged the depo-
sitions had "brought to light" who was responsible for the *Life* article. The complaint omitted Random House, Pocket Books, and Paramount Pictures; the suit
was now against Time, Inc. and Hayes, Erskine, and The Desperate Hours Company. The complaint alleged that "defendants Hayes, Erskine, and the Desperate
Hours Company had knowledge . . . that defendant Time, Inc. intended to identify the plaintiffs Hill and their children as the specific family portrayed in *The
Desperate Hours*, and nevertheless . . . thereafter collaborated with and made it
possible for defendant Time, Inc. to prepare and publish said article."[28]

The amended complaint alleged that the article was not merely a distorted
depiction of the Hills; it was entirely false. The "*Life* magazine article of February 28, 1955 was intended to, and actually did convey the impression that the

plaintiffs Hill and their children were the family fictionally depicted in the novel, play and motion picture *The Desperate Hours*, and [those] works constituted a dramatic portrayal of plaintiffs and a reenactment of the true life incident in which plaintiffs Hill and their children were involved, which to the knowledge of defendants . . . was false and untrue."[29] "The use of the plaintiffs' name and portrait . . . was primarily for advertising, entertainment, and trade purposes, and designed to thrill, astonish, and move the readers of *Life* magazine by reporting the fact of the opening of the play in such manner as to falsely and sensationally link said fictional work directly with one specific family and one actual event out of the past." Garment now asked for $600,000 punitive damages, bringing the total amount of requested damages to $900,000: $450,000 from Time, Inc. and $450,000 from Hayes, Erskine, and the Desperate Hours Company.[30]

Jerome Malino wrote to his co-counsel Berman: "The action always had a serious aspect to it but it is becoming extremely complex and cumbersome and I think that our clients should be apprised of what is going on and of the legal costs that are mounting up, and they should pay an additional retainer at this time." Hayes and Erskine were becoming panicked. Berman reassured his clients that despite the aggressive maneuvers of the plaintiff, "we have excellent chances to lick this case."[31]

≈

Hill v. Hayes unfolded against the backdrop of intense criticism of the news media. Although hating the press had long been a national pastime, passions soared in the 1950s. "If you are possessed with eyes and ears that hear, you must have noticed that the American press has been subjected to an unusual amount of astringent criticism," noted one critic. "Darts have been flying, needles have been dug into veins, cannons have been fired."[32] "Across the land, citizens are fretful about the performance of the mass media of communication," *Christian Century* observed in 1959. "In California, in New York, in way stops in between, they have formed volunteer groups to police the gaudy offerings of the newsstands."[33] When they wrote the constitutional guarantee of freedom of the press, the framers did not envision "the newspaper in its gossip activities, the emotional sensationalism, the cameraman prowling among faces contorted, by grief, terror, horror, vacuousness, and fear."[34]

A major complaint, as in the past, was excessive sensationalism and invasions of privacy. In the prosperous postwar decades, publishers and broadcasters faced competition for audiences with more time and money to spend on news and entertainment.[35] Newspaper circulation reached historic highs; in 1950, there were 1,780 daily newspapers that ran 55 million copies each day, and by 1960, 1.3 newspapers per American.[36] A paperback revolution made books available for only twenty-five cents, and book sales in the country increased by 450 percent.[37] Only 9 percent of homes had television sets in 1950; 87 percent did by 1960.[38]

Using shocking, at times disturbing, tactics, publishers courted the attention of an increasingly distracted, jaded, media-saturated populace. Crime news took up more space in newspapers, and tabloids and true crime magazines with titles like *Official Detective Stories, Current Detective, Uncensored Detective,* and *Women in Crime* became popular. The *National Enquirer* was founded in 1956,[39] and the television show *Candid Camera,* which debuted in 1953, broadcast hidden camera footage of ordinary people being confronted with unusual, highly embarrassing situations.[40] "The moments in life which ought to be private, the property of the individual experiencing whatever is happening to him, are recorded on film and transferred to the pages of several million copies of magazines," wrote critic Anthony Harrigan in 1958.[41] The press respected neither privacy nor propriety: "Readers of news magazines have thrown up before their eyes each week picture stories which show theologians in undershirts heavy with sweat, a bride changing her clothes after the wedding service, the reaction of a pregnant woman to the result of a saliva test used in determining the sex of the unborn child, [and] an exhausted athlete vomiting under the stands after a grueling race."[42]

Before the war, many publications had internal policies against subjecting private citizens to gratuitous publicity, especially around sensitive topics such as illnesses and crimes. Some newspapers had "office rules" "not to print details of local divorce suits, statutory assaults, and other local stories in court and out involving the sex question."[43] Scenes of funerals and burials were generally taboo, and "four letter words related to sex and bodily functions" were shunned.[44] As one managing editor wrote in 1940, "There is one thing that all editors do without exception: they protect the names of virtuous women and of young boys of good family."[45] "We do not name juvenile offenders, we do not name illegitimate children, or their parents, or persons accused of attempting suicide, if they fail in their attempt."[46] By the mid-1950s, this polite self-regulation was on the decline. It had become common practice to reveal the pasts of people who had served prison sentences, even if they had rehabilitated and were living reformed lives. Newspapers printed the names and addresses of first offenders, even when charges were set aside. Sometimes names of relatives were divulged. In cases where the press did withhold names of criminals and crime victims, so many clues were included in the story that readers could infer the person's identity.[47]

Aided by new technological inventions, news-gathering techniques were becoming more aggressive and intrusive. The fall before the Hills' hostage incident, film director Billy Wilder had issued *Ace in the Hole*, a vicious attack on "scoop mad" reporters and the media frenzy around accidents, crimes, and other tragic events. In the movie, a wisecracking, ambitious reporter learns about a man who has become trapped in a cave while collecting ancient Indian artifacts. Sensing a golden opportunity, the reporter delays the rescue effort and calls in the press. Cameramen descend on the town, frantically snapping pictures. In the end, the man dies from the delay.[48] Pocket-size tape recorders "either carried in a shoulder holster or elsewhere secreted on the body" had become standard equipment among reporters, noted one journalism text. Reporters may "steal photographs, peek through windows, climb fire escapes to effect entrances into apartments, waylay servants, relatives, and friends, and virtually besiege the dwelling of someone reluctant to be interviewed."[49]

Corporate greed drove this sensationalism, pandering, and distortion, said critics. By the end of World War II, a significant portion of the nation's newspapers, magazines, and broadcast stations were owned by corporations.[50] Of the nearly two thousand newspapers published in the United States, eighteen publications had 24 percent of the nation's circulation.[51] Over two-thirds of radio stations in the country belonged to one of four major networks.[52] "The marketplace of ideas is not closed, but the cost of renting a stall in that marketplace is sky-high," noted the *Antioch Review* in 1953.[53] When "media behemoths"—the Luces, Scripps, and Hearsts of the world—were responsible for the news, the facts were treated roughly, and the truth became a casualty in the race for circulation and profit. "Facts must be given hypodermic injections to make them zestful and sparkling enough for appearance in circulation-building headlines—the ones which leave a flavor of doom or crisis lingering in the breakfast coffee." For most journalists, "the news has come to mean something different from important new information. [What] the journalist means by 'news' is something that has happened within the last few hours which will attract the interest of customers."[54]

Opinion polls revealed that a significant percentage of the public was dissatisfied with the press and supported restrictions, including legal restrictions, on broadcasting and publishing. In 1952, a national study found "widespread criticism and disapproval" of journalists for sensationalism and bias.[55] A sociologist in 1958 noted that there was "widespread indignation" when media gossip "exceeds certain bounds."[56] Forty-six percent of respondents in a 1957 poll opposed printing photographs of bodies of dead people, and half would prohibit the publication of divorce hearings. Only 36 percent would permit the reproduction of a painting of a nude.[57] Less than half of students at Purdue University thought that "newspapers and magazines should be allowed to print anything they want except military secrets."[58] Sixty percent said that the police and other groups should have the right to censor or ban books and movies. A Gallup poll found that half of Americans were in favor of "freedom of speech for everybody," but 45 percent would limit or qualify the right.[59] Concluded one journalist in 1957, "Public opinion, in growing degree, angrily reacts to violations of privacy by journalists."[60]

~

A reflection of this antipress sentiment, a number of attempts were made to legally crack down on the press in the 1950s. Law professors, legislators, judges, and critics offered proposals for increased government involvement in the operations of the media, including more vigorous libel laws, stricter obscenity and "indecent literature" laws, laws against group defamation, and taxes on publications with large circulations. One critic suggested that the "government hold newspapers responsible civilly or criminally for . . . false or unqualified statements of fact or half-truths."[61] Some states proposed measures that declared the "newspaper, magazine, and periodical publishing business" to be "clothed with a public interest" and subject to regulation.[62] In 1956, Georgia passed a law that made it easier for plaintiffs to sue the press for libel and win damage awards.[63] "More stringent application of libel laws" had become socially accepted, noted the *UCLA Law Review*.[64]

Plaintiffs brought an increasing number of libel suits against the press and claimed greater damage awards. The volume of libel cases in the 1950s more than doubled that of any previous decade.[65] "The law of libel and slander has undergone a . . . revitalization, with a marked acceleration in the rate of institution of cases," observed an experienced trial lawyer.[66] Famed plaintiffs' lawyer Melvin Belli observed that awards for libel, slander, and invasion of privacy were exceeding the value of the most horrible personal injury cases: "A man's reputation is worth more before a jury than his limbs—even his life."[67] Commentators observed the "vicarious satisfaction" of juries "in helping a libel case plaintiff to the pot of gold at the end of the rainbow."[68]

Privacy suits were also on the rise. By the mid-1960s, there were more than three hundred reported privacy cases on the books, most of them involving the media, and many of them successful.[69] In one case from 1952, a photographer had taken a picture of a couple at an ice cream shop in Los Angeles. The picture showed the man and woman seated at a counter with the man's arm around the woman. The photo was used in *Harper's Bazaar* to illustrate an article titled "And So the World Goes Round," a short commentary reaffirming "the poet's conviction that the world could not revolve without love." Observers thought the picture was flattering. But the couple alleged that it misrepresented them, and they sued. The California Supreme Court concluded that there had been an invasion of the couple's privacy. Their "amorous pose" was a personal, "private" matter, even though it had taken place in public.[70] In *Metzger v. Dell Publishing*, from 1955, a New York trial court held that the publishers of *Front Page Magazine* violated the New York privacy statute when they published a photograph of the plaintiffs, young men, in conjunction with a story titled "Gang Boy," about crime among Brooklyn teenagers. The youths had no connection with crime and were simply "dragged into the article" by the misfortune of being present when the reporter appeared in the neighborhood in search of "local color."[71]

When a commercial flight developed engine trouble, a Navy commander on board helped land the plane. NBC ran a televised dramatization of the incident in 1956, altering the details and portraying him foolishly: "praying during the course of the emergency landing . . . wearing a Hawaiian shirt . . . [and] repeatedly smoking a pipe and cigarettes." A federal court determined that a jury could potentially find in the distorted broadcast an "offensive invasion of privacy."[72] Torts scholar William Prosser, in a seminal 1960 law review article, described these "false presentation" cases, involving the portrayal of true facts in a distorted light, as actions for "false light" invasion of privacy, in contrast to cases involving the "public disclosure of private facts," where injury had been caused by the publication of embarrassing, truthful personal material.[73]

Even some famous people were winning privacy claims against the press. In 1961, the baseball player Warren Spahn sued a publisher under the New York privacy statute over an unauthorized biography of him that he claimed was false. The biography depicted him as a war hero who had been awarded the Bronze

Star. Spahn had served in the Army but had not been decorated. The book also inaccurately portrayed his relationship with his father, who appeared in the story as a kind mentor and coach, and it incorporated false, invented dialogue. Spahn found this offensive; he was embarrassed at the way his military experience had been glorified and was concerned that people would think he fabricated the story to make himself look heroic. A trial court determined that the biography constituted a false, fictionalized use of Spahn's identity for commercial, non--newsworthy purposes; the publication was enjoined, and Spahn won a substantial damage award.[74]

〜

Yet at the same time privacy liability was expanding, courts in several jurisdictions continued to reject privacy claims in the name of freedom of the press and the "public's right to know." Antipress sentiment notwithstanding, there was a growing civil liberties, free-speech consciousness in the 1950s, fueled by recent memories of Nazi atrocities, the suppression of free expression in Communist nations, and political repression at home. During the anti-Communist hysteria of the late 1940s and 1950s, publications were banned for their allegedly subversive content. Federal, state, and local governments required loyalty oaths, attempted to outlaw the Communist Party, and denied government benefits to people suspected of being disloyal to the United States.[75] As in times of increased conservatism, there were campaigns to clean up so-called indecent movies and literature. Comic books, linked to violence, juvenile delinquency, and crime, were banned in some states and cities.[76] In 1951, the *New York Times* noted an "increase in efforts by private individuals and public officials to impose censorship on the book publishing industry."[77] "Books, radio, television, magazines, newspapers, schools, libraries, as well as films, are all feeling increasing pressure from advocates of censorship," the *Times* noted in 1953.[78]

An anticensorship movement gained momentum. Across the country, there were protests against literary censorship and rallies for academic freedom, many organized by the American Civil Liberties Union. A study in 1953 found a growing number of Americans who wanted to eliminate restrictions on publishing. Organizations denounced the "outbreak of censorship of paper-bound books and other media," which were posing "a threat to our fundamental liberties."[79] This movement was strengthened by several First Amendment rulings of the U.S. Supreme

Court. In 1952, *Burstyn v. Wilson* declared mandatory government prescreening and licensing of films, practiced in several states, to be an abridgment of freedom of the press.[80] In 1957, the Court overturned convictions of Communists who had been jailed for membership in the Communist Party, concluding that mere advocacy of communist ideas did not constitute a "clear and present danger."[81] In *Speiser v. Randall* (1958), the Court invalidated, on First Amendment grounds, a state law requiring a veteran to show that he had not advocated the overthrow of government as a condition for receiving government benefits.[82]

Many state and federal judges were becoming sensitive to free press issues and the burdens that libel and privacy law imposed on publishing. In libel cases, some courts were giving the press greater leeway for the publication of erroneous, defamatory statements of fact on public affairs made without "malice," or knowledge of their falsity.[83] In privacy law, some courts interpreted the "newsworthiness" privilege broadly.[84]

In *Waters v. Fleetwood*, from 1956, the Supreme Court of Georgia held that a newspaper that published and sold photographs of a girl who had been murdered by being drowned in a river did not violate the privacy of the girl and her family. Even though the photos showed the decomposition of the girl's body and displayed the body as "an object of public curiosity," the newspaper had a privilege to print and sell the picture because the murder was a matter of public interest.[85] In 1954, a federal district court concluded that a *Saturday Evening Post* photograph of a man on the Golden Gate Bridge attempting to persuade a woman not to jump off the bridge did not invade the man's privacy because it dealt with a subject that was "newsworthy" and of "general public interest."[86]

In 1951, the Massachusetts Supreme Court rejected a privacy claim brought by the parents of a girl who had been killed in a car accident and whose mutilated body was depicted in a Boston newspaper. The court determined that the publication was newsworthy. "Doubtless many persons at such a time would be distressed or annoyed by a publication of the sort here involved," it noted. "But if the right [to privacy] asserted here were sustained, it would be difficult to fix its boundaries. . . . A newspaper could not safely publish the picture of a train wreck or of an airplane crash if any of the bodies of the victims were recognizable. The law does not provide a remedy for every annoyance that occurs in everyday life."[87]

~

On May 16, 1958, Time, Inc. served its answer to Garment's amended complaint. It claimed that the Hills' story was a matter of "public knowledge and record" and that the *Life* article was a "subject of legitimate news interest," in "every respect a subject of general interest and of value and concern to the public at the time of its publication."[88]

Time, Inc. argued that there was no falsification in the story because the connection between *The Desperate Hours* and the Hill incident was essentially true. Time's lawyers created a diagram, what they described as a "parallel column display," that listed side by side the similarities between *The Desperate Hours* and the Hills' experience. Among them: "Mr. Hilliard, a man in his early forties. Mr. Hill, a man in his early forties. Mrs. Hilliard, an attractive woman in her early forties. Mrs. Hill, an attractive woman in her early forties. A teenage daughter (on both sides). The play had a ten-year-old son; the real-life incident had an eleven-year-old son." "Both incidents, the real and the fictional, took place at approximately 8:30 am, in an isolated suburb of a large city." "Joseph Nolen, elder of the two convict brothers, in his mid-twenties. Acted as spokesman for the three while in the Hills' home." "Glenn Griffin, elder of the two convict brothers, in his mid-twenties. Acted as spokesman for the three while in the Hilliards' home."[89]

In 1960 Time, Inc. moved to dismiss the case, alleging that the publication was "news" and therefore immune under New York's privacy law. Garment insisted that the identification of the Hills with *The Desperate Hours* involved both "fictionalization and a promotional scheme" and was therefore not newsworthy. It had long been recognized under New York law that the "deep social interest in favor of unhampered news reporting . . . does not extend to fiction disguised as news." "The evolution of the *Life* article makes it clear the plaintiffs were dragged into said article and back into the public eye without the slightest news justification."[90] The *Life* article was "nothing more than ballyhoo in disguise—a false contrivance serving the mutual commercial interests of the publisher and the subject."[91]

The court denied Time, Inc.'s motion. Judge Henry Epstein concluded that there were significant questions as to whether the *Life* article was legally "newsworthy" and that the case should be sent to trial to resolve the question. Epstein thought that the *Life* article seemed like a fabrication, a "piece of commercial fiction." *Life* appeared to have created a "wholly fictitious display for commercial advertising and trade purposes, using plaintiffs' names and family as the basis for a 'true-life thriller.'" The use of the Hills' name and a picture of their former home gave the story a "verisimilitude of truth and accuracy" that was "wholly unwarranted." The evidence did "not warrant a conclusion that defendant Time, Inc. [had] been sedulous in its adherence to the concept of a free press news story."[92]

Time appealed, and on June 27, 1961, New York's intermediate appeals court, the Appellate Division, affirmed the lower court's denial of the motion for summary judgment.[93] Six years after the case began, it finally proceeded to trial.

CHAPTER NINE

The Trial

The trial of *Hill v. Hayes* started on April 4, 1962, in Manhattan in the New York Supreme Court, a state trial court, and it lasted two weeks. Garment would argue that *Life* falsified the relationship between the Hills and *The Desperate Hours* and that the publication was thus for commercial rather than news purposes, in violation of New York's privacy law. Time, Inc.'s lawyers insisted that the article was news, and, in stating that the play was a reenactment of the Hills' experience, was essentially true; the article was a "newsworthy" report on a "matter of public concern." If "reenactment" was an error, it was a minor one and did not justify liability, according to Time.

Though the legal case turned on issues of truth and falsity, larger questions loomed in the background about the individual's right to privacy against the media's right to report the news. Could the press thrust people before the spotlight, with impunity, in the name of the public's "right to know"? Should people be forced to sacrifice their privacy for the sake of a newsworthy story? Could people tell the media *hands off, no more, leave me alone,* and could they call on the law to help them?

~

Of course, the legal arguments mattered, but the emotional strategies in this high-stakes trial were even more important. Here Garment clearly had the upper hand. In Garment's words, "Both I and my calmly competent trial assistant, Don Zoeller, then a recent Fordham Law night school graduate . . . saw what our job was. We knew the judge and jury might well wonder why the Hills were so bothered by *Life*'s article." So "we saw that we had to get the jury as angry as we were at Time, Inc. and to help them see the issue not as libel but as an act of commercial exploitation, an invasion of the privacy of private persons. To the squadron of *Life* staffers and editors who spent weeks meticulously devising, editing, and polishing their article, the Hills were simply names in the news, one dimensional journalistic props, not flesh and blood people. In short, we bet our case on the theme of ice-cold institutional indifference."[1]

The irresponsibility of *Life*'s editors was the principal theme, and Garment took every opportunity to hammer it home. The Mudge lawyers wrote in their trial memorandum:

> Plaintiffs will show that there is no legitimate free press issue in this case—that the *Life* article was an utterly irresponsible piece of commercial fiction disguised as journalism and manufactured with cold deliberation by defendant Time, Inc. . . . that it involved a publicity device formulated in collaboration with the promoters of *The Desperate Hours*, that it was consciously viewed by Time, Inc. as a gimmick when formulated, that it was devised, written, edited, and published by Time, Inc. with actual knowledge of its falsity and with complete indifference to the rights and feelings of the plaintiffs and their children.

"In our view, the *Life* article in question is one of the most irresponsible acts of journalism that ever came to light in a courtroom."[2]

"The real significance of this case will come from the evidentiary details surrounding the development of the *Life* article," Garment asserted. "We propose to show that the *Life* article was prepared at the highest editorial levels of Time, Inc. and that deliberate professional care was taken to involve the Hill family with *The Desperate Hours* in the most direct and dramatic fashion possible. Further, we propose to show that the invasion of privacy . . . was a product of Time, Inc.'s editorial policy and not some haphazard or inadvertent error on the part of subordinate personnel of the magazine."[3]

Garment announced to the jury that this was going to be an important case in which privacy rights would trump freedom of the press. "There are matters of vital interest in this case in addition to the vindication of the plaintiffs' rights and the redress of their injuries," he said. "The press issue that will be drawn into focus by the evidence involves the abuse of the freedom of the press by one of the nation's great publishing institutions. An organization as vast and resourceful as Time Inc. has the capacity to cause immense harm to individuals under the cloak of constitutional immunities. An irresponsible press is a threat to the idea of a free press, for it destroys respect for that institution."[4]

Because the press was not able to respect fundamental human rights, the law had to intervene. "We must look to private actions like the present one, where the individual is willing to pit himself against the power of the press in a public forum, for some check to be placed on unlawful acts by the press." "We will be asking for punitive damages for [*Life*'s] callous, reckless, total indifference to the rights and feelings of a group of human beings."[5]

~

The showdown took place in the courtroom of Judge Arthur Klein. Born in New York City in 1904, Klein had been elected as a Democrat to the U.S. House of Representatives, where he served from 1941 to 1956. Eventually tiring of life in Washington, he resigned his congressional seat to run for a position on the New York Supreme Court in 1957.[6] As a judge, Klein was perhaps best known for his 1963 decision throwing out the state's ban on the sale of *Fanny Hill*, ruling that the erotic book was not technically obscene under the standards determined by the U.S. Supreme Court and that the ban was unconstitutional. "While the saga of Fanny Hill will undoubtedly never replace 'Little Red Riding Hood' as a popular bedtime story, it is quite possible that were Fanny to be transposed from her mid eighteenth century Georgian surroundings to our present day society, she might conceivably encounter many things which would cause her to blush," Klein had written.[7] In *Hill v. Hayes*, this pleasant, mild-mannered judge found himself overwhelmed by two highly skilled lawyers with strong personalities.

The Cravath lawyer who argued the case, Harold Medina Jr., was a well-known specialist in media law. His father, Harold Medina Sr., was a federal judge. The elder Medina was famous for a 1949 ruling involving eleven leaders of the U.S. Communist Party charged with advocating the violent overthrow of the government. The jury found all of the defendants guilty, and Medina, sitting on the federal court for the Southern District of New York, sentenced most of them to prison. The following year, he was appointed to the Second Circuit Court of Appeals, succeeding to the position vacated by Judge Learned Hand.[8]

Harold Medina Jr.'s polished upbringing was a far cry from Leonard Garment's hardscrabble background. Born in New York in 1912, Medina attended the private Hill School and graduated summa cum laude from Princeton in 1934. At Princeton he had been a middleweight boxing champion and on the varsity debating team. After earning a law degree at Columbia in 1937, he joined Cravath,

Swaine & Moore, where he spent his entire career. His colleagues described him as articulate, brilliant, and cocky, with a "jaunty boxer's demeanor."[9] By the time of the *Hill* trial, Medina had argued dozens of libel, privacy, copyright, and trademark cases for Time, Inc.[10] Medina also did extensive work for other national publications, including *Look*, *Esquire* magazine, and the *Saturday Evening Post*.

One of Medina's early claims to fame was his representation of Time, Inc. columnist Whittaker Chambers in the Alger Hiss case. In 1948, Chambers had accused Hiss, a government attorney, of having been part of the Communist Party and engaging in espionage for the Soviets. Chambers, himself a former Communist Party member, had been called to testify before the House Un-American Activities Committee. Chambers later stated on a national radio program that Hiss was a Communist. Hiss sued Chambers for defamation, and Medina represented Chambers.[11] A young Republican congressman from California, Richard Nixon, was appointed to head a subcommittee to investigate the Chambers-Hiss allegations. The zeal with which Nixon pursued the case raised his public stature and led to his nomination as vice president in 1952.

∾

On the second day of the trial, Garment's opening address to the jury set the tone for the next two weeks: "There may be a question in your mind today as to what this right of privacy has to do with freedom of the press, what line there is between the so-called freedom of the press and the individual's right of privacy. And I want to talk briefly about that."[12]

"The press has the right to write about anyone or anything that is newsworthy, and that includes matters ranging from affairs of state to the Twist." That right was available to the "*New York Times* equally as it is to any gossip magazine." "There is an enormous area in which the press can operate without any restraint except its own inherent sense of what is right and proper and fair. Now, out of that enormous area the law has carved out one small area, one small island for the individual, and that's called the right of privacy. . . . It is a limited right of the individual as against freedom of the press." "Because the right is limited, because that island or that area is so small, it's all the more precious, it's all the more important, it's all the more worth preserving."[13]

Garment told the jury, "Suppose I were trying a personal injury case in this courthouse and one day I was driving back to my house in Brooklyn, and over the

Brooklyn Bridge I had an accident and I was injured, somebody else was injured, and reporters came and photographed the accident. Now, that's news. That could be reported everywhere."[14] But if that same account were "dramatized . . . fictionalized . . . embellished with a lot of matter out of some writer's imagination . . . if it were so embellished as to really give you a distorted impression of what actually happened . . . that would not be news."[15] "Well, ladies and gentlemen, in general terms, that's what this case is about." "We say that there is no question but that this article was false from beginning to end insofar as its use of the Hills' name was concerned." The family was "dragged back into the public eye as part of a phony news article."[16] "They did it in order to have a lively article. . . . That's what they do and look for in every article. And they do it with the greatest skill because they have the best, the finest, the most talented people that money can hire."[17]

Garment continued: "Now I told you that Mrs. Hill wasn't a well woman when the *Life* article came out, and you will hear the evidence about that. She had an active, busy life. She had five children. She had been through this experience. She had her problems. She was in her middle forties. But she was functioning. She was not disabled." "The *Life* article . . . crippled this woman. It struck a blow at the heart of this family. Wait to see what publicity can do to a family."[18]

Medina's words were compelling but lacked Garment's emotional punch. Medina insisted that *Life*'s editors were acting in "perfectly good faith in coming out with an article on this newsworthy event in the present, the play, and the newsworthy event in the past, the crime." "All we did was to put those together, something that the Hills' friends and family had for some months put together."[19] He then continued, "We, as a publication going throughout this country, are entitled to report on newsworthy events. That is a right guaranteed to us by the Constitution of the United States. People tend to sneer at rights these days, you know, but the fact remains that if we are going to have a press that reports correctly events which occur and newsworthy happenings, that right should be observed."[20]

Garment and Medina were both seasoned, skilled trial attorneys in the prime of their careers. Garment was known for his vivid delivery and animated techniques; in his presentation he raised his voice, gesticulated wildly, and even threw books. The Mudge lawyers had created a huge, magnified posterboard display of various drafts of the *Life* article, showing the tightening of the relationship between *The Desperate Hours* and the Hills in successive versions of the article. Garment set the display up in the courtroom in a way that closed in on the witnesses, creating an ominous and intimidating effect. Garment pointed to the posters repeatedly during his presentation, as if the enormity of the blown-up articles would somehow drive home the magnitude of *Life*'s distortion and the harm to the Hill family.[21] When Medina accused Garment of being histrionic and overblown, Garment replied: "When Mr. Medina says that Mr. Garment gets worked up and shouts and throws books, I admit to you that I do all of that, and I do it because I am human and I have feelings, and in the face of [Time's] kind of contempt and arrogance you are not human unless you have feelings of anger and throw books."[22]

These passionate outbursts disguised what was in reality an immense amount of self-control and disciplined preparation. According to Don Zoeller, Garment "had done his homework." He had prepared for every angle of Time's attack, even to the point of calling James Hill and asking him about his extramarital affairs. James traveled most of the year on business, and Garment wanted to know if he was seeing women in other cities. Garment thought that Time, Inc.'s lawyers would try and dig up dirt on James's private affairs in an attempt to discredit him; they would argue that Elizabeth's sufferings were not the product of *Life*, but rather a bad husband. James told Garment—truthfully—that he wasn't having any affairs. As Zoeller recalled, Garment "taught me one of the basic elements of trial technique: prepare your case by looking into the other side's case."[23]

~

The examination of witnesses started with James Hill. Garment asked James to carefully recount the events of September 11, 1952. Through his questioning, he portrayed James as a courageous, loving father, not unlike Dan Hilliard in *The Desperate Hours*. Just as Dan Hilliard had risked himself to protect his family from violence, James tried to shield his family from the aggressions of the press. James recounted the many requests for interviews he had denied and his efforts to rebuff reporters, columnists, and photographers in the weeks after the hostage incident.

In Medina's telling, the Hills were hypersensitive, greedy, and litigious. Insofar as they willingly spoke to the press, they were "public figures" who had voluntarily put themselves in the spotlight and given up their right to privacy. Medina also suggested that a profit motive was behind the lawsuit. Why didn't James contact Time, Inc. before he contacted a lawyer? Why didn't he write to Hayes objecting to the book, or to Paramount Pictures complaining about the film? "So the first thing you did with respect to any of these defendants was the instituting of this action by the service of a summons and complaint in October 1955, is that not correct?"[24]

Garment asked Judge Klein for permission to show the jury the film *The Desperate Hours* to demonstrate the contrast between Hayes's story and the Hills' real-life experience. "From the point of view of injury, from the point of view of damage, the film is an essential vehicle for demonstrating what the American public saw according to *Life* magazine," he told the judge. Hayes's lawyer objected, arguing that the film would prejudice the jury since it was not at issue in the case. Klein permitted the showing, telling the lawyers that he would soften the movie's impact by telling the jury that there were "liberties which were taken in the production of the film to make it more dramatic" than the play and the book. Klein believed that the film would "enlighten the jury" as to whether the Hills' story had been distorted in *Life*. "The thing the jury must find was whether the *Life* article was a pure fiction of the play's relationship to this particular incident. And I can't think of a better way for this jury to determine that fact than to see the film," he said.[25]

The film was shown in the middle of James's testimony, which in Garment's recollection was "something less than a tour de force."[26] James was not a compelling speaker, and the jury was getting bored. But after the movie, something "magical" happened. In Garment's words, "the plaintiff magically became Fredric March, and the jury followed his testimony with rapt fascination from that point on."[27]

It was during the trial, Garment recalled, that he really came to understand what his clients had suffered. As he listened to James describe the family's emotional turmoil, he realized why the Hills were so devastated by the *Life* article. Even if the portrayal was complimentary, the Hills were right to be outraged at the magazine's distortion of their experiences and identities. As Garment wrote many years later, "We have beliefs about ourselves, images in our own minds, that . . . are our own intimate and personal property, even if they are silly or vain or distorted." A person's self-image was "a small enough place of private territory in an invasive world and is as important as anything else." Being publicly misrepresented, even if it was not unflattering or critical, could be more hurtful to a person's sense of self than the "cruelest print libel."[28]

～

After James Hill's testimony, Joseph Hayes took the stand. Garment tried to convince the jury that Hayes was a co-conspirator in the *Life* article—that he collaborated with the *Life* editors by tracking down the location of the home and paying the actors to take part in the photo shoot. He also got Hayes to admit that *The Desperate Hours* was not really about the Hills—that the work was largely a product of Hayes's imagination, culled from stories of various hostage incidents, and that *Life*'s description of the play as a "reenactment" was an outright lie.

> Garment: . . . Would it be fair to say altogether, Mr. Hayes, that out of all of these elements—the classic hostage theme, the many news and magazine accounts of homes, houses, and families held prisoner by convicts and criminals, and your own personal location near a penitentiary, out of all of these elements, *The Desperate Hours* was shaped?
>
> Hayes: I would say from those elements and others. . . .[29]
>
> Garment: It was not your intention and you did not depict any person whatever who was involved in the Hill incident, either the convicts or the members of the family or anyone else involved in the actual Hill incident?
>
> Hayes: No I did not.[30]

Garment's key witness was Tom Prideaux. Garment grilled the editor for a day and a half and succeeded in making him look arrogant, effete, and callous. Garment got Prideaux to admit that he never bothered to ask Hayes about the relationship between the Hills and *The Desperate Hours*. He also tried to prove that Prideaux knew that *The Desperate Hours* was not really about the Hills. Garment brought into evidence the reference file, or "clipping file" that Prideaux had before him when he wrote the article. In it were the *New York Times* article on the Hills from September 1952, Hayes's *New York Times* piece "Fiction Out of Fact," and *Time*'s own news article on the Whitemarsh incident. Because Prideaux apparently knew the differences between *The Desperate Hours* and the real-life story but nonetheless described the play as a "reenactment," punitive damages were justified, according to Garment.

> Garment: Weren't you concerned, Mr. Prideaux, with finding out what the relationship was between *The Desperate Hours* and this real-life family that were going to be involved in this article?
>
> Prideaux: We were pretty well convinced by this time that it was a very strong relationship.[31]
>
> Garment: Did you ask the author?

Prideaux: I assumed, again—the author and I knew our mutual feelings about this. That was the assumption of our relationship.

Garment: You spent time with Mr. Hayes . . . didn't you?

Prideaux: That's right.

Garment: And in the course of that you never asked him whether this was sparked off, triggered off, inspired or what by this incident in Philadelphia?

Prideaux: A specific question of that nature was never asked, but a discussion of the play itself, what the play was about, in the light of my own knowledge of what the true incident was about, confirmed in my mind beyond any doubt that there was a relationship, and Mr. Hayes' presence was tacit proof of that.[32]

Garment then asked Prideaux to "take his time" and point out any parts of the article that indicated a difference between the play and the real-life incident. "I am telling you to take your time and to point out one clash, to point out one clash in points of the time of the actual incident as opposed to the time sequence of the play, to point out anything about the size of the family that would indicate that there was a clash, to point out anything about the events that took place, anything in any picture, in any caption, anything in the text.

Prideaux: That would be a waste of everybody's time for me to do that.

Garment: Answer my question and tell me whether there is a single clash, anything in that article that would indicate to the reader that there was any difference at all between *The Desperate Hours* and the so-called desperate ordeal of the Hill family.

Prideaux: Yes. I think the word "inspires" takes care of that.[33]

Prideaux's performance on the stand was disastrous. Even Medina's examination of the *Life* editor backfired horribly. Prideaux told Medina that he felt it was "obligatory" for the magazine to point out the "connection" between the Hills and the play. Garment then asked:

Garment: You told Mr. Medina that when *The Desperate Hours* came out you felt it was obligatory to connect this family with *The Desperate Hours*. Is that right?

Prideaux: Yes.

Garment: Did you feel it was obligatory to involve them in this kind of vio-
    lence and display?

Prideaux: No. . . .

Garment: Did you give any thought to it?

Prideaux: A great deal of thought . . . to what we were saying, what impression
    we were creating, and we took special pains to identify the scenes that
    were from the play itself as being from the play itself.

Garment: You didn't give one single thought to the Hill family while this
    whole article was being prepared, did you?

Prideaux: That is not true.[34]

As Garment wrote in his autobiography, "In perhaps the trial's crowning moment
of journalistic insensitivity, Prideaux testified that since there was a 'connection' between the Hill incident and *The Desperate Hours*, *Life* felt 'it was an obligatory thing
to do, to point out this connection.' And that, kiddies, is the kind of unguarded
hubris that produces chillingly large punitive damage verdicts against the press."[35]

~

Elizabeth Hill attended the trial, but she was not called to testify, given her
fragile emotional state. Relating her experiences was her psychiatrist, Stanley
Dean, who offered a dramatic and disturbing story. Dean asserted that the *Life*
article was the "direct precipitating cause" of Elizabeth's mental condition. "Here
we have an average American woman, an American housewife, a mother of five
children, an active member of her community, in good health, able to function in
a very adequate and normal way." When her name was connected with the "terrifying and frightening events of the book and the play . . . this proved to be such
a shock to her nervous system that she couldn't take it. She simply broke down."
"This woman has been sick, and at times seriously sick, for almost seven years. I
am afraid . . . that this is a chronic condition which will require her to have some
psychiatric observation and treatment for the rest of her life."[36]

According to Medina, Elizabeth's ailments were nothing more than the effects
of menopause. Medina read to the jury the symptoms of menopause: depression,
delusions, anxiety, agitation, restlessness, insomnia, fatigability, irritability.

Medina: Isn't it a fact, Doctor, that, in general, the menopause occurs on an
    average at the age of forty-seven?

Stanley Dean: On an average it occurs at the age of fifty, sir. The span could be from the late forties until the middle fifties, but the average is around fifty.

Medina: And isn't it a fact that in menopause depression and extreme melancholia may become a most serious manifestation?

Dean: It may, yes.

Medina: And in menopause there may be little interest in life?

Dean: That's very true.

Medina: And the patient may avoid other people, have little confidence in herself, be fearful and worried about trifles?

Dean: In general, that is possible, in some cases, rather, it's possible.

Medina: And with the menopause there may even be suicidal tendencies, sometimes carried to actual accomplishment; is that not correct?[37]

The only person responsible for the Hill family's sufferings was James Hill, Medina argued in his closing statement. If James truly wanted the family to be left alone, he never would have spoken to the press. It was foolish for him to think that as crime victims, the family was "not newsworthy, the family should forget it, [that] no one was ever going to mention this again." James should have known that he could never "retire from his newsworthy position" any more than a person who had been on the *Titanic*, or "the man who ran the wrong way in the Rose Bowl."[38]

"There is nothing wrong with this play, nothing lurid about it. The family are unharmed. They are heroes in it. But [James] keeps thinking things are much worse than they really are and dressing them up. And all you have to do is read the play to know that."[39] James knew that Elizabeth was going through menopause, and yet he was away on business most of the time. "May I suggest . . . that if perhaps there was a little less of bad judgment on the part of her husband, Elizabeth would be a better woman today."[40]

In the end, Medina returned to his newsworthiness argument: "You have a best selling novel made into a motion picture that's being held up and a Broadway play about to open." "If that isn't a newsworthy event in the entertainment field, I will eat my hat."[41]

"So you had two newsworthy events and you had a very real connection between the two. And of course putting the two newsworthy events together was a matter of interest. It's not a crime to make things interesting . . . that is the reason for having these media. This was no publicity stunt."[42]

~

Garment's summation to the jury was powerful. "We charged this most powerful of all news publications in the world with having done this deliberately, with knowledge of falsity, and we charged them with having brought about the permanent disability of a human being by reason of their action." "For seven years, ladies and gentlemen, this greatest of all news institutions persisted in claiming that what they did was legally justified by freedom of the press." "The freedom of the press was their defense from the beginning to the end."[43]

To Prideaux and the others who worked on the story, the Hill family had no "real existence." "The *Life* editors couldn't think of them as people who lived in a community, who had friends, who had children, who might be offended, might be degraded, might be shocked and upset by this kind of involvement of them in a magazine of this kind of reputation, prestige, standing, and circulation."[44] He explained, "They were dealing with private individuals. They were dealing with people who didn't count. They were dealing with people who were not celebrities. They were dealing with people who they felt would do nothing about this and therefore they went the whole hog and drew them completely into this nightmarish work of fiction."[45]

"I say to you, ladies and gentlemen, that it was beneath them; that they are removed from the reality of life by the power of the printing presses that they hold in their hands; that they have taken the freedom of the press and degraded that great amendment to our Constitution; that they consider themselves immune from legal process; that they consider themselves above logic and common sense; that they consider themselves detached from the community."[46] "Here is the most powerful of news media, proceeding with the most arrogant and complete indifference to a family of seven human beings and dragging them into the dirt and filth of *The Desperate Hours* for their own selfish commercial purposes."[47]

"Now, there are not many people who have the stamina or the will or the energy to fight indifference, to fight this kind of wrong when it appears in the public press. These people have done it." He exhorted the jury to make an award "that is heard not only in this courtroom but in every editorial room throughout the country. You must award punitive damages in an amount that shocks the newspaper industry."[48]

~

The jury was hyped up, and Judge Klein tried to soothe them. "One of the lawyers has said or indicated to you that this is an important case, either very important or important," he told the jurors. "In fairness to all the lawyers, I might say that, of course, it is important, just as every case is important. It is no more important, it is no less important than any other case that has been tried in this court." "There is one other point," he added. "It is called to my attention one of the jurors has been reading a book by a prominent lawyer" on libel and privacy suits. "If you have read anything outside that may conflict with what I tell you, with all due modesty, I might say I am right and the writer of the book is wrong."[49]

Klein then charged the jury:

> It is for you to determine . . . whether, in publishing the article, the defendant Time, Incorporated altered or changed the true facts concerning plaintiffs' relationship to *The Desperate Hours*, so that the article, as published, constituted substantially fiction or a fictionalized version for trade purposes; that is to amuse, thrill, astonish or move the reading public so as to increase the circulation of the magazine or for some other material benefit. If you feel that the defendant Time, Incorporated did publish the article, not to disseminate news, but was using plaintiffs' names, in connection with a fictionalized episode as to plaintiffs' relationship to *The Desperate Hours*, your verdict must be in favor of the plaintiffs.[50]

"If you find a verdict against defendant Time, Inc. . . . . then you will consider whether the evidence proves that these so-called theatrical defendants collaborated with the employees of Time, Inc. in the publication of the article." The jury was instructed that liability could not be found "merely because of some incidental mistake of fact, or some incidental incorrect statement."[51]

"You may only award exemplary or punitive damages . . . if you find from the evidence that [the defendants] knowingly referred to the plaintiffs without first obtaining their consent, and falsely connected plaintiffs with *The Desperate Hours*, and that this was done knowingly or through failure to make a reasonable investigation," Klein said, adding, "You do not need to find that there was any actual ill will or personal malice toward the plaintiffs if you find a reckless or wanton disregard of the plaintiffs' rights."[52]

The jurors entered their deliberations at around 10:50 a.m. and returned at 11:55 with a question for the judge. They were unclear about the definition of "trade purposes" in the privacy statute. Klein told them, "When the [statute] mentions the word trade, it means what you might call a commercial use; in other words, was it to the material advantage of the defendant Time to write this article in such a way as to enhance or increase the circulation of the magazine."[53]

Medina protested. "A news use in a normal newspaper, or news magazine, does not come within the statute," he told the judge. "I want to make sure the jury understands that, because I think that is what is troubling the jury." Klein clarified: "Before the plaintiffs can be entitled to a verdict against the defendant Time, Incorporated, you must find that the statements concerning the plaintiffs in the article constituted fiction, as compared with news or matters which were newsworthy, and that they were published for purposes of trade, that is, to increase the circulation or enhance the standing of the magazine with its readers."[54]

The three-woman, nine-man jury went back and returned five hours later.[55] Don Zoeller knew the outcome when the court attendant opened the door to the jury room and gave him a big thumbs-up.[56] Although the jury concluded that Joseph Hayes and Howard Erskine were not co-creators of the *Life* article and therefore not liable to the Hills, it determined, by a vote of ten to two, that Time, Inc. had falsely portrayed the Hills' story in the *Life* article on *The Desperate Hours* and thus violated their privacy under New York law. The jury awarded James $50,000 compensatory damages and $25,000 punitive damages; Elizabeth received $75,000 compensatory and $25,000 punitive damages.[57] Some of the jurors wanted to give the Hills the full amount they had asked for, but one of them, a former journalist, convinced them to hold down the award. At $175,000, it was the biggest invasion-of-privacy verdict in history.[58]

Klein thanked the jurors for taking part in the intense two-week ordeal: "I'm sure none of you feels you have wasted your time."[59]

PART III

Privacy and Freedom of the Press

CHAPTER TEN

The Privacy Panic

The Hills' lawsuit against Time, Inc. took place at a time of great anxiety around personal privacy. In the 1950s and 1960s, privacy, in all its meanings and senses, was seemingly under assault by an array of forces: the media, the government, researchers, advertisers, and marketers, armed with new surveillance and monitoring technologies. There was a "privacy panic" in the postwar era, and it influenced the course of the case.

$\sim$

Although privacy concerns were intense in the 1950s, they were hardly new. Americans had been complaining about the loss of their privacy for a long time. In small villages and towns during the colonial era, gossip and "snooping" into other people's affairs were decried as "invasions of privacy."[1] European visitors in the eighteenth century noted that "privacy was out of the question" in American towns, and observed the "annoyance of the inquisitorial habits of New England and the impertinence of American curiosity."[2] In the eighteenth and nineteenth centuries, the privacy of the mails became a worry, as sealed letters were sometimes purloined and opened by postal employees.[3] The decennial census, which began in 1790, was described as an intrusion into personal life; in the early 1800s the development of telegraph communications, which could be easily intercepted, brought concerns with privacy to new heights.[4]

With urbanization, industrialization, and the development of new communication technologies in the late nineteenth century, the nation experienced its first, large-scale "privacy panic." As we've seen, invasive journalism was regarded as one of the primary enemies of privacy; new technologies for recording sound and visual images, such as cameras and dictaphones, also imperiled the "right to be let alone."[5] In 1902, the *New York Times* complained that "kodakers lying in wait"—people who stood in the street and took photos of passers-by with Kodak cameras—were a threat to privacy that demanded legal control.[6] Telephones were a feature of many homes by 1900, and with the telephone came the phenomenon of telephone tapping.[7] In the early days of the telephone system, all calls were routed through manual switchboards staffed by telephone operators, and operators often listened in on calls.[8]

The sensory conditions of city life—crowds, dirt, lights, sounds, odors—were denounced as especially destructive to privacy. As people moved from the country to the city and lived close to each other in thin-walled apartments, there were fears that personal intimacies would no longer be secret. A critic in 1897 complained of "certain sorts of street music that are nothing more and nothing less than hideous assaults on the privacy and comfort of humanity."[9] In 1894, when the Brooklyn Common Council ordered a street to be lighted with arc electric lamps, the residents embarked on a protest, calling the lights a "great annoyance" and an "invasion" of their privacy.[10] The wealthy became obsessed with protecting the privacy and security of their homes with high fences, locks, gates, and curtains to shield out noise, lights, dust, and intruders.[11]

The 1930s—a decade that saw the growth of the mass media, a burst of new technologies, and the expansion of state and federal governments—witnessed another wave of concerns with privacy. Although invasions of privacy by the media remained an issue, "information privacy"—large-scale data collection—emerged as a major source of public anxiety. The federal government's data collection under the auspices of various New Deal programs led to privacy concerns. Although a purpose of such information gathering was ostensibly benign—the provision of welfare and Social Security benefits, for example—there were complaints that collecting information on people's personal affairs, especially their financial data, was unjustified snooping. "The Federal Government last year sent out 135,000,000 questionnaires seeking exhaustive data . . . on the personal habits, condition, and conduct of citizens," lamented one magazine author in 1935. "Each state, city, and county relief board . . . has snooped into tenement squalor to document the misery of millions of the nation's poor who are on relief."[12] Questions about income were at the heart of a national protest against the 1940 U.S. census. Citizens formed "antisnooping" groups and refused to answer offending questions.[13]

In the 1930s, businesses and research institutions began collecting data on individuals and their personal affairs. Starting in 1935, the Gallup poll surveyed 200,000 Americans each year on subjects ranging from, "How are you going to vote?" to their opinions on important national issues. Market researchers rang the telephones in millions of homes, asking questions like, "Does your husband use a deodorant?" and what laxatives they gave their children.[14] The growth of the social sciences led to further forays into personal life. Professors "are getting awfully nosy of late," complained one writer in 1930. "They are always sending out questionnaires inquiring into your private life. . . . They seem to feel that they must know just how much we eat, what we do with our spare time, and how we like our eggs."[15] By the end of the 1930s, the "death of privacy" had become a familiar refrain. Privacy was said to have been killed by "the telephone . . . the long eared wiretapping apparatus; the radio with its ubiquitous microphone; the current flood of questionnaires; the spread and mushroom growth of keyhole journalism; the prying eyes of the candid camera," in the words of *Scribner's* magazine.[16] Once "sacred," quipped the *New York Times* in 1931, privacy had become a mere "memory."[17]

∿

Although wartime exigencies temporarily quieted privacy concerns, the 1950s saw the resurgence of privacy as a pressing issue. One historian notes "the stunning emergence" of the topic of privacy in the 1950s, in a "variety of locations," ranging from journalistic exposés to "television programs, law review articles, mass market magazines, films . . . poems, novels, [and] autobiographies."[18] Privacy had never been more yearned for and coveted, yet in a commercialized, bureaucratic, technologically mediated society—one increasingly preoccupied with surveillance, monitoring, predicting, organizing, categorizing, and selling—"the right to be let alone" was seemingly more imperiled and besieged than ever before.

An immediate cause of the postwar privacy panic was the advent of new electronic surveillance technologies. Wartime and Cold War–era defense research had produced an array of devices that could be used for surreptitious recording and monitoring, including telephoto lenses, infrared film, closed-circuit TV, hidden microphones, remote taps on telephone lines, and long-range "parabolic mikes" that could pick up conversations from over three hundred feet away. In 1955, a magazine wrote about "a microphone that can be held against a wall to pick up conversations in an adjoining room, a briefcase recorder that starts operating when a person begins to talk, [and] a combination radio receiver and recorder that can be carried in an overnight case."[19] The world of science fiction was becoming real. "Miniature 'still' cameras can be hidden within a room to take films," observed privacy scholar Alan Westin. "'Television eyes' now come in small units (3 inches by 9 inches) . . . and can be hidden on the premises and can send a picture of the room to a remote receiver located a block or two away."[20] These recording devices could be made totally undetectable, designed to look like lumps of sugar, lipstick tubes, or cigarette lighters.[21]

Official monitoring of citizens went into overdrive, propelled by national obsessions with communism and crime. Although law enforcement wiretapping dates back to the early twentieth century, it reached unprecedented proportions after World War II. In 1960, the New York City police were said to be tapping as many as twenty thousand telephone lines a year without court orders.[22] By the early 1960s, at least fifty federal agencies employed more than twenty thousand investigators engaged in various forms of electronic surveillance for purposes ranging from ferreting out tax cheats to investigating "subversives" in government.[23] J. Edgar Hoover testified that the FBI had between fifty and two hundred wiretaps on any given day in cases involving alleged Communist sympathizers and foreign government informants.[24] Loyalty security programs at federal, state, and local levels permitted searching investigations of the backgrounds of government employees, who could be fired if any derogatory information, including untrue and uninvestigated charges of Communist Party affiliations, turned up in their files.[25]

Not only the government was spying on citizens. The proliferation of surveillance technologies unleashed voyeuristic impulses on a mass scale. Though illegal in most states, electronic eavesdropping was being practiced by a broad sector of the populace. "Wiretapping is epidemic; even where it is illegal, it flourishes, and some authorities believe that the number of telephones being monitored on any given day runs into the hundreds of thousands," observed Richard Rovere in the *American Scholar* in 1957.[26] In 1955, the press carried front-page stories about a New York wiretapping ring that was monitoring over 100,000 phone lines.[27] Business intelligence, divorce proceedings, and dirty politics were among the most common reasons for bugging and "snooping."[28] "Each day in every major city of the nation, private telephone conversations are being listened to and recorded by unknown and unsuspected persons. . . . the practice is shockingly widespread and is growing from year to year," Senator Thomas J. Dodd of Connecticut announced on the Senate floor in 1961.[29] By that time, nearly seven hundred private detectives were in business around the country.[30]

Presaging our own time, electronic surveillance was becoming a regular feature of everyday life. Employers installed video cameras in office cubicles, at entrances and exits to buildings, and in restrooms. The *New York Times* reported that AT&T had set up a camera in an air-conditioning duct in the men's restroom in its New York headquarters that snapped pictures every seven seconds.[31] One corporate official, seeking to eavesdrop on his female employees, arranged for miniature radio transmitters to be put inside the plastic rollers of the toilet paper holders in the women's restroom.[32] Electronic surveillance was also being used for sales and marketing purposes. Restaurants planted tiny mikes beneath tables to gauge diners' reactions, and two-way mirrors observed customers in stores. "These days a housewife shopping in a supermarket may be filmed by a hidden movie camera while she gives her rapt attention to a new display or a new product. The camera eye might observe her facial expressions, gestures, the length of time it takes her to make her selection," observed journalist Myron Brenton.[33] Hospital rooms were being set up so nurses could listen in on patients, and apartment buildings were equipped with microphones and TV cameras, "so that the superintendent may keep tabs on various parts of the building and watch for burglars—or if he chooses, amuse himself and his friends."[34] Even children were being watched and probed. A magazine reported that some classrooms had been bugged so principals could "flip a switch and listen in" at any time.[35]

Americans also feared losing the privacy of their minds—the sanctity of their secrets and innermost thoughts. By the early 1960s, businesses and governments were using various forms of psychological evaluation for personnel selection.[36] These included polygraph tests and personality testing, described by one scholar as the "use of written or oral examination to discover traits of personality for purposes of judging an individual's psychological strength, especially to predict his future performance in some role such as employment."[37] As many as 70 percent of American companies were estimated to be using psychological tests for employee evaluations.[38] Junior and senior high schools began giving personality tests as part of their evaluation and guidance procedures. The *New York Times* reported in 1960 that almost 130,000 tests had been given to students that year, or nearly three tests for every child in the first grade through college.[39] All of this information became part of the child's permanent school record.[40] As one sociologist summarized, the observation of private behavior without the explicit consent of the person being observed had become one of the most disturbing phenomena of the times.[41]

~

Even more than physical surveillance or media invasions of privacy, information privacy became the focus of the nation's privacy concerns. The disclosure of personal data had become a prerequisite to obtaining an array of public and private benefits and services, ranging from welfare to driver's licenses, social security, public education, medical treatment, and consumer credit. Wrote Alan Westin:

> To help himself, to help science, and to help society run efficiently, the individual now pours a constantly flowing stream of information about himself into the record files—birth and marriage records, public school records, census data, military records, passport data, government and private employment records, public-health records, civil-defense records . . . income-tax returns, social-security returns . . . automobile registration records, post-office records, [and] psychological and psychiatric records. As our industrialized system has grown more complex, as government regulatory functions have increased, and large bureaucratic organizations have become the model in our private sector, as social science has committed itself heavily to data-collection and analysis, we have become the greatest data-generating society in human history.[42]

Employers, insurance companies, and federal and state governments were amassing extensive dossiers on individuals, made up of data compiled from an array of private and public sources.[43] In the early 1960s, the U.S. Civil Service Commission had 7.5 million files on individuals, and the House Un-American Activities Committee had a card file of more than 1 million names. These files were sold to third parties, and files generated information for other files.[44] By the early 1960s, governments, businesses, charities, and political parties were spending over $400 million a year to buy and use personal data. A thriving mailing list industry did over $2 billion of business a year compiling names from public and private sources and selling them to marketers to use in targeted advertisements.[45] Anyone who was interested could order lists of "earthworm growers . . . racetrack bettors . . . people with double listings in the Manhattan phone book, and thoracic surgeons under 65 in private practice."[46]

The invention and popularization of credit cards led to the massive transfer of personal data. The nation's first multipurpose credit card was issued in 1950 by Diners Club, and by the end of the decade, several businesses were issuing their own cards. Credit bureaus compiled files on every account holder; the Associated Credit Bureau, a nationwide organization of twenty-two hundred local credit groups, had files on over 6 million adults, and the Retail Credit Company had 23 million dossiers. A typical file contained information ranging from one's age, occupation, spouse, children, and education, to "personal habits, comments by neighbors and employers, notes on any tendency to gamble or drink excessively, an estimate of marital bliss, evidence of ability or inability to live within an income, police record, judgments, litigation, and collection suits."[47] These dossiers were accessible to employers, government investigators, private detectives, and even potential mates. A magazine told the chilling story of a young man who one day visited his fiancée as they were approaching marriage. Her father called the marriage off, reading out loud "an awesome, detailed report" on the man "from his birth to his most recent paycheck four days before." The report listed his salary, that he was forty days overdue on his car payment, and the amount of his bank balance. According to the file, he had C grades in college, suffered a minor heart ailment, and had his driver's license suspended for speeding. The dossier had been purchased by the woman's father from a local credit bureau for $6.50.[48]

Data collection and aggregation was facilitated by advancements in computing technology. The first commercial digital computers were introduced shortly after World War II, and by the early 1960s, banks, insurance companies, credit card companies, personnel departments, airline companies, and federal agencies were heavily dependent on computer data processing.[49] The standardization of computer languages permitted computers to communicate with one another in networks, leading to data pools and data banks.[50] In 1961, the president of a computer company foresaw the future of privacy when he noted that more and more information about Americans was being collected and stored on computers and predicted that it would all add up to an "almost embarrassingly intimate picture of each citizen." "Someday somebody—or some machine—will reach the logical conclusion that all these data should flow into one computer or one computer center. When that happens, individual privacy and liberty will be at the 'mercy of the man who pushes the button to make the machine remember.'"[51]

As it became a nation of big business, big government, big research, and big data, America was becoming a tracked society, a monitored society, and a watched society. Commentators described a pervasive feeling of "nakedness," a sense of being constantly exposed, subject to relentless, total surveillance. "Whether you like it or not anyone who chooses to do so can know everything—both true and false—that it is possible to know about you," observed sociologist Ashley Montagu in 1956: "The files of the Congressional Committee on Un-American Activities are open to anyone who cares to use them. Then there are the manpower lists, the biographical reference works, specialty lists, credit ratings, telephone books . . . the scandalmongering yellow press, private eyes, public eyes, FBI's, wiretapping, TV and radio brainwashing, and so on." "Today we have gossip sheets with huge circulations which specialize in the exposure of the most intimate details of the individual's life. . . . Innumerable individuals have set themselves up in everything ranging from one-man vigilante committees to group organizations dedicated to the investigation of the private life of any and every individual whom they choose to pillory. . . . Telephoto lenses are now able to pick up scenes over great distances, and . . . it is now possible to do this with television and sound and other recording devices." Social scientists were discussing the possibility of keeping "central files of standardized photographs of the entire population." "And, of course, these photographs will be in the nude. Thus will the last of our privacies be stripped from us."[52]

~

New technologies and surveillance practices spurred the postwar privacy panic; another cause of the panic was actually increased privacy. Despite incursions on their privacy, postwar Americans, in many respects, had more privacy than any previous generation. Prosperity had led to conditions of greater physical seclusion and isolation for many Americans, as well as more "privacy" in the sense of greater choice, freedom, and autonomy in different realms of life. As *Time* magazine noted presciently, "The affluent society [was] on the verge of providing every American with as much or little privacy as he chooses."[53] The more privacy Americans had, the more privacy they came to expect, and the more sensitive they were to perceived intrusions on their privacy. Then, as now, Americans' privacy anxieties were not only a response to lost privacy, but also to increased privacy and increasing expectations of privacy.

The GI Bill offered subsidies for higher education and, for many veterans, the possibility of first-time home ownership. By the early 1950s, large numbers of the middle class had migrated to the suburbs and life in single-family homes. Home ownership became an important element of public identity; young families "secured a position of meaning in the public sphere through their new found social identities as private land owners," writes one historian of the decade.[54] With its big yards and gated communities, suburbia was a landscape of privacy. When describing the suburbs, a 1953 issue of *Harper's* suggested that it represented a "new form of social cohesion that allowed people to be alone and together at the same time."[55]

There was a near-obsession with separation from one's neighbors using tall fences, thick curtains, and carefully placed hedges. Suburbanites sought privacy not only between homes but within homes. In the 1950s, home builders were following buyers' demands to erect more walls between rooms, and a "privazone" dual bathroom separated toilets and bathtubs from dressing areas for increased privacy.[56] Psychologists advised parents to give each child his or her own room in the interest of the child's psychological development and emotional health. In a culture of "freedom," "every person has a right to privacy," wrote one housing specialist. "At every age, from six months on, privacy of the individual must be respected for his well-being. This means that even babies of six months should have their own room for their proper emotional development." Teenagers, especially, should have their own space: "Every age group and individual needs a place of retreat from today's tensions." According to experts, families in homes with too little privacy were prone to fights and "breakdowns."[57]

Suburbia was made possible by widespread car ownership and mass communications, which allowed a connection to public life while living distant from population centers. Cars and mass media, especially television, invited retreat into the individual, familial, private sphere. Automobiles gave people near-total control of their mobility; they personalized travel and enabled a sense of "privacy in public."[58] The setting for personal conversations, family bonding, and other intimate experiences, cars became, for many, an extension of the private home. Television also encouraged remote and isolated experiences. By the end of the 1950s, almost every family had a TV set, and the nation was experiencing the world from the privacy and intimacy of their living rooms.

While politicians and officials curried the public's favor by denouncing the loss of privacy in America, they also invoked the expanding privacy of the middle class as a tribute to the nation's prosperity, ingenuity, and freedom. In the midst of the Cold War, the private, suburban, nuclear family, enjoying television in their living rooms and excursions in the family car, was held up as a testament to the virtues of capitalism and democracy. In his famous 1959 "kitchen debate" with Soviet premier Nikita Khrushchev, Vice President Richard Nixon described well-appointed suburban residences with abundant appliances and glamorous housewives as evidence of the nation's superiority over the Soviets. A comfortable domestic life was the pinnacle of success; the private life was the "good life."[59]

Despite their complaints about the loss of privacy, middle-class Americans had never before lived so privately, observed critic August Heckscher in 1959. Heckscher observed a "cult of the home"—a withdrawal from the public sphere and a "retreat into privacy." In suburbia, "the kitchen seems to take a higher rank than the school; the car than the highway upon which its usefulness depends."[60] The public's experiences of privacy and attachment to privacy were "even more than in previous times."[61]

~

The postwar era's concerns with privacy also reflected a growing emphasis on the individual in American culture. In the affluent society, where people had time, energy, and money to focus on nonessential pursuits, Americans were turning inward, toward the self. An array of practices, industries, and institutions were focusing their attention on the person—his or her comfort, prestige, leisure, health, well-being, and opportunity.

Consumerism flourished in the booming economy, and a vast, sophisticated advertising industry promoted the acquisition of products as a means to fulfillment, status, and recognition. Psychology, oriented around the goal of "self-realization," was exerting a major influence over popular thought. The era saw what has been described as a "therapeutic culture."[62] Psychological themes and concepts suffused popular discourse, and the individual's feelings were vaunted to a position of paramount importance.[63] From birth to death, Americans were taught to concentrate on themselves, on their "individual struggle in life," observed one anthropologist of the time.[64] "The child grows up needing time to himself, a room of his own, freedom of choice, freedom to plan his own time and his own life." He would spend his adult life pursuing his own pleasure and privacy, using his wealth to install "private bathrooms in his house, buy a private car, a private yacht, private woods and a private beach, which he will then people with his privately chosen society."[65]

Opportunity, choice, and freedom became ideals in a country that was said to be the richest, most egalitarian, and successful on earth. The United States had become a "republic of choice," in the words of historian Lawrence Friedman.[66] Middle-class Americans could choose from among thousands of models of cars and an array of products on department store floors and grocery shelves. There was not only more choice, but a belief in a right to choose: postwar Americans came to believe that there should be a "'hyperdiversity of choices' in the selection and design of practically all [their] wants, everything from the cradle to the grave," observes one political scientist.[67] A writer in the *New York Times* in 1962 spoke of the "obstinate striving" of Americans "to assert their primary right to be and to choose, to achieve or defend an area for private living, and to respect the same desire among their fellow men."[68] Commentators noted the link between the emphasis on privacy and the individualistic, therapeutic bent of American culture. "Privacy became valued as individualism and the ego became valued," observed *Time*. "In earlier times, retreating into solitude was a religious act; now privacy became a devotion in the new secular religion of the self."[69]

"Privacy," circa 1960, meant not only seclusion, isolation, and being let alone, but autonomy, choice, and personal freedom. The ideal of privacy had become a symbol of postwar America's self-image as a land of possibility, independence, and self-creation. Privacy was the essence of the American dream, noted William Faulkner in a 1955 essay in *Harpers'* magazine.[70] Privacy meant the protection of the autonomous self, imperiled by the homogenizing forces of the consumer culture, the information society, and the modern military industrial complex with its vast, totalizing, impersonal institutions—in the words of one writer, "an increasingly urban, socialistic, mechanized, computerized, electronic society" made up of "depersonalizing forces."[71] Anthropologist Margaret Mead, writing in 1965, described privacy as "closely bound up with our sense of individuality and our belief in the value of personal choice." "The desire for a personal life of one's own choosing" had been part of the ideal of the "open frontier," and it kept Americans searching for greater possibility and freedom of choice in their lives.[72]

Privacy was every person's right to possess and define himself, to make his own decisions about his life, and to pursue his own peace, comfort, and self-interest. "Privacy says, 'This is mine.' It gives a person something to call his own. That something is, of course, his individual and unique self. The decline of privacy, then, is in significant measure the story of the decline of individualism," wrote journalist Myron Brenton.[73] "Intrusions on privacy are baneful because they interfere with an individual in his disposition of what belongs to him," observed sociologist Edward Shils. "The social space around an individual, the recollection of his past, his conversation, his body and its image, all belong to him. He does not acquire them through purchase or inheritance. He possesses them and is entitled to possess them" by virtue of his own unique selfhood.[74] Amid public fears of "de-personalization and manipulation" through media voyeurism, electronic surveillance, and mass data collection, the right to privacy—the right to control and possess one's "private personality"—was the "last defense of individuality."[75]

CHAPTER ELEVEN

Appeals

In the midst of public animus toward the press and heightened sensitivity around privacy issues, the verdict in *Hill v. Hayes* made headlines. The Associated Press issued a story that appeared in newspapers throughout the country in April 1962. A "jury has awarded a hosiery executive and his wife $175,000 after ruling the privacy of the former Pennsylvanian was invaded in an article published in *Life* magazine. The Hills charged that the *Life* article exposed them to 'extensive and undesirable publicity' and that they suffered 'great emotional embarrassment.'"[1] The AP story made it to the *New York Times* but not the front page, leading Leonard Garment to quip that he was "dismayed that the *New York Times* did not feature a page one story about the miraculous triumph of the people over the press."[2]

Time's rival, *Newsweek*, ran an alarmed article in its April 30, 1962, edition. "What is invasion of privacy?" it asked.

> Traditionally, newsmen have assumed that stories about a legitimate news event, presented in legitimate fashion, do not constitute invasion of privacy— even when the articles appear long after the event. Under this premise, *Life* magazine, reporting the opening of a play called "The Desperate Hours" in 1955, recounted briefly the actual experience on which the show was based: the 1952 invasion of the James J. Hill residence near Philadelphia by three convicts, who held the family hostage for 19 hours. The widely reported story seemed harmless enough when *Life* reran it, but last week a New York . . . jury ruled that the *Life* article had exposed Mr. and Mrs. Hill, who had not consented to the *Life* story, to illegal invasion of privacy.

"To journalists, the decision, which will be appealed by Time, Inc., seemed significant on two counts," *Newsweek* noted. "The first, of course, was the large amount of the award." The second was an even more critical issue: What constituted legitimate news?[3]

From the moment the decision was handed down, it was clear that Time, Inc. was not going to rest with the judgment. The publisher was deeply troubled by the outcome and vowed to appeal. The $175,000 verdict brought out just how threatening privacy law was to the publishing industry. The *Hill* case was turning into a test case, one that Time, Inc. intended to pursue to the fullest to clarify the law of privacy and establish important free speech precedent.

In spring 1962, Cravath filed an appeal with New York's intermediate appeals court, the Appellate Division, seeking a dismissal of the complaint or, alternatively, a new trial.[4] It again argued that the publication was "newsworthy." "Since the primary subject of the *Life* article was current news . . . and the matter related to it (the ordeal of the James Hill family) was itself of contemporary general interest, an almost absolute privilege arose." Time, Inc.'s lawyers further alleged that the showing of the film at the trial had prejudiced the jury and that the $175,000 verdict was "grossly excessive." "The defendant is not alone in its amazement at the size of the verdict—one need only query any member of the Bar." With judgments like the one in *Hill v. Hayes*, "New York as the center of the publishing industry will not remain long."[5]

Cravath's brief also contested what it described as erroneous and misleading jury instructions. Judge Klein told the jury that it had to determine whether *Life* had "altered or changed the true facts concerning plaintiffs' relationship to *The Desperate Hours*, so that the article . . . constituted a fictionalized version . . . to amuse, thrill, astonish or move the reading public so as to increase the circulation of the magazine."[6] If the instruction were correct—that any alteration of true facts, however slight, rendered material "fictionalized" and unprotected by the news privilege—"the guaranty of a free press would be emasculated."[7] "Should Time, Inc. be required to pay $175,000 in damages because it said it 'reenacted' . . . when it should have said 'based,' or 'inspired' when it should have said 'triggered?'" Cravath's brief asked. "The day that judgments in a right of privacy action can be upheld on semantic distinctions of that illusory nature is the day that a free press becomes a thing of the past."[8]

Cravath now admitted there was an error in the story—the account of the play as a "reenactment"—but described it as unintentional and harmless. To punish a negligent misstatement like the one in the *Life* article would infringe on freedom of the press. If a single careless mistake subjected a publisher to liability, "every newspaper and magazine in the country would run an incalculable risk every day in the week as a glance at any recent edition, including numerous instances in which error might appear, will so readily disclose."[9]

On May 14, 1963, the appeals court upheld the judgment against Time, Inc. As the majority noted, at the time of the hostage incident, the Hills were undoubtedly newsworthy. But over time, the incident had been "relegated to the outer fringe of the public consciousness." "Although the play was fictionalized, *Life*'s article portrayed it as a reenactment of the Hills' experience. It is an inescapable conclusion that this was done to advertise and attract further attention to the play, and to increase present and future magazine circulation as well. It is evident that the article cannot be characterized as a mere dissemination of news, nor even an effort to supply legitimately newsworthy information in which the public had, or might have, a proper interest." The falsity of the article took it out of the category of "news" and justified the verdict against Time, Inc.[10]

Yet the court agreed that the showing of the film to the jury constituted "substantial prejudicial error." "The emotional impact of viewing a highly charged, tense, dramatic film portrayal of incidents of the nature here involved, with accompanying sound effects, was inflammatory and undoubtedly served to influence the jury improperly," wrote Judge Harold Stevens. The court also thought the verdict was excessive—"grossly excessive"—and ordered a new trial to reassess damages.[11]

Judge Benjamin Rabin wrote a concurring opinion, one that would play a significant role in the Supreme Court's later ruling on the case.[12] The article "portrayed the previous Hill incident in a highly sensational manner and represented that the play was a true version of that event. It was not. It was fictionalized and the jury so found." He then added a curious comment: "if it can be clearly demonstrated that the newsworthy item is presented, not for the purpose of disseminating news, but rather for the sole purpose of increasing circulation, then the rationale for exemption no longer exists. In such circumstance the privilege to use one's name should not be granted even though a true account of the event be given—let alone when the account is sensationalized and fictionalized."[13] Rabin seemed to be suggesting that if a true, newsworthy item was published solely for the purpose of increasing circulation, it could be an actionable invasion of privacy. Rabin's view had far-reaching implications: if read literally, it could bankrupt the press.

Bernard Botein, a noted free speech advocate, issued a dissent.[14] "The article complained of was a report upon a new play, traditionally a newsworthy subject. . . . To point out, in an article of that nature, a relation between the play and the concededly newsworthy incident in which plaintiffs had been involved creates no cause of action." He admitted that there were "elements of inaccuracy or exaggeration in the article." But "can it be said that such flaws are of so extravagant a nature as to convert into fiction an informative presentation of legitimate news?" he asked. "In my opinion not; we are in a domain where 'the lines may not be drawn so tight as to imperil more than we protect.'" Botein also took issue with Rabin's concurrence: "To hold, as suggested in the concurring opinion, that a violation of [the New York privacy law] may be established by a showing that a newsworthy item has been published solely to increase circulation injects an unrealistic ingredient into the complex of the right to privacy, and would abridge dangerously the people's right to know. In the final analysis, the reading public, not the publisher, determines what is newsworthy, and what is newsworthy will perforce tend to increase circulation."[15]

Legal journals and law reviews noted the Appellate Division's decision.[16] The decision received a good deal of unfavorable commentary in publishing trade journals, including the prominent *Publishers' Weekly*. The brilliant, sharp-tongued Harriet Pilpel, a *Publishers' Weekly* columnist, lawyer for literary interests, and influential member of the ACLU, railed against the Appellate Division's ruling: "Now everyone knows you can't have . . . complete and absolute freedom of expression. As Justice Holmes pointed out, no one should be free to call 'fire' in a crowded theater. But the refinements of the restrictions enunciated in . . . recent cases are a far cry from Justice Holmes' classic example." Decisions like *Hill v. Hayes* portended "a press that is less than free."[17]

In an attempt to preserve some of the award in case of a successful appeal, Garment entered negotiations to settle with Time, Inc. on Elizabeth's claim. Time's lawyers, in a breach of its usual policy, settled with Elizabeth Hill for $60,000.[18] Elizabeth was subsequently dropped from the case; James was now the only plaintiff. At the new trial on damages in 1963, the court eliminated the punitive damage award and granted $30,000 in compensatory damages to James Hill.[19]

∾

Less than a year later, the U.S. Supreme Court issued a decision that transformed First Amendment law, the law of libel, and the Hills' case. *New York*

Times v. Sullivan was a major victory for the publishing industry, the culmination of its long efforts to free itself from the burdens of liability for libel.

The *Sullivan* case grew out of the violence of the civil rights movement. By 1964, that battle had taken on epic proportions. The struggle that started in the early 1950s with the fight against school segregation had grown into a massive interracial, nonviolent movement challenging segregation on multiple fronts by 1960. In the early 1960s, the northern press began covering the movement and the backlash it spawned. On the front pages of newspapers and on the evening news, Americans watched southern officials turn attack dogs, police forces, and hoses on peaceful protesters, including children as young as six. The media spotlight galvanized the South, which redoubled its efforts to maintain racial separation using billy clubs, tear gas, and law books.[20]

On March 29, 1960, a civil rights group, the Committee to Defend Martin Luther King and the Struggle for Freedom in the South, published a full-page advertisement in the *New York Times*. The committee included several civil rights notables and prominent public figures such as Harry Belafonte, Marlon Brando, Jackie Robinson, and Eleanor Roosevelt, as well as four black Alabama ministers. The group was put together in response to an indictment by an Alabama grand jury against Martin Luther King Jr. in 1960 for perjury in connection with filing Alabama tax returns. The advertisement was an appeal for funds to defend King from the spurious charges.[21]

The advertisement, titled "Heed their Rising Voices," began: "As the whole world knows by now, thousands of Southern Negro students are engaged in widespread non-violent demonstrations in positive affirmation of the right to live in human dignity as guaranteed by the U.S. Constitution and the Bill of Rights. In their efforts to uphold these guarantees, they are being met by an unprecedented wave of terror by those who would deny and negate that document which the whole world looks upon as setting the pattern for modern freedom." The ad went on to describe a series of violent acts by Alabama authorities against civil rights protesters. In one paragraph, it stated: "In Montgomery, Alabama, after students sang 'My Country, 'Tis of Thee' on the State Capitol steps, their leaders were expelled from school, and truckloads of police armed with shotguns and tear-gas ringed the Alabama State College Campus. When the entire student body protested to state authorities by refusing to re-register, their dining hall was padlocked in an attempt to starve them into submission." Another paragraph asserted: "Again and again the Southern violators have answered Dr. King's peaceful protests with intimidation and violence. They have bombed his home almost killing his wife and child. They have assaulted his person. They have arrested him seven times— for 'speeding,' 'loitering' and similar 'offenses.' And now they have charged him with 'perjury'—a felony under which they could imprison him for ten years."[22]

Because the advertisement was placed by a responsible group and bore the signatures of prominent individuals, the *Times* ignored its own policies and published it without confirming its accuracy. However, the newspaper's own files would have revealed that some of the allegations were false. Although nine students were expelled by the state board of education, it was for demanding service at a lunch counter in the Montgomery County Courthouse, not for leading the demonstration at the capitol. The dining hall was never padlocked. The police never surrounded the campus, nor were they called to the campus in connection with the state capitol demonstration. Martin Luther King had been arrested four, not seven, times.[23]

L. B. Sullivan, the Montgomery commissioner for public affairs, responsible for overseeing the police in the city, alleged that the *Times*, in publishing the ad, had defamed him. Although the ad did not mention him by name, he claimed that the word *police* referred to him as the supervisor of the police department, so that he was accused of "ringing" the campus with police. He also alleged that the ad imputed to the police—and therefore to him—the padlocking of the dining hall to starve the students, the bombing of King's home, and the perjury charges.[24] Sullivan's suit was one of many brought over the advertisement. Alabama governor John Patterson filed a $1 million libel suit against the *Times*, and Montgomery mayor Earl James, city commissioner Frank Parks, and former city commissioner Clyde Sellers each filed suits for $500,000.[25]

In Alabama, libel was a strict liability tort, permitting no latitude for negligent errors of fact. It was also based on a presumption of falsity—a statement deemed to be libelous per se was assumed to be false unless the defendant proved it true. Damages were presumed, meaning that the plaintiff did not have to show how— or if—he had actually been harmed. Under these rules, an Alabama trial court held that the *Times* had committed a libel in publishing the advertisement and awarded half a million dollars in damages to Sullivan. The judgment was affirmed by the state's supreme court.[26]

Southern opponents of the civil rights movement had discovered the power of libel law as a weapon against the press. After the *Sullivan* suit was initiated, the

Montgomery Advertiser ran an article headlined: "State Finds Formidable Legal Club to Swing at Out-of-State Press." The day after the verdict in *Sullivan*, the *Alabama Journal* predicted that the award could "have the effect of causing reckless publishers of the North to make a re-survey of their habit of permitting anything detrimental to the South and its people to appear in their columns."[27] In addition to the "Heed Their Rising Voices" ad, the *New York Times* was defending itself in ten separate lawsuits, with claimed damage awards totaling more than $6 million, over an article by reporter Harrison Salisbury, "Fear and Hatred Grip Birmingham."[28] The *Times* withdrew its reporters from Alabama; facing labor unrest and earning small profits at the time, the *Times* might have actually gone out of business if it had to pay the judgments. As the *Nation* noted in a 1960 editorial after the *Sullivan* verdict, "The Montgomery formula is so simple and effective that it is certain to be applied elsewhere. It has always been possible for a community to apply murderous pressures to a local publication, but it has not been so easy to bring the 'outside' publication to heel. Now this loophole has been closed." "Just as Commissioner Sullivan is not the real plaintiff in Montgomery, so the *Times* is not the real defendant; the unnamed defendant is the press itself, in all sections of the country, South as well as North. A dangerous precedent is in the making."[29]

Louis Loeb, a partner in the firm Lord Day & Lord, was the principal lawyer for the *Times*. Loeb came every day to the *Times* office, where he consulted with editors and reporters. Assisting Loeb on the *Sullivan* case were two senior partners, Thomas Daly and Herbert Brownell, former attorney general under President Eisenhower. Loeb invited Herbert Wechsler, a professor at Columbia Law School, to join the defense of the *Times*, and Wechsler took over the task of appealing the case to the Supreme Court. Wechsler convinced the *Times*'s executives that it should appeal on the basis of First Amendment issues rather than easier, more obvious grounds that would not have affected libel law or First Amendment jurisprudence. The *Times* could have argued that there was nothing in the ad that could be understood as a defamation of Sullivan, or that the Court could not exercise personal jurisdiction over the *Times*. Instead, it argued that the common law of defamation, as it existed in Alabama and many other states at the time, abridged the freedom of the press guaranteed by the First Amendment.[30]

Wechsler knew that one of his main obstacles would be convincing the Court that there was a constitutional question for it to consider. As we know, it had long been the Court's position that libel was an area outside the First Amendment—

that defamatory statements were unprotected by the Constitution. In his petition for certiorari and briefs to the Court, Wechsler argued that libel did not "enjoy a talismanic insulation from the limitations of the First and Fourteenth Amendments." Insofar as it restricted the right to protest and criticize official conduct, "the decision of the Supreme Court of Alabama gives a scope and application to the law of libel . . . that . . . abridges freedom of the press."[31]

Although libel laws didn't suppress speech outright like a censorship law, they infringed on freedom of the press because they forced publications to self-censor for fear of liability, Wechsler argued. The rules of liability applied by the Alabama courts in libel cases—the presumption of falsity, presumed damages, and strict liability—infringed "basic constitutional rights in their most pristine and classic form." The Alabama law impaired the right of the public and the press "to assure unfettered interchange of ideas for the bringing about of political and social changes desired by the people."[32] Insofar as it could be used as a device for "insulating government against attack," the common law of libel was repugnant to the Constitution.[33]

Wechsler analogized the common law of civil libel to the crime of seditious libel, long regarded as unconstitutional under the First Amendment. In 1798, Congress passed the Sedition Act, which declared it a crime for "any person to write, print, utter or publish . . . any false, scandalous and malicious writing or writings against the government of the United States, or either house of the Congress . . . , or the President . . . , with intent to defame the said government, or either house of the said Congress, or the said President, or to bring them or either of them, into contempt or disrepute." Wechsler argued that Alabama's libel law was even worse than seditious libel, which required that the defendant's purpose was to bring the "official into contempt or disrepute." Under Alabama's rules, criticism of public officials was presumed to be false and malicious. "We submit that such a rule of liability cannot be reconciled with this Court's rulings on the scope of freedom of the press safeguarded by the Constitution. . . . Those rulings start with the assumption that one of the prime objectives of the First Amendment is to protect the right to criticize all public institutions."[34]

The American Civil Liberties Union, which filed an amicus brief, emphasized the "chilling effect" produced by Alabama's policy of strict liability for defamatory errors of fact.[35] "If newspapers are to be liable without fault to heavy damages for unwitting libels on public officials in political advertisements, the freedom of dissenting groups to secure publication of their views on public affairs and to seek support for their causes will be greatly diminished."[36] They argued for the adoption, as a First Amendment requirement, of the conditional privilege for "matters of public concern" that existed in some states: "Where 'matters of public concern, public men, and candidates for office' are involved, 'anyone claiming to be defamed by the communication must show actual malice'"—reckless disregard of the truth—"'or go remediless.'"[37] Time, Inc.'s Harold Medina was familiar with the privilege, having come across it in a libel case in Michigan. Medina, who knew Wechsler, mentioned it to Wechsler while he was working on the *Sullivan* brief.[38]

The *Times*'s petition emphasized the importance, in the turbulent political climate, of the issues in the *Sullivan* case. "This is not a time when it would serve the values enshrined in the Constitution to force the press to curtail attention to the racial tensions of the country or to forego dissemination of its publications in the area where tension is extreme. Here, too, the law of libel must confront and be subordinated to the Constitution. The occasion for that confrontation is at hand."[39] As the ACLU framed the legal question, "the issue is whether the state of Alabama can, under the label of libel, penalize these petitioners by a $500,000 judgment in favor of a public official because of publication by them of an appeal for political and social change." "Acceptance for publication of appeals by minority groups is a duty of the press—particularly in a time in which mass communication, such as the daily press provides, is one of the only effective means for communication of ideas."[40]

Sullivan's lawyers insisted that libel had never been protected by the First Amendment, and that to accept the *Times*'s position would be to change hundreds of years of established law. "The Times and its powerful corporate newspaper friends obviously realize that history and precedent support the holding below that this libelous advertisement is not constitutionally protected." "Throughout its entire history, this Court has never held that private damage suits for common law libel in state courts involved constitutional questions." Sullivan's lawyers accused the *Times* of asserting "at least for themselves and others who conduct the business of mass communication, an absolute privilege to defame all public officials."[41]

The Supreme Court granted certiorari. It was one of only a few times in the Court's history that it had taken a libel case.[42] The Court was motivated to hear the *Sullivan* case in part by the civil rights issue, one of the signature issues of the Warren Court, which ten years earlier had issued the landmark desegregation decision in *Brown v. Board of Education*. But *New York Times v. Sullivan* was not only about race and civil rights. Several of the justices were deeply concerned with free speech and freedom of the press, imperiled by anti-Communist witch hunts and the civil rights backlash, as well as the recent surge of libel suits against the press. *Times v. Sullivan* came before the Court when three of the Court's most liberal justices—Black, Douglas and Brennan—were engaged in a lively and acrimonious public debate about the meaning of freedom of speech—whether free speech rights could be balanced against such state interests as national security, or if the First Amendment was an absolute, forbidding any government action that burdened freedom of expression.

The press and the civil liberties community watched the *Sullivan* case closely. As Norman Dorsen of the ACLU wrote not long after the Court's decision to hear the case, "The United States Supreme Court will soon decide a free speech case in which, for once, the petitioner does not represent the isolated and marginal in American society. . . . The petitioner this time is the New York *Times*, . . . anchor of the Establishment. The *Times* now seeks for itself what its editorial columns have so often sought for others—the protection of the First Amendment of the Constitution." "The chief questions raised by the *New York Times* litigation involve the extent to which defamation laws impose limitations on free speech, and the self-censorship that would hamstring bold journalism if the present vogue of astronomical libel judgments were permitted to become a national custom."[43]

$\sim$

In a 9–0 decision, issued on March 9, 1964, the Supreme Court, in an opinion by Brennan, reversed the judgment against the *Times*. The Court agreed with the publisher that state libel judgments were not exempt from constitutional scrutiny—that "libel can claim no talismanic immunity from constitutional limitations." "Like insurrection, contempt, advocacy of unlawful acts, breach of the peace, obscenity, solicitation of legal business, and the various other formulae for the repression of expression that have been challenged in this Court, libel . . . must be measured by standards that satisfy the First Amendment."[44] Brennan accepted Wechsler's seditious libel analogy. The public's right to criticize its leaders freely was the "central meaning" of the First Amendment.[45] "We consider this case against the background of a profound national commitment to the principle that debate on public issues should be uninhibited, robust, and wide-open, and that it may well include vehement, caustic, and sometimes unpleasantly sharp attacks on government and public officials. . . . The present advertisement, as an expression of grievance and protest on one of the major public issues of our time, would seem clearly to qualify for the constitutional protection." Alabama's libel law "failed to provide the safeguards for freedom of speech and of the press that are required by the First and Fourteenth Amendments in a libel action brought by a public official against critics of his official conduct."[46]

Times v. Sullivan eliminated the strict liability rule in libel cases involving public officials. Criticism of public officials containing erroneous statements of fact was protected by the First Amendment, provided that the errors were not made with "actual malice"—with knowledge that the statements were false or with reckless disregard of their truth or falsity. Following the *Times's* lead, the Court constitutionalized the common law privilege that existed in a minority of states for false and defamatory speech on "matters of public concern,"[47] making it a formal First Amendment requirement. "Erroneous statement is inevitable in free debate, and . . . must be protected if the freedoms of expression are to have the 'breathing space' that they need . . . to survive," Brennan wrote.[48] Newspapers would cease reporting on public officials and controversial issues if minor, careless errors subjected them to liability.

Brennan also took issue with the presumption of falsity under Alabama law and the defendant's burden to prove the truth. "A rule compelling the critic of official conduct to guarantee the truth of all his factual assertions—and to do so on pain of libel judgments virtually unlimited in amount—leads to . . . 'self-censorship,'" Brennan wrote. "Allowance of the defense of truth, with the burden of proving it on the defendant, does not mean that only false speech will be deterred. . . . Under such a rule, would-be critics of official conduct may be deterred from voicing their criticism, even though it is believed to be true and even though it is in fact true, because of doubt whether it can be proved in court or fear of the expense of having to do so. They tend to make only statements which 'steer far wider of the unlawful zone.'. . . The rule thus dampens the vigor and limits the variety of public debate. It is inconsistent with the First and Fourteenth Amendments."[49]

Hugo Black wrote a concurrence, joined by William Douglas, in which he agreed with the Court's reversal of the judgment but rejected the actual malice standard: "I base my vote to reverse on the belief that the First and Fourteenth Amendments not merely 'delimit' a State's power to award damages to 'public officials against critics of their official conduct' but completely prohibit a State from exercising such a power." The *Times* had an "absolute, unconditional constitutional right to publish . . . criticisms of the Montgomery agencies and officials," Black wrote. "We would, I think, more faithfully interpret the First Amendment by holding that at the very least it leaves the people and the press free to criticize officials and discuss public affairs with impunity."[50] Justice Arthur Goldberg, a liberal recently appointed by President Kennedy, wrote a concurrence in which he similarly advocated an "absolute, unconditional privilege to criticize official conduct despite the harm which may flow from excesses and abuses."[51]

New York Times v. Sullivan was immediately recognized as a landmark case, the most important First Amendment decision of the twentieth century, if not all time. In the opinion of University of Chicago law professor Harry Kalven Jr., the decision may "prove to be the best and most important" free speech ruling the Court had ever produced. Kalven believed that in defining a "central meaning" of the First Amendment, and a domain of speech—speech on political officials and public affairs—that received the Constitution's strongest protection, the opinion made "a notable shift in constitutional idiom and could provide a new start for consideration of free speech problems."[52]

Justice Brennan became a press celebrity, the media's favorite son. "'Publish and be damned!' is a brave slogan that most newspaper editors aspire to in principle," wrote *Newsweek* shortly after the decision. "Publish and be sued, however, has long been a fact of journalistic life. . . . But last week the U.S. Supreme Court handed down a decision that greatly strengthens American journalism." "The threat of libel as a means to censor publications had been considerably weakened."[53] The *New York Times* praised the decision as a "victory of first importance in the long—and never-ending—struggle for the rights of a free press."[54] "The Supreme Court has, in a very real sense, given legal voice to the creed by which all good newspapers have continued to live and prosper to the glory of the public interest."[55]

With *New York Times v. Sullivan*, freedom of the press was revolutionized and, at the same time, seriously complicated. The monumental decision raised more questions than it answered. The Court made clear that libel involving public officials fell under the Constitution's purview. But who was a public official? Should the *Sullivan* rule extend to libelous speech on public figures—individuals who were prominent and socially influential but did not hold public office? The

Sullivan opinion emphasized what was implicit in many of the Court's earlier free speech decisions: that the freedom to discuss public officials and public issues was the central meaning, the core concern of the First Amendment. But what was a "public issue"? Did the First Amendment protect only the discussion of governmental affairs, or did it reach beyond political criticism to protect publications on "matters of public concern" in its broadest sense—anything that concerned or interested the public? What about libel involving private citizens—ordinary people who played no role in public affairs? If the tort of libel was to be brought under First Amendment scrutiny, why not the closely related tort of invasion of privacy?

∿

William J. Brennan Jr. was appointed to the Supreme Court by President Eisenhower in 1956. In the opinion of many Supreme Court historians, Brennan was not only the most important intellectual influence on the Warren Court, but perhaps one of the greatest Supreme Court justices in the nation's history. He exerted his influence not only through his intellect, but even more, his "personality, friendliness, political instincts, and his uncanny ability to define a liberal consensus that could bring in centrists and even some conservatives," in the words of historian Melvin Urofsky.[56] Although he cared deeply about theory and doctrine, Brennan was also "a politician, an operator who conceived of his role in a completely different fashion from that of most judges," according to one biographer. "He worked the justices the way Lyndon Johnson worked the floor of the Senate."[57]

Brennan, an Irish Catholic Democrat, was the second of eight children born to working-class parents who had immigrated to the United States in the 1890s. As a child, Brennan worked as a grease monkey in a garage and delivered milk in a horse-drawn wagon. After attending Harvard Law School, he returned to New Jersey to practice law with a prominent firm in the 1930s. Following Army service in World War II and a return to private practice, Brennan was appointed to the state's trial court in 1949. Three years later, he was appointed to the state's supreme court, where he served for four and a half years. *Life* described him as "hard working, [and] respected by lawyers, who have often found themselves discomfited because [he] sometimes catches you off guard." Brennan was "a moderate liberal and a strict judge," "one of the keenest, quickest judicial minds in the country."[58] Brennan's ascent to the Court was unexpected. "Almost everybody in the country was . . .

surprised at his appointment," noted *Life* in 1957. "He was not a nationally known jurist and he was totally unknown as a political figure." He was not even a Republican, but rather "a lifelong, city-bred Democrat, a genial, outgoing, even garrulous man, much more like a successful toastmaster than a sobersided jurist."[59]

With Brennan's appointment, which filled the traditional political requirement of having a Catholic on the Court, Eisenhower unwittingly created a judicial revolution. When Eisenhower assumed the presidency in 1953, only two of the justices—Black and Douglas—were outspokenly liberal. Within three years, the Republican president gave them two allies: Brennan and Chief Justice Earl Warren. Eisenhower would regret these choices. Brennan quickly distinguished himself as a crusader for civil liberties and civil rights, a justice with a "passionate concern with the rights of persons accused of crimes."[60] He was also liberal on free expression, which became one of his most ardent causes.[61]

During his tenure on the Court, Brennan would pioneer several key concepts in modern First Amendment jurisprudence, including the idea of "self-censorship." Brennan believed that laws regulating speech could be unconstitutional even if they didn't directly limit speech; they could violate the First Amendment if they encouraged people to censor themselves in order to avoid getting in trouble with the law. In the majority opinion in *Speiser v. Randall* (1958), Brennan wrote that a California law that required applicants for government benefits to show that they had not been involved in the Communist Party had an unconstitutional "chilling effect" on speech. The burden of proof should have been on the state, not the applicant: "a man who knows that he must bring forth proof and persuade another of the lawfulness of his conduct necessarily must steer far wider of the unlawful zone than if the State must bear these burdens."[62] *Smith v. California* (1959) considered a Los Angeles ordinance that imposed criminal penalties on booksellers for the mere possession of obscene writings, even if they were unaware of their content. Writing for the majority, Brennan declared that the law was unconstitutional because it inhibited the sale of books that were not obscene, for "if the bookseller is criminally liable without knowledge of the contents . . . he will tend to restrict the books he sells to those he has inspected; and thus the State will have imposed a restriction upon the distribution of constitutionally protected as well as obscene literature."[63] Because First Amendment "freedoms are delicate and vulnerable," the "threat of sanctions may deter their exercise almost as potently as the actual application of sanctions."[64]

Brennan's closest allies on the Court—Black, Douglas, and Chief Justice Earl Warren—diverged greatly in temperament, background, and personality. Hugo Black had been appointed to the Court in 1937 by President Franklin Roosevelt. Black hailed from the Alabama backcountry—he described himself as a "hillbilly." Despite never having graduated from college, he went on to become a successful trial lawyer, police judge, and county prosecutor and was elected to the U.S. Senate in 1926. He was famous for carrying the Constitution in his jacket pocket, imitating the manner in which evangelicals carried copies of the Bible.[65] He read the Constitution as literally as scripture; he believed that the guarantees of the Bill of Rights were to be followed to the letter and that its provisions were unambiguous in meaning.[66] "I cherish every word of [the Constitution], from the first to the last," he said, "and I personally deplore even the slightest deviation from its least important commands."[67] At the same time Black was a strict constructionist, he was a civil libertarian and judicial activist who believed that the Constitution commanded the Supreme Court to enforce individual rights and liberties "no matter what legislators may have thought, and no matter what the consequences."[68] Personally, Black was a gracious man with a soft manner and slow southern drawl. At the same time, he had a fearsome drive and tenacity of conviction that came through in his tennis game, his judicial opinions, and his often tense relationships with his fellow justices.[69] "You can't just disagree with him," commented Justice Robert Jackson to a *New York Times* columnist. "You must go to war with him if you disagree."[70]

William Douglas was one of the most eccentric men ever to sit on the Supreme Court. Douglas grew up in Washington State; his father died when he was a boy, and the family was impoverished. Having contracted polio as a child, he began mountain climbing to strengthen his body. His love of nature and feelings of being a loner and outsider produced a brooding and intense personality. Douglas rose quickly in his legal career, becoming chairman of the Securities and Exchange Commission and a Yale Law School professor. He was appointed to the Court by President Roosevelt in 1939. Dazzlingly brilliant, Douglas produced some of the Warren Court's most influential opinions, particularly in the area of civil rights and civil liberties. Despite his accomplishments, he never fully exercised his talents. Douglas harbored ongoing political ambitions, radical philosophies put forth in over thirty popular books, and a penchant for womanizing, which contributed to the undoing of his judicial potential. Writes Supreme Court historian Jeffrey Rosen, "Douglas was distracted for much of his tenure, devoting his energies instead to angling for the vice presidency and to compulsive bouts of drinking and adultery with college students, flight attendants, or any other women who crossed his path."[71] "It's hard to avoid the suspicion that Douglas often scribbled his opinions on the back of a cocktail napkin. Breezy, polemical, and unconcerned with the fine points of legal doctrine, they read more like today's blog entries than carefully reasoned constitutional arguments."[72]

Like Black and Douglas, Earl Warren came from humble roots. Born in Los Angeles, he was the son of a Norwegian immigrant who worked for the Southern Pacific Railroad. After working his way through college and law school and a brief period in private practice, Warren served for thirteen years as a district attorney for Alameda County, and then for four years as California's attorney general. In 1943, he was elected governor of California, and during his ten years in office, he pushed forward a broad program of progressive social reform. In 1948, he ran for vice president on the unsuccessful Republican ticket headed by Thomas Dewey. He was at the start of his third term as a progressive Republican governor of California when he was appointed to the Supreme Court in 1953.[73] A "practical politician" who "worked magic in small groups," Warren had no clear judicial philosophy; he was a pragmatic instrumentalist who used the law to reach the result he favored in a given case, usually one that favored individuals over authorities.[74] His approach to cases was human and personal; he had a tendency to personalize legal issues and "saw litigants before the Court as people, not abstractions," in the words of one former law clerk.[75] Upon his retirement, Warren said that he hoped the Court under his leadership would be remembered as "the People's Court."[76]

By the time of *Sullivan*, Warren's Court had revolutionized American life in precisely that manner, protecting individual and minority rights in criminal justice, voting rights, employment, housing, transportation, and education.[77] When Warren left the Court in 1969, decisions under his leadership had outlawed school segregation, announced the "one-man, one-vote" doctrine, made most of the Bill of Rights binding on the states, ruled out compulsory prayer in public schools, curbed wiretapping, upheld the right against unreasonable searches and seizures, secured the right to counsel, and barred racial discrimination in voting, marriage laws, and housing sales and rentals. As law professor Fred Rodell observed in the *New York Times* in 1964, "For the first time in the Court's 175 year history . . . a consistent majority of the justices [Warren, Black, Douglas, Brennan, and Goldberg], scorning self-restraint where individual liberties are at issue, are determined to enforce the Bill of Rights (plus the Fourteenth Amendment) against any government action, state or federal, that disregards or infringes its guarantees. From the protection of equal voting rights to the protection even of obscene literature from censorship, it is this determination which has brought down on the Court's head the current storm of protest."[78]

Opposition to the Court, particularly in the South, had been sparked by the 1954 *Brown* decision and fueled by its opinions on obscenity, school prayer, redistricting, and criminal procedure.[79] In 1957, a coalition of southern congressmen introduced legislation that would have curbed the Court's power by reversing all or part of particular decisions, curtailing its general appellate jurisdiction, and changing the qualifications for service on the Court. In 1964, a congressional committee was considering no fewer than 147 proposals to undo the school prayer decisions. Thirteen states approved a proposed constitutional amendment to reverse the voting reapportionment rulings. In the early 1960s, the right-wing John Birch Society launched a national campaign to drive Warren from the Court. Billboards calling for Warren's impeachment appeared on American roads and highways.[80] The notorious Birch Society campaign "was both irrelevant and historic. At no point did it reach anything close to the support required to bring articles of impeachment against Warren, so its threat was abstract," writes Warren biographer Jim Newton. "Nevertheless, its breadth and duration revealed the intense animus that the Court inspired in those years."[81]

~

Until the early 1960s and the retirement of Felix Frankfurter, the Warren Court was not especially liberal on freedom of expression. Although there were exceptions, on balance, the Court's First Amendment decisions in the 1950s tended to be conservative. At the height of the anti-Communist hysteria in the late 1940s, Frank Murphy and Wiley Rutledge, civil libertarian allies with Black and Douglas, died within two months of each other. President Truman tried to appeal to the right wing by appointing Tom Clark and Sherman Minton, who became part of the conservative wing led by Frankfurter. As a result, the Supreme Court during the McCarthy era approved a series of state and federal laws that curtailed freedom of expression.[82]

The "preferred position" concept that had once prevailed, in which speech rights were given the highest judicial solicitude, largely disappeared from the

Court's free speech cases.[83] In the 1950s, its dominant approach to the First Amendment became an ad hoc balancing approach, in which the litigant's interest in free speech was weighed against the government's interests in restricting speech.[84] One of the best-known examples of ad hoc balancing was *Dennis v. United States* (1951), in which eleven leaders of the American Communist Party were convicted under the Smith Act for being members of an organization whose teachings advocated the violent overthrow of the government. A majority of six justices upheld the conviction. The leading opinion, by Chief Justice Fred Vinson, purported to use the clear-and-present-danger test, but in reality it used a balancing test; Vinson determined that the government's rationale for the measure, national security, justified the repression of expression.[85] Civil libertarians attacked the *Dennis* decision. "Treated by the balancing test, 'the freedom of speech' protected by the First Amendment is not affirmatively definable," wrote one critic. "It is defined only by the weight of the interests arrayed against it and it is inversely proportional to the weight accorded to those interests. When this approach is taken, there can be no floor beneath which that freedom may not be allowed to sink."[86]

Dissatisfaction with the Court's free speech decisions led to a national discussion on the state of the First Amendment in the early 1960s.[87] As Yale law professor Thomas Emerson noted in 1963, "[No] one concerned with freedom of expression in the United States today can fail to be alarmed by the unsatisfactory state of First Amendment doctrine. Despite the mounting number of decisions and an even greater volume of comment, no really adequate or comprehensive theory of the First Amendment has been enunciated, much less agreed upon." "Not only are courts and the legal profession in sharp conflict but the public is seriously confused and the First Amendment is threatened with disintegration."[88]

Liberal judges and legal scholars offered alternatives to the ad hoc balancing approach, and "absolutism" gained currency as a free speech methodology. Alexander Meiklejohn, a noted political theorist and president of Amherst College, advanced a particular kind of free speech absolutism that he described in several articles and in a 1948 book, *Free Speech and its Relation to Self-Government*. Meiklejohn's thesis was that civil liberties were "not all of one kind."[89] Economic rights could be regulated, but the government was forbidden to restrict freedom of speech and freedom of religion. Freedom of speech was an "absolute" when it came to "public speech." "Public speech" was essential to democratic self-governance; it was through "public discussions of public issues" that citizens maintained a democratic society. Meiklejohn defined speech on public issues broadly; it incorporated a wide range of material, including philosophy, science, art, literature, and entertainment.[90] "Private speech" included obscenity, incitement, and libels against private citizens, which had "no relation to the business of governing" and were unprotected by the First Amendment.[91]

Brennan was influenced by Meiklejohn, and the philosopher's views can be seen in the *Sullivan* opinion.[92] In *Sullivan*, Brennan described speech on public officials and political issues as the heart of the First Amendment, subject to the Constitution's strongest protection.[93] Yet unlike Meiklejohn, Brennan thought some speech on public issues could be restricted.[94] While Meiklejohn would have done away with liability for libels on public officials, Brennan's *Sullivan* opinion limited recovery but did not eliminate it. The state's interest in protecting reputations against reckless attacks, even the reputations of political figures, was not to be disregarded entirely.[95]

Hugo Black became an outspoken proponent of another kind of First Amendment absolutism—a true absolutism, in which the government was completely prohibited from regulating speech. "Nothing that I have read in the Congressional debates on the Bill of Rights indicates that there was any belief that the First Amendment contained any qualifications," he told an audience at New York University.[96] "I am for the First Amendment from the first word to the last. I believe it means what it says, and it says to me, 'Government shall keep its hands off religion. Government shall not attempt to control the ideas a man has. Government shall not attempt to establish a religion of any kind. Government shall not abridge freedom of the press or speech. It shall let anybody talk in this country.'"[97]

Black's position became the subject of national controversy when he delivered a public lecture at New York University in 1960. The speech, noted *Harper's* magazine, was "perhaps the most forceful statement of one side of a controversy . . . which . . . has divided the judiciary, split the Supreme Court, and posed troubling issues for those concerned with the preservation of individual freedom in America."[98] In the lecture, Black announced that "one of the primary purposes of the Constitution with its amendments was to withdraw from the Government all power to act in certain areas—whatever the scope of those areas may be. If I am right in this then there is, at least in those areas, no justification whatsoever for 'balancing' a particular right against some expressly granted power of Congress. If the Constitution withdraws from Government all power over subject matter in an area, such as religion, speech, press, assembly, and petition, there is nothing over which authority may be exerted."[99]

In an interview in 1962 with Professor Edmond Cahn of New York University, published in that school's law review, Black explained his position further. "I understand that it is rather old fashioned and shows a slight naiveté to say that 'no law' means no law. . . . I have to be honest about it. I confess not only that I think the Amendment means what it says, but also that I may be slightly influenced by the fact that I do not think Congress should make any law with respect to" speech. He went as far as to say that he "had no doubt" that liability for libel was unconstitutional. With the First Amendment, the framers "intended that there should be no libel or defamation law in the United States under the United States Government, just absolutely none."[100]

Cahn was astonished at Black's position. Did that mean, Cahn asked, that one was "free to say or print anything, anywhere, any time, and get away with it?" Black said: "My view is, without deviation, without exception, without any ifs, buts or whereases, that freedom of speech means that you shall not do something to people either for the views they have or the views they express or the words they speak or write."[101]

～

Within weeks of the *Sullivan* decision, Time, Inc. appealed to New York's highest court, the Court of Appeals. The publisher repeated its argument that the story about the Hills was "news." "The opening of a play destined for Broadway, such as the *Desperate Hours*, is as newsworthy an event in the field of drama as can possibly be imagined," read Time, Inc.'s brief. "There can be no question but that *Life* magazine had a news privilege to report on that play, its settings, its actors, its author, and any other fact having a relevant connection with it—and so to report through words, photographs, or any other method of communicating with the public."[102]

The brief highlighted the constitutional issue: the judgment against Time, Inc. violated "constitutional guaranties of free press and free speech." "As recently stated by the Supreme Court in *The New York Times Co. v. Sullivan* . . . 'erroneous statement is inevitable in free debate and . . . it must be protected if the freedoms of expression are to have the "breathing space" that they need to survive.'"[103]

"That pronouncement, made in the context of a case concerning defamatory criticism of a public official, is applicable, a fortiori, to any 'erroneous statement' made in free debate regarding a Broadway play, where the 'factual error' is not even of a derogatory, let alone defamatory nature." The lower court's "premising of liability on mere 'factual error' [was] clearly erroneous, and the decision should be reversed on that ground alone, if for no other."[104]

Time, Inc. also argued that the New York privacy statute was, on its face, unconstitutional. "On its face, the statute is clearly incompatible with the First Amendment of the Constitution of the United States," "for all newspapers are published for profit (and, accordingly, in ordinary usage, for 'purposes of trade') and invariably 'use' both the names and pictures of persons associated with newsworthy events. Under a literal interpretation of the statute, the daily press would be subjected to criminal fines and civil recoveries for the publication of virtually every line in print."[105]

According to the Hills' lawyers, *Sullivan* had no bearing on the case. *Sullivan*, a libel action, was "limited to criticisms of public officials in regard to their official conduct."[106] Even if *Sullivan* did apply, *Life* demonstrated reckless disregard for the truth about the Hills. "The record in this case overwhelmingly establishes that *Life*, through its editorial staff, knew that the association of respondent and his family to *The Desperate Hours* was basically false. Appellant prepared and published said article with either knowledge or reckless indifference to the fact that the article was basically false and would in all likelihood be highly offensive to respondent and his family."[107] Hill "and his family were used as the basis for a staged publicity article for a commercial event, and the effect of the article was to introduce them into the fictional episodes of a novel, play, and motion picture."[108] In a per curiam opinion, issued by the court as a whole, without any explanatory text, a majority of the Court of Appeals in April 1965 affirmed the judgment against Time, Inc.[109] Judge Stanley Fuld dissented, taking Time, Inc.'s position that the article was newsworthy. "There can be no doubt that the play certainly bore a close and legitimate relationship to the real-life incident," he wrote. "I do not believe that [the New York privacy law] may be availed to create a cause of action against those who published an article reporting a new play, unquestionably a subject worthy of press comment, and pointing out that there was a relationship between the play and an actual event, also concededly newsworthy, in which the plaintiff some years before had been involved."[110]

"Court Says 'Life' Invaded Privacy: Appeals Bench Affirms Other Decisions on Family in 'Desperate Hours.'" "Exploitation Is the Key: Magazine Account Written 3 Years after the Ordeal Held Not Newsworthy," announced the *New York Times* the day after the decision.[111] Harriet Pilpel devoted an entire *Publishers' Weekly* column to the decision, describing it as an "unwarranted and threatening" expansion of the right of privacy.[112] Pilpel noted that while liability for libel diminished with *Sullivan*, privacy liability was expanding: "The laws of libel and privacy seem to be on opposite ends today of the see-saw which represents permissible private limitations on freedom of expression."[113]

"With the great liberalization of the laws of libel and obscenity . . . the privacy doctrine today looms as the greatest single threat we face to a free marketplace of ideas," she wrote. "Throughout the land this . . . basic conflict between freedom of utterance and the individual's right of privacy is arising with increasing frequency. How it is resolved will fundamentally affect all writing, publishing, and even living in the USA from now on."[114]

CHAPTER TWELVE

Griswold

In May 1965, immediately following the New York Court of Appeals decision, Time, Inc.'s lawyers announced their plan to appeal to the U.S. Supreme Court, challenging both the publisher's liability and the constitutionality of the New York statute under the First and Fourteenth Amendments. The media and the public watched the petition closely. It was hoped that the case would clarify two ambiguous and contested areas of law: the First Amendment rights of the press and legal protections for the right to privacy.

Shortly after Time, Inc. announced its intent to appeal, the Supreme Court in June 1965 issued its decision in *Griswold v. Connecticut*, announcing a "right to privacy," found in "penumbras" and "emanations" of the Bill of Rights. Like *New York Times v. Sullivan*, *Griswold* complicated the *Hill* case. Not only a right protected by tort law, privacy was now potentially a broad, general right guaranteed by the Constitution.

≈

The period between 1964 and 1967 was, by all accounts, a watershed in the national debate over privacy. Scholars produced a number of important writings on privacy, among them Alan Westin's treatise *Privacy and Freedom*, an issue of the respected journal *Law and Contemporary Problems* devoted to the topic of privacy, and articles by eminent legal scholars Harry Kalven Jr. and Edward Bloustein.[1] Two books on privacy hit best-seller lists—Myron Brenton's *The Privacy Invaders* and Vance Packard's *The Naked Society*, which became the subject of public discussion and commentary.[2] By 1965, three congressional subcommittees were investigating aspects of Americans' imperiled privacy.[3] "Millions of Americans are living in an atmosphere in which peering electronic eyes, undercover agents, lie detectors, hidden tape recorders, bureaucratic investigators, and outrageously intrusive questionnaires are becoming commonplace, if often only suspected facts of life," wrote Vance

Packard.[4] According to an article in *Christian Century*, "If the socializing, depersonalizing forces continue undiminished," the time would come "when a man can no longer enter a closet to pray in secret, enjoy solitude, keep a trust, hold an unconventional opinion, [or] cover from public view some private part of his being."[5]

Newspapers and magazines carried exposés on the latest technologies for surreptitious watching and listening. A television station in Pittsburgh ran a series on privacy that included episodes such as "Bugging in the Automobile World," "Telephones and Intercoms," and "Motel Bugging." The use of surveillance technology for "industrial espionage" was discussed in articles with titles such as "How Spies Steal Business Secrets."[6] In 1964, the New York City Bar Association produced a study on the "flood" of new privacy-invading devices, including laser lights, "truth drugs," and hidden TV cameras and recorders.[7] "Can personal privacy survive the ceaseless advances of the technological juggernaut?" asked the *New York Times*. "Many in public and private life now fear to use telephones for conversations they would keep confidential, while the variety of electronic bugs available to eavesdrop on even whispered communications staggers the imagination. And young lovers would be well advised to remember that the skies are increasingly full of sputniks equipped with cameras capable of taking extraordinarily detailed pictures of what transpires under the moon as well as on it."[8]

With the growth of television as a news medium, media invasions of privacy reached new levels of intimacy and intensity. Commentators complained about "the relentless video pursuit of bereaved individuals," "disgraceful and tasteless attempts to interview grief-stricken people who lost members of their families in . . . tragedies," and "spot news stories when television reporters and cameramen rush to the scene of a story" and "try to pry into the deeper personal feelings of defenseless persons suddenly thrust into the news."[9] Magazines, newspapers, and television reporters were making extensive use of the new surveillance technologies. In 1960, CBS persuaded the chairman of an "Ike Day" celebration to wear a hidden wireless microphone when he greeted the president, who was not informed; his remarks were broadcast to the nation. The *Cleveland Press* secreted a camera in a brothel and snapped pictures of members of the Cleveland police force having lunch there. CBS was reported to have used concealed microphones at an airport meeting between the governors of Oregon and New York.[10]

Of all the threats to privacy, large-scale data collection and processing remained perhaps the most fearsome. Journalistic exposés and congressional investigations revealed the mushroom growth of the computerized "dossier society." In addition to federal and state governments, private companies and organizations had begun extensive file sharing over computer networks. In 1962, the Internal Revenue Service built a regional data processing center that would employ 1,800.[11] In 1965, the New York Stock Exchange announced plans to set up a computer center for its members.[12] Personal injury claims records were being aggregated for use by insurance and health companies.[13] "At this midway point between *1984* and 1984, a new image has been coupled to that of Orwell's closed-circuit television camera: it is the image of the electronic data bank, where a complete dossier for every one of us is literally at the fingertips of the console operator," wrote law professor Kenneth Karst.[14] "Computers have become so efficient and so sophisticated . . . 'a terrifying array of personal information' becomes available at the push of a button."[15]

In 1965, 1984 got a little closer when a consultant for the U.S. Bureau of the Budget authored a memo recommending that the federal government create a centralized "data service center" to store and analyze all of the information collected by the government.[16] The data center, which ultimately never materialized, would compile all of the statistics collected by more than twenty federal agencies, and the information would be made available to research firms, businesses, state and local governments, and a variety of other outside organizations.[17] The pooled information could include a person's educational history, military service, credit rating, court and police records, income, and employment.[18] There was also discussion of a medical data bank, which would compile the medical histories of all Americans.[19]

These proposals set off massive criticism. In hearings by a House subcommittee on invasion of privacy, representatives called the proposed national data center a "monster," "octopus," and "great expensive electronic garbage pail"[20] that would mean "the effective end of privacy."[21] Critics discussed the possibility of a "record prison," in which a person was permanently wed to his or her past. "Let's assume an individual had a nervous breakdown years ago, with subsequent complete recovery. Or even that the person contracted a social disease in his youth." "Is this medical record to pop out of a computer at the touch of a button, say, by that person's employer?"[22] "We are establishing a doctrine of no second chance, no forgiveness, one life, one chance only," law professor Charles Reich testified before Congress.[23]

Americans had become privacy conscious. According to one survey of more than three hundred newspaper editorials on electronic eavesdropping, there was near-unanimous agreement that both private and official eavesdropping had "reached proportions unbearable for a free society."[24] Alan Westin noted that statements "deploring the erosion of privacy and the tactics of 'Big Brother'" were "issuing steadily from every position along the ideological spectrum."[25] A psychological test given to New York primary school students containing embarrassing questions about sex was protested as an invasion of privacy and ultimately thrown out.[26] Nude protesters, with signs stating "Computers Are Obscene," were picketing IBM offices.[27] Campaigns sought to make it illegal for stores to sell clients' names and addresses to third parties, in the interest of protecting "the right to privacy."[28] When Santa Clara County announced its plans to create a centralized computer system containing dossiers that would be available to authorized inquirers within seconds or minutes, citizens raised complaints about "invasions of privacy" and a "big brother" society.[29] There were outcries around the federal census, a twelve-page questionnaire that included such queries as the number of bathrooms in one's home, the value of one's property, one's income, and the number of cars one owned. Failure to respond could lead to a penalty or jail time. One prominent political figure protested the questionnaire as "uncivilly inquisitorial and absolutely unconstitutional." He was jailed, and the Supreme Court refused to hear his petition.[30]

"Privacy is a ringing word in the American vocabulary, whether it stands for a tangible line drawn against the world . . . or for an intangible circle surrounding the individual," noted *Time* magazine in 1966. It observed the nation's desperate search for privacy and the measures some were taking to preserve their privacy: "Some seek physical solutions—better-planned cities, apartment buildings with thicker walls, atrium houses that turn their backs on the street, telephones that truly turn off. Others seek psychological solutions: psychiatric therapy to make up for the loss of privacy, or the secular equivalent of religious retreats."[31] Privacy seekers were urged to pull out their telephones, put their money in a cookie jar, "keep one eye peeled for hidden TV transmitters," and pay cash for everything.[32] "Everyone cannot, of course, electronically sweep his home and office every day," noted a Columbia University sociologist. "But the next time a credit agency calls to inquire about a neighbor, or one is asked to fill out a questionnaire on his sex life, he can simply say what no one seems to say anymore: 'It's none of your business.'"[33] "Privacy must be fought for resolutely step by step: the door closed, the questionnaire ignored, the mass resisted, the electronic eye out-stared, the moment of silence stolen and cherished."[34]

⌒

Americans increasingly sought legal solutions to their privacy problems. In the 1960s, citizens filed lawsuits over a variety of invasions of privacy, ranging from unwanted media exposure to wiretapping, surreptitious video recording, telephone solicitation, mailing list trafficking, unauthorized data collection, and surveillance by private detectives. In one noted case from 1964, *Hamberger v. Eastman*, a husband and wife in New Hampshire sued the landlord of their apartment for invasion of privacy when he installed a microphone near the headboard of their bed, connected by wires to the landlord's house. The landlord's motion to dismiss the case was denied.[35] Between 1964 and 1966, more than a dozen civil lawsuits for electronic eavesdropping were pending.[36] In 1964, a New York assemblyman representing Manhattan sought the repeal of a state law that permitted the state to sell copies of auto registration forms for use in compiling commercial mailing lists. He described the selling of names and personal data as "an obvious violation of civil rights," an attack on personal privacy.[37]

Privacy suits against the media surged, and many were successful. In one case from Alabama, a forty-four-year-old woman had gone into the funhouse at a county fair. As she left, her dress was blown up by air jets. A photographer from the local paper got a snapshot, and the picture of the woman in her panties ran on the front page. Even though the picture was taken in a public place, the trial court made an award of several thousand dollars, upheld by the state's supreme court in 1964.[38] The *Miami Daily News* published an article that contained the statement, "Wanna hear a sexy telephone voice?" It gave instructions to call a particular phone number and "ask for Louise." "Louise" filed suit for invasion of privacy, alleging that the article led to "many hundreds of telephone calls by various and sundry persons seeking to talk to and listen to the plaintiff." A Florida appeals court denied the newspaper's motion to dismiss the privacy claim.[39]

The right to privacy, as conceived by Warren and Brandeis, was a tort right, established by state statutory or common law. Whether there was a right to privacy in the federal Constitution remained a matter of ongoing debate. Until the 1950s, the Constitution's protection of privacy was housed primarily in two provisions: the Fifth Amendment's privilege against self-incrimination and the Fourth Amendment's protection against unreasonable search and seizure. The Fourth Amendment was limited to physical trespass and did not cover wiretapping and electronic surveillance. In *Olmstead v. U.S.* (1928), the Supreme Court had concluded that the use as evidence of wiretapped conversations obtained without a warrant did not violate the Fourth Amendment.[40]

Between the 1920s and the early 1950s, the Court alluded to other constitutional or quasi-constitutional privacy rights, such as a right to privacy in one's religious beliefs,[41] a "privacy" right to be free from excessive noise from blaring sound trucks,[42] a right against unwanted solicitation by door-to-door salesmen,[43] and "family privacy," protecting a "realm of family life which the state cannot enter."[44] In *Kovacs v. Cooper*, from 1949, the Court upheld a municipal law prohibiting sound trucks, noting that "in his home or on the street [the citizen] is practically helpless to escape this interference with his privacy by loud speakers except through the protection of the municipality."[45] In *Breard v. Alexandria* (1951), the Court upheld a municipal antisolicitation ordinance, praising the law for protecting "citizens against . . . practices deemed subversive of privacy and of quiet."[46] The source and scope of these "privacy" rights was unspecified and vague.[47]

When Earl Warren took his position as Chief Justice in 1953, the Supreme Court had yet to articulate a distinct constitutional jurisprudence or theory of privacy. By the time Warren left the Court in 1969, the Supreme Court had become a major force protecting privacy rights. Prior to 1953, the word *privacy* appeared in 88 Supreme Court opinions. It was in 107 opinions during Warren's fifteen-year tenure.[48]

The 1952 case *Public Utilities Commission of the District of Columbia v. Pollak* involved the use of recorded music and advertisements by a municipal company inside its buses. The plaintiffs argued that their free speech and due process rights were violated by being forced to listen to the recordings. A majority upheld the broadcasts.[49] William Douglas dissented, arguing that to force a "captive audience" to listen to broadcasting violated the citizen's right to privacy under the due process clause of the Fifth Amendment and the First Amendment's guarantee of "the sanctity of thought and belief." The right to privacy "should include the right to pick and choose from competing entertainments, competing propaganda, competing political philosophies," he wrote. "The right to be let alone . . . is the beginning of all freedom."[50]

In the late 1950s and early 1960s, the Supreme Court identified new privacy rights under the First and Fourteenth Amendments. A First Amendment right of "associational privacy" was declared in *NAACP v. Alabama* in 1958, holding unconstitutional Alabama's attempts to require the NAACP to turn over its membership lists in order to be admitted as an out-of-state corporation.[51] *Sweezy v.*

New Hampshire (1957) held unconstitutional the state's efforts to force a lecturer at the state university to disclose his political preferences, noting "the right of a citizen to political privacy, as protected by the Fourteenth Amendment."[52] The Warren Court also expanded the right to privacy under the Fourth Amendment. *Silverman v. United States* (1961) prohibited the introduction of evidence obtained by a "spike microphone," a listening device with a foot-long metal rod.[53] *Mapp v. Ohio* (1961) extended to state courts the exclusionary rule regarding illegally seized evidence, an "essential part of the right to privacy."[54]

Perhaps the most significant development in the Supreme Court's privacy jurisprudence involved birth control and "marital privacy." *Poe v. Ullman* (1961) challenged an 1879 Connecticut statute that made the use of contraceptives a criminal offense. A general statute also made it unlawful to "assist, abet, counsel, cause, hire, or command another to commit any such crime." Two married couples and a doctor contested the provision. The Court held that they lacked standing to bring the case because the law had never been enforced. Douglas and Harlan issued dissenting opinions. Both thought there were justiciable issues and agreed that the act was unconstitutional. Douglas believed that the law violated the physician's right to freedom of expression and also deprived married couples of a right to privacy, guaranteed to them under the due process clause of the Fourteenth Amendment. The right to privacy, he said, was "implicit in a free society," "emanat[ing] from the totality of the constitutional scheme under which we live."[55] Harlan found the Connecticut act a violation of the due process clause of the Fourteenth Amendment, insofar as it invaded "marital privacy," a fundamental right, a part of the "ordered liberty" protected against state action by the Fourteenth Amendment.[56]

In response to *Poe v. Ullman,* the Planned Parenthood League of Connecticut opened a clinic at which it gave contraceptive advice to married couples. The state arrested the executive director of the center and one of the participating physicians, and their convictions were upheld by the state's appeals courts. They appealed to the U.S. Supreme Court in 1964, basing their claim on a right to privacy in the First, Third, Fourth, Fifth, Fourteenth, and Ninth Amendments. Their brief argued: "The Connecticut statutes violate due process in that they constitute an unwarranted invasion of privacy. Whether one derives the right of privacy from a composite of the Third, Fourth and Fifth Amendments, from the Ninth Amendment, or from the 'liberty' clause of the Fourteenth Amendment, such a constitutional right has been specifically recognized by this Court. Although the boundaries of this constitutional right of privacy have not yet been spelled out, plainly the right extends to unwarranted governmental invasion of (1) the sanctity of the home, and (2) the intimacies of the sexual relationship in marriage. These core elements in the right to privacy are combined in this case."[57]

A majority of the justices in *Griswold v. Connecticut* agreed that the antiquated law had to be struck down but couldn't agree on the method. Douglas was assigned to write the opinion. He initially based it on freedom of association under the First Amendment—the right of the husband and wife to associate freely. As he wrote in a draft opinion in April 1965, "Marriage does not fit precisely any of the categories of First Amendment rights. But it is a form of association as vital in the life of a man and a woman as any other and perhaps more so." Marriage involved both freedom of association and the "interchange of ideas": "It is the main font of the population problem; and education of each spouse is the ramification of that problem, the health of the wife, the well being of the family, is central to family functioning. These objects are the end products of free expression and these Acts intrude on them."[58]

Harlan and Byron White agreed with the outcome but disagreed with the reasoning, arguing that it was ridiculous to implicate a "right of association" in marriage and that the Connecticut law should be overturned on the basis of the liberty protected by the Fourteenth Amendment. Brennan intervened to try and gather a majority. He wrote a memo to Douglas: "Dear Bill: I have read your draft opinion in *Griswold v. Connecticut* and, while I agree with a great deal of it, I should like to suggest a substantial change in emphasis for your consideration. . . . If a suitable formulation can be worked out, I would prefer a theory based on privacy, which . . . is the real interest vindicated here."

> Your opinion suggests, I think, a more fruitful approach, more closely tailored to the real interest at stake. You point out that, in creating a right to association, the Court has invoked the First Amendment to protect something not literally within its terminology of speech and assembly, because the interest protected is so closely related to speech and assembly. Instead of expanding the First Amendment right of association to include marriage, why not say that what has been done for the First Amendment can also be done for some of the other fundamental guarantees of the Bill of Rights?
>
> In other words, where fundamentals are concerned, the Bill of Rights guarantees are but expressions or examples of those rights, and do not preclude

application or extensions of those rights to situations unanticipated by the Framers. Whether, in doing for the other guarantees what has been done for speech and assembly in the First Amendment, we proceed by an expansive interpretation of those guarantees or by application of the Ninth Amendment admonition that the enumeration of rights is not exhaustive, the result is nearly the same. The guarantees of the Bill of Rights do not necessarily resist expansion to fill in the edges where the same fundamental interests are at stake.

Based on that reasoning, the Connecticut statute would "run afoul of a right to privacy created out of the Fourth Amendment, and the self-incrimination clause of the Fifth, together with the Third, in much the same way as the right of association has been created out of the First. Taken together, those amendments indicate a fundamental concern with the sanctity of the home and the right of the individual to be let alone," Brennan wrote.[59]

Following Brennan's lead, Douglas rested his opinion in *Griswold v. Connecticut* on a constitutional "right to privacy," fashioned out of extensions or "emanations" from different provisions in the Bill of Rights. Douglas conceded that there was no specific, constitutionally enumerated right to privacy but spoke of "zones of privacy" created by the Bill of Rights. Specific guarantees in the Bill of Rights have "penumbras, formed by emanations from those guarantees that help give them life and substance." "The right of association contained in the penumbra of the First Amendment is one, as we have seen. The Third Amendment in its prohibition against the quartering of soldiers 'in any house' in time of peace without the consent of the owner is another facet of that privacy. The Fourth Amendment explicitly affirms the 'right of the people to be secure in their persons, houses, papers, and effects, against unreasonable searches and seizures.' The Fifth Amendment in its Self-Incrimination Clause enables the citizen to create a zone of privacy which government may not force him to surrender to his detriment. The Ninth Amendment provides: 'The enumeration in the Constitution, of certain rights, shall not be construed to deny or disparage others retained by the people.'"[60] It was the first time the Court had cited the Ninth Amendment to invalidate a statute.[61]

Seven justices voted in favor of the petitioner, Griswold. Douglas's position secured five votes. Harlan and White concurred in the result but located the right to privacy in the due process clause of the Fourteenth Amendment.[62] "In my view, this Connecticut law, as applied to married couples, deprives them of liberty without due process of law, as that concept is used in the Fourteenth Amendment," White argued.[63] Arthur Goldberg's concurrence, joined by Warren and Brennan, agreed that the Connecticut birth control statute intruded on the right of "marital privacy" and described privacy as a fundamental right protected by the due process clause of the Fourteenth Amendment and also the Ninth Amendment. "The Ninth Amendment shows a belief of the Constitution's authors that fundamental rights exist that are not expressly enumerated in the first eight amendments and an intent that the list of rights included there not be deemed exhaustive," he wrote.[64] "As the Ninth Amendment expressly recognizes, there are fundamental personal rights such as this one, which are protected from abridgement by the Government, though not specifically mentioned in the Constitution."[65]

Griswold fueled ongoing disputes on the Court over "incorporation," which guarantees of the Bill of Rights were made applicable to the states through the due process clause of the Fourteenth Amendment, and the related debate over whether the due process clause protected fundamental rights that were not specifically elaborated in the Bill of Rights. Hugo Black had long argued that the Fourteenth Amendment made all of the Bill of Rights applicable to the states and that there was no basis for a judicial formulation of any other fundamental rights. This was his concept of "total incorporation."[66] Black dissented in *Griswold*, denying a broad right to privacy in the Constitution. He noted that privacy was an "abstract, and ambiguous concept" mentioned nowhere in the Bill of Rights or the Fourteenth Amendment: "I get nowhere in this case by talk about a constitutional 'right of privacy' as an emanation from one or more constitutional provisions. I like my privacy as well as the next one, but I am nevertheless compelled to admit that government has a right to invade it unless prohibited by some specific constitutional provision."[67] In a footnote, Black accused Douglas of attempting to elevate the tort of privacy into a constitutional doctrine: "This Court, which I did not understand to have power to sit as a court of common law, now appears to be exalting a phrase which Warren and Brandeis used in discussing grounds for tort relief to the level of a constitutional rule which prevents state legislatures from passing any law deemed by this Court to interfere with privacy."[68]

Much of the public favorably received the *Griswold* decision. "*Griswold v. Connecticut* contains the clearest articulation to date . . . of the constitutional foundations of a yearning for privacy, which constitutes a major component of the 'American Dream,'" noted one law professor shortly after the decision.[69]

Editorials agreed that the constitutional privacy right was "vital to the present American era."[70] But not everyone was satisfied with the "penumbras and emanations" formulation, criticized as vague, "kaleidoscopic," and "uncertain and ambiguous." As the *Boston Herald* put it, "The Court's opinion is a rather fuzzy one. It sets up a new 'right of privacy' which is nowhere mentioned in the Constitution. And it refers to no less than six amendments."[72] "With the court's nebulous dicta in the *Griswold* case, an entire new field of constitutional law appears dimly in the haze."[73]

The *Griswold* opinion was indeed hazy, and it left important questions unanswered. How far did the constitutional right to privacy extend, if at all, outside the context of "marital privacy"? Could it apply to other kinds of invasions of privacy—wiretapping, electronic eavesdropping, unwanted media publicity, computerized data collection? Where in the Constitution was the right to privacy to be found, and which interests, if any, outweighed the privacy right?

To privacy advocates, *Griswold* created a host of possibilities. In declaring a potentially broad right to privacy "emanating" from the Bill of Rights, or in the Fourteenth Amendment, the Supreme Court seemingly offered a blank check for a range of constitutional privacy claims. As the *New York Times* noted not long after the decision, *Griswold* was "being used as a peg to support a variety of legal claims of privacy. Since the word 'privacy' does not appear in the Constitution, lawyers and judges were previously hard put to uphold it, because this usually involved rejecting an opposing right that was well-established in the law. But now they can merely cite the Douglas opinion as proof of the right—and indications are that they are rushing to do so." "On all sides," lawyers were turning to *Griswold* "to support widely differing claims" to privacy. A twenty-five-year-old man working for the FBI, dismissed from employment because he allowed his girlfriend to stay overnight in his apartment, sued the agency under the theory that its surveillance of his activities violated his "right to privacy." A Baltimore court ordered harassing picketers to stay away from a woman's home, citing *Griswold* and noting that in the balance between the picketers' free speech and the woman's right to privacy, "the balance favors the privacy of the home."[74]

Legal experts predicted that *Griswold* could lead to the outlawing of wiretapping and other forms of electronic eavesdropping.[75] The Douglas "penumbra" argument could be used to establish that emanations from the Bill of Rights forbade electronic surveillance, suggested one law professor: "If there is a right to marital privacy in the home, why should there not be as well a right of privacy in the home or place of business against the unwelcome intrusion of uninvited participants in conversations intended to be private?"[76] *Griswold*, some speculated, could be used to outlaw virtually any intrusion on privacy and liberty, ranging from direct mail soliciting, polygraph tests, intrusive questionnaires, loyalty oaths, and employee background checks.[77] Observed Thomas Emerson, who argued the case for the birth control clinic in *Griswold*, "it would not be surprising to see the concept of privacy employed in a number of other situations to safeguard the private sector of our lives from government encroachment":

> Various kinds of police practices, not technically covered by the search and seizure guarantees of the Fourth Amendment, would easily fall within an expanding concept of the right to privacy. Efforts by government officials to compel the production of private information through legislative committees, lie detector tests, or other similar means may gradually be brought within the constitutional doctrine. Release of official records of arrests not resulting in conviction might be curtailed. Finally, the whole field of social welfare legislation and administration may be forced into procedures and practices more compatible with human dignity and integrity.
>
> [These are] indicative of some of the areas that may be encompassed within an expanded concept of the right to privacy. Undoubtedly the Court will proceed slowly, developing the right to privacy on a case-by-case basis. The essential point is that the key constitutional doctrine has been enunciated, and many forces in our society will press hard toward fuller realization of its great potential.[78]

"If the right of privacy is as broad as Samuel D. Warren and Louis Brandeis claimed when they first suggested it in 1890—immunity of the person—the right to one's personality, a right against the world—then [*Griswold*] could be just the beginning."[79]

For the press, *Griswold* represented a potential threat. Although the guarantees of the Bill of Rights technically applied only to government actions, publishing industry lawyers predicted, rightly, that plaintiffs suing the media under state privacy tort laws would attempt to use *Griswold* to buttress their claims.

Indeed, this is what the Hills' lawyers would argue—they claimed that *Griswold* established privacy as a constitutional right that not only shielded individuals from assaults and intrusions by the state but also justified legal protections against invasions of privacy committed by private actors such as the press. After *Griswold*, the conflict between freedom of the press and the right to privacy, previously a clash between a constitutional right and a weaker tort right, could now be cast as a conflict between two constitutional rights.[80]

In fall 1965, a few months after the *Griswold* decision, Time, Inc. filed its appeal with the Supreme Court.[81] It asked that the judgment be reversed as an abridgment of freedom of the press, as the *Life* article reported on a "news" event and the judgment rested on a statute that was unconstitutional on its face. The New York privacy law abridged freedom of the press "when . . . construed to permit the award of damages for invasion of privacy by the publication of a review of a play that resembled a prior incident involving a private person, the review and accompanying photographs being inaccurate in some particulars."[82]

Time, Inc. continued to parallel the case to *Sullivan*, in which a minor and careless error in a report on a newsworthy issue resulted in a large damage award against a publisher. "The question, then, is whether New York can properly impose . . . liability upon a publisher who connects without malice a non-public figure to a current news event in a report containing factual errors that could have been obviated by a more diligent investigation. The recital of that question suggests its inevitable answer under the First Amendment. To require the press to be totally accurate at its peril is precisely the kind of self-censorship that was so roundly condemned in the *Times* opinion."[83] Like the law of libel before *Sullivan*, privacy law had a "chilling effect" on the press: "Like the citizen critic, who has a duty to judge his government, the fourth estate has a duty to report the news. If that duty is encumbered by liabilities arising out of factual error or exaggeration, then it will not always be fully discharged, and the entire community suffers."[84]

Just as *Sullivan* subjected libel law to the First Amendment's purview, the Court should constitutionalize the tort of invasion of privacy. The "time ha[d] come" "for a decision making it clear that the First Amendment is present in what has traditionally been considered 'tort territory.' Now that the tort territory of defamation has been made to yield to the First Amendment by the decision in

New York Times v. Sullivan, the tort territory of privacy at the very least demands a searching constitutional examination."[85] "It is hardly necessary to assert now that the analogue to defamation, the law of privacy, is as central to First Amendment considerations as the problem faced in the *Times* case."[86]

Time, Inc. asked the Court to constitutionalize the state law newsworthiness privilege: "The Court [should] extend a general constitutional protection to the press against damage awards and criminal and prior restraints under the law of privacy, at least so long as the publication reveals some logical connection between the person named and the public event and makes some contribution to the dissemination of information or ideas, that is, to what is most broadly conceived to be news."[87] There would be an exception, as in libel, for falsehoods made with actual malice: "The protection would yield upon proof that the non-public figure [plaintiff] was connected to the news item because of actual malice on the part of publisher towards that person or because of the publisher's flagrant and reckless disregard for the truth. Such a rule would protect the press from self-censorship, but at the same time would not destroy the privacy tort, especially in cases in which advertisers make use of names for endorsement purposes without consent, the precise situation for which the tort remedy was created." [88]

The Hills' lawyers argued that the judgment did not present a First Amendment question and that the *Sullivan* decision had no bearing on the case: "*Life* magazine's fabricated photo-article is a far cry from the publication involved in *Sullivan*."[89] They invoked *Griswold*: "This Court has recently noted that the individual's 'right to be let alone' is a privilege which falls within the penumbra of constitutional protection. In *Griswold* the Court struck down a state statute which, if applied, would have invaded the individual's privacy. The New York Privacy Law, which safeguards the individual's right to be let alone, consistent with the free dissemination of news, accords highest respect to the overall design of the Bill of Rights."[90] On December 6, 1965, the Supreme Court announced that it would take the case to consider the "important constitutional questions" involved.[91]

CHAPTER THIRTEEN

Nixon

In 1965, the Hills acquired an unexpected advocate. Two years earlier, the former senator, vice president, and presidential candidate Richard Nixon joined the Mudge law firm, which renamed itself Nixon, Mudge, Rose, Guthrie, and Alexander. Nixon would argue the Hills' case before the Supreme Court. The case became an integral part of Nixon's efforts to rehabilitate his public image during his "Wilderness Years," the six-year span between his failed run for the California governorship in 1962 and his election as president in 1968.

∾

In his long political career, Richard Nixon traveled far from his humble roots. Richard Milhous Nixon was born in 1913 in Yorba Linda, California, to a family of Quakers who worked as farmers and grocery store owners. Nixon attended local Whittier College, then moved east in 1934 to attend law school on scholarship at Duke University. He returned home to Whittier after graduation to practice law at a local firm, then a few years later began a position at the Office of Price Administration in Washington. Nixon enlisted as an officer in the Navy and served through World War II, rising to the rank of lieutenant commander.

In 1946, Nixon ran for Congress in California's Twelfth District and won. During his term in Congress, Nixon gained notice as a Cold Warrior, serving in the House Un-American Activities Committee and doggedly pursuing former State Department official and accused Communist Alger Hiss. Nixon went on to win a seat in the Senate, and within a short period was chosen as the vice-presidential running mate for Dwight Eisenhower. Nixon initially caused problems for the Republican ticket when the press discovered that he had a slush fund that made it appear as if he was receiving gifts from wealthy supporters. Though he was pressured to resign to ease the tension on Eisenhower, Nixon chose instead to give his infamous "Checkers" speech, in which he assured the public that the only gift he had received was a puppy, which his daughters had named "Checkers." The public was convinced, Nixon stayed on the ticket, and Eisenhower and Nixon won the 1952 election.[1]

Nixon served as vice president for two terms under Eisenhower, then unsuccessfully ran for president against John F. Kennedy in 1960 and failed in his attempt to become California's governor in 1962. He blamed these losses, in part, on the press, which had antagonized him since the beginning of his career. Nixon's trouble with the press began during his campaigns for the House and the Senate, when liberal publications like the *New Republic* and the *Nation* attacked his red-baiting campaign tactics. Those outlets pilloried him during the Hiss hearings, and the press was largely responsible for the "fund scandal." According to an executive for the *New York Herald Tribune*, by the end of the 1950s, Nixon had come to believe that "freedom of the press was often a handy refuge for subtle as well as overt character assassination."[2]

Reporters hounded Nixon during the 1960 presidential campaign, when the majority of the press supported Kennedy. In 1962, after losing the governor's race, Nixon gave what he called his "last press conference," accusing the press of covering only their favored candidates.[3]

> The last play. I leave you gentlemen now and you now write it. You will interpret it. That's your right. But as I leave you I want you to know—just think how much you're going to be missing.
>
> You won't have Nixon to kick around any more, because, gentlemen, this is my last press conference and it will be one in which I have welcomed the opportunity to test wits with you. I have always respected you. I have sometimes disagreed with you. But, unlike some people, I've never canceled a subscription to a paper and also I never will.
>
> I believe in reading what my opponents say and I hope that what I have said today will at least make television, radio, the press, first recognize the great responsibility they have to report all the news and, second, recognize that they have a right and a responsibility, if they're against a candidate, give him the shaft, but also recognize if they give him the shaft, put one lonely reporter on the campaign who will report what the candidate says now and then.

This spiteful attack was a public relations disaster. Barring a miracle, Nixon's political career was over.[4]

Nixon then decided to leave California and move to New York in the hope of making a fresh start. He confided to his friend Elmer Bobst, retired chairman of the Warner Lambert Pharmaceutical Company and known as the "Vitamin King," his interest in returning to politics, possibly becoming secretary of state. With his political aspirations in mind, Nixon turned down offers of the chairmanships of Chrysler and Pepsi Cola International, and he refused invitations to become the president of a midwestern university and national commissioner for baseball.[5] Bobst and Nixon had worked together during the 1950s when Nixon was vice president, and Bobst served as honorary national chairman of the United States Savings Bond committee. Almost thirty years older than Nixon, Bobst had taken a fatherly interest in Nixon and was one of his closest confidants. Nixon's daughters referred to Bobst as "Uncle Elmer."[6]

Bobst suggested that Nixon pursue work on Wall Street in corporate law. In the previous hundred years, six presidential candidates had come from Wall Street law, and two Wall Street lawyers had become president of the United States.[7] Early in April 1963, Bobst called the senior partners at Mudge, where Bobst took his legal work, with the suggestion that they should invite Nixon to join the firm. "You need new blood at the top . . . someone who can serve to bring the firm into the eyes of Wall Street and to the attention of industry throughout the country," he said. Bobst arranged for several of the partners to meet Nixon over golf in New Jersey the following Saturday. They invited Nixon to a formal lunch at the firm's Broad Street office the following day. As Nixon recalled:

> We lunched in the conference room. I particularly remembered they had candles, lighted candles, for lunch which to me was quite impressive. My God, candles in the middle of the day! So we had a good lunch and a very good talk and I remember the sell was not particularly hard. . . . We talked about it and I just had a good feeling about them.[8]

The firm's leaders offered Nixon a $220,000 base salary and a position as one of the leading partners at the firm, whose name would be changed to Nixon, Mudge, Rose, Guthrie, and Alexander.[9] Nixon was asked if he had given up politics, and he said yes. As he told partner John Alexander, "John, if you knew anything about politics, you'd know that a politician doesn't give up his base. My base is California. When I come to New York, all that's behind me—I intend to do what I can for the firm."[10] He told reporters, "As for using New York as a base for politics, or injecting myself into local politics, you may quote me as saying emphatically it is not so. I am not coming to New York for any political reason whatsoever."[11] "I'm going to New York for the purpose of practicing law and not for practicing politics."[12] This was a lie. Nixon joined the firm because he needed to make money and also because he felt it could serve as a launching pad for his political ambitions.

News broke in early May 1963 that Nixon would be moving to New York and had made plans to join the firm.[13] His public relations aide issued Nixon's statement at the Waldorf Astoria Hotel: "On June 1, 1963, I shall move my residence to New York City and shall become counsel to the firm of Mudge, Stern, Baldwin & Todd. After I have met the six months' residency requirement of . . . New York . . . I shall apply for admission to the New York Bar. When admitted I shall become a general partner in the firm. Pending my admission to the New York Bar, I shall engage principally in matters relating to the Washington and Paris offices of the firm."[14] Nixon passed the bar easily; the requirement for admission to the New York bar was a 500-word statement discussing the question, "What do you believe the principles underlying the form of government of the United States to be?" The chairman of the state's Committee on Character and Fitness described Nixon's essay as the finest he had seen in twenty-eight years and asked permission from the state judiciary to make the essay public, something that had never been done before.[15]

Nixon purchased a $135,000 cooperative apartment on Fifth Avenue, in the same building as Governor Nelson A. Rockefeller's apartment.[16] This apartment, which could host up to seventy-five guests, became a site for parties and social gatherings, where Nixon entertained guests by playing the piano. By December 1963, Nixon was reported by the *New York Times* to be a "happy New Yorker. He chats with cab drivers about children. He walks two dogs—the famous Checkers and a poodle—in Central Park. He goes to football games and movies and Broadway shows." Nixon owned a 1963 Oldsmobile and was driven to work by a Cuban refugee whose wife worked as the Nixons' cook. "Mr. Nixon takes a briefcase of law work home. He has a dictaphone at home and at the office," wrote the *Times*. "He reaches his law office at 8:30 am [and] stays until 6 pm, missing the main stream of traffic both ways." He belonged to fashionable in-town clubs and country clubs and sat on the boards of directors of several important companies and organizations, including the insurance company Mutual of New York and the Boys' Club of America.[17] Nixon was becoming a man about town, and for someone who had spent his life in politics, the experience was new and thrilling.

Nixon was delighted to be on what he called the "fast track," surrounded by art, culture, taste, "the big deals and money of corporate America, and . . . the most influential brains in the country."[18]

Nixon quickly proved himself as a lawyer. According to biographer Stephen Ambrose, he went at the job just as he went after political office, "aggressively, with an equal emphasis on hard work and personal contacts."[19] He gave the firm a higher profile and brought in new accounts; among them was the Pepsi Cola account, which was directly attributable to Nixon's relationship with Pepsi's chairman, Don Kendall. Years before, when he was vice president, Nixon had agreed to appear in the kitchen of a model home in Moscow, in which a six-pack of Pepsi was placed on the kitchen counter. That became the site of the famous "kitchen debate" with Soviet leader Nikita Khrushchev.[20] Nixon, Mudge took on litigation and acquisition work for clients such as Studebaker, Warner Lambert, General Cigar, and Precision Valve, all of whose chairmen considered themselves close to Nixon. Businessmen flocked to the firm, some simply for the prestige of working with a former vice president. Nixon himself remarked on this phenomenon: "I never realized how easy it is to make money. I just got twenty five thousand dollars for telling a bunch of stupid jerks something they could have learned from the newspapers." Nixon described his activities during this period in this way: "Believe me, it's an excruciatingly difficult thing. You go to board meetings and you go to dinners and you talk to people that you would rather, frankly, not talk to. You work and work and work."[21]

Much of Nixon's work for the firm was not strictly legal but business—advising clients on dealings overseas or negotiating with foreign governments.[22] He also recruited for the firm. In 1965, he joined the Mudge recruiting team on five law school campuses, including Columbia, Yale, and Harvard. Hundreds of law students signed up to have a twenty-minute interview with Richard Nixon. At Harvard, Nixon spoke to the Graduate Students' Young Republican Club and invited them to see him in New York. Five students took him up on the invitation; they enjoyed cocktails at Nixon's apartment, dinner (featuring filet of sole bonne femme and baked Alaska for dessert), and cigars and brandy in his den after the meal.[23]

Within two years of moving to New York, Nixon was enjoying success, financial prosperity, and a good deal of contentment. He was earning more than $250,000 a year, plus income from the royalties on his book *Six Crises* and other writings.[24] He was also establishing the base for his return to politics. In 1965 and

1966 he flew around the country campaigning for Republican candidates and gave lectures worldwide.[25] The law firm was sympathetic to Nixon's aspirations and gave him plenty of time for his political activities. Nixon described his time in New York as his "Wilderness Years." The period was "one of the most remarkable of his life," in which he "fought for his reincarnation," observes biographer Jonathan Aitken. "The key elements in that fight were achieving professional success in the legal world . . . exercising astute judgment to position himself in the center of the Republican hierarchy, and campaigning like a warrior in the cause of his party during the leanest of years." Nixon "prepared himself for his comeback with the discipline of a former heavyweight champion returning to the ring."[26]

Although friendly and well liked at the firm, Nixon was introverted and private and did not spend much time cultivating what he called "buddy-buddy" relationships.[27] The only person he got close to was Leonard Garment. It was an odd alliance, given their backgrounds: Garment, a gregarious liberal Democrat, jazz clarinetist, and critic of the Establishment, and the dour, brooding, Republican Nixon.[28] Garment described his relationship with Nixon as a combination of "amusement and affection. We were sort of friends. We didn't go to basketball games together, but we were close." Garment dropped by Nixon's office daily, offering a "flood of memos on every imaginable subject, ranging from restaurant and theater recommendations to appraisals of the war in Vietnam," and "a continuous stream of advice on politics, the media, show business, and the law."[29] Both he and Nixon came from humble working-class roots—"similar backgrounds on the wrong side of the tracks," Garment recalled. "The animating force in our lives was the work ethic. Our driving force was that we so much wanted to succeed." "Instinctively we knew that we could be instruments for each other's purposes. We had the synergy of two live wires."[30]

In 1964, Garment and several other lawyers at the firm had started an impromptu campaign team for Nixon. Sometime that year, Garment hit on the *Hill* case as a possible vehicle for Nixon's political rehabilitation. Garment recalled the first time he mentioned the case to Nixon: "Nixon listened carefully to my description of the case. The magazine wasn't out to injure the Hills, he remarked; it just didn't give a good goddamn about them. It was only interested in selling its goddamn magazine. That's what makes it so infuriating, he went on. All that fancy First Amendment talk—just a lot of pious bullshit while they exploit the hell out of you."[31]

Garment envisioned Nixon arguing the case before the Supreme Court. While Garment would remain involved in the case, Nixon would serve as *Hill*'s public face. This could cast Nixon in a new light, as a principled crusader for the besieged privacy rights of ordinary Americans rather than the rejected politician and sore loser. Wrote Garment: "The Court's decision to hear the case established that large public issues were involved. It also summoned up for me what seemed to me an attractive picture—for the case and for Richard Nixon's future—of Nixon, who had apparently passed from the political scene, defending the right of privacy against one of the nation's largest publishers." The Hills were receptive to Garment's suggestion and urged that Nixon argue the case.[32]

Nixon had doubts about getting involved in the case, now designated *Time, Inc. v. Hill*. He thought he ran a risk: some of his oldest political enemies sat on the Court, most notably Earl Warren. During the 1952 Republican Convention, Nixon promised to support Warren's candidacy for the presidency but instead supported Eisenhower. Ever since, Warren had a contempt for Nixon that was almost a "visceral repugnance," according to Warren biographer Bernard Schwartz.[33] The case would also pit Nixon against one of the most powerful publishing empires in the country, which could make it seem that he was still waging his war against the press.[34] Eventually Garment convinced Nixon that his appearance before the Supreme Court could become part of the public's perception of him as a "New Nixon," "a disciplined advocate respectful of constitutional principles, not the bitter politician lashing out at journalists in his famous 'last press conference.'"[35] Nixon agreed to argue the case, realizing the significant consequences for the law as well as his own future.[36]

~

The Nixon, Mudge firm began gearing up for the Supreme Court phase of the case in late 1965. Garment and a team of young associates assisted by a distinguished elderly partner, Goldthwaite Dorr, worked to dismantle Time, Inc.'s claims: that the *Life* story was "news," that the error in the *Life* article was negligent rather than intentional, and that *New York Times v. Sullivan*, with its actual malice rule, negated liability for the press based on negligent errors of fact.

The Nixon lawyers tried to demonstrate that *Sullivan* had no relevance to *Hill*. The *Life* article—a false, commercial publication that invaded the privacy of ordinary citizens—did not implicate the First Amendment's "central meaning," as described in *Sullivan*. No one could say that the opening of *The Desperate Hours* was "a matter of pressing public concern, nor that in 1955 it involved . . . a public issue or a matter upon which 'vigorous and uninhibited public debate' should be encouraged," read a memo circulated around the firm in early 1966.[37] "The *Life* article would involve a 'public issue' only if that definition were extended to the utmost limit, i.e., to all matters of general public interest, whether or not involving a general public debate." A "public issue for purposes of applying a qualified privilege as required by the First Amendment should include matters involving the public welfare."[38] The Hills were not public figures like the plaintiff in the *Sullivan* case, a "public official in the center of a current public controversy." "How could it be said that someone who had never actively participated" in a public event—"who was being introduced involuntarily into the subject"—was a public figure? "That would be a farfetched and unrealistic definition of 'public figure.'"[39] Garment wrote to Nixon, "If the court accepts Cravath's argument and equates the *Life* article (and the law of privacy) with the *New York Times* advertisement (and the law of libel) it will have made an enormous extension in the New York Times doctrine."[40]

Even if the actual malice standard applied, *Life* had recklessly disregarded the truth when it described *The Desperate Hours* as a "reenactment." Read one memo: "The evidence shows deliberate alteration of the facts, i.e., a meticulously precise statement of a false relationship between the Hill incident and *The Desperate Hours*. The equating of the Hill incident with the brutality and heroics of *The Desperate Hours* resulted from a typically skillful Time, Inc. blend of text, captions, and photography, tied together by staging in the former Hill home. . . . The end product (not unlike a composite photograph) was a journalistic hoax."[41] "Appellant's editorial and research talent—second to none in the publishing world—were directed solely to making the absolutely false point that *The Desperate Hours* was the story of the Hill incident. We rely on the fact that the editor of *Life* had before him, when he wrote the *Life* article, a prior article by the author of *The Desperate Hours* which made it absolutely clear that the story of *The Desperate Hours* was not the story of the Hills—or any other actual family."[42] "Intentional falsehood and hoaxing are concededly not protected by the First Amendment."[43]

Griswold, the Nixon lawyers argued, had given the right to privacy a new, elevated constitutional stature. The decision was "valid precedent for [*Hill*] because it recognizes that the Bill of Rights protects the privacy of an individual."[44] Like other laws that protected privacy, the New York privacy statute was concerned with "encroachments on the dignity and self-respect of the individual." Strong legal protections for privacy were critical at a time when "the right to be let alone" was being imperiled, eroded by the sensationalistic press, the "miniaturized microphone and tape recorder, the one-way mirror, the sophisticated personality test, the computer with its enormous capacity for the storage and retrieval of information about individuals and groups, behavior controlling drugs, the miniature camera, the polygraph, the directional microphone, infrared photography, and other . . . devices."[45] "Privacy is an important right and has been recognized as such by federal governments," and a "ruling against privacy and permitting disclosure would have a deleterious effect throughout our entire governmental system and adversely affect important interests of our society."[46]

Because *Hill* was such a high-profile case and the only case that the firm had ever argued before the Supreme Court, the firm invested substantial resources in its preparation—hundreds of associate hours. Four associates were involved in writing the briefs in the *Hill* case and helping Nixon prepare for his oral argument: Donald Zoeller, who had assisted Garment at the *Hill* trial in 1962; Douglas Parker, a recent Cornell Law graduate; a 1964 Ohio State law graduate, Allen Rule; and a recent Harvard Law graduate, Cyrus Abbe. Rule was the "intellectual backbone" of the team and did extensive research into First Amendment theory and doctrine. Nixon admired Rule's work and spoke highly of the young associate.[47] The associates "communicated" with Nixon through Garment, who had regular discussions with Nixon about the case, and through various memoranda and drafts of the briefs. The associates who worked on the case referred to their time sheets as "the Desperate Blotters," a pun on *The Desperate Hours*.[48]

The firm's associates prepared memo upon memo for Nixon to digest and lists of "essential reading" on privacy and free speech, including writings by Meiklejohn and other legal scholars, published talks by Justice Brennan on the First Amendment, treatises on balancing and absolutist approaches to the First Amendment, popular literature on privacy such as Packard's *The Naked Society*, and dozens of privacy cases. In preparation for Nixon's oral argument, the associates also investigated the backgrounds, philosophies, and personalities of the Supreme Court justices and predicted their positions on the issues in case.

Earl Warren, they speculated, would vote for the Hills. "Warren has taken a strong position in defense of the rights of an individual criminal accused or arrestee who is often helpless to defend himself against the collective power of society; in *Hill* he may be . . . predisposed to protect an individual injured by a more powerful social force," noted one memorandum.[49] Potter Stewart, a moderately conservative Eisenhower appointee, and Tom Clark, former attorney general under President Truman and known for his conservative leanings, would also probably vote for the Hills.[50] So would John Marshall Harlan. Harlan, appointed by Eisenhower, was perhaps the most conservative member of the Court. A mellow, old-fashioned Princeton gentleman, deeply intellectual, Harlan was a believer in judicial self-restraint and a skeptic about the Court's powers.[51] Harlan, who advocated a balancing approach to the First Amendment, had written noted opinions upholding government restrictions on speech; he had rejected free speech claims by individuals held in contempt by the House Un-American Activities Committee and who were denied admission to the bar for refusing to respond to questions concerning alleged Communist activities.[52] Yet Harlan had also taken more libertarian positions on the First Amendment. He joined the majority in *New York Times v. Sullivan*, and in 1957 construed the Smith Act to permit prosecution of Communist party leaders only for speech amounting to incitement to action rather than "abstract doctrine" advocating overthrow.[53]

Byron White's position on the First Amendment was unclear. A former professional football star and deputy U.S. attorney general appointed by President Kennedy in 1962, White was characterized in the press as a "moderate, centrist, [and] swing vote." Journalists described him as "cautious and colorless," "less concerned with the individual than with authority," and "tending towards the conservatives."[54] A memo circulated around the Nixon firm speculated that White's "anti-libertarian inclinations" would lead him to accept the argument that "*Hill* belongs in that class of cases not entitled constitutional protection for reasons developed in *Chaplinsky* and its progeny."[55] White, who in his years as a sports star grew uncomfortable with the media spotlight, disliked and distrusted the press. He concurred with the Court's decision in *Sullivan*, but would spend much of his later career trying to cabin the protections for the press that grew out of that case.[56]

Black, with his First Amendment absolutism, would obviously go for Time, Inc., as would Douglas, who joined Black in his free speech libertarianism. Brennan, "the most important First Amendment spokesman on the Court," was difficult to predict. Brennan defended the press in *Sullivan*, yet his position on the First Amendment was not an absolutist one. Personally Brennan had mixed feelings toward the press. He was a devoted consumer of journalism and read at least two newspapers each morning and watched the evening news at night. Yet he had had bad run-ins with journalists; on several occasions he had declined to speak with reporters, claiming that "there is just too much risk of being misquoted or misunderstood."[57]

Abe Fortas, who replaced Arthur Goldberg in 1965, was a wild card. Fortas—Douglas's former student at Yale, who also served under Douglas at the Securities and Exchange Commission—was a former Yale professor and prominent lawyer in private practice before his appointment to the bench. Fortas came from a lower-middle-class Jewish family in Memphis, Tennessee. A founding partner at the prestigious Washington, D.C., law firm Arnold, Fortas, and Porter, Fortas argued landmark public interest cases, including *Durham v. United States* (1954), which reformed the insanity defense, and *Gideon v. Wainwright* (1963), in which the Supreme Court declared a constitutional right to counsel.[58] During the red scare of the early 1950s, Fortas had come to public notice as the defense attorney for Owen Lattimore, a professor accused by Joseph McCarthy of being the top Russian espionage agent in the United States.[59]

Fortas had a close relationship with President Lyndon Johnson, whom Fortas represented during his contested 1948 election to the Senate. Johnson had won the Democratic primary by only eighty-seven votes, and his opponent, the former governor of Texas, persuaded a federal judge to issue an order taking Johnson's name off the general election ballot while the primary results were being contested. Johnson asked Fortas for help, and Fortas persuaded Hugo Black, with the entire Supreme Court on vacation, to void the court order as an improper intrusion into state political affairs.[60] Fortas was described in the press as "abrasive, aggressive, ambitious, brilliant, clever, cold, cryptic, decisive, deliberate, delightful, determined, discreet, distant, dynamic, enigmatic, hardboiled, high powered, imaginative, [and] incisive." Fred Rodell, in a sympathetic article in the *New York Times*, believed that despite his fearsome media image, Fortas was also "generous, gentle, human, and warm," a complex character, "never embarrassed, never taken by surprise," with a "slowly mobile smile, [and] a deep, velvet-smooth voice." He was "tender-hearted" as well as "tough-minded."[61]

Fortas was perhaps "the least predictable justice on First Amendment questions," observed a memo in March 1966. He was part of the Court's liberal bloc, but he had also decided against civil liberties, voting with the majority in *Ginzberg v. United States* (1966), upholding an obscenity conviction against the publisher of an erotic magazine. "Fortas' work in *Gideon* . . . may predispose him, like Warren, to give greater weight than Brennan" to the interests of sympathetic figures like the Hills, the memo concluded. [62]

Nixon had his own suspicions. In early 1966, Nixon hosted social gatherings at his apartment where the firm's lawyers discussed the case and took odds on its outcome. Doug Parker, an associate at the firm, recalled one party in which all agreed that Black would rule against the Hills on the basis of his absolutist views. Fortas, Nixon believed, would vote "[against us] because he's a very partisan Democrat." Nixon was confident that Warren would go in his favor: "He hates me, but he's a strong family man and he'll appreciate what this did to the Hill family."[63]

~

Goldthwaite Higginson Dorr had recently joined Nixon, Mudge through a merger with his own law firm. A tall, stately ninety-year-old, Dorr, who served in the Spanish American War and had graduated from Columbia Law School in 1904, had a long and distinguished legal career as an assistant U.S. attorney, an assistant director of munitions during World War I, and the founder of his own firm specializing in railroad law.[64] He had developed a deep personal interest in the *Hill* case and took a lead role in preparing the Supreme Court briefs and assisting Nixon's oral argument.

A formal gentleman of the old school, Dorr believed that the right to privacy was the essence of a civilized society. He lamented the loss of privacy and dignity in what he saw as an aggressive, sensationalistic, materialistic culture, and he believed that the law could be a force for their restoration. Dorr praised the New York privacy law, with its protection against gratuitous publicity and commercial exploitation of the persona. "The instinctive feelings which prompted the enactment of this statute were sound at the time of enactment," he wrote in a memo to the firm. "Experience over 60 years has not shown them to be unsound. Instead, they now appear more valid than ever. The inevitable changes in our human relationships and habits by our current extreme technological and commercial developments in communication make it all the more reasonable for the law to clothe the individual with at least some shreds of privacy."[65]

In early 1966, Dorr contacted the American Civil Liberties Union, which had filed an amicus brief in *Griswold* on behalf of the birth control clinic. Dorr hoped to convince the ACLU to file an amicus brief with the Court on behalf of the Hills. He wrote to ACLU lawyer Aryeh Neier: "Because of my long acquaintance with those who have devoted so much of their effort to the Civil Liberties Union, going back to Arthur Garfield Hays [the ACLU's cofounder] in Law School days, I know something of its instinct over the years for the protection of the individual in freedom of thinking and expression, and I also know its interest in one aspect or another of the protection of the privacy and personality of the individual."[66] Dorr also wrote to Ernest Angell, president of the ACLU: "Whatever the law may ultimately prove to be in this case, it is difficult to conceive how anyone could have been put in a more cruelly false light than Hill and his family were by the *Life* publication by its false praise of their heroism." "The Supreme Court in the *Griswold* case seems to have been searching for constitutional protection for a right to privacy—and a strong majority found one avenue or another to find that protection. I was glad to see that the Civil Liberties Union by its Amicus Curiae Brief was helpful in this search."[67]

Angell's response was less than Dorr had hoped for. Angell admitted that the Hills had a potentially viable claim for invasion of privacy but that it was a "close case, on the borderline" and did not "indubitably fall within the scope of previously determined ACLU policy in matters such as this." Although Angell's personal sympathies lay with the Hills, and the organization had been active in campaigns for privacy rights—efforts to decriminalize birth control and abortion and to curb official and private wiretapping—many in the noted free speech organization would likely come out in support of Time, Inc. and freedom of the press, Angell observed.[68] Ultimately the ACLU never got involved in *Time, Inc. v. Hill*.[69]

Dorr, who was known around the firm as "G.H.," was a "stubborn old bird," recalled Doug Parker. "Dorr was a shrewd . . . gentleman and, despite his years, displayed remarkable energy and an even more remarkable tenacity in arguing and re-arguing his point of view." Parker remembered an all-day meeting in which the members of the *Hill* team went over the final version of the Supreme Court brief, which had gone through many drafts. The meeting lasted from 9:00 a.m. to 8:00 p.m., with G.H. repeatedly raising points that he felt strongly about, even points that had been previously been resolved.

Garment, who was in his forties, went home that night and said, "God, I feel seventy." His wife, Grace quipped, "You know, G.H. is home looking in the mirror and saying 'I feel seventy again.'"[70]

⁓

Nixon was not directly involved in the *Hill* case until three weeks before the oral argument in April 1966. According to Garment, Nixon viewed his appearance before the Court as "a 'crisis' such as had periodically marked his career," and he met it with "stunningly meticulous" preparation.[71]

Nixon prepared obsessively for his performance. He memorized the trial record, relevant precedents, and dozens of law review articles. As the oral argument neared, he set up "skull sessions"—question-and-answer sessions with his colleagues simulating court argument.[72] As Nixon recalled, "I locked myself up in my office for two weeks. No phone calls. No interruptions. It [took] a tremendous amount of concentration."[73] Goldthwaite Dorr commented, "He did his homework. A lot of them don't, you know. But he made it his own, digested everything. Didn't care if he exposed his own ignorance to learn a thing. He had to know it."[74] According to a profile in *Harper's* magazine, Nixon "lived, breathed, talked, and thought sixteen hours a day about the case . . . he was to argue before the Supreme Court."[75] Nixon was driven to give the best possible performance in his return to the public stage; whether or not he admitted it, he was also enacting his vendetta against the press.

According to Pat Buchanan, a young conservative journalist who had been hired by the "campaign team" to oversee Nixon's political efforts, Nixon found himself "bored to death" with corporate law. He brought Buchanan into his office for long discussions on foreign policy and politics, noting that if he had to practice law for the rest of his life, "I would be mentally dead in two years and physically dead in four." When Nixon was assigned to the argument in *Time, Inc. v. Hill*, his attitude changed. Wrote Buchanan, "The challenge of pleading a case before the Court and his old antagonist Chief Justice Earl Warren . . . and the intense study and time of testing before the Supreme Court—this was an aspect of his legal profession that did capture Nixon's interest."[76]

Throughout his career, Nixon was notorious for his scribbling on long, lined yellow legal notepads. Nixon's "closest friend was the always available, always compliant, always silent yellow pad," Garment recalled. "It . . . served as a kind of door through which he could walk and shut out the world. When Nixon took out his yellow pad and unscrewed his pen, you knew it was time to move on."[77] Nixon worked on his preparation for the oral argument during lunches, dinners, and trips to meet with clients. Luncheons with friends and colleagues would often veer onto the topic of privacy, allowing Nixon to work out some of the theories he would argue in the case. On plane trips, he immersed himself in his legal pads, jotting down notes, arguments, and turns of phrase that he planned to deliver during his hour-long performance before the Court. This was Nixon's famous strategy, one that he employed in many of his speeches and public addresses: he painstakingly outlined and reoutlined his address on his yellow pads, and when he had memorized the key phrases, he put the notes aside and spoke extemporaneously.[78]

Nixon developed an arsenal of provocative attacks on *Life* that he planned to deliver at the oral argument. "I like my magazine newsy, exciting, and stimulating, but not at the cost of invading the privacy of a just ordinary middle-class family by using their name in a fictional setting for commercial gain."[79] "With the Hills they threw caution to the winds to get maximum impact for the benefit of the magazine and the collateral event—the show."[80] He described *Life*'s technique of fabricating "news" as "hoaxing." "Such hoaxing neither educates nor informs, and therefore does not present a First Amendment problem," he wrote.[81]

Nixon's presidential archives contain literally hundreds of yellow pages with his notes on the *Hill* case in his scrawling, cramped hand. As he wrote on March 14, 1966, commenting on Cravath's "weak points":

1) They equate Hills with public figures!

2) Attempt to extend Sullivan—no reasoning.

3) Fiction by definition is deliberate untruth.[82]

Nixon observed:

Laudatory falsehood is as damaging as defamatory falsehood. Defamatory falsehood affects what others think of you. Laudatory falsehoods affect what you think about yourself—a man's self-respect—his integrity is affronted by the knowledge he has been placed in a false laudatory light.

Shall we allow the use of persons as commercial props by the mass media? he asked.

Without a strong right to privacy, "how can an individual remain an individual in a mass communication society?"[83]

❧

We don't know with certainty what Nixon thought about the *Hill* case. According to two of the lawyers who worked with Nixon, Don Zoeller and Doug

Parker, Nixon said hardly anything about the case and gave little indication of his feelings about it. Parker believed that Nixon was a "principled lawyer" and that he would have given his all for Time, Inc. if asked to represent it.[84]

It would not be a stretch to conclude that Nixon was personally on the Hills' side. Nixon was a genuinely private person, and he obviously hated the press.[85] His yellow-pad jottings and memoranda indicate strong sympathies for the Hills, hard-working, ordinary "silent Americans" and fellow "victims" of the media. Nixon was no friend of free speech, as made clear during a recent kerfuffle involving Eugene Genovese, a Marxist professor at Rutgers University who during a campus "teach-in" had advocated a Vietcong victory in Vietnam. Nixon attacked Genovese in a public speech and in a letter to the *New York Times*, alleging that he was actually arguing for the preservation of academic freedom by "defending the system of government which guarantees freedom of speech to individuals." ("So much for their fucking sophistication!" Nixon said to Garment, commenting on the shocked reaction of the press to his statements. "Oh I know you and the rest of the intellectuals won't like it—the men back at the firm won't like it either—but somebody had to take them on.")[86] Journalist Jules Witcover speculated that one reason Nixon wanted to get involved with the *Hill* case was because of the Genovese incident. In the academic community, the law firm, and the liberal New York legal community, the Genovese debacle "had left a cloud hanging over Nixon's views on individual freedom." The *Hill* case offered an ideal opportunity to "dispel the cloud in a forum certain to receive national attention," according to Witcover.[87]

Despite his unrestrained use of profanity, Nixon was in many ways a prude; he deplored sensationalism and railed against the Warren Court's decisions expanding First Amendment protections for profane and obscene speech, particularly opinions by Justice Brennan.[88] Nixon was overtly offended by *The Desperate Hours* and the "constant use of profanity in the play." Quipped Garment, "Nixon, as the world learned from the Watergate tapes, was quite capable of using profanity in public. Public display was the place where he, with some consistency, drew the line."[89] As would become strikingly clear in his post–*Time, Inc. v. Hill* career, Nixon had no problem with—indeed, welcomed—the use of the law to quash speech he disliked, disagreed with, or felt offended or threatened by. Nixon's attacks on Time, Inc. during his oral argument, it is safe to say, were more than just lawyerly posturing.

PART IV

Time, Inc. v. Hill

CHAPTER FOURTEEN

At the Court

"A proper Philadelphian with a distaste for publicity set the stage this week for the first Supreme Court test of a modern legal concept—the right of privacy," noted the *New York Times* in a December 1965 article by the legal reporter Fred Graham, titled "Free Press vs. Privacy: An Issue for the Court." "Last Monday the Supreme Court announced that it will review the [*Hill v. Hayes*] decision later in this term. This comes at a time when powerful considerations support the right to be let alone, as well as freedom of expression."[1]

As the *Times* noted, Time, Inc. was asking the Court not only to reverse the judgment for the Hills, but for a decision declaring unconstitutional "all right of privacy judgments against members of the news media," so long as the publication had a connection to a newsworthy event. The result, Graham observed, could "knock out virtually all recoveries against news publications, and . . . relegate right of privacy actions to suits over outright advertisements and libels." If the justices adopted Time, Inc.'s view, "the story of James J. Hill, a man with a stubborn desire for anonymity, will be famous as long as lawyers recall the case that spelled the decline of the legal right of privacy."[2]

≈

Against the backdrop of cultural concerns with privacy and press ethics, and in the shadow of *Sullivan* and *Griswold, Time, Inc. v. Hill* came to the Court freighted with a good deal of significance. The case tapped into pressing social issues: the future of privacy in the "naked society," the meaning of "the news," the boundaries of freedom of the press in the age of big media. It also raised questions of constitutional doctrine that were contested on the Court: the status of the constitutional right to privacy, the absolutism-balancing debate in First Amendment law, and possible extensions of *New York Times v. Sullivan*. The presence of Nixon heightened the stakes and raised intrigues that swirled beneath the legal debates.

How would Nixon fare before the Supreme Court? What would happen when Nixon confronted Warren? Would Nixon's hatred for the press come through in his argument? Why was Nixon arguing the case, anyway?

Since *New York Times v. Sullivan*, the Court had been concerned with its implications and potential applications to different kinds of plaintiffs and subject matter. As the *New York Times*'s lawyer Herbert Wechsler had written presciently, "One could not fairly ask the Court to foresee in one opinion all the problems that would evolve from this demarche in constitutional law."[3] It was unclear whether the privilege should extend beyond high-level public officials to lower-ranked officials, if it should apply to libel cases involving a broader class of "public figures," and perhaps even to all publications on "public affairs."

At the same time as *Hill*, the Court heard two cases in which it extended the *Sullivan* rule in the libel context. In *Rosenblatt v. Baer* (1966), heard during the same term as *Time Inc. v. Hill*, the Court defined "public officials" for the purpose of the conditional privilege as those who have "substantial responsibility for or control over the conduct of governmental affairs."[4] In 1967, in *Curtis Publishing v. Butts* and *Associated Press v. Walker*, the Court extended *Sullivan* to libel cases brought by public figures "involved in issues in which the public has a justified and important interest."[5]

Sullivan had announced a broad commitment to the idea that debate on public issues should be "uninhibited, robust, and wide open."[6] Law professor Harry Kalven Jr. suggested that such language implicitly invited an extension of the *Sullivan* actual malice rule in a "dialectic progression" from speech on public officials to "government policy to public policy to matters in the public domain"—potentially to all "newsworthy" material.[7]

∼

When Time, Inc. appealed to the Supreme Court, Earl Warren's clerks had urged him to vote against taking the case. Law clerk Michael Smith wrote in a memo to Warren, "I agree with [Time, Inc.] that eventually the law of privacy, like the law of libel, will probably have to be brought under constitutional restraints to protect freedom of speech and press. This is not an appropriate case, however, for [James Hill] is not a public person . . . and the fictionalization indulged in by [Time, Inc.] comes very close to recklessness if it does not actually reach that point."[8]

Warren did not need persuading. He was convinced that the decision of the New York Court of Appeals was correct and that there was no constitutional question for the Court to consider. James Hill "was not a public figure—nor were his children—the state has an interest in protecting the privacy of its citizens," he jotted in a handwritten note.[9] Along with Warren, Fortas, Stewart, and Clark voted not to hear Time, Inc.'s appeal—a significant lineup, given the eventual outcome of the case.[10]

～

Time, Inc.'s Supreme Court brief was a forceful summation of its earlier position:

> The law of privacy in New York . . . now imposes damages and criminal and prior restraints upon members of the press who mention a private person in a news article . . . whenever the article is factually inaccurate, that is . . . "fictionalized." This is startling doctrine . . . in a nation that prides itself on freedom of expression, and specifically in this case, freedom of the press. It has come about because the law of privacy, although a late starter, has been the product in New York and elsewhere of a common law development, subject to the discretion and varying content furnished by judges in a climate that did not feel the presence of the First Amendment. Like the common law rule of *Coleman v. MacLennan*, rendered constitutional by *New York Times Co. v. Sullivan*, the tort remedy for invasion of privacy was created before there was full appreciation that the First Amendment guarantees even applied to the states.[11]

Time, Inc. called for the *Sullivan* actual malice standard to apply to all speech on "matters of public concern" regardless of whether it involved public officials, public figures, or private citizens. It argued that the Court should prohibit liability under the New York statute for the publication of "newsworthy" matters unless the plaintiff could demonstrate that the material was false and the error made with reckless disregard of the truth. There should be "general constitutional protection to the press against damage awards and prior restraints under the law of privacy, at least so long as the publication . . . makes some contribution to the dissemination of information or ideas, that is, to what is most broadly conceived to be news."[12] "In the present case, appellant reviewed a current newsworthy event which bore a substantial connection to a newsworthy event that had occurred some two and one-half years before. Such a publication, without more, is entitled to constitutional protection."[13]

The publisher emphasized the social importance of the *Life* article.[14] The *Desperate Hours*, and the *Life* article on the play, "like the advertisement in *New York Times,* dealt with one of our major public issues. Attention in the United States given to civil rights has been rivaled by attention given to crime. . . . In our society, these issues must be put to the public and eventually resolved by the public. But their resolution demands more than a front-page newspaper inventory of anti-social acts and nameless victims. It requires a sustained examination of how criminals think and behave, their fears and motivations, and how ordinary Americans react to their behavior. The *Desperate Hours* is such an examination; it makes a contribution to public understanding of the problem of crime."[15] "Dr. Meiklejohn concluded that literature and the arts have a social importance and what he called a 'governing importance'. . . . Where defamation or obscenity is not present, we submit, a fortiori, that public discussion of the form involved here is guaranteed prima facie protection under the First Amendment."[16]

Time, Inc. conceded that there was a constitutional right to privacy—a fundamental right, "perhaps comparable to the Fourth and Fifth Amendment guarantees against government action"—and that it must be balanced against freedom of the press.[17] "Because of its importance and collision here with the demands of the First Amendment, we recognize that the Court may wish to provide something less than absolute protection in this field, that is, to carve out a limited exception [protecting privacy] where the publication has little redeeming social value." "It may be, for example, that the right of privacy will be paramount in cases where purely private facts are raked up in such a way as to be shocking to community notions of decency. Or if an individual is depicted in a totally false light, that is, if his identification has no logical connection to the news event described, it is arguable that the protection under the First Amendment should give way."[18] In this case, because the *Life* article was "news" with "redeeming social importance," *Life*'s right to publish trumped the Hills' interest in being left alone, Time, Inc. asserted.

The brief for the Hills emphasized the harms suffered by the family. "Before a national audience, in one of America's most influential and widely-read newsmagazines," James Hill and his family were "falsely identified with the violence, terror, and lurid events depicted in the novel, play, and motion picture *The Desperate Hours*." "The contrast between the complete submissiveness of [Hill] and his family in 1952, and the fictional feats of breathtaking 'heroism' for which *Life* bestowed accolades in 1955 could not have been more grotesque."[19]

> Although the circumstances of this case are unusual, the injury to the Hill family illustrates the consequences of recklessness and irresponsibility in the use of mass media. Victims of disasters or crimes may be deeply affected by their experiences even if they escape without physical harm. Public reminders of such events—particularly in false or distorted form—can mobilize disabling anxieties and fears. The law of privacy does not protect victims of real life events from reminders of their experiences through legitimate news dissemination . . . but a line is properly drawn, we submit, at false, exploitative publicity like the *Life* article.[20]

The First Amendment, they wrote, did not protect "false and injurious statements made for commercial purposes."[21]

While Time Inc.'s lawyers tried to align the case with *New York Times v. Sullivan*, the Hills' lawyers cast it in the image of *Griswold*. The *Hill* case was about the disappearance of privacy in America and much-needed legal protections for the "right to be let alone." Drawing on academic and theoretical works on privacy, as well as contemporary popular writings such as the best-selling *The Naked Society*, the Hills' brief was an emotional tribute to the importance of privacy to the individual's autonomy, dignity, and sense of self.[22] "The right to privacy is fundamental to our constitutional system. Like the freedom to speak and write and print, it is vital to the growth of the individual and the enrichment of society. Protection of privacy from unreasonable intrusion by government or individuals is . . . recognized as a social interest of the highest order in our constitutional plan."[23]

"Whether a particular privacy has specific protection, as in the Fourth and Fifth Amendments, or has other more general protection under the Constitution, [as in *Griswold v. Connecticut*], it derives meaning from the unifying concept of the essential dignity and worth of every human being—a concept at the root of any decent system of ordered liberty."[24] "The law of privacy affirms a conviction that, even in a society increasingly characterized by powerful and impersonal organizations of government and commerce, the personality of the individual is worth protecting."[25]

The Hills' lawyers asserted that the constitutional right to privacy not only shielded people from invasions of privacy by the government, but also justified laws that protected people against privacy invasions committed by private actors such as the press. "The Constitution, by definition and implication, recognizes protected privacies and secures them from governmental intrusions. No less central to our constitutional plan is the power and responsibility of the individual states to protect their citizens from unreasonable intrusions and injury at the hands of individuals."[26] "The right of privacy which the Constitution protects from government intrusions, and the right of privacy which the states, through their tort law, protect from individual intrusions, are in substance the same. Each derives from the concept of an inviolate human personality; each protects areas of private life involving man's thoughts, emotions, and sensations that the law says should be left alone."[27]

∽

At dawn on April 27, 1966, Nixon and Garment flew from New York to Washington. Arriving at the Supreme Court around 9:00 a.m., they waited for the justices to arrive for the day's arguments.[28] Just before the Court was to convene, Garment summoned Nixon, flipping nervously through his yellow pads, from the lawyers' lounge. When Garment tried to push Nixon forward, Nixon said, "Never rush into a public place." The two lawyers walked slowly to their seats.[29] According to the *New York Times's* Fred Graham, who sat in an assigned seat squeezed into the narrow space between the attorneys' table and the justices' bench, Nixon seemed "nervous and uncomfortable."[30]

At 10:00 a.m., the justices began hearing the day's cases. The first case of the day was an antitrust case in which the government was trying to force the Pabst Brewing Company to give up another beer brewer it had acquired.[31] Shortly before noon, it called the lawyers for *Time, Inc. v. Hill.* The tension in the courtroom was palpable. "Staring up at his old rival [Warren], reflecting on the indignities each had served on the other over the years, Nixon had to blanch at how thoroughly Warren once again controlled his destiny," writes a Warren biographer.[32] But Nixon came to Washington on a high tide of confidence, fueled by the good wishes of many supporters, including James Hill, who sent Nixon a handwritten note a week before the argument:

Dear Dick, Just wanted you to know that we are glad you are with us in the final round of our fight. If we don't lick them next week in Washington I'll be glad to barnstorm the country with you to see if public opinion can't do what proper legal channels should have taken care of years ago. Am sure this won't be necessary. Will be in Washington next week pushing with you.[33]

The courtroom was packed with media correspondents. Nixon's argument had received a lengthy buildup in the press.[34] "Richard M. Nixon held center stage at the Supreme Court Wednesday as he urged the justices to expand the newly discovered constitutional 'right to privacy,'" wrote the *Miami Herald*.[35] "On a number of counts, it's an apt case for the former Vice President, now a New York lawyer," observed the *Los Angeles Times*. "Some of the cast of characters involved were key players in the Nixon-Eisenhower era. There's Robert Montgomery, who was once Eisenhower's TV advisor. There's Time, Inc., one-time Nixon backer. . . . And of course Earl Warren." Nixon's arguments "may offer ammunition for both his foes and his fans. Some may regard his stance as a defense of the civil right of privacy against one of the major corporate mass communications media. Others may see it as an attempt to restrict freedom of the press."[36]

$\backsim$

Harold Medina addressed the Court first. "Your Honors, we started out with a newsworthy event, a play on Broadway, a play which has been a novel . . . [and] made into a motion picture. When we're recording on that fact . . . I say we can report anything as relevant to that and that no one can say snag."

Medina admitted that there was an error in the article: "I come to this Court saying . . . Alright, we made a mistake." But "the fact we made out a mistake constitutionally is unimportant."[37]

Medina recounted the Whitemarsh incident. He alleged that James Hill, after the hostages left, came out on his front porch and with a microphone held a "press conference."

Brennan, interrupting: Are you suggesting that he called a press conference?
Warren: Why do you call this a press conference? If the press descends on a man's home, and he agrees to talk to them, and they urge him to talk over the microphone, do you call that a press conference?

Warren, Brennan, Stewart, and Fortas were visibly hostile to Medina. Fortas was the most aggressive of all. When Medina claimed that the play was "identical" to the *Life* article, Fortas pushed back:

Fortas: Are you going to describe to us the differences between the play and the book and the real life incident?

Medina: I'm not going to try that in detail Your Honor, it will take too long.

Fortas: . . . There were some rather ugly incidents that took place in the house . . . that did not take place in real life. . . . [There was] some indication in the novel and the play of sexual danger so far as the daughter was concerned.

Medina denied that there were any "ugly incidents."

"You deliberately sent a photographer out," Fortas said. "There was a staging of incidents there. This was something that was created." "And isn't it possible that there is a difference . . . for purposes of the First Amendment between the creation of that kind of a news item" and real news?

Fortas, Warren, and Stewart made clear that they were thinking about privacy more expansively than the narrow terms of the New York statute. Did the press have a right to record a married couple in their bedroom and broadcast the recording if it was "newsworthy"? Stewart asked. Could the press dredge up long-hidden facts about a person and publish it if it there was public interest in it? Warren asked Medina: "Do you suggest that if there was publicity concerning some event in a person's life particularly when he had done nothing wrong, that a publication could follow him every place he went in the country and over a period of years dig that up to his detriment?"

"I say the New York courts have done three things which are unconstitutional," Medina concluded his argument. "First, they've said that there can be privacy for a public fact and this was a public fact. Secondly, they said that the test is truth or falsity and I say that has no relationship to privacy." Referring to the concurring opinion of Judge Rabin from the Appellate Division, he noted, "Thirdly, they've said that the test must be motivation to increase circulation and I say that it cannot constitutionally be the test as to whether we're going to be held for having done something wrong to somebody."[38]

∽

Dressed in a black suit and starched collar[39] and "appearing as comfortable in the role of Wall Street lawyer as he did in public life,"[40] Nixon delivered a skilled and professional argument. "Was this a reenactment?" he asked. "When we look at the Hill incident and the play, we have incidents that instead of being similar, except as for the cast of characters and the stage setting are concerned, are as far apart as they could possibly be."

"Let's look at the Hill incident for a moment. What made it a particularly unusual hostage instance? What made it [a] particularly unusual hostage incident was the fact that it had an absence of violence. Now what made the play a hit?" The play succeeded because of its violence.

Nixon asked the justices to examine the photographs that were printed with the *Life* article. "Now the members of this Court know *Life* magazine tells its stories through pictures. And also the members of this Court are aware of the fact that *Life* magazine, being the most popular of the picture magazines, does not use pictures that relate superficial events. They go to the heart of the case."

> Nixon: If you will [turn] your attention for the moment to the pictures, there are six which are used in this article. Now, understand this is the article about the play which [Time, Inc.] says is a reenactment in which the differences are superficial. There are six pictures.

The first picture showed two convicts haranguing the fictional daughter Cindy in the "Hilliards'" living room while the mother "watches helplessly." "That didn't happen in the Hill incident," Nixon said. He then instructed the justices to "go to the second page entitled 'True Crime, Three Crises at a Backdoor.'" In that picture, "daughter Cindy stalls off her beau from entering the home." "That didn't happen," Nixon said again.

> Nixon: Let me emphasize again that the reason that *Life* magazine did this is [that] it was a good gimmick. They were using these people as props. They were using them as props for the purpose of making the article more readable and for selling more magazines.

Nixon made clear that the Hills had done everything in their power to protect their privacy. In response to Medina's "press conference" statement, Nixon insisted that the Hills were "involuntarily in the news." "It's ridiculous to believe that [James Hill] called a press conference and brought out his little microphone out from the house," Nixon said. "The evidence clearly demonstrates that this is a classic case of privacy—not only did they not seek publicity, they refused to go on the Ed Sullivan Show. Mr. Hill wrote a letter to one author who wanted to write an article and share the proceeds with him, and why? Not because they were interested in the price that they were going to get for privacy but because privacy to them was priceless."[41]

Nixon's argument was filled with dramatic lines he had written out carefully on his yellow pads and committed to memory. *Life* was "completely unconcerned about the Hills, knew nothing about them, and made no effort to find out what actually had happened during the incident," he said. "*Life* lied and it knew it lied" was a favorite phrase.[42] He reminded the Court of the importance of the case: privacy was "an area of the law which deserves a paramount measure of protection because . . . it's an area where you have the fundamental problem that confronts all Americans today . . . how does an individual remain an individual in our mass communications society?"[43]

Warren was clearly pro-privacy and for Nixon. So was Fortas. His handwritten notes during the oral argument illustrate that he had been swayed early on by Nixon's comments. "This is fiction, not news. It was staged and contrived," Fortas had written.[44] Douglas, the author of *Griswold*, said nothing during either Medina or Nixon's presentations. Brennan's comments were brief and noncommittal. Only Hugo Black was openly against Nixon. Why wouldn't the New York statute potentially cover "every news item . . . or every editorial"? he asked. "Doesn't any publication made about a human being affect his privacy?" "Every newspaper" was published for "purposes of trade," wasn't it?[45]

The statements by Warren and Fortas were surprising to Nixon, given how much both men opposed Nixon's politics. Nixon later commented that because Warren and Fortas had both been in the public eye before coming to the Court, they knew how brutal the press could be when it went after a target.[46]

As Medina spoke, Nixon took notes with a pencil on two yellow pads.[47] The courtroom was crowded with lawyers, secretaries, law clerks, and spring tourists.[48] At the end of his argument, Nixon's wife, Pat, and their two daughters, who were in the courtroom—the daughters having taken a day off of school—congratulated Nixon, and so did Medina.[49] As he left the courtroom, Nixon scooped up four of the goose-quilled pens on the counsel tables to give to his daughters.[50]

The *New York Times*'s Fred Graham praised Nixon's performance. He thought Nixon's argument was devoid of the "self-important posturing" that other political figures adopted when they argued before the Court. Worried that he might play into the "Tricky Dick" image of his political past, "Nixon was at times candid to a fault," Graham noted.[51] Nixon faltered only once—he had tried to explain a California court decision by declaring that it was a common law decision.[52] Warren informed him that there was no common law jurisdiction in California.

Nixon grinned awkwardly, accepted Warren's comments, and went ahead with his argument.[53]

Nixon received letters of praise from around the country. Former Supreme Court justice Stanley Reed attended the oral argument and sent Nixon accolades: "Win or lose you presented the case in the best possible light for your client. It was a clear and persuasive piece of advocacy."[54] Journalists, judges, lawyers, and professors sent him congratulations and requests for copies of the briefs. The press commentary on Nixon's performance was overwhelmingly positive. The *Washington Post*'s Supreme Court reporter described Nixon's presentation as "one of the better oral arguments of the year." At a Court luncheon shortly after the argument, the justices expressed surprise that Nixon had done so well. According to one of his clerks, Justice Brennan deeply admired the oral argument.[55] Fortas believed that Nixon had made one of the best arguments that he had heard on the Court and that Nixon could develop into one of the "great advocates of our times."[56]

~

The next morning Garment found on his desk a five-page, single-spaced memorandum addressed to him from Nixon. Upon arriving at his Fifth Avenue apartment the evening after the oral argument, Nixon dictated a tape of commentary, transcribed by Nixon's secretary. "Now that the case is over, here are some of the points I believe deserved more emphasis in the oral argument," read the memo. "I only wish there were some way we could ethically transmit some of these thoughts to the clerks who will be helping the justices write their briefs!"[57]

Nixon criticized his own performance. He thought he should have stressed the brutality and "ugly incidents" in the *Desperate Hours*, which would have brought home the seriousness of the offense to the Hill family:

> I think it would have been most effective after completing my analysis of the *Life* pictures to turn to Justice Fortas and to have directly replied to the question he asked Medina as to whether there had been some rather "ugly incidents" in the play. Medina, as you recall, answered that question in the negative. I could have then briefly recounted in a most effective way the murder of the trash man, the killing of two of the convicts [and other violent incidents] . . . and the constant use of profanity in its ugliest forms during the play.[58]

Nixon also acknowledged the weakness of his privacy argument. He admitted that *Griswold* was not technically on point, since the state was not infringing on the Hills' privacy: "Here the question is not the power of the state to infringe on a right but the power of the state to recognize and implement a right."[59]

I think what would have been most helpful to the Court in writing the opinion would have been a brief statement clearing up Medina's fuzzy reference to a right of privacy being a constitutional right emanating from the Fourth, Fifth, Ninth, and other Amendments (in other words, using the *Griswold* analogy). This kind of analysis, if followed to its conclusion, is both inaccurate and dangerous from a constitutional standpoint. In *Griswold*, it was essential to find that there was a constitutional right to privacy in marriage since the issue there was the power of the state to impair that right. Here the question is not the power of the state to infringe on a right but the power of the state to recognize and implement a right.[60]

Nixon was concerned that the attempt to locate a right to privacy in the Ninth Amendment, as in *Griswold*, might backfire. "If we should contend that there is a right of privacy under the Ninth Amendment, the Court would have the problem in every case to determine whether the right of privacy under the Ninth Amendment or the right of free expression under the First Amendment should prevail when the two come into conflict." Nixon thought it might have been wise to "downgrade" the Hills' right to privacy from a freestanding constitutional right to "one of those areas where the state had the power under the Ninth and Tenth Amendments to give redress to private citizens where they are injured by other private citizens."[61] "While this analysis would tend to downgrade the right of privacy for which we were contending in our case (below even the position Medina in his rather vague and muddy way was implicitly recognizing) it would give . . . the Court a hard-rock base of reasoning for recognizing the privacy tort in a very definite, limited, constitutionally defensible way."[62]

A good portion of the memo is devoted to Nixon's concerns about media publicity. Nixon believed—mistakenly—that "there were no columnists or nationally known reporters present." He thought this was an indication of an attempted "blackout" by the "press establishment"—in particular, Time, Inc. Nixon suspected that the "Time/Life crowd" had talked to the *New York Times*, the top officials of the Associated Press and the United Press, as well as the "*Newsweek*

crowd" and "warned them about the consequences of giving any significant publicity to our presentation." He worried about not getting "the publicity which we
deserve which might bring us more clients in the future" and "help us in terms of
other considerations which are broader than our purely 'commercial' interests"—a
reference to his political ambitions.[63]

Nixon thanked Garment for letting him argue *Time, Inc. v. Hill:* "Your step-
ping aside when you yourself could have handled the matter in brilliant fashion
demonstrated a selflessness which is very rare in our firm or any other firm for
that matter," he wrote. "I only hope that you will get some much deserved 'divi-
dends' in the future!"[64]

When he assumed the presidency, Nixon appointed Garment to the position
of special consultant to the president. From 1968 to 1973, Garment worked on
White House projects in the areas of civil rights and the arts. Garment would
play a central role in Watergate; Nixon appointed him to the position of White
House counsel after the dismissal of former White House counsel John Dean for
his involvement in the Watergate cover-up. Garment discouraged Nixon from de-
stroying White House tapes, pushed unsuccessfully for the president's resignation,
and recommended to Nixon's successor, Gerald Ford, that Nixon be pardoned.
Garment would be remembered as a "voice of conscience in a White House that
had lost its ethical bearings."[65]

CHAPTER FIFTEEN

Decisions

Two days after the oral argument, on April 29, 1966, the justices met in private conference, the secret session where they gathered around a green-felt-topped table in a book-lined conference room and voted on the outcome of the cases heard that week. Warren, who led the meetings, started with his own brief statement on a case. He then gave the other justices five minutes each to present their views, in order of seniority. After that, the issues were opened to the group for discussion and debate. Finally, there was a vote, with the junior justice going first.[1]

Warren began the conference on the *Hill* case by announcing his vote to affirm the New York Court of Appeals. The *Life* article was not "news," he said. "The article was fiction—it was false in material respects."[2] Warren was the leader of the Court's liberal bloc, but his position on speech was less libertarian than that of his colleagues. Warren's thinking on freedom of speech was dominated by his lifelong discomfort with obscenity and also his distrust of the press. After years in public life, he had seen plenty of bad reporting, and "he could not bring himself to sanction it any more than he could stomach the actions of pornographers," writes his biographer.[3]

Fortas also voted for Nixon and the Hills, having made up his mind during the oral argument. Clark, Stewart, and Harlan also voted to affirm the New York Court of Appeals. Harlan agreed that the *Life* article was not news; it was "not a mere comment on the play. . . . It is a fictionalized account invading privacy."[4]

Brennan joined the majority affirming the New York courts. According to a handwritten note in Brennan's papers at the Library of Congress, in the early stages of the case, Brennan thought *Hill* was outside the scope of *Sullivan*. As private citizens, the Hills deserved more protection for their privacy than public officials did for their reputations, and the rationales for protecting the press were weaker in *Hill* than in *Sullivan*. "*Times* can be distinguished on a multifactor approach," Brennan wrote. The *Hill* case involved a "1) non-governmental—political issue;

2) not *daily* reporting—i.e., no need for haste; 3) Hill did not thrust himself into 'the vortex'—i.e., voluntariness or assumption of risk; 4) Quasi-promotional—[Life] had available sources, working with play's producers, etc. and had sources to check."[5]

Douglas, White, and Black voted to reverse. Black asserted that a newspaper "can use fiction under the First Amendment," and that the judgment was a "flagrant violation of the First Amendment."[6] Nixon had succeeded; the vote was 6-3 for the Hills.

∼

Traditionally the Chief Justice decided who would write the Court's opinion in each argued case in which he was in the majority. Warren assigned the opinion to Abe Fortas, whose feelings about the case were as strong as his. Fortas circulated an initial version of his majority opinion on June 8, 1966. The twenty-page Fortas draft opinion is an extraordinary document, perhaps the bitterest critique of the press in any Supreme Court opinion. Fortas adopted Nixon's argument wholesale, along with Nixon's hostility to the press.

Fortas began with what he described as the "unavoidably distressing" facts of the case—the *Life* editors' conscious, willful manipulation of the truth about the Hills.[7] While "Prideaux's first draft reflected recognition that the play was not an account of the Hill family's experience," "writers write and editors revise." "A senior editor thought the draft of the article was not 'newsy enough.' So he rewrote it in critical respects. Caution and restraint were discarded. . . . The total effect is of violence in which the son and daughter [were] involved."[8]

Fortas recognized the importance of a "broad and generous application" of freedom of the press. "This Nation is prepared to pay a heavy price for the immunity of the press in terms of national discomfort and danger in the tolerance of a measure of individual assault," Fortas wrote, referring to the protection given the press to defame public officials in *New York Times v. Sullivan*.[9] But "needless, heedless, wanton and deliberate injury of the sort inflicted by *Life's* picture story" was "not an essential instrument of responsible journalism":

> Magazine writers and editors are not by reason of their high office relieved of the common obligation to avoid inflicting wanton and unnecessary injury. The prerogatives of the press—essential to our liberty—do not preclude

reasonable care and avoidance of casual infliction of injury to others totally unexplainable by any purpose or circumstance related to its function of reporting or discussing the news or publishing matters of interest to its readers. They do not confer a license for pointless assault.[10]

Citing the Hills' brief, Fortas wrote that the injury to the Hill family inflicted by *Life* illustrated "the consequences of recklessness and irresponsibility in the use of mass media."[11]

The centerpiece of the Fortas opinion was the right to privacy. "There is . . . no doubt that a fundamental right of privacy exists, and that it is of constitutional stature," Fortas wrote. Quoting from Goldberg's concurring opinion in *Griswold v. Connecticut*—"the right to privacy is a fundamental personal right, emanating from the totality of the constitutional scheme under which we live"—as well as other rulings on Fourth, Fifth, and First Amendment privacy, including *Mapp v. Ohio* (1961; "the right to privacy" was "basic to a free society"), *Boyd v. United States* (1886), *Wolf v. Colorado* (1949), and the Brandeis dissent in *Olmstead v. United States* (1928) (the right to privacy is the "most comprehensive of rights and the right most valued by civilized men"), Fortas described the constitutional right to privacy in more sweeping terms than anyone else on the Court had ever done.[12] Fortas extrapolated from *Griswold* and the Court's other privacy cases to infer something that had never been clearly articulated in any Supreme Court decision—a broad, general right to privacy in the Constitution.[13]

The right to privacy "is not just the right to a remedy against false accusation," Fortas wrote. "It is not only the right to be secure in one's person, house, papers, and effects. . . . It embraces the right to be free from coercion, however subtle, to incriminate oneself; it is different from, but akin to the right to select and freely to practice one's religion and the right to freedom of speech; it is more than the specific right to be secure against the Peeping Tom or the intrusion of electronic espionage devices and wiretapping. All of these are aspects of the right to privacy, but privacy reaches beyond any of its specifics. It is, simply stated, the right to be let alone; to live one's life as one chooses, free from assault, intrusion, or invasion except as they can be justified by the clear needs of a community living under a government of law."[14]

Fortas continued, "If . . . privacy is a basic right, whether one considers it derived from the First, Fourth, Fifth, or Ninth Amendments, or otherwise, it follows that the States may, by appropriate legislation and within proper bounds, enact laws to vindicate that right." He cited the 1949 case *Kovacs v. Cooper*, sustaining a local ordinance regulating the use of sound trucks, and *Breard v. Alexandria* (1951), upholding a state law restricting solicitation of magazine subscriptions in private homes. Both opinions had referenced a "right to be let alone."[15] "Difficulty presents itself because the application of such state legislation almost inevitably threatens to impinge upon conflicting rights of those accused of invading the privacy of others. But this is not a fatal objection."[16]

In each potential clash between the right to privacy and another conflicting right, the problem must be "carefully and precisely diagnose[d]." In the *Hill* case, the reconciliation of privacy and freedom of the press was "reasonably clear," Fortas wrote. New York had achieved a proper balance between the two rights with its "newsworthiness" standard.[17] The New York courts had consistently excluded truthful, newsworthy material from the statute. It was only when a publisher engaged in "fictionalization" that it could be liable for invasion of privacy. Fortas conceded that if truthful, newsworthy material were punishable under New York law, there would be a constitutional problem. Insofar as it punished only falsified facts, the New York privacy law did not abridge freedom of the press. Fortas implied, though did not explicitly state, that *Sullivan* applied to the case. The jury's conclusion that there had been "fictionalization" was a sufficient finding of "deliberate or reckless departure from substantial accuracy," a reckless disregard of the truth.[18]

"We cannot conclude that this application of New York's right-to-privacy statute is in fatal collision with freedom of the press," Fortas concluded. "The deliberate, callous invasion of the Hills' right to be let alone—this appropriation of a family's right not to be molested or to have its name exploited and its quiet existence invaded—cannot be defended on the ground that it is within the purview of a constitutional guarantee designed to protect the free exchange of ideas and opinions. This is exploitation, undertaken to titillate and excite, for commercial purposes. It was not a retelling of a newsworthy incident or an event relating to a public figure. It was not such an account. It was not so designed. It was fiction: an invention, distorted and put to the uses of the promotion of *Life* magazine and of a play. Many difficult problems may arise under the right-to-privacy statute, but we conclude that the present case, on its facts and on the New York law as construed by the courts of that state, does not permit the appellant to claim immunity from liability because of the First Amendment."[19]

⁓

Like Nixon, Fortas hated the press. According to his biographer, Laura Kalman, Fortas "feared and loathed the press" due to his own unpleasant encounters with it, as well as those of his friend and benefactor, Lyndon Johnson.[20] During his time in private practice in the McCarthy years, Fortas had represented many clients whose names were smeared in the press. The Walter Jenkins scandal of 1964, in which a top Johnson aide was ruined by press reports on his homosexual affairs, deepened Fortas's conviction that the press was overly intrusive.[21] Fortas described reporters as "mongers" who were "dirty" and "crooked" and "misused" the information they obtained. While in private practice, Fortas was once so upset by an article about one of his clients that he sent the reporter a letter containing only the salutation and his signature. He later explained that he started to dictate a responding letter, "but then I thought about the laws of libel and just signed it and sent it on."[22] By 1966, Fortas was actively seeking to narrow the scope of press freedom as set out in *Sullivan*. According to Kalman, Fortas "could not understand the insistence of Justices Black and Douglas on First Amendment rights." Fortas regarded Black and Douglas's protection of the press "with the same bemusement with which another individual would have contemplated a defender of the rattlesnake's right to strike."[23]

Fortas was also genuinely moved by the injustice to the Hills. As Garment noted, the fact that Richard Nixon was advocating for the Hills mattered little to either Warren or Fortas—"whatever political baggage the former vice president might be carrying, he also happened to be bearing the right message."[24] According to Fred Rodell, two "outstanding components" of Fortas's judicial temperament were "his tremendous respect for the right of privacy and his almost physical abhorrence of violence." Fortas believed that when "words were used as instruments of aggression and personal assault," as in the Hills' case, they lost their constitutional immunity.[25]

For all its force, the Fortas opinion was cryptic. Fortas, even more than his mentor Douglas, disdained the explanatory process. He had "the opportunistic outlook of a good lawyer," observes one legal scholar. "Once he knew his desired outcome, he couldn't care less how he got there."[26] Though Fortas seemed to concede that *Sullivan* applied to the case, he also suggested that negligent or incidental falsehoods could potentially offer a basis for liability. Fortas admitted that a privacy right that infringed on the reporting of truthful news events would be unconstitutional. Yet he also implied that the New York courts had erred in defining the "news" too broadly. Fortas would draw the lines between public and private speech, between newsworthy and nonnewsworthy material, in a much less speech-protective fashion than many of the state court decisions had done.

Fortas had written that the article on the Hills was not newsworthy because it was false. At the same time, he suggested that *Life's* reporting on the family was not newsworthy for other reasons—because of the topic's unimportance to public affairs, because it was published two and a half years after the hostage incident, and because of the serious injury it inflicted on the family. In forcing the Hills to relive their misfortunes and in turning the family into a public spectacle, *Life* committed a "deliberate, callous invasion of the Hills' right to be let alone" and forfeited its constitutional protections. Thrusting the Hills before the public gaze for no real public purpose was an unwarranted invasion of a "family's right to not be molested or to . . . have its quiet existence invaded." The right to privacy trumped the right of the press when it published material that created severe injury and had no real function as "news."

$\sim$

The brash Fortas opinion led to immediate reactions. Clark, on June 9, wrote a note to Fortas after the draft was circulated, indicating his support for it: "Good going. Join me."[27] Although Brennan joined the opinion, his penciled notes on his copy of the opinion make clear that he thought Fortas had gone too far. He was unhappy with Fortas's use of the word titillate to describe *Life's* motivation for the article and thought Fortas might have been "distorting the record" in his account of the facts.[28] According to a 1966 term history written by Brennan's clerks, Brennan felt that the Fortas opinion was "replete with invective for the press," and Brennan, the author of *Sullivan*, was offended. Fortas's opinion, his clerks wrote with alarm, "never once mentioned a First Amendment standard."[29]

Douglas circulated a dissent on June 9, 1966. He claimed that the material was newsworthy and asserted his absolutist view that "state action to abridge freedom of the press is barred by the First and Fourteenth Amendments where the discussion concerns matters in the public domain. The episode around which this book was written had been news of the day for some time; the novel did not make it such. A fictionalized treatment of the event is, in my view, as much in the public domain as would be a watercolor of the assassination of a public official." Referencing *Griswold*, Douglas wrote that "it would be one thing if the press were battering down barricades to the sanctuary of our home," but here, he believed, there was no invasion of privacy. "A private person is catapulted into the news by events over which he had no control. He and his activities are then in the public domain as fully as the matters at issue in *New York Times Co. v. Sullivan*. Such privacy as one normally has, ceases when a person's life has ceased to be private. . . . Some might well want to let a sad public event be lost in memory. But I see no qualification of the First Amendment that permits it."[30]

Douglas challenged Fortas's characterization of privacy as an expansive constitutional right. According to Douglas, the "privacy" in *Griswold* protected the home and the marital bedroom; it was not a broad right to dignity or peace of mind, as Fortas suggested. Black agreed with Douglas's position in the dissent but not his reference to the hated *Griswold* opinion: "I would like to agree with you but do not want to suggest an association such as you do with *Griswold* . . . I hope you can take it out," he wrote to Douglas. Douglas agreed, and Black joined the dissent.[31]

Harlan circulated a concurrence. Regardless of whether it was "news," the *Life* article was "comparatively unimportant to the public," he wrote. "The Hill incident had never involved someone of public interest; it was no longer any part of current affairs, and its reappearance was largely window dressing for a review of the play. At best, this is poles apart from the interests so scrupulously guarded" in *New York Times v. Sullivan*. The article was also "materially false in imparting an aura of violence and brutality to the Hill incident," and the falsity was "in good part due to what was at best undeniable carelessness in the writing and editing process."[32]

Byron White, who had voted in favor of Time, Inc., saw a chance to undermine the majority. On June 8, 1966, he sent a typewritten draft of a "rough and incomplete" dissent to Brennan in which he brought up an issue Fortas had not mentioned in his opinion.[33] White later circulated a more polished version of the dissent on June 9. He observed that when the New York Court of Appeals affirmed the Appellate Division's ruling in favor of the Hills, it affirmed both the main opinion and the concurring opinion by Judge Rabin. White was concerned by Rabin's implication that truthful material, if published for "circulation-generating" purposes, could be actionable as an invasion of privacy under New York law.[34] White also thought that the jury instructions suggested that Time, Inc. could be liable even if the misrepresentations in the story were innocent. "There are inherent difficulties in ascertaining the 'truth' in many, many cases, difficulties which cannot be surmounted in the context of the work of an ordinary newspaper attempting, as it does, to report an endless stream of varied events. The press of time and concepts of current newsworthiness make it wholly impractical, if not impossible, to produce news which is factually accurate in every detail. Deadlines and certitudes will never be a perfect mix."[35] "The law of privacy should not be permitted to stifle the reporting of the news or educational or entertainment materials by extending a cause of action for invasion of privacy without requiring the allegation and proof of deliberate or negligent falsehood," he wrote.[36]

Brennan was not convinced by White's dissent. Next to a passage where White wrote, "I think the Court should make it unmistakably clear that the First Amendment will not permit the imposition of liability for publishing a truthful account of the news of general public interest," Brennan scribbled in the margin of his draft of the opinion, "Can't disagree . . . —but doesn't require reversal." Next to White's sentence stating that "the statement of the Appellate Division, affirmed by the Court of Appeals, that an otherwise newsworthy item, truthfully reported, loses its privileged character if the jury finds it was published for the purposes of trade is an obvious license to impose liability whenever the jury wishes to do so," Brennan wrote one word: "Bad." Brennan criticized White for assuming that "fictionalization does not by definition require deliberation or recklessness," which was one of Fortas's main points.[37]

In response to White, on June 14, 1966, Fortas circulated another draft of the majority opinion with extensive revisions. In an attached note, he expressed his appreciation for "the help which many of you gave me which caused me to realize the deficiencies of my first draft."[38] "Attached is a new draft of my opinion in this case. The legal part of it has been completely rewritten and various changes have been made in the first portion of the opinion. I very much regret burdening all of you with this drastically revised opinion."[39]

The revised draft emphasized that the Rabin concurrence was not a correct statement of New York's law. Liability under the New York statute required "deliberate, willful, and knowing fabrication," and that "standard was properly applied by the trial judge's charge to the jury."[40] Although the New York courts did not specifically refer to the First Amendment in their decisions, they "nonetheless demonstrated an awareness that careful limitations must be set to the operations of the privacy statute lest it come into fatal collision with the pervasive protection accorded freedom of the press."[41]

Fortas concluded: "We do not believe that such a statute, so construed and applied, can or will inhibit the press. It does not penalize mere error. It places no restraint upon comment and discussion. It is not an overhanging danger. It cannot ensnare the unwary or even the negligent. It reaches only those who deliberately circulate an account which is pervasively fictionalized and is falsely and deliberately attributed to a living person."[42] "We cannot say that the First Amendment prohibits a state from enacting a statute so confined."[43]

~

Hugo Black was seething over the Fortas opinion. He claimed it was the worst First Amendment opinion he had seen since 1952 and scribbled angry notes in the margins of his copy of the opinion.[44] He marked up every one of the twenty pages that Fortas had circulated.[45]

In his handwritten notes, Black accused Fortas of reading into the record "every possible inference adverse to what the press has done." The Fortas opinion made Time, Inc. look like an "ogre" and a tyrant by calling its "rather ordinary article an 'exploitation.'" In saying that *Life* "deliberately inflicted 'wanton and unnecessary injury' the Court usurp[ed] a jury function" and encouraged "the public to charge a court vendetta against Time." Louis Brandeis, the architect of the tort right to privacy, "never ever intimated much less asserted that he was elevating a right to privacy to a constitutional plane on a level with the First Amendment." To give judges the "power to change the Constitution" as Fortas was doing was the hallmark of a "totalitarian regime."[46]

Next to Fortas's statement that "Mrs. Hill became seriously ill" as a result of the *Life* article, Black quipped, "Just as she might have had serious typhoid fever!" Fortas had written that psychiatrists testified that the article was the "direct precipitating cause of her condition"; Black wrote smugly that such diagnoses could be "a new field for psychiatrists." In the opinion, Fortas noted that James Hill resisted the impulse to commit physical violence against Hayes and the *Life* editors and instead initiated legal action. Black scrawled next to this, "Did Hill testify he was tempted to commit physical violence?" "Is this evidence the result of the mind-reading of the Court?"[47]

Black was incensed by Fortas's sweeping description of the right to privacy. Privacy was a "popular idea but not one embodied in any constitutional provision," Black wrote. The fact that privacy may have been a "basic" right did not mean it was a constitutional one. "There is no such broad . . . constitutional right. Justice Brandeis will not say so." In response to Fortas's sentence, "We do not believe that such a statute, . . . can or will inhibit freedom of the press," Black noted, "This will inhibit freedom of the press . . . it is an overhanging danger . . . a great exaggeration."[48]

According to Fortas biographer Bruce Murphy, Black welcomed the bitter and sweeping Fortas opinion. Black planned to write a magnificent dissent, a treatise on his First Amendment absolutism, but he needed more time for his project. He thought that it would take him all summer to write his dissent, which would be the "greatest dissent of his life."[49] Black took advantage of Fortas's extensive revisions of the draft, and he wrote a "petulant" note to Fortas in which he insisted that because of the alterations, he needed extra time to write his response. The term was about to end; Black proposed that the case be held over to the following term so that he could properly address his concerns with the opinion.[50]

Black's entreaty, together with White's doubts about the privacy statute, persuaded Fortas to agree to have the case held over to the next term and reargued. On June 16, 1966, Fortas issued an order requesting that Medina and Nixon return to the Court in the fall to address four questions: "1) Is the truthful presentation of a newsworthy item ever actionable under New York's statute as construed or on its face?; 2) Should the per curiam opinion of the New York Court of Appeals be read as adopting the (Rabin concurrence)?; 3) Does the concept of fictionalization require reckless disregard of truth or falsity as a condition of liability?; 4) What are the First Amendment ramifications of the respective answers to the above questions?"[51]

Nixon geared up for another round of questioning. He interrupted his cross-country campaigning for Republican candidates in the 1966 midterm elections—an effort that would prove critical to his reemergence as a presidential candidate—and devoted three weeks to focusing on the arguments.[52]

∾

Over summer 1966, Hugo Black remained upset about the *Hill* case. He was troubled by what he saw as the strident and accusatory Fortas opinion and the majority's efforts to constrain constitutionally protected speech through its "weighing and balancing" approach, weighing the worth of Time, Inc.'s speech against the value of the Hills' privacy. He began to write a dissent that he planned to circulate right before the reargument. Throughout the summer, he worked diligently on it, often staying up until the early morning hours. Black's wife was both impressed and concerned by his devotion to the case. She wrote in her diary on August 12, 1966: "Hugo has been working until around 1:30 every night. He is working on this case he is so interested in. It's one that Abe Fortas got out about a week before the Court adjourned. Hugo told me them he was going to write a dissent this summer, so they agreed to get it reargued this fall."[53]

Black was not only was upset with Fortas's seeming disregard for the First Amendment and his expansive view of a "right to privacy" that Black found nowhere in the Constitution. Black, who was eighty and becoming more irascible and abrasive in his old age, disliked Fortas personally. He believed that Fortas was using judicial power in "all the wrong directions" and was a purely "results-oriented" justice who had no regard for the Constitution. Fortas was a "wheeler dealer . . . totally unprincipled and intellectually dishonest," Black claimed.[54]

Fortas had come on strong in his first two years on the Court, with a confident, "know-it-all attitude," and Black felt threatened. Black viewed Fortas as a "pretender to the throne of leadership."[55] All of the justices were openly disturbed by Fortas's ongoing connections to Lyndon Johnson, including offering advice to the president about Vietnam, domestic unrest, and other issues.[56] Shortly after Fortas joined the Court in 1965, Black began to attack him on several occasions, including outbursts toward him in Court sessions.[57] One particularly nasty clash between Black and Fortas involved *Brown v. Louisiana* (1966), in which Fortas wrote a majority opinion to overturn the convictions of five black men who refused to leave a segregated library. In his dissent, Black accused the majority of being distrustful of the ways of the South; Fortas accused Black of racism.[58]

Black wrote an initial draft of his sixteen-page memorandum on August 24, 1966, but held off circulating it until the day before the reargument, on October 17, 1966.[59] Bernard Schwartz characterized the memo as the "most eloquent statement" of Black's views on the First Amendment and "more scathing in its condemnation of the weighing process than anything else ever published by Justice Black."[60]

Black's memo began by attacking Fortas, Harlan, and White for their balancing approach to the First Amendment and their "gross, flagrant refusal to give Time the benefit of the First Amendment."[61] Even White, who would have reversed the judgment for the Hills, seemed "perfectly willing to subordinate constitutional press freedom to a 'new right of privacy' fashioned not by the people in their Constitution and not even by legislators under their power to make laws, but fashioned by judges based upon their 'strong judicial sentiment that some segments of the press and mass media have abused their privilege and must in some respects be curbed.'"[62]

"By legal legerdemain," the majority had transmuted "the First Amendment's promise of unequivocal press freedom . . . into a debased alloy—transmuted into a freedom which will vacillate and grow weaker or stronger as the Court personnel is shifted from time to time," Black wrote. "The weighing process makes it infinitely easier for judges to exercise their newly proclaimed power to curb the press. For under its aegis judges are no longer to be limited to their recognized power to make binding *interpretations* of the Constitution. That power . . . has . . . become too prosaic and unexciting. So the judiciary now confers upon the judiciary the more 'elastic' and exciting power to decide, under its value-weighing process, just how much freedom the courts will permit the press to have."[63]

Black attacked the majority's "rhapsodical descriptions of the great value of the 'right to privacy,' said to be an individual's 'right to be let alone.'" "Describing it as a right 'which the Court derived by implication from the specific guarantees of the Bill of Rights' yet proclaiming that it 'reaches beyond any of its specifics,'" the majority improperly held that the privacy right was "so basic to a free society" that its . . . value outweighed "the constitutional right of Time and the public in general to a free press:"[64]

> Neither the "right to be let alone" nor the "right to privacy," while appealing phrases, were enshrined in our Constitution as was the right to free speech, press, and religion. Government can coexist with unfettered freedom of speech, press, and religion, and the First Amendment stands as a monument to the Founders' belief that these freedoms are essential to the existence of a democratic society like ours. But the very existence of Government negatives any claim that citizens have a general, unconditional, unequivocal "right to privacy" or "to be let alone." If every person carries with him an unconditional right to privacy or to be let alone, the burglars, rapists, robbers, murderers, and other law violators would be completely immune from all governmental investigations, arrests, trials, and punishments.[65]

Black admitted that the Constitution protected privacy rights in certain discrete contexts. The Third, Fourth, and Fifth Amendments could each be "loosely said to result in protecting man's right to privacy or right to be let alone unless proceeded against in accord with these explicit Bill of Rights safeguards." But for judges to attempt to extrapolate from those guarantees a "general, all-embracing constitutional provision guaranteeing a general right to privacy" was "fantastic."[66]

Black insisted that the *Life* article was "news," "news no one I think will deny who has ever turned the pages of a newspaper or news magazine to find out what theatre or play he might enjoy."[67] Many of the "sharp criticisms and invectives" against Time, Inc. were "completely unsupported by the record," Black wrote. Fortas's "staccato-like repetition" of accusations against Time, Inc.—"caution and restraint were discarded," "heedless, wanton, and deliberate injury," "recklessness and irresponsibility in the use of mass media," "pointless assault"—"could hardly be pointed to as models of understatement even in an advocate's brief."[68] Black criticized the majority for reading the facts of the case in a way that drew "every possible inference adverse to what the press has done."[69] "The more despicable *Life*'s conduct, the easier to balance away freedom of the press in favor of Hill's right to privacy."[70]

"After mature reflection I am unable to recall any prior case in this Court that offers a greater threat to freedom of speech and press than this one does, either in the tone and temper of the Court's opinion or in its resulting holding and judgment," Black wrote.[71] "One does not have to be a prophet . . . to foresee that judgments like the one in this case can frighten and punish the press so much that publishers will cease trying to report news in a lively and readable fashion as long as there is—and there always will be—doubt as to the complete accuracy of the newsworthy facts. Such a consummation hardly seems consistent with the clearly expressed purpose of the Founders to guarantee the press a favored spot in our free society."[72]

Shortly after the memo was circulated, Fortas went to Black's home, hurt and angered. According to Black biographer Roger Newman, Fortas went to Black to demand an apology because Black had viciously parodied Fortas's writing style.[73] According to Elizabeth Black, the two men talked it out and "Abe left feeling OK."[74]

~

When Nixon and Medina appeared before the Court on October 18, 1966, they were unaware of the bitter exchanges between the justices. Nixon was, in Garment's opinion, even better and more relaxed than he had been in the first argument.[75] According to the *New York Times*'s Fred Graham, Nixon was "much more confident and knowledgeable in the second argument."[76] Yet Nixon's opposition, led by Black, White, and Brennan, was much fiercer. Both Garment and Nixon sensed that the Court's take had changed since the first argument—"and from our point of view . . . for the worse."[77] The reporter for the *Washington Post* noted that "while Nixon took a tougher line, Medina seemed to score more points with key Justices over involved questions of New York's invasion of privacy law."[78]

Medina spoke first. He detailed Time, Inc.'s responses to the four questions that had been posed to the parties for reargument. Medina argued that truthful presentations of newsworthy items had in fact been held actionable under the New York statute, that the Court of Appeals adopted Rabin's concurring opinion in the Appellate Division when it affirmed the decision, that New York did not require reckless disregard of truth or falsity as a prerequisite to liability, and that "the New York statute and its application to the present facts cannot be reconciled with the demands of the First Amendment."[79] Medina admitted that there was an error in *Life's* use of the word reenactment, an "unintentional error." But the article, he insisted, was essentially true: "If this true crime didn't inspire this tense play, I am an Eskimo. It certainly did. That's the basic point."[80]

White and Brennan expressed doubts about the statute's constitutionality. Brennan seemed receptive to Medina's invitation to strike down the New York law.[81] Fortas remained hostile to Time, Inc.'s position, and he continued to express concerns about media irresponsibility and the dangers of an expansive definition of the "news":

> Fortas: Let's suppose the *New York Times* . . . published a boudoir picture of
> certain people taken in their own bedroom. . . . Would that be a breach
> of this statute, a violation of this statute? . . . You wouldn't call that news,
> would you?[82]

Warren was also clearly against Medina:

> Warren: Were those horrendous things detailed in the article and in the picture true?
> Medina: Of course not, your honor.
> Warren: How can the article be true?[83]

Medina concluded by thanking the Court "for the courtesy of allowing us this reargument, because I think this case is of great importance in an endeavor to do in privacy what you did in libel." "We have gone through this case for 11 years. I had been talking about the Constitution through the New York courts. Until we got to this Court, no one realized the Constitution of the United States had anything to do with this case. And I say it is time that this Court made it quite clear to the state courts that the Constitution does have something to do with this."[84]

~

At the start of his fifty minutes of argument, Nixon spoke for several minutes without any interruptions from the justices.[85]

> Nixon: Mr. Chief Justice, may it please the Court. We have come far afield from the first time that we argued this case this spring. Then, the question before the Court was whether or not the judgment in this case impinged on the First Amendment. Now, we have the problem of whether or not the judgment in all of the New York cases, going back over 63 years, may have impinged upon the First Amendment.[86]

Citing extensively from New York case law, Nixon argued that the privacy law had never been used to penalize truthful accounts of the news and that the statute did not pose a conflict with the First Amendment.[87] As he did in his first argument, he emphasized *Life*'s calculated, intentional falsehoods:

> Nixon: It is our contention that in this case as it was argued by the plaintiff, it was established by the evidence, it was charged by the court, it was found by the jury, and it was held by the courts of New York in their appeals courts, that *Life* magazine lied. And that *Life* magazine knew it lied. That is the proposition that I contend for here.
>
> . . . *Life* magazine presented to its millions of readers the proposition that the Hill incident was the same as the *Desperate Hours* play. That was not true. We argued that proposition previously in the spring, but the best and most eloquent proof that it was not true is that *Life* tells its pictures not only by its words, but primarily by its pictures, and in telling its story by pictures, the six pictures that it select[ed] on this play present[ed] incidents, none of which occurred to the Hills; all of which, of course, had happened in the play. This was not simply incidental falsity. It was substantial falsity, and it was complete falsity in every one of those instances.

. . . Not only did *Life* make this false statement, but . . . its editors, in this case its picture editor, made the statement with knowledge that it was false . . . in the story file of the defendant there were not only current statements and stories that had been carried at the time the Hill incident occurred, but there was an article by the author himself in which he specifically stated that his play was not based on any specific incident, but was based on many incidents occurring in several different situations, and that when he completed his story it was different from any of the hostage incidents about which he had read.[88]

Brennan asked Nixon about the Rabin opinion. Nixon admitted that while Rabin's concurrence was part of the New York Court of Appeals' affirmance of the judgment for the Hills, the discussion of "commercial purpose" in the opinion was dictum—an expression of opinion that was not essential to the decision and not binding as precedent. Brennan said, "It may very well be a dictum," and made the audience laugh when he added, "Indeed if this were an opinion of one of my brethren, I would say it was." Brennan asked Nixon whether the Supreme Court could declare that a state court's interpretation of a state statute was not central to its ruling. Nixon said that the Court could do so because the language in Rabin's opinion had never been used by another New York court.[89]

Hugo Black went after Nixon:

Nixon: The point that we are making in this case is that the *Life* article is false, false in stating by picture, by every editorial device—with no qualification whatever—that the Hill incident was reenacted in *The Desperate Hours*, that the *Desperate Hours* family is the Hill family, that the violence that occurred in *The Desperate Hours* . . . all of these incidents, all of them that were in *The Desperate Hours*, and made it the hit that it was, did not occur to the Hills.

Black: That was a blending of fiction with fact.

Nixon: It was stating fiction was fact. It was more than that; it was fictionalizing the Hills. It was using the Hills as commercial props for the purpose of selling more magazines. It was creating a story, rather than reporting a story. And that is the heart of the tort under the New York law. If it had stated that this was reminiscent of this item, and then had described the

Hill incident as it occurred, then *Life* magazine would not have been liable. But I should also point out, *Life* magazine would not have had a story.

Black: Why wouldn't it?

Nixon: Why, it wouldn't have had the story because it wouldn't have been newsworthy.

Black: They could certainly have referred to other things in this play?

Nixon: Let us go, then, to why? Why *Life* magazine—when I refer to "*Life* magazine," I am referring, of course, to an institution, 24 senior editors, 41 other managing editors, and two hundred and eight. . . .

Black: You don't think they are all liable?

Nixon: But what I am suggesting is, I am referring to any one of the individuals who may have worked on the article; but in this particular instance, *Life* magazine, as far as checking on this item, did not do so. And they did not do so because *Life* magazine knew what the truth was.

. . . It was [described by *Life*] as a gimmick, an editorial gimmick. And the question is: Are private persons, involuntarily drawn into the vortex of a public issue. . . . are private persons by this Court to be allowed, in effect, to be used as gimmicks for commercial purposes in a falsified situation in which, I would suggest here, an editorial organization, the largest in the world, with more resources to question the facts than any other, used them in a fictionalized situation?

Black: The commercial purpose you refer to is selling magazines? Selling magazines for profit?

Nixon: Magazines are sold for profit.

Black: Is there anything wrong with that?

Nixon: Not at all.[90]

Nixon pointed out that the Hills were not public figures, and that if the Court applied *Sullivan*, private figures would receive less protection for their privacy than for their reputations. Under the Court's libel doctrine at the time, the reckless disregard standard applied only to statements on public officials; the Court left intact the common law, strict liability rule for "private libels." Medina's proposal would create a discrepancy between libel and privacy law. Why was the interest in privacy worth less than the interest in reputation? Nixon asked.[91]

Fortas's notes from the second argument indicate that he remained on Nixon's side. He wrote down, approvingly, several of Nixon's phrases: "*Life* lied and knew it lied," "None of the pictures used by *Life* shows the incident that happened to the Hills," *Life* "was using the Hills as commercial props to sell more magazines."[92]

Nixon had flown in to Washington that morning from New York. The arguments ran over the allotted time and had to be continued the following day. On the first evening, instead of having the case behind him, Nixon was rehearsing it again in his hotel room. The next morning, he rose early again and faced the justices for another hour of questioning and argument.[93]

Nixon's second appearance before the Supreme Court received some publicity in the press, although less than the first argument. The *Christian Science Monitor* noted that Nixon's appearance caused relatively "little stir in town." A few reporters attempted, unsuccessfully, to interview him as he left the courtroom. When they tried to stop him at the elevator, he said, "I'm sorry, but I'm due in San Francisco at 2 o' clock. I'm going to argue a little politics." Would it be a relief to get back to politics? Nixon was asked. "Well, there won't be as many tough questions," he replied. "Not that the press won't be tough," he added, as the elevator door closed.[94]

~

Two days after the reargument, in the Court's second conference on the case, the votes had switched. The initial vote had been six to three for the Hills; it now shifted to seven to two against the Hills. The dramatic Fortas opinion and the critical Black memorandum had led to a reversal. As Leonard Garment later noted, the great irony of the *Hill* case was that after all the musings about how the Court would react to Nixon, the animosity that shaped the outcome involved not Nixon but the conflict between Black and Fortas.[95]

Warren maintained his vote in favor of the Hills. He admitted that the New York law was "not too clear" but that the "specific holding below was correct," and the Court should put an end to the litigation, which had gone on for over eleven years. In the statute's limited application to the *Life* story, there was no violation of the First Amendment. False, fictionalized publications had no value as "news."[96]

Fortas held to his original position, insisting that the jury had found the *Life* article to be "knowingly, recklessly, willfully false." Between the first and the second votes, Stewart, Harlan, Brennan, and Clark changed their minds. Stewart believed that New York could not "hold [a] paper liable for anything other than a deliberate falsification" and that the jury had not been instructed on this standard. Clark also thought the law was too broad and that the jury "instructions were bad." Black asserted that the law was "unconstitutional as being too broad and vague" and "also violates the First Amendment." Clark, White, Douglas, Brennan, Stewart, Harlan, and Black would reverse the decision and remand the case to the New York courts for a new trial in which the jury would be instructed to apply the *Sullivan* rule to the falsity issue.[97]

Brennan and Black would have gone as far as to strike down the New York privacy statute. This might have happened had the New York Court of Appeals not issued its decision a week later in *Spahn v. Julian Messner, Inc.* In that case, it will be recalled, the famous baseball player Warren Spahn had sued a publisher for invasion of privacy under the New York privacy statute when his name and identity were used in a biography that he claimed was false and "fictionalized." The Court of Appeals in *Spahn* confirmed Nixon's reading of the privacy statute—under New York case law, truthful, newsworthy material was privileged even if published for commercial or "circulation-generating" purposes.[98] The Rabin concurrence was not a correct statement of the law.[99] *Spahn* also made clear that there was no intent requirement under the New York statute. The New York Court of Appeals had been asked by the publisher to apply the *Sullivan* actual malice standard to *Spahn* and refused to do so.[100]

With the Chief Justice no longer in the majority, Black, as the senior majority justice, assigned the opinion, and he gave it to Brennan. "Hugo told me he had assigned five cases Friday. He evidently got the Court on his Time magazine case!" Black's wife noted in her diary on Saturday, October 23, 1966. "How he has worked. Abe and the Chief the only ones against him."[101]

~

Brennan issued the first draft of his opinion on December 1, 1966. His clerks usually wrote his opinions, but because he felt so strongly about the issues, Brennan wrote much of *Time, Inc. v. Hill*. When it came to the First Amendment, his clerk recalled, he wanted to "speak in his own voice."[102] That same day, Fortas indicated that he would soon circulate a dissenting opinion.[103]

The decision in *Spahn* led Brennan to believe that the statute need not be struck down on its face—New York law respected "newsworthy" material.[104]

However, he believed that New York could not impose liability for innocent or negligent falsehoods, and a new trial was needed in which the jury would be instructed with the proper standard. He disagreed with Fortas that the jury had already been instructed on that standard and found reckless disregard in its conclusion that the *Life* article was fictionalized.[105]

At first, White was the only one to join the opinion. Immediately after the opinion was circulated, he wrote to Brennan saying that he had "a good deal of enthusiasm for the job you have done."[106] On December 22, Fortas circulated a dissent.[107] Aware of how much he had offended Brennan with his first opinion, he sought to make amends. Fortas sent a copy of his dissent to Brennan with a handwritten note on it: "Please let me know if any of this bark is too bitey. I'll change it. I will not circulate until I hear from you."[108] Warren joined the dissent, and so did Clark, who had retreated from the majority. Clark's clerk, Stuart Philip Ross, had written to him that Fortas's dissent "is well written and I think makes more sense than the majority opinion." Clark wrote to Fortas on January 2, 1967: "Join me, please. Well done."[109] On January 3, Harlan circulated his partially concurring, partially dissenting opinion.[110]

On December 1, 1966, Douglas sent his concurrence to Black, asking him if he had any suggestions before he circulated it. Black wrote, "I told [Brennan] I would approve but would probably also write myself."[111] Black drafted an opinion, which he showed only to Douglas on December 27. Douglas made suggestions for revision, and Black circulated the revised opinion on December 30.[112] Stewart then became the deciding vote. Brennan lobbied him, and he agreed to reverse. Brennan had won Stewart's allegiance by adding a paragraph, in a January 5 version of the opinion, clarifying that the holding would apply only to privacy cases under the New York statute, not libel cases involving private citizens, which had been a particular concern of Stewart.[113] Stewart wrote to Brennan, agreeing to join Brennan's opinion: "I think you have written a fine opinion, and I am glad to join it."[114]

CHAPTER SIXTEEN

January 9, 1967

The 6–3 decision in *Time, Inc. v. Hill* was issued on January 9, 1967.[1] Justice Brennan wrote for the majority: "We hold that the constitutional protections for speech and press preclude the application of the New York statute to redress false reports of matters of public interest in the absence of proof that the defendant published the report with knowledge of its falsity or in reckless disregard of the truth."[2] The trial judge's charge to the jury had failed to indicate that intentional or reckless falsehood was a prerequisite to liability.[3] The Court reversed the decision and remanded the case to the New York Court of Appeals for "further proceedings not inconsistent with this opinion."[4]

Brennan took the *Sullivan* rule on false and defamatory statements about public officials and applied it to false and nondefamatory statements about private citizens connected to nonpolitical subjects. This was a major extension of *Sullivan* and not explained by *Sullivan*'s rationale of protecting the public's ability to discuss public officials and political issues.[5] Brennan, notes his biographer, had a "seize the moment" approach to the Constitution.[6] In *Hill*, he saw a chance to extend the First Amendment gains he had made in *New York Times*, and he took the opportunity to announce an expansive terrain of protected expression encompassing more than strictly political affairs.

"The guarantees for speech and press are not the preserve of political expression or comment upon public affairs, as essential as those are to healthy government," Brennan wrote.[7] He quoted a 1941 case, *Thornhill v. Alabama*: "Freedom of discussion, if it would fulfill its historic function, must embrace all issues about which information is needed or appropriate to enable the members of society to cope with the exigencies of their period."[8] Brennan then referenced *Winters v. New York* (1948), in which the Court had overturned, on First Amendment grounds, the conviction of a bookseller under an "indecent exposure" statute for distributing a magazine containing "accounts of . . . bloodshed, lust, or crime." "The line between the informing and the entertaining [was] too elusive" to make that boundary the test for freedom of the press, the *Winters* Court had concluded.[9] Brennan wrote: "We have no doubt that the subject of the *Life* article, the opening of a new play linked to an actual incident, is a matter of public interest."[10] It was not the function of the courts to make judgments about media content, especially nondefamatory material; comic books, human-interest stories, gossip— the "vast range of published matter" in the press, including material that exposed people to unwanted publicity—were protected by the First Amendment.[11]

Freedom of the press meant more than protecting political discourse and criticism, said Brennan. Freedom of the press meant freeing the press from damage awards, with their inevitable "chilling effect." "We create a grave risk of serious impairment of the indispensable service of a free press in a free society if we saddle the press with the impossible burden of verifying to a certainty the facts associated in news articles with a person's name, picture, or portrait, particularly as related to non-defamatory matter," he wrote. "Even negligence would be a most elusive standard, especially when the content of the speech itself affords no warning of prospective harm to another through falsity. A negligence test would place on the press the intolerable burden of guessing how a jury might assess the reasonableness of steps taken by it to verify the accuracy of every reference to a name, picture or portrait."[12]

"Erroneous statement" was no less inevitable in reporting stories like the *Life* article than in the case of "comment on [political] affairs," Brennan wrote. "Sanctions against either innocent or negligent misstatement would present a grave hazard of discouraging the press from exercising the constitutional guarantees. Those guarantees are not for the benefit of the press so much as for the benefit of all of us. A broadly defined freedom of the press assures the maintenance of our political system and an open society. Fear of large verdicts in damage suits for innocent or merely negligent misstatement, even fear of the expense involved in their defense, must inevitably cause publishers to 'steer . . . wider of the unlawful zone' . . . and thus 'create the danger that the legitimate utterance will be penalized.'"[13]

According to Brennan, the facts of the case would support either a jury finding of innocent or negligent misstatement, or a finding that *Life* portrayed the play as a reenactment of the Hill family's experience with reckless disregard of the truth, or with actual knowledge that the statement was false. A jury could reasonably conclude from the evidence that the *Life* editors knew it was untrue that *The Desperate Hours* "reenacted" the Hill family's experience. On the other hand, a jury could find innocent or negligent misstatement on the testimony that a freelance photographer linked the play to the Hill incident, that Hayes cooperated in the photo shoot, and that Prideaux thought "beyond doubt" that the essence of the play was the Hill incident.[14]

What about privacy? Brennan dismissed the Hills' privacy argument by ignoring it. The only mention of privacy in the opinion came in a passage that suggested that the Hills should have no expectation of privacy, at least when it came to media publicity: "One need only pick up any newspaper or magazine to comprehend the vast range of published matter which exposes persons to public view, both private citizens and public officials. Exposure of the self to others in varying degrees is a concomitant of life in a civilized community. The risk of this exposure is an essential incident of life in a society which places a primary value on freedom of speech and of press."[15]

~

In his concurrence, Black agreed to apply the *New York Times* standard but held to his absolutist views. He asserted that the *Times* doctrine was "bound to pass away as its application to new cases proves its inadequacy to protect freedom of the press from destruction in libel cases and other cases like this one. The words 'malicious' and particularly 'reckless disregard of the truth' can never serve as effective substitutes for the First Amendment words: '. . . make no law . . . abridging the freedom of speech, or of the press.'"[16]

As he had in his poison memorandum, Black attacked the "recently popularized weighing and balancing formula" as a "Constitution-ignoring-and-destroying technique." "The 'weighing' doctrine plainly encourages and actually invites judges to choose for themselves between conflicting values, even where, as in the First Amendment, the Founders made a choice of values, one of which is a free press." "If the judicial balancing choice of constitutional changes is to be adopted by this Court, I could wish it had not started on the First Amendment. The freedoms guaranteed by that Amendment are essential freedoms in a government like ours. That Amendment was deliberately written in language designed to put its freedoms beyond the reach of government to change while it remained unrepealed. If judges have, however, by their own fiat today created a right of privacy equal to or superior to the right of a free press that the Constitution created, then tomorrow and the next day and the next, judges can create more rights that balance away other cherished Bill of Rights freedoms."[17]

In a separate concurrence, Douglas agreed with Black that the *Sullivan* exception for knowing or reckless falsity was an abridgment of speech barred by the First and Fourteenth Amendments. He insisted that the *Life* article was newsworthy: "The episode around which this book was written had been the news of the day for some time. The most that can be said is that the novel, the play, and the magazine article revived that interest." He agreed with Brennan that the Hills had no legitimate interest in privacy: "It seems to me irrelevant to talk of any right of privacy in this context. Here a private person is catapulted into the news by events over which he had no control. He and his activities are then in the public domain as fully as the matters at issue in *New York Times Co. v. Sullivan*."[18]

In a partially concurring, partially dissenting opinion, Harlan agreed to reverse the New York Court of Appeals on the basis of the jury instruction but proposed a more lenient standard of liability, one that was less friendly toward the press. He admitted that error was inevitable in news reporting, especially when abstract matters were being discussed, "illustrated here in the difficulty to be encountered in making a precise description of the relationship between the Hill incident and *The Desperate Hours*."[19] Yet he rejected Brennan's "sweeping extension" of *Sullivan* and would apply a negligence standard on remand to the New York courts. "The distinction between the facts presented to us here and the situation at issue in the *New York Times* case and its progeny casts serious doubt on that grant of immunity and calls for a more limited 'breathing space' than that granted in criticism of public officials," he wrote. The Hills could prevail if they could show that *Life* was merely careless, rather than reckless, in its research and fact checking.[20]

Harlan worried that a recklessness standard was insufficient to protect private citizens against the abuses of the press. Public officials were a hardy breed of individuals who had assumed the risk of irresponsible publicity—of "exposure to charges, innuendoes, and criticisms"—but ordinary people like the Hills had not. "Mr. Hill came to public attention through an unfortunate circumstance not of his making rather than his voluntary actions and he can in no sense be considered to have 'waived' any protection the State might justifiably afford him from irresponsible publicity. Not being inured to the vicissitudes of journalistic scrutiny such an individual is more easily injured and his means of self-defense are more limited," Harlan wrote.[21]

While public officials and public figures could defend themselves from false or hurtful accusations in the "marketplace of ideas," when it came to private figures, "we cannot avoid recognizing that we have entered an area where the 'marketplace of ideas' does not function." Unlike public officials, the Hills lacked access to a public platform and were helpless to defend themselves. "It would be unreasonable to assume that Mr. Hill could find a forum for making a successful refutation of the *Life* material or that the public's interest in it would be sufficient for the truth to win out by comparison as it might in that area of discussion central to a free society. Thus the state interest in encouraging careful checking and preparation of published material is far stronger than in *New York Times*." Harlan continued:[22]

> The coincidence of . . . factors in this situation leads me to the view that a State should be free to hold the press to a duty of making a reasonable investigation of the underlying facts and limiting itself to "fair comment" on the materials so gathered. Theoretically, of course, such a rule might slightly limit press discussion of matters touching individuals like Mr. Hill. But, from a pragmatic standpoint, until now the press, at least in New York, labored under the more exacting handicap of the existing New York privacy law and has certainly remained robust. Other professional activity of great social value is carried on under a duty of reasonable care and there is no reason to suspect the press would be less hardy than medical practitioners or attorneys for example.

Harlan concluded, "The 'freedom of the press' guaranteed by the First Amendment, and as reflected in the Fourteenth, cannot be thought to insulate all press conduct from review and responsibility for harm inflicted. The majority would allow sanctions against such conduct only when it is morally culpable. I insist that it can also be reached when it creates a severe risk of irremediable harm to individuals involuntarily exposed to it and powerless to protect themselves against it." He ended his concurrence with a warning to the majority of the long-term consequences of extending *Sullivan*: in relieving the press of even "minimal responsibility" for accuracy, the *Times* doctrine was "ultimately harmful to the permanent good health of the press itself. If the *New York Times* case has ushered in such a trend it will prove in its long-range impact to have done a disservice to the true values encompassed in the freedoms of speech and press."[23]

~

Fortas's dissent, joined by Warren and Clark, remained angry, though less strident than his draft opinion. "Perhaps the purpose of the [majority] decision . . . is to indicate that this Court will place insuperable obstacles in the way of recovery by persons who are injured by reckless and heedless assaults provided they are in print, and even though they are divorced from fact," he began. "If so, I should think that the Court would cast its decision in constitutional terms. Short of that purpose, with which I would strongly disagree, there is no reason here to order a new trial. The instructions in this case are acceptable even within the principles today announced by the Court."[24]

Fortas conceded that First Amendment freedoms were "delicate and vulnerable, as well as supremely precious" and that the First Amendment must be construed broadly.[25] "But I do not believe that whatever is in words, however much of an aggression it may be upon individual rights, is beyond the reach of the law, no matter how heedless of others' rights—how remote from public purpose, how reckless, irresponsible, and untrue it may be." Fortas did not believe that the First Amendment "preclude[d] effective protection of the right of privacy—or, for that matter, an effective law of libel. I do not believe that we must or should, in deference to those whose views are absolute as to the scope of the First Amendment, be ingenious to strike down all state action, however circumspect, which penalizes the use of words as instruments of aggression and personal assault."[26]

In an earlier draft version of the dissent, Fortas was even more forceful in his attack on the press: "The courts may not and must not permit either public or private action that censors or inhibits the press. But part of this responsibility is to preserve values and procedures which insure the ordinary citizen that the press is not above the reach of the law—that it is not a tyrant whose lash must be endured, regardless of circumstances."[27] In another passage that he removed from the final version, Fortas said that he wrote his dissent to correct the majority's "unwillingness to cope with the problem of determining the limits of the First Amendment." His colleagues, particularly Black and Douglas, showed "an excessive readiness to sacrifice competing values to its supposed absolute and universal mandate, and an excessive readiness to condemn state statutes where the domain of the First Amendment is implicated."[28]

As he had in his majority opinion, Fortas highlighted the Hills' constitutional right to privacy. In the dissent, however, he scaled back his earlier, sweeping description of the scope of the right to privacy. Although Fortas maintained that privacy was a "basic right," he no longer claimed that the "right of privacy reaches beyond any of its specifics."[29]

He wrote: "There are great and important values in our society, none of which is greater than those reflected in the First Amendment, but which are also fundamental and entitled to this Court's careful respect and protection. Among these is the right to privacy, which has been eloquently extolled by scholars and members of this Court." "A distinct right of privacy is now recognized, either as a 'commonlaw' right or by statute, in at least 35 States. Its exact scope varies in the respective jurisdictions. It is, simply stated, the right to be let alone; to live one's life as one chooses, free from assault, intrusion or invasion except as they can be justified by the clear needs of community living under a government of law." Fortas again cited *Griswold* as precedent for a general constitutional right to privacy: in *Griswold*, the Court "held unconstitutional a state law under which petitioners were prosecuted for giving married persons information and medical advice on the use of contraceptives. The holding was squarely based upon the right of privacy which the Court derived by implication from the specific guarantees of the Bill of Rights."[30]

Fortas attacked the majority's reversal on the basis of the jury instruction:

The Court today does not repeat the ringing words of so many of its members on so many occasions in exaltation of the right of privacy. Instead, it reverses a decision under the New York "Right of Privacy" statute because of the "failure of the trial judge to instruct the jury that a verdict of liability could be predicated only on a finding of knowing or reckless falsity in the publication of the *Life* article." In my opinion, the jury instructions, although they were not a textbook model, satisfied this standard. . . .

Such drastic action—the reversal of a jury verdict by this remote Court— is justified by the Court on the ground that the standard of liability on which the jury was instructed contravenes the First Amendment. But a jury instruction is not abracadabra. It is not a magical incantation, the slightest deviation from which will break the spell. Only its poorer examples are formalistic codes recited by a trial judge to please appellate masters. At best, it is simple, rugged communication from a trial judge to a jury of ordinary people, entitled to be appraised in terms of its net effect. Instructions are to be viewed in this commonsense perspective, and not through the remote and distorting knothole of a distant appellate fence. . . .

"Fictionalization" and "fiction" to the ordinary mind mean so departing from fact and reality as to be deliberately divorced from the fact—not merely in detail but in general and pervasive impact. The English language is not so esoteric as to permit serious consequences to turn upon a supposed difference between the instructions to the jury and this Court's formulation. Nor is the First Amendment in such delicate health that it requires or permits this kind of surgery, the net effect of which is not only an individual injustice, but an encouragement to recklessness and careless readiness to ride roughshod over the interests of others.[31]

Fortas concluded with a warning to the majority of the dangers of its view of the First Amendment's "absolute and universal mandates," which obscured the importance of the interest in privacy and the harms caused by unrestrained press freedom:

The courts may not and must not permit either public or private action that censors or inhibits the press. But part of this responsibility is to preserve values and procedures which assure the ordinary citizen that the press is not above the reach of the law—that its special prerogatives, granted because of its special and vital functions, are reasonably equated with its needs in the performance of these functions. For this Court totally to immunize the press—whether forthrightly or by subtle indirection—in areas far beyond the needs of news, comment on public persons and events, discussion of public issues and the like would be no service to freedom of the press, but an invitation to public hostility to that freedom. This Court cannot and should not refuse to permit under state law the private citizen who is aggrieved by the type of assault which we have here and which is not within the specially protected core of the First Amendment to recover compensatory damages for recklessly inflicted invasion of his rights.[32]

Fortas expressed concern for the well-being of the Hills, who had endured the lawsuit for over a decade. "Presumably, the appellee is entitled to a new trial. If he can stand the emotional and financial burden, there is reason to hope that he will recover damages for the reckless and irresponsible assault upon himself and his family which this article represents. But he has litigated this case for 11 years. He should not be subjected to the burden of a new trial without significant cause. This does not exist."[33]

That trial never came to pass. Nixon announced that the Hills would seek a new trial, but shortly after the Court's decision, Time, Inc. settled with James Hill. The amount of the settlement was not part of the public record; it appears in a memo that Garment wrote to Nixon and has been preserved in Nixon's papers. "The Hill case is settled," Garment wrote to Nixon. "Time, Inc. has agreed to pay $75,000 (in addition to the $60,000 previously paid to settle Mrs. Hill's claim). Jim Hill is gratified with this outcome and relieved that another trial is avoided. Medina is likewise relieved. I think this is an honorable settlement, and, under the circumstances, a sensible step for all concerned."[34]

Elizabeth Hill continued to struggle with severe depression caused in part by the publicity in *Life* magazine. A few years after the Supreme Court's decision in *Time, Inc. v. Hill*, she committed suicide.[35]

CHAPTER SEVENTEEN

The Aftermath

Time, Inc. v. Hill transformed the meaning of freedom of the press and the scope of the right to privacy in the United States. The 1967 decision, often overlooked in the shadow of *New York Times v. Sullivan*, was important in its own right. As a technical matter, the holding in *Time, Inc. v. Hill* applied only to a narrow set of cases: privacy claims involving questions of truth and falsity under the New York privacy statute. Yet the implications of the Brennan opinion were far-reaching. *Time, Inc. v. Hill* set forth an expansive vision of freedom of the press and dimmed the potential for a strong right to privacy that could be invoked against the press.

As *New York Times v. Sullivan* constitutionalized the law of libel, *Time, Inc. v. Hill* constitutionalized the privacy tort. Once regarded as an area of speech outside the First Amendment, "invasions of privacy" were now protected by the Constitution. Publishers could not be made to pay damages for using people's identities, life stories, photos, or personal information so long as they related to "newsworthy" matters and were not knowingly or recklessly falsified.

The majority opinion adopted the most expansive view of the newsworthiness privilege under state law and implied that it was a constitutional requirement. If material was of "public interest," it was presumptively newsworthy and privileged. A "matter of public interest," Brennan suggested, was anything that the public was "interested" in, whether news about politics, celebrity gossip, or human interest stories. In this view, the press could create curiosity in an issue by publicizing it, then point to the interest it generated and claim that the material was "of public interest" and a privileged "news" item. This capacious and circular definition of newsworthiness essentially gave the press the ability to determine what was privileged and to relieve itself from liability. Even false, newsworthy material was protected under the First Amendment unless the falsehood was knowing or reckless.

Newsworthy material defined not only the privacy law privilege, but the scope of freedom of the press. The majority opinion announced a broad vision of the

First Amendment as protecting all newsworthy "matters of public interest." This went beyond *Sullivan*, with its more limited terrain of political affairs. As Harry Kalven Jr. wrote not long after the decision, "The Brennan thesis" was that "newsworthiness defines the ambit of constitutional concern. The *Life* report in the [*Hill*] case was newsworthy. It is therefore within the sphere in which state-law remedies for aggrieved individuals are subject to judicial review under the First Amendment."[1]

In declaring the public discussion of "matters of public interest" the operative dynamic of participatory democracy, Brennan—drawing on Time, Inc.'s brief—adopted the views of Alexander Meiklejohn. It will be recalled that Meiklejohn's vision of First Amendment protected speech incorporated a wide range of material, including philosophy, science, art, literature, and entertainment. Through public discussion of these "public issues," citizens of a democracy governed themselves.[2] As the *Columbia Journalism Review* noted, there were "striking parallels" between Brennan's opinion in *Hill* and Meiklejohn's writings.[3] "*Time, Inc. v. Hill* . . . indicate[s] that the Court has pretty much adopted Meiklejohn's delineation of the public and private spheres."[4] Outside of the Black/Douglas absolutist position, which never commanded a majority, Brennan's description of protected First Amendment speech was one of the broadest issued by the Supreme Court to that time. The Court took a "giant step" expanding freedom of the press "without being forced to an explicit justification for it and without openly invoking *New York Times*," Kalven observed.[5]

Perhaps the most significant result of *Time, Inc. v. Hill* was that it diminished a right to privacy that could be mobilized against the press. What seemed like a possibility in the pro-privacy climate of the 1960s—a right to privacy, under both federal constitutional law and state tort law, that would permit people like the Hills to recover damages for invasive media publicity—had been undermined.

In many respects, privacy law developed significantly since the *Hill* case. In the decade after *Hill*, the Supreme Court expanded the scope of the right to privacy under the Fourth Amendment. *Katz v. United States* (1967), notably, extended the Fourth Amendment to electronic eavesdropping.[6] The Court also expanded the *Griswold* "autonomy" or "fundamental liberty" right to privacy. In *Eisenstadt v. Baird* (1972), the Court, citing *Griswold*, invalidated a law prohibiting the distribution of contraceptives to unmarried persons, noting that "if the right of privacy means anything, it is the right of the individual, married or single, to be free from unwarranted governmental intrusion into matters so fundamentally affecting a person as the decision whether to bear or beget a child."[7] *Roe v. Wade* (1973) drew on *Griswold* to extend constitutional protection to abortion rights.[8] In *Whalen v. Roe* (1977), the Court for the first time recognized a right to information privacy, noting that the constitutionally protected zone of privacy involved the individual interest in avoiding disclosure of personal matters and the interest in "independence in making certain kinds of important decisions."[9] Since the 1970s, there have been major statutory developments in the protection of privacy. In 1974, Congress passed the Privacy Act, which regulates the collection and use of records by federal agencies and gives citizens the right to access and correct their personal information.[10] Other federal and state laws protect the privacy of financial information, health records, video rental records, and educational records.[11]

But as a right that could be invoked against the media, privacy stalled with the *Hill* case. As one commentator noted, "The First Amendment protection afforded the press [in *Hill*] raises the possibility that the constitutional [newsworthiness] privilege will engulf much of the law of privacy. The slight chance that a statement will be published that cannot be considered to be a matter of public interest leads to the conclusion that the instant decision has severely restricted the protection of privacy by state law."[12] "By extending the public interest privilege to a constitutional level, *Hill* seems likely to limit considerably the future usefulness of 'privacy' as a tort."[13] As Harvard Law professor Arthur Miller speculated, "*Hill* may well have aborted much of the doctrinal growth capacity of the law of privacy."[14] "The ability of a privacy invasion victim to avoid the effect of the First Amendment has been substantially limited by the Supreme Court's decision in *Time, Inc. v. Hill.*"[15]

∽

In January 1967, *Time, Inc. v. Hill* sparked major debate. The decision was covered extensively in the nation's media outlets. "The Supreme Court ruled . . . that 'newsworthy' persons, including those who do not seek publicity, have only a limited right to sue for damages for false reports that are published about them," observed the *Washington Post*.[16] *Editor and Publisher* described the "decision of the U.S. Supreme Court in the *Life* magazine case" as a "landmark in the ever-increasing number of invasion of privacy cases."[17] The opinion substantially "extends the guarantee of freedom of the press established by the Constitution," noted the *Hartford Courant*.[18] Wrote the *Des Moines Register*, "The U.S. Supreme Court took a significant step recently towards resolving the conflict between the right of the individual to privacy and the guarantee of free press in a ruling that comes down forcefully on the side of the public's right to be informed." "News media have a vital stake in presenting accurate information . . . But no news organization is free of unintentional misstatements of fact. The Supreme Court ruling is assurance that punishment in such a case will not be a heavy damage award."[19]

The *New York Times* gave extensive coverage to the decision, running excerpts of the opinion under the headline, "Supreme Court Supports Press on a Privacy Issue."[20] It also published an editorial praising the Court for giving the press "breathing room" to "inform and criticize":

> By its . . . decision in a case involving *Life* magazine, the Supreme Court has extended the freedom and intensified the responsibility of the American press. The Court has ruled that an individual's right to privacy does not entitle him to damages for reports containing false information or impressions unless there is proof that the errors were published knowingly or recklessly.
>
> Unquestionably, the Court's doctrine—when applied to private persons, as against public officials—does represent a considerable invasion of traditional concepts of privacy. The extent of the breach is bound to disturb many Americans in a period when the circumscriptions on privacy are already omnipresent.[21]

In a shamelessly self-congratulatory move, *Time* magazine published an article in its January 20, 1967, issue titled "A Vote for the Press over Privacy." The article noted the 1890 article that launched the right to privacy, attacking "yellow-press invasions of the sacred precincts of private and domestic life. The denunciation contained obvious merit; over the years, thirty-four states have guaranteed personal privacy in varying degrees. The denunciation also bore the seeds of conflict with the First Amendment guarantee of freedom of the press. Sooner or later, the Supreme Court would obviously have to settle a basic question: To what extent does the First Amendment immunize the press from observance of state privacy laws?"

"Last week the Court answered that question for the first time," *Time* continued. "Out went a New York privacy judgment against Time Inc., publisher of *Life* magazine. In came a new standard: the First Amendment protects the press against privacy suits for false news reports—unless the plaintiff manages to prove conclusively that the report was deliberately or recklessly false." "The rulings strike the concept of privacy a considerable blow, but 'freedom of discussion' takes priority, said Brennan."[22] The president of Time, Inc. issued a public statement praising the Court for upholding the "vital principle of a free press."[23]

While the press celebrated the decision, public opinion was on the other side. Leonard Garment believed that many ordinary Americans saw the *Hill* decision as an example of the "arrogance of journalists and intellectual elites in riding heedless over the interests and values of more ordinary folk."[24] In 1967, the American press was approaching the height of its power as an institution, on its way toward its peak influence in the mid-1970s. With the rise of investigative journalism and bold coverage of Vietnam, civil rights, and antigovernment protest, the press was a major, opinionated force in the nation's political and social affairs. While some supported the media's powerful voice, many Americans continued to believe that media institutions abused their authority, engaged in needless sensationalism, took dangerous liberties with the truth, and ran roughshod over privacy.[25]

At a time when the public was sensitive to privacy issues, the Court's decision "cavalierly undercut[ting] a basic right" was "especially disturbing," noted one commentator. The decision in the *Hill* case was one more insult to the "right to be let alone" at a time when "privacy is being increasingly threatened in a 'naked society.'"[26] After *Griswold*, *Mapp v. Ohio* (1961), and the Warren Court's other privacy-protecting decisions, Americans had come to see the Supreme Court as a defender of personal privacy against powerful and unjust social forces. *Hill* failed that expectation and left many feeling disappointed and betrayed.

Law reviews and legal journals attacked the Brennan opinion. Wrote legal scholar Marshall Shapo in the *Texas Law Review*, "To pardon the invasion of privacy of [James Hill] . . . is to allow the massed power of the media to run unchecked against isolated and helpless individuals."[27] "Are we here simply, or largely, as spectators, to be regaled and entertained by the misfortunes of our fellows as reported by the media of information, marvelous in their technical accomplishment?" asked legal scholar Willard Pedrick. "Are the tragedy and heartbreak of individuals, who have sought no role in the direction of our society, to be the stuff served up to beguile the rest of us?"[28] "The fact that what allegedly happened to the Hill family was news should not in the name of the First Amendment justify an obliteration of society's commitment to the value of privacy," commented media lawyer and law professor Melville Nimmer.[29] "What social interest worthy of constitutional protection" appeared in the *Life* article? "What purpose is served, besides the creation and satisfaction of idle curiosity?"[30]

Critics assailed the application of *Sullivan* to the different, unrelated facts of the *Hill* case. "However absolute the freedoms of press and speech may be, the political settings in *New York Times* . . . presented a much greater need for free speech than did *Hill,*" noted the *North Carolina Law Review.*[31] "If the rationale of *New York Times* is taken seriously, political speech—discussion of issues about which governments make decisions—deserves fullest constitutional protection." *Hill* could not "reasonably be put into that category."[32] Argued law professor Edward Bloustein, "If the central meaning of the First Amendment involves a proscription against any legal bar to political defamation, why should it be used to bar the attempt of a private person to recover damages for a use of his name or likeness in a mass publication where that use in no way contributes to the discussion of issues of general or public interest?"[33] "Was it relevant to the purposes of self-government to publish in a mass medium the name of the family that was linked to the play by something that had happened three years previously?" "What real purpose other than titillation of the magazine reader's urge to pry into other people's lives was served by identifying the family involved?"[34]

The expansive definition of newsworthiness or "matters of public interest" was the most criticized aspect of the decision.[35] "In using the words 'public interest,' the Court in *Hill* seems to have defined them as matters in which the public (or at least the news media) is interested," noted the *William and Mary Law Review.*[36] "More than two years after their brief and highly unwelcome moment in the public eye, the Hill family was a "matter of public interest" only because of the very *Life* magazine article about which they complained," commented the *Harvard Law Review.* "The Court's tests . . . make the press the arbiter of its own constitutional protection: by the very act of printing an article sufficiently sensational to arouse public interest, the press . . . insulate[s] itself from liability."[37] The *Hill* decision "points towards a time when anything that the press decides to print will be held newsworthy and therefore within the First Amendment's protection and beyond the law of privacy."[38] "Newsworthiness will almost certainly become a descriptive and not a normative term. In brief, the press will be the arbiters of it and the Court will be forced to yield to the argument that whatever the press prints is by virtue of that fact newsworthy."[39]

~

Time, Inc. v. Hill's effects on the law were significant and felt immediately. By the early 1970s, the decision had touched "a wide variety of cases, including cases involving false statements and those involving true statements," observed the *Washington Law Review*.[40] Although *Hill's* holding was technically limited to cases under the New York privacy statute, by describing newsworthiness as a category of constitutional proportion, the Court strengthened the news privilege in common law privacy cases, weakening the privacy tort.[41] Since *Hill*, the newsworthiness privilege has become so expansive that it is extremely difficult to win a privacy suit against the media for the publication of either true facts or false, nondefamatory facts.[42]

In the years after the Supreme Court's decision, courts declared a wide array of material to be newsworthy and exempt from liability for invasion of privacy. In 1968, the Second Circuit Court of Appeals deemed a graphic and sensational story in the *National Enquirer* about a gruesome murder suicide, "why the happiest wife and mother in the neighborhood suddenly decided to kill her three children and herself," to be newsworthy and a "legitimate matter of public concern."[43] In 1970, an article about two children who suffocated by trapping themselves in a refrigerator was described as a newsworthy "matter of public concern."[44]

The *Des Moines Register* published the name of a young female victim of involuntary sterilization in a story on the misadministration of a mental health facility. In 1977, the Iowa Supreme Court concluded that the paper was not liable for invasion of privacy, even though publication of the girl's identity was unnecessary to the story and caused her distress. According to the Iowa Supreme Court, the publication of the girl's name was "newsworthy" because it enhanced the appeal and readability of the story, offering "a personalized frame of reference to which the reader could relate." Citing *Hill*, the court observed, "Publicity need not be informative, entertaining, timely or important to be entitled to First Amendment protection. At the very least news includes discussion of 'all issues about which information is needed or appropriate to enable the members of society to cope with the exigencies of their period.'"[45]

When a gay Vietnam veteran, Oliver Sipple, foiled an assassination attempt on President Gerald Ford in 1975—Sipple struck down a woman who tried to shoot Ford as he was speaking at a rally– the man became an instant celebrity. Newspapers discussed his sexual orientation; several speculated that Ford's failure to promptly thank Sipple for his act was because he was gay. Sipple had concealed his homosexuality from his family, and when they read the news articles and found out, Sipple was ostracized and humiliated. Sipple sued the publisher of the *San Francisco Chronicle* for invasion of privacy. Referencing *Hill,* the California Supreme Court held that his sexual orientation was "newsworthy"—it was connected to a legitimate public issue, namely, the issue of Ford's delayed thanks. The court described the newsworthiness privilege as being constitutionally mandated, of "constitutional dimension based upon the First Amendment."[46]

A newspaper published a photo of a soccer player during a game, with his genitalia inadvertently exposed from his shorts. He sued; the court concluded that the photo was newsworthy, since it was published with an article about the game. "Publication in a newspaper does not lose its protected character simply because it may embarrass the persons to whom the publication refers," the court observed.[47] Citing *Hill,* it noted that "exposure of the self to others in varying degrees is a concomitant of life in a civilized community," and "the risk of . . . exposure" "is an essential incident of life in a society which places a primary value on freedom of speech and of press."[48]

~

Since *Hill,* the Supreme Court has heard only a few cases involving the First Amendment implications of tort liability for invasion of privacy. In them, the Court strongly suggested that liability for the publication of truthful facts is categorically unconstitutional under the First Amendment, though it never definitively ruled on the issue. In *Smith v. Daily Mail* (1979), the majority concluded that although there might be limited contexts where a privacy interest could override the right to publish true facts, in general, if a newspaper "lawfully obtains truthful information about a matter of public significance, then state officials may not constitutionally punish publication of the information, absent a need to further a state interest of the highest order."[49] The Court invoked the *Hill* "reckless disregard" standard in its first and only "false light" privacy case, *Cantrell v. Forest City Publishing* (1974). In that case, a newspaper published blatant falsehoods about a family, victims of a bridge disaster, including an interview with a woman that was totally fabricated. A jury found reckless disregard of the truth, and the Supreme Court affirmed on that standard.[50]

Time, Inc. v. Hill also influenced the law of libel. In the first few years after the decision, several lower courts read *Hill,* erroneously, to apply the *Sullivan* standard to false and defamatory statements on any "matter of public concern."[51] Technically, *Hill* did not affect libel law; *Sullivan* and two cases decided the same term as *Hill, Curtis Publishing Co. v. Butts* and *Associated Press v. Walker*, confirmed that the malice privilege in libel cases depended on the status of the plaintiff—whether he or she was a public figure or a private figure—rather than on the "newsworthiness" of the subject.[52] Yet in 1971, the Court extended *Hill* to the libel context. In *Rosenbloom v. Metromedia*, an opinion by Justice Brennan held that the actual malice standard applied whenever the subject matter of the libel was a "matter of public or general interest." "If a matter is a subject of public or general interest, it cannot suddenly become less so merely because a private individual is involved, or because in some sense the individual did not 'voluntarily' choose to become involved," he wrote.[53]

Three years later, in *Gertz v. Robert Welch*, the Court returned to the "status of the plaintiff" approach in defamation cases. Concluding that private individuals, unlike public figures, did not voluntarily expose themselves to an increased risk of injury from defamatory falsehoods and were therefore more deserving of recovery than public figures, *Gertz* adopted a minimum requirement of negligence for compensatory damages in libel cases involving private figures and matters of public interest.[54] Brennan dissented in *Gertz*, insisting that the proper accommodation between "avoidance of media self-censorship and protection of individual reputations" demanded that the *Sullivan* standard apply to libel actions "concerning media reports of the involvement of private individuals in events of public or general interest."[55] After *Gertz*, some courts continued to apply *Hill* in privacy cases involving private figures, matters of public interest, and false statements of fact—"false light" privacy cases—while others applied *Gertz*.[56] The *Gertz* approach, acknowledging a distinction between public and private figures, was essentially Harlan's position in *Hill*.

The Court has used the *Hill* "matters of public interest" or "newsworthiness" concept to protect speech in a variety of contexts under the First Amendment. In *Pickering v. Board of Education* (1968), a majority held that a public school teacher had a right to speak on issues of "public concern" without being dismissed unless knowing or reckless falsehood could be shown.[57] In *Connick v. Myers* (1983), the Court indicated that the "matters of public concern" standard used to judge public employee speech was the same as in *Hill*.[58] A matter of "public concern is something that is a subject of general interest and of value and concern to the public at the time of publication."[59] When a majority upheld the firing of an assistant district attorney in *Connick* for circulating a questionnaire on coworkers' attitudes toward employment policies, Justice Brennan dissented, stating that the majority had defined "public concern" too narrowly: "The Court's narrow conception of which matters are of public interest is . . . inconsistent with the broad view of that concept articulated in our cases dealing with the constitutional limits on liability for invasion of privacy."[60]

Most recently, "matters of public concern" was invoked by the majority in its decision for the Westboro Baptist Church in the 2011 case *Snyder v. Phelps*. The antigay hate group had picketed the funeral of a soldier with signs reading "God Hates the USA/Thank God for 9/11," "America Is Doomed," and "God Hates Fags." Citing *Hill*, the Court concluded that however hateful, the picketing involved speech on a "matter of public concern," speech that could be "fairly considered as relating to any matter of political, social, or other concern to the community," and that was a subject of "legitimate news interest; that is, a subject of general interest and of value and concern to the public." "While these messages may fall short of refined social or political commentary, the issues they highlight—the political and moral conduct of the United States and its citizens, the fate of our Nation, homosexuality in the military, and scandals involving the Catholic clergy—are matters of public import."[61]

∾

In reducing the potential for liability for invasions of privacy, *Time, Inc. v. Hill* emboldened the press. Like *New York Times v. Sullivan*, the *Hill* decision may have encouraged diminished caution and restraint in news reporting, and deeper and more intrusive journalistic forays into personal lives.[62] In Leonard Garment's view, the decision in *Hill* led journalists to believe that the "First Amendment's writ ran without limit."[63] Privacy scholar Robert Ellis Smith believed that had the *Hill* decision gone the other way, "the excessive tabloidism of the 1980s and 1990s" might have been stemmed.[64]

Though it's impossible to draw a precise correlation between the law and media content, one can't help but notice the rise of increasingly voyeuristic and sensational journalism at the same time as expanding protections for the press in privacy and libel cases. The 1980s and 1990s, dubbed the "Tabloid Decades,"[65] saw ruthless exposures of politicians' private lives and extensive disclosures of the habits, quirks, health conditions, family troubles, and misfortunes of both celebrities and ordinary people in tabloids and quasi-tabloids like the *National Enquirer* and *People*, TV shows like *A Current Affair* and *Hard Copy*, and cable news programs.[66] One legal scholar has noted the "convergence of tabloid and serious journalism" since the 1990s, both characterized by "sensationalism, salacious sinfulness, the seamlessness of public and private life," and "gossip, innuendo, and rumor."[67] As the *New York Times* noted in 1992, there was a "rising tide of advocacy for personal privacy" at the same time as a "glut of publications and television programs devoted to the most intimate details of people's lives."[68] Stories like the *Life* article on *The Desperate Hours*, dramatic and exciting in 1955, had become downright quaint.

One of the most eminent observers of the law and the press, the *New York Times*'s Supreme Court journalist, Anthony Lewis, attributed the late twentieth-century media's relatively cavalier attitudes toward privacy in part to *Time, Inc. v. Hill*. For decades, Lewis wrote and spoke extensively about the *Hill* decision, maintaining that it was wrong: "If your life is ruined by the press, you should have some kind of recourse," he told a public audience in 2008.[69] "What did James Hill, a private person, have to do with the reasoning of *New York Times v. Sullivan* . . . and its lesson that the central meaning of the First Amendment is the right to criticize those who govern us? My answer is—nothing. I think the Court in *Time, Inc. v. Hill* applied the compelling logic of *Sullivan* in a situation where it was quite inapposite."[70] "James Hill was not a public person of the kind for whom the *Sullivan* rule was imposed, someone who should have stayed out of the kitchen if he could not stand the heat. Nor was Mrs. Hill. I do not think the Hills of this world should have to jump such high hurdles in order to make a modest legal point about their privacy."[71]

"The American press has largely been triumphant in its resistance to the law of privacy," Lewis observed. "But the press should not be too comfortable—too arrogant . . . in its court victories against privacy claims. The public, coarse as its tastes have become, may react against disclosure for disclosure's sake if pressed too far against the powerless. . . . 'The right to know,' that phrase chanted by some editors as if it were a magic incantation, is not the only value in a democratic society, not even one as committed to freedom of expression as ours. Privacy is also a crucial value . . . . a[n] essential component of a civilized life."[72] "In a world that has known Orwell's Big Brother, and that now lives with electronic networks tracking our lives, many would resist the proposition that 'exposure of the self to others' is a necessary part of living in a 'civilized community.'"[73]

~

At a time when privacy had emerged as a major social issue, and when the Warren Court was expanding constitutional protections for privacy in different contexts, the *Hill* majority seemingly diminished the importance of privacy. Brennan, who had forwarded a relatively expansive vision of privacy in *Griswold*, declined to take a broader view of privacy in *Hill*. Why did a Court that was so respectful of privacy in many regards reject the Hills' privacy claim?

One reason, alluded to in the Brennan opinion, is that the majority did not see the case as really involving "privacy," since it concerned what was arguably a public fact. Since they were connected to a newsworthy event—the hostage incident—the Hills had no "right to privacy" in the sense of a right to avoid the public gaze. The only "privacy" right the Hills had, at least under New York law, was a right to not be presented falsely in the media, which was not a true "privacy" interest. Some of the justices were skeptical about the injury to the Hills. Were the Hills overreacting to *Life*'s use of their names? Wouldn't some people enjoy being the subject of media attention, especially publicity that cast them in a flattering light?

The dissenters, by contrast, were sensitive to the emotional and dignitary harms that can come from unwanted, distorted publicity. While Fortas admitted that the Hills had no privacy when it came to newsworthy publications, he implied that *Life*'s use of the family in its story did not constitute legitimate "news." As private citizens, the Hills had a right to not be thrust into the spotlight three years after their misfortune, a right to not have their "quiet existence" disturbed for a relatively frivolous article with no real public purpose. There was a privacy right to not be gratuitously exposed, a right to not be paraded before the public for titillation and entertainment, a right that *Life* violated when it used the Hills in their publicity scheme.

In the majority's view, even if *Life* had invaded the Hills' privacy, it was in the name of a greater good. The loss of personal privacy, Brennan suggested, is the price we all must pay for a free society. For better or worse, we all assume the risk of having our privacy invaded by the media—a risk that for most of us is fairly small. In return, we get something much greater—the freedom to know the "news" and a press that is unafraid to publish; the freedom to read and see what we want; the freedom to criticize and comment; the freedom to think independently and speak our minds.

Fortas, Warren, Clark, and Harlan did not dispute the importance of freedom of the press, but they did not see its benefits as going solely to the public. As a profit-generating enterprise, the benefits of freedom of the press go disproportionately to the press. As a business profiting from the sales of its product, the press should pay for the harms it creates, no less than those who offer other goods and services to the public must compensate victims for injuries they cause. If doctors and lawyers can be liable for malpractice, as Harlan asked in his opinion, why can't the press be held to a comparable standard? To quote Harry Kalven Jr., writing on the case, "If the risk of jury judgments under a negligence standard is not too inhibiting for other useful activity, why is it an undue burden on communication?"[74]

The majority would exempt the press from the ordinary rules of tort liability. To Brennan, Black, and Douglas, the press deserved special treatment under the law because of its centrality to the functioning of democracy. The press should have more latitude to create injuries, without consequence, because of the harm that would ensue if the media curtailed its activities for fear of liability. Press restraint, or anything beyond minimal restraint, was anathema to the public good; public discourse was at its best and most productive when it was "wide open and robust"—nearly unrestrained.

The dissenters, including Justice Harlan, disagreed that an unrestrained press best serves the interests of democracy and freedom. To Fortas, Warren, Clark, and Harlan, there was no danger to a free press in forcing the media, under the threat of liability, to police itself and take responsibility for its words. Requiring the press to bear the burdens of its injurious speech was in the public's interest: a self-conscious, self-aware, self-limiting press was more conducive to meaningful public discourse than a potentially reckless press, one that injured individuals, disregarded the facts, and lost the trust and confidence of its readers. Democracy does not need a free press so much as it needs a thoughtful press, one that thinks before it speaks. A press that earns the public's confidence for its reliability, transparency, and high regard for its audiences is a boon to the public, even if that behavior is induced in part by the pressures of the law.

∾

For Earl Warren, *Time, Inc. v. Hill* represented a great failure. Warren had long believed in the importance of curbing certain kinds of harmful speech, such as obscenity, and he was disturbed that he had been unable to persuade the Court to follow his views in *Hill*.[75] To Warren and Fortas, the case was not so much about free speech or privacy as it was about "nontechnical justice," in Leonard Garment's words—"two ordinary American parents touched by near-tragedy and trying to shield themselves and their five young children from the cheapening effects of unwanted and distorted publicity."[76]

Fortas won praise for his dissent from the public and the legal community.[77] Yet he remained bitter about the *Hill* case for the rest of his life. Many years later, he told Garment that no other case during his time on the Court had bothered him so much or so offended his sense of justice.[78] "It was a bad result, and terribly unfair to the Hill family. I offer you my apologies for not being more effective," he said to Garment.[79]

Hill cursed Fortas in other ways. In 1968, Warren was resigning, and a departing President Johnson had tried to put Fortas in the position of Chief Justice to avoid the possibility of a Nixon appointment.[80] But Fortas was undone by a series of scandals. The nomination was blocked in part by revelations that Fortas had given Johnson a good deal of political advice. In May 1969, a *Life* magazine article also revealed that Fortas had accepted a $20,000 honorarium from the financier Louis Wolfson, who was being investigated by the Securities and Exchange Commission. Entitled "Fortas of the Supreme Court: A Question of Ethics," the article was subtitled, "The Justice . . . and the Stock Manipulator." It featured two large pictures of Fortas and Wolfson above a caption asking: "Why would a man of his legal brilliance and high position do business with Louis Wolfson, a well-known corporate stock manipulator known to be under federal investigation?"[81]

Fortas wrote an angry letter to Time, Inc., in which he condemned *Life* for its "brutal and savage assault" against a "defenseless subject." He never mailed the letter.[82] For years, Fortas maintained to friends and colleagues that the *Life* article had been Time, Inc.'s punishment for his role in the *Hill* case.[83] One of the lawyers who worked on the case encountered Fortas many years later, and Fortas said to him: "I'll never forget the *Hill* case and let me tell you, *Life* magazine never forgot it either."[84] When President Nixon found out about the accusations against Fortas, he replied, "Fortas ought to be off of [the Supreme Court]." Spurred by the Nixon administration, the press hounded Fortas.[85] Fortas resigned from the Court in May 1969.

Despite the outcome of the case, *Time, Inc. v. Hill* emboldened Nixon. The praise he received for his oral argument was empowering and encouraging to him.

According to biographer Jonathan Aitken, "Nixon's appearance before the Supreme Court in the *Hill* case marked the zenith of his legal career. In his own mind he had now proved himself on the fast track of the New York bar. This made him feel ready to return to the even faster track of national politics."[86] Bob Haldeman, who had been Nixon's scheduler in the 1960 presidential campaign and his unsuccessful 1962 gubernatorial effort in California, believed that Nixon's years practicing law in New York were "enormously valuable in developing a sense of security that he could compete . . . and that he proved himself."[87] Although Nixon and his impromptu "campaign team" at the law firm had been laying the foundations for a presidential run, Nixon, chronically insecure, remained doubtful about his prospects. Aitken suggests that *Time, Inc. v. Hill* helped Nixon find the confidence he needed to announce his 1968 presidential bid.[88] One of the major themes in his campaign was his opposition to the Warren Court, particularly the Court's criminal procedure decisions. Nixon accused Earl Warren of "coddling criminals."[89] In 1968 Nixon won a narrow victory over Hubert Humphrey, carrying thirty-two states.

With Fortas and Warren departing, Nixon would get to appoint two justices. He appointed Warren Burger Chief Justice and Harry Blackmun to replace Fortas. In 1969, on the last day Warren appeared on the Court before his retirement, Nixon gave an unprecedented address to the Court by a sitting president. He joked, "In 1966, as a member of the Bar, I appeared on two occasions before the Supreme Court. I can say, Mr. Chief Justice, that there is only one ordeal which is more challenging than a Presidential press conference, and that is to appear before the Supreme Court of the United States."[90]

Right after the decision, Nixon had told reporters that he was "pleased" that the Court had upheld the New York privacy law. "From this standpoint," he said, "the court's decision is a historic vindication of the rights of the individual as against abuses of freedom of the press."[91] In reality, he was outraged and offended. Nixon felt he had lost his "war" on the press. As he said to Garment, "I always knew I wouldn't be permitted to win . . . against the press." Nixon told Garment that he "never want[ed] to hear about the *Hill* case again."[92]

Nixon nevertheless continued to think about the *Hill* case into his presidency. A discussion of the *Hill* case appeared in the White House tapes from Watergate. According to a transcript made by the House Judiciary Committee in its impeachment inquiry, Nixon's counsel, John Dean, said that the threat of a libel suit against the press could have a "very sobering effect on several of the national magazines," making them think again before printing "this Watergate junk." This conversation followed:

> Nixon: Well, you of course know, that I said at the time of the Hills' case—well, it is God-damned near impossible for a public figure to win a libel case anymore.
>
> Dean: Yes, sir, it is. To establish 1) malice, or reckless disregard of—no, they're both very difficult.
>
> Nixon: Yeah. Well, malice is impossible, virtually. . . .
>
> Dean: Tough. That's a bad decision, Mr. President. It really is. It was a bad decision.
>
> Nixon: What the hell happened? What's the name of that? I don't remember the case, but it was a horrible decision.
>
> Dean: New York Times v. Sullivan.
>
> Nixon: Sullivan case.
>
> Dean: And it came out of the South on a civil rights. . . .
>
> Nixon: Selma. It was talking about some, some guy that was—yeah, he was a police chief or something. Anyway, I remember reading it at a time when—that's when we were suing Life, you know, for the Hills. When Life was as guilty as hell.
>
> Dean: Did they win it?
>
> Nixon: Supreme Court—four to three. There were a couple of people who couldn't—no, five, five to four, five to three and a half.[93]

Time, Inc. v. Hill also surfaced in a conversation between Nixon and Chief Justice Warren Burger at the beginning of 1973 as Burger was considering the case *Miller v. California*, which dealt with the definition and legality of pornography:

> Burger: I am struggling with this pornography thing. I don't know how we are coming out. I am coming out hard on it.
>
> Nixon: Good, good . . . . Of course I am a square . . . I mean a square in the sense that I read those [obscenity] cases when I did the Hill versus Time thing.
>
> Burger: Yeah.
>
> Nixon: And you know because it related to the whole freedom of the press thing, and let's face it, it's just gone overboard, that's all. It is always a question of balance.[94]

Nixon didn't know that he almost won the *Hill* case.

In 1985, law professor Bernard Schwartz published the draft opinions from *Time, Inc. v. Hill* in his book *The Unpublished Opinions of the Warren Court,* including the Black memorandum and the unpublished Fortas majority opinion.[95] Schwartz obtained this material as he was doing research for a biography of Earl Warren. Anthony Lewis's review of the book for the *New York Times* led with the material on the *Hill* case: "With the background material supplied by Mr. Schwartz, they tell the fascinating story of how the Supreme Court, in the course of deciding the *Hill* case, changed its mind."[96]

One midmorning on a Tuesday in January 1986, shortly after the book came out, Garment got a phone call from Nixon. "Did you see [Anthony] Lewis's review of that book in the Sunday Times?" he asked. "Maybe we'll find out what really happened in that case."[97]

The issue of privacy remained a theme throughout the rest of Nixon's life and career. During his presidency, Nixon installed an elaborate taping system in the White House, broke into the offices and bugged the phones of his rivals, and authorized secret investigations of the sexual and drinking habits of his political enemies. At the same time that he freely invaded others' privacy, he was deeply protective of his own privacy and fought against any kind of exposure. As president he punished journalists who invaded his privacy by having them audited by the IRS and canceling their White House privileges.[98]

In February 1974, in his State of the Union Address, Nixon announced a broad national initiative to "define the nature and extent of the basic extent of the right to privacy" and a proposal to protect citizens from "wiretapping, bugging, and other forms of invasion of privacy."[99] Shortly after, Nixon—revealed by investigative journalists to have been complicit in the bugging of his political opponents and his own staff, and covering up those efforts—resigned the presidency in disgrace. Congress took up the privacy issue, noting in a report the "additional impetus" that came from the "recent revelations connected with Watergate-related investigations, indictments, trials, and convictions."[100] The passage of the 1974 Privacy Act and the Freedom of Information Act were in part responses to Watergate.

Nixon remained a passionate defender of his own privacy. In 1977, upset about having to surrender tape recordings and papers from his presidency under a federal statute that required national archivists to examine information accumulated by the president, Nixon challenged the act's constitutionality on the grounds that it violated his right to privacy. In an opinion by Justice Brennan in *Nixon v. Administrator of General Services*, the Supreme Court upheld the statute, noting that as a public figure, Nixon had surrendered his privacy.[101] Nixon later threatened to sue ABC in connection with the television network's planned presentation of "The Final Days," on Nixon's last months as president. Nixon alleged an invasion of his privacy. A critic in the *New York Times* trenchantly observed that "the decision in *Time, Inc. v. Hill*, though underscoring the emptiness of Mr. Nixon's threats to ABC, should lead us to reconsider his reputation for mirthlessness, for the lawyer who unsuccessfully argued James Hill's case in the Supreme Court . . . was Richard M. Nixon."[102]

≈

Time, Inc. v. Hill represented a lost opportunity for the Court. Despite being handed an ideal set of facts—an innocent, all-American family victimized by one of the nation's most powerful media empires—the Court missed a chance to seriously contemplate the privacy rights of private citizens against the press.

The New York statute, which conditioned liability on commercialization and falsity, obscured the privacy issue in the case. Personal animus also colored the Court's deliberations—Black's dislike of Fortas and Fortas's dislike of the press. The outcome in *Hill* was complicated by the legal confusion around *Griswold* and the dispute over the source and status of the constitutional privacy right.

Coming to the Supreme Court only a year after *Sullivan*, the timing of the case distorted it. Harry Kalven Jr. thought that the Court was "handicapped" by timing. "*Hill* was a curiously difficult case to handle so soon after *New York Times*," he wrote shortly after the decision.[103] As Leonard Garment commented in a 1989 article on the *Hill* case in the *New Yorker*, the case might have gone the other way if Time, Inc. hadn't appealed when it did. "Might the *Hill* decision have been affirmed if Time's appeal to the Supreme Court had not followed so quickly on the heels of *Sullivan* and the surrounding pro-press enthusiasm of . . . the courts?" he asked.[104]

"Would the *Hill* case have engendered an earlier and more constructive exploration of appropriate distinctions between the protection of private and public figures from press comment, as Justice Harlan suggested, if the case had not been distorted by a bitter personal vendetta by one Justice towards another?" Garment wrote. "What might have happened if Watergate had not apotheosized the investigative journalist and made the idea of restraint, self-imposed or court-imposed, anathema to dominant journalistic opinion?" Garment said that the case left him with a "permanent collection of what-ifs."[105] Me too.

What would have happened had the decision gone the other way? Would the press have been "chilled"? Would the coverage of important news have been impaired?

Would the right to privacy have a stronger presence in American law?

Would we have a more respectful culture, with the press leading the way? Could the voyeurism of our twenty-first-century media have been avoided? Could we have reduced the casualties of invasive media exposure?

We can't know for sure. One thing we do know, and that the story of *Time, Inc. v. Hill* makes clear, is that the law's priority of the press over privacy wasn't inevitable but rather a conscious choice. The Court made a choice, but it isn't set in stone.

Acknowledgments

I thank the many individuals who assisted me with this project. I am particularly indebted to Alan Hruska, Stephen Goodman, Don Zoeller, and Douglas Parker, who allowed me to interview them about their experiences with the *Hill* case.

Stephen Wermiel kindly offered his insights from his research on Justice Brennan. Jeffrey Frank shared material from his research on Richard Nixon and the history of Nixon's law firm. I am also grateful to Suzanne Garment for permission to view Leonard Garment's papers held at the Library of Congress.

Fred Konefsky and Jack Schlegel read the manuscript in its entirety and offered constructive comments. I am especially grateful to Fred for his interest in this work.

Many thanks go to the researchers, archivists, and librarians who assisted me with materials at the Library of Congress, the Richard Nixon Presidential Archives, the Mudd Manuscript Library at Princeton University, the Manuscripts and Archives Division at the Yale University Library, the Lilly Library at Indiana University, the Tarlton Law Library at the University of Texas, and the Appellate Division Fourth District Law Library in Rochester.

The librarians at the SUNY Buffalo Law School played an enormous role in making this book happen, as did talented research assistants Kelsey Till, Sarah Handley-Cousins, Katie Horn, and Tara Ward. A grant from the Baldy Center for Law and Social Policy at the SUNY Buffalo Law School helped me with archival research.

As ever, my deepest gratitude goes to Mike Scanlon for his tireless encouragement.

Notes

Introduction

1. Restatement (Second) of Torts § 652D comment g (1977).

2. See Diane L. Zimmerman, "Requiem for a Heavyweight: A Farewell to Warren and Brandeis's Privacy Tort," *Cornell Law Review* 68 (1983): 291; Jonathan Mintz, "The Remains of Privacy's Disclosure Tort: An Exploration of the Private Domain," *Maryland Law Review* 55 (1996): 425, 426; Samantha Barbas, "The Death of the Public Disclosure Tort: A Historical Perspective," *Yale Journal of Law and Humanities* 22 (2010): 171.

3. 47 U.S.C. § 230. Part of the motivation behind the act was to keep the Internet, then an emerging medium, a free and open domain for communication; if web hosts feared being sued for every statement that appeared on their sites, it would have a "chilling effect" on speech and publication. See Anthony Ciolli, "Chilling Effects: The Communications Decency Act and the Online Marketplace of Ideas," *University of Miami Law Review* 63 (2008): 137–268.

4. See Jeanne Hauch, "Protecting Private Facts in France: The Warren and Brandeis Tort Is Alive and Well and Flourishing in Paris," 68 *Tulane Law Review* (1994): 1221; James Q. Whitman, "The Two Western Cultures of Privacy: Dignity Versus Liberty," *Yale Law Journal* 113 (2004): 1169–70; Barbara McDonald, "Privacy, Princesses, and Paparazzi," *New York Law School Law Review* 50 (2005): 205; Ronald J. Krotoszynski Jr., "Reconciling Privacy and Speech in the Era of Big Data: A Comparative Legal Analysis," *William and Mary Law Review* 56 (2015): 1289–90, 1298–1309; Robin Barnes, *Outrageous Invasions: Celebrities' Private Lives, Media, and the Law* (New York: Oxford University Press, 2010).

5. Gert Brüggemier, Aurelia Colombi Ciacchi, and Patrick O'Callaghan, eds., *Personality Rights in European Tort Law* (Cambridge: Cambridge University Press, 2010), 203–205.

6. See David Streitfeld, "European Court Lets Users Erase Records on Web," *New York Times*, May 13, 2014, A1.

7. The article credited with "inventing" the invasion of privacy tort is Samuel D. Warren and Louis D. Brandeis, "The Right to Privacy," *Harvard Law Review* 4 (1890): 193.

8. See, e.g., Daily Times Democrat v. Graham, 276 Ala. 380, 383 (Ala. 1964); Leverton v. Curtis Publishing Co., 97 F. Supp. 181, 182 (E.D. Pa. 1951); Gill v. Hearst Publishing Co., 239 P.2d 636, 638 (Cal. 1952).

9. Griswold v. Connecticut, 381 U.S. 479, 484 (1965).

10. See, e.g., Harriet Pilpel, "Laws of Libel and Privacy Opposite on the See Saw," *Publishers Weekly*, August 31, 1964, 296.

11. William L. Prosser, "Privacy," *California Law Review* 48 (1960): 394.

12. New York Times Co. v. Sullivan, 376 U.S. 254, 273 (1964).

13. Draft opinion, Time, Inc. v. Hill, June 14, 1966, Abe Fortas Papers, Box 31, Folder 699, Yale University Manuscripts and Archives.

14. Ibid., 9–10.

15. Ibid.

16. Justice John Marshall Harlan wrote a partially concurring, partially dissenting opinion.

17. Time, Inc. v. Hill, 385 U.S. 374, 388 (1967).

18. Donald M. Gillmor and Jerome A. Barron, *Mass Communications Law, Cases and Comment* (Minneapolis, MN: West Publishing Co., 1969), 487.

19. The most thorough chronicler of the case was Leonard Garment, the lawyer for the Hills. See Leonard Garment, *Crazy Rhythm: From Brooklyn and Jazz to Nixon's White House, Watergate, and Beyond* (New York: Times Books, 1997), chap. 4; Leonard Garment, "The Hill Case," *New Yorker*, April 17, 1989, 90–110. Law professor and Supreme Court historian Bernard Schwartz wrote a chapter on the case, and the late *New York Times* journalist Anthony Lewis included the story of the case in his book on the *New York Times v. Sullivan* decision and its aftermath. Bernard Schwartz, *The Unpublished Opinions of the Warren Court* (New York: Oxford University Press, 1985), 240–303; Anthony Lewis, *Make No Law: The Sullivan Case and the First Amendment* (New York: Vintage Books, 1991), 184–90. See also Lee Levine and Stephen Wermiel, *The Progeny: Justice William J. Brennan's Fight to Preserve the Legacy of* New York Times v. Sullivan (Washington, D.C.: American Bar Association, 2014), 55–64.

20. On libel, privacy, and freedom of the press between 1900 and 1960, see David Rabban, *Free Speech in Its Forgotten Years, 1870–1920* (Cambridge: Cambridge University Press, 1997); Margaret A. Blanchard, *Revolutionary Sparks: Freedom of Expression in Modern America* (New York: Oxford University Press, 1992); Norman Rosenberg, *Protecting the Best Men: An Interpretive History of the Law of Libel* (Chapel Hill: University of North Carolina Press, 1990); Eric Easton, "The Colonel's Finest Campaign: Robert R. McCormick and Near v. Minnesota," *Federal Communications Law Journal* 60 (2008); Norman Rosenberg, "Taking a Look at 'the Distorted Shape of an Ugly Tree': Efforts at Policy-Surgery on the Law of Libel during the Decade of the 1940s," *Northern Kentucky Law Review* 15 (1988): 11–56; Norman L. Rosenberg, "The New Law of Political Libel: A Historical Perspective," *Rutgers Law Review* 28 (1975) 1141–84.

Major writings on the history of privacy law in the United States include Alan F. Westin, *Privacy and Freedom* (New York: Atheneum, 1967); Robert Ellis Smith, *Ben Franklin's Website: Privacy and Curiosity from Plymouth Rock to the Internet* (Providence, RI: Privacy Journal, 2004); Frederick S. Lane, *American Privacy: The 400-Year History of Our Most Contested Right* (Boston: Beacon Press, 2009); David J. Seipp, "The Right to Privacy in American History" (PhD diss., Harvard University, 1978).

Chapter 1

1. Transcript of Record (TR), Hill v. Hayes, 15 N.Y.2d 986 (1965), 26.

2. U.S. Census, 1910, 1930, 1940; James Jay "Jipper" Hill, *Orlando Sentinel*, March 3, 1993; University of Kansas Yearbooks, 1926–1928.

3. TR, 25–26.

4. Yearbooks, University of Colorado at Boulder, 1927–1930.

5. TR, 27.

6. Fredrick Miller, Morris Vogel, and Allen Davis, *Philadelphia Stories: A Photographic History, 1920–1960* (Philadelphia: Temple University Press, 1988), 281.

7. "Wife Describes 19 Hour Captivity," *Philadelphia Bulletin*, September 14, 1952, 3.

8. Wini Breines, *Young, White, and Miserable: Growing up Female in the Fifties* (Chicago: University of Chicago Press, 1992), 3.

9. Ibid., 4.

10. Inger L. Stole, *Advertising at War: Business, Consumers, and Government in the 1940s* (Urbana: University of Illinois Press, 2012), 179; David Farber, *The Age of Great Dreams: America in the 1960s* (New York: Hill and Wang, 1994), 9.

11. David E. Sumner, *The Magazine Century: American Magazines since 1900* (New York: Peter Lang, 2010), 117.

12. Farber, *Age of Great Dreams*, 9.

13. Paul Levine and Harry Papasotiriou, *America since 1945: The American Moment* (New York: Palgrave Macmillan, 2011), 71.

14. See Elaine Tyler May, *Homeward Bound: American Families in the Cold War Era* (New York: Basic Books, 1990), 3.

15. Allan C. Carlson, "Luce, *Life*, and 'The American Way,'" *This World* 13 (Winter 1986): 69.

16. Joanne Meyerowitz, "Beyond the Feminine Mystique: A Reassessment of Postwar Mass Culture, 1946–1958," *Journal of American History* 79 (1993): 1455, 1460.

17. See generally William Whyte, *The Organization Man* (New York: Simon & Schuster, 1956).

18. Sloan Wilson, *The Man in the Gray Flannel Suit* (New York: Simon & Schuster, 1955), 272.

19. Douglas Miller and Marion Nowak, *The Fifties: The Way We Really Were* (Garden City, NY: Doubleday, 1977), 136.

20. C. Wright Mills, *White Collar: The American Middle Classes* (Oxford: Oxford University Press, 1951); David Riesman, *The Lonely Crowd: A Study of the Changing American Character*, with Nathan Glazer and Reuel Denney (New Haven, CT: Yale University Press, 1950).

21. Miller and Nowak, *The Fifties*, 10.

22. Ibid.

23. Quoted in Breines, *Young, White, and Miserable*, 3.

24. "The American and His Economy," *Life*, December 29, 1952, 31.

25. August Heckscher, "The Invasion of Privacy (II): The Reshaping of Privacy," *American Scholar* 28 (1959): 11–20.

26. "Posse Hunts Three Convicts South of Maryland Border," *Philadelphia Bulletin*, September 14, 1952, 1; "FBI Joints Search," *Philadelphia Bulletin*, September 13, 1952.

27. "Three Escaped Convicts Seize Family, Hold Home 19 Hours to Elude Hunt," *New York Times*, September 13, 1952, 1.

28. "FBI Joins Search."

29. "House Party," *Time*, September 22, 1952, 30; TR, 24.

30. "Three Prison Fugitives Hold Family Captive," *Philadelphia Bulletin*, September 13, 1952.

31. "Wife Describes 19 Hour Captivity."

32. "House Party," 30.

33. "Wife Describes 19 Hour Captivity."

34. TR, 27–28; "Wife Describes 19 Hour Captivity."

35. "House Party," 30.

36. TR, 30–33; "Wife Describes 19 Hour Captivity."

37. TR, 33.

38. James Hill deposition, September 1956, 4, Box 15, Joseph Hayes Papers, Lilly Library, Indiana University.

39. Ibid., 12.

40. Ibid., 4.

41. Breines, *Young, White, and Miserable*, 87–88.

42. Hill deposition, 5.

43. Ibid.

44. TR, 34.

45. "Pardon Me," *Norristown Times-Herald*, September 13, 1952.

46. "House Party," 30.

47. *Norristown Times-Herald*, September 13, 1952, 2.

48. "Three Convicts Elude Posses, Hunt Bogs Down," *Chicago Daily Tribune*, September 15, 1952, C8; "Convict Hunt Abandoned at Pen Mar, Md.," *Washington Post*, September 15, 1952, 13.

49. "Three Escaped Convicts Seize Family"; "Three Escaped Convicts Sought in 4 States," *New York Times*, September 14, 1952, 67.

50. "Two Escapees Slain in Gunfight," *Philadelphia Inquirer*, September 21, 1952.

51. "Schuer, Slain Nolen Brothers Denounced as Mad Dogs," *Philadelphia Bulletin*, September 22, 1952.

52. Hill deposition, 13.

53. "Rendezvous with Death in NYC," *Philadelphia Bulletin*, September 22, 1952.

54. TR, 49, 57.

55. TR, 65.

56. TR, 40.

57. "Hills to Leave Whitemarsh Home Where They Were Kept Captive by Three Escaped Convicts," *Conshohocken Recorder*, November 20, 1952.

58. "Captive Family Moving to Connecticut," *Philadelphia Bulletin*, November 23, 1952.

59. "Hill Unhurt. Car Wrecked in Crash," *Conshohocken Recorder*, November 25, 1952.

60. TR, 51.

Chapter 2

1. "Wife Describes 19 Hour Captivity," *Philadelphia Bulletin*, September 13, 1952.

2. Ray Banta, *Indiana's Laughmakers: The Story of over 400 Hoosiers: Actors, Cartoonists, Writers, and Others* (Indianapolis: PennUltimate Press, 1990); Joseph Hayes and Marrijane Hayes, *And Came the Spring* (New York: Samuel French, 1942), 143; "Joseph Hayes, 88, Author of The Desperate Hours, Dies," *New York Times*, September 20, 2006, C13.

3. Banta, *Indiana's Laughmakers*, 84; N. M. Goodwin, "The Desperate Hours Story," *Hartford Courant*, July 3, 1955, SM6.

4. Brooks Atkinson, "At the Theatre," *New York Times*, January 22, 1949, 10; Sam Zolotow, "Leaf and Bough Dropped $97,500," *New York Times*, January 24, 1949, 16.

5. Transcript of Record (TR), Hill v. Hayes, 15 N.Y.2d 986 (1965), 97.

6. TR, 172–77; "Two Bandits Finally Trapped: Washed-Out Bridge Ends Wild Flight," *San Bernardino County Sun*, June 8, 1949, 1–2; "Catch Gunmen Trio: Wreck Near Here Aids In Nabbing Pair, Third Surrenders; Hitchhiker Also Hurt In Crackup," *Beatrice Daily Sun*, June 7, 1949, 1.

7. "Burglar Terrorizes Family; Uses One Woman for Shield . . . Group Surprises Intruder upon Arrival Home," *Lincoln Star*, October 2, 1947, 11; "Burglar Uses Woman as Shield as He Escapes," *Estherville Daily News*, October 2, 1947, 1.

8. "Gunman Shielded by Hostage Is Shot," *New York Times*, October 10, 1947, 52.

9. TR, 102. "Desperado Is Slain, 2 Caught, in Siege," *New York Times*, March 17, 1951, 13.

10. TR, 100, 155–56.

11. "Escaped Felon Slays Girl Hostage as Policemen Trap and Shoot Him," *New York Times*, June 12, 1952, 11.

12. TR, 157, 158.

13. Mark Zaloudek, "Former Sarasota Author Dies at 88," *Sarasota Herald-Tribune*, September 24, 2006, BV1.

14. James Oliver Brown to Hayes, April 12, 1951, June 13, 1951, Box 15, Joseph Hayes Papers, Lilly Library, Indiana University.

15. Joseph Hayes, "Fiction out of Fact," *New York Times*, January 30, 1955, X1.

16. Hayes to Brown, July 14, 1954, Box 15, Hayes Papers; Bob Thomas, "Hayes Tells How Fortune Is Made from Misfortune," *Odessa American*, August 30, 1954, 4.

17. Joseph Hayes, *The Desperate Hours* (New York: Random House, 1954), 19.

18. Ibid., 20.

19. Ibid., 42.

20. "The Desperate Hours" (Glen Theatre advertisement), *Joplin Globe*, November 16, 1955, 12.

21. Wini Breines, *Young, White, and Miserable: Growing Up Female in the Fifties* (Chicago: University of Chicago Press, 1992), 9.

22. Hayes, "Fiction Out of Fact," X1.

23. "Desperate Fugitive Trio Holds Family in Suspense," *Washington Post*, April 18, 1954.

24. Richard Coe, "Still Exciting, Those Hours," *Washington Post*, November 10, 1955.

25. Whitney Bolton, "Looking Sideways," *Pampa Daily News*, March 14, 1954.

26. "Desperate Fugitive Trio Holds Family in Suspense."

27. Hayes, "Fiction out of Fact."

28. Joseph Hayes, "About the Desperate Hours," *Wings*, March 1954, in TR, 483–84.

29. "The Desperate Hours: Holds Fans Hostage," *Los Angeles Times*, September 25, 1955, D1–2.

30. "Convicts Hide in Home, Hold Family as Hostages," *Philadelphia Inquirer*, February 21, 1954, in TR, 354.

31. "New Hayes Novel Interests Bogart," *New York Times*, May 19, 1954, 36.

32. Louella O. Parsons, "Humphrey Bogart to Make Third Movie, 'The Desperate Hours,' at Paramount," *Lubbock Morning Avalanche*, June 2, 1954, 7; Thomas, "Hayes Tells How Fortune Is Made From Misfortune," 4.

33. Gabriel Miller, *William Wyler: The Life and Films of Hollywood's Most Celebrated Director* (Lexington: University Press of Kentucky, 2013), 320.

34. Press release, Paramount Studios, Joseph Hayes Papers, Lilly Library, Indiana University.

35. "Broadway Drama for Montgomery," *New York Times*, June 19, 1954, 9.

36. TR, 231.

37. "New Thriller on Broadway Is Top Notch," *Chicago Daily Tribune*, February 12, 1955, 15.

38. *Time*, February 21, 1955, 54.

39. Whitney Bolton, "Looking Sideways," *Cumberland Evening Times*, February 22, 1955, 4.

40. Shawn Levy, *Paul Newman: A Life* (New York: Crown, 2009), 105–106.

41. Jack Gaver, "Up and Down Broadway," *Terre Haute Tribune*, March 9, 1955, 4.

42. "Joseph Hayes, 88, Author of The Desperate Hours, Dies," C13.

43. "New Picture," *Time*, October 10, 1955, 116.

44. Miller, *William Wyler*, 320.

45. Coe, "Still Exciting, Those Hours."

46. "The Current Cinema," *New Yorker*, October 15, 1955, 152.

47. L.K., "Spectators Feel Impact in Suspense Play at Tenthouse," *Rhinelander Daily News*, July 3, 1957, 8.

48. "Desperate Hours," *Saturday Review*, October 22, 1955, 30.

49. "New Picture," *Time*, October 10, 1955, 116.

50. Stefan Kanfer, *Tough without a Gun* (New York: Knopf, 2011), 204.

51. Brooks Atkinson, "Theatre," *New York Times*, February 11, 1955, 20.

52. Quoted in Amnon Kabatchnik, *Blood on the Stage, 1950–1975: Milestone Plays of Crime, Mystery, and Detection* (Lanham, MD: Scarecrow Press, 2011), 169.

53. Whitney Bolton, "Looking Sideways," *Cumberland Evening Times*, February 28, 1955, 20.

54. "Two Big Hits in Color" (Osocales Theatre ad), *Santa Cruz Sentinel*, February 3, 1956, 10; "The Desperate Hours" (Lyric Ludington theater ad), *Ludington Daily News*, November 12, 1955, 10; "The Desperate Hours" (Orpheum theater ad), *Atchison Daily Globe*, December 4, 1955, 2.

55. TR, 302.

56. Brief of Appellant, 15 N.Y.2d. 986 (1965), 12.

57. James Hill deposition, September 1956, 43–44, Box 15, Joseph Hayes Papers, Lilly Library, Indiana University.

58. Ibid, 41.

59. Ibid., 47.

60. TR, 61.

61. Ibid., 57–58.

62. Ibid., 369.

63. Transcript of Record, Hill v. Hayes, 18 A.D.2d 485 (N.Y. App. Div. 1963), 639.

Chapter 3

1. James Baughman, "Who Reads Life?" in *Looking at Life Magazine*, ed. Erika Doss (Washington, D.C.: Smithsonian, 2001), 42.

2. Otha Cleo Spencer, "Twenty Years of Life: A Study of Time, Inc.'s Picture Magazine and Its Contributions to Photojournalism" (PhD diss., University of Missouri, 1958), 275.

3. Ibid., 275–76.

4. Baker quoted in Baughman, "Who Reads Life?" 41.

5. Wollcott Gibbs, "Time, Fortune, Life, Luce," *New Yorker*, November 28, 1936, 20. On Time, Inc., see also Robert Vanderlan, *Intellectuals Incorporated: Politics, Art and Ideas in Henry Luce's Media Empire* (Philadelphia: University of Pennsylvania Press, 2011); James L. Baughman, *Henry R. Luce and the Rise of the American News Media* (Baltimore, MD: Johns Hopkins University Press, 2001).

6. Raymond Fielding, "Time Flickers Out: Notes on the Passing of the 'March of Time,' " *Quarterly of Film, Radio and Television* 11 (1957): 354, 357.

7. See Loudon Wainwright, *The Great American Magazine: An Inside History of Life* (New York: Ballantine Books, 1988), 33; Alan Brinkley, *The Publisher: Henry Luce and His American Century* (New York: Vintage Books, 2011), 208–16; Doss, *Looking at Life*, 1–4; Robert Elson, *Time, Inc.: The Intimate History of a Publishing Enterprise*, vol. 1 (New York: Atheneum, 1968), 280–98.

8. William Brinkley, *The Fun House* (New York: Random House, 1961), 258.

9. David Welky, *Everything Was Better in America: Print Culture in the Great Depression* (Champaign: University of Illinois Press, 2008), 98.

10. Hedley Donovan, *Right Places, Right Times* (New York, Touchstone, 1991), 157–62. The standard biography on Luce is Brinkley, *The Publisher*.

11. Theodore White, *In Search of History: A Personal Adventure* (New York: Harper-Collins, 1979), 206.

12. Richard Clurman, *Beyond Malice: The Media's Years of Reckoning* (New York: Transaction Books, 1988), 2.

13. Luce, "Original Picture Magazine Prospectus," quoted in Elson, *Intimate History*, 279.

14. Wainwright, *Great American Magazine*, 33.

15. Elson, *Intimate History*, 344.

16. Wainwright, *Great American Magazine*, 116.

17. Elson, *Time, Inc.*, 294.

18. Brinkley, *The Fun House*, 392; Allan C. Carlson, "Luce, Life, and the American Way," *This World* (Winter 1986): 56–74.

19. Spencer, "Twenty Years of Life," 393.

20. Ibid., 396.

21. Elson, *Time, Inc.*, 418.

22. Wainwright, *Great American Magazine*, 193.

23. Stanley Rayfield, *How Life Gets the Story: Behind the Scenes in Photojournalism* (New York: Doubleday, 1955).

24. Wainwright, *Great American Magazine*, 33.

25. Baughman, *Henry R. Luce*, 151; Wendy Kozol, *Life's America: Family and Nation in Postwar Journalism* (Philadelphia: Temple University Press, 1994), 5.

26. "The American and His Economy," *Life*, January 5, 1953.

27. Wendy Kozol, "The Kind of People Who Make Good Americans," in *Looking for America: The Visual Production of Nation and People,* ed. Ardis Cameron (Oxford: Blackwell, 2005), 178.

28. Alfred Politz Research, *A Study of Four Media* (New York: Time, Inc., 1953), 18.

29. Jeanne Harman, *Such Is Life* (New York: Thomas Crowell, 1956), 8.

30. Spencer, "Twenty Years of Life," 307.

31. Ibid., 312.

32. Elson, *Time, Inc.*, 419.

33. Transcript of Record (TR), Hill v. Hayes, 15 N.Y.2d 986 (1965), 184.

34. Carol Channing, *Just Lucky I Guess: A Memoir of Sorts* (New York: Simon & Schuster, 2002), 111.

35. Doss, *Looking at Life*, 14 (noting that most *Life* staffers came from the professional managerial class; disproportionately represented were graduates from Harvard and Yale).

36. Wainwright, *Great American Magazine*, 184; Yale Yearbooks, 1928–1930; "Prideaux, Ex-Hillsdaleite, Man on Aisle at 4,000," *Hillsdale Daily News*, November 26, 1963, 9.

37. "Man on the Aisle at 4000 Plays," *Life*, November 22, 1963, 3.

38. Wainwright, *Great American Magazine*, 223.

39. Hamblin, *That Was the Life*, 274.

40. On Smith, see Sarah Boxer, "Bradley Smith, 87, Champion of the Rights of Photographers," *New York Times*, September 7, 1997, 52.

41. Letter, n.d., from Smith to A. J. Malino, Box 3, Folder 1, Hayes Papers, Lilly Library, Indiana University.

42. N. M. Goodwin, "The 'Desperate Hours' Story," *Hartford Courant*, July 3, 1955, SM6.

43. TR, 192. See also Bradley Smith to A. J. Malino, February 26, 1957, Joseph Hayes Papers, Lilly Library, Indiana University.

44. Ibid., 122.

45. Ibid., 180.

46. Ibid., 280.

47. Ibid., 199.

48. Piri Halasz, *A Memoir of Creativity: Abstract Painting, Politics and the Media, 1956–2008* (Bloomington, IN: iUniverse, 2009), 51.

49. Dwight Macdonald, "Time, Fortune, Life," *Nation*, May 22, 1937, 585. The researchers were derisively called "eeck girls" by male staff. They were said to exclaim "eeck" "in bursts of enthusiasm" when something pleased them. Edward K. Thompson, *A Love Affair with Life and Smithsonian* (Columbia: University of Missouri Press, 1995), 40.

50. TR, 128.

51. Ibid., 198.

52. Ibid., 205.

53. Wainwright, *Great American Magazine*, 180.

54. On Thompson, see Hamblin, *That Was the Life*, 203–17; Wainwright, *Great American Magazine*, 177–90.

55. Wainwright, *Great American Magazine*, 177; Charles Champlin, *A Life in Writing: The Story of an American Journalist* (Syracuse, NY: Syracuse University Press, 2006), 130.

56. Elson, *Time, Inc.*, 189.

57. Wainwright, *Great American Magazine*, 162.

58. Ibid., 189.

59. TR, 204.

60. Brinkley, *The Fun House*, 9.

61. TR, 216.

62. Ibid., 207.

63. Dwight Macdonald, "Time and Henry Luce," *Nation*, May 1, 1937, 501.

64. David E. Sumner, *The Magazine Century: American Magazines since 1900* (New York: Peter Lang Publishing, 2010), 63.

65. John K. Jessup, ed., *The Ideas of Henry Luce* (New York: Atheneum, 1969), 70.

66. Clurman, *Beyond Malice*, 2, 87, Donovan, *Right Places, Right Times*, 333.

67. Ibid., 3.

68. Jessup, *Ideas of Henry Luce*, 71.

69. "Canons of Journalism," *Annals of the American Academy of Political and Social Science* 109 (September 1923): 305–306.

70. Robert D. Leigh, ed., *A Free and Responsible Press: A General Report on Mass Communication: Newspapers, Radio, Motion Pictures, Magazines, and Books* (Chicago: University of Chicago Press, 1947), 21.

71. On "dotting," see Champlin, *A Life in Writing*, 128; W. A. Swanberg, *Luce and His Empire* (New York: Scribner, 1972), 261–64.

72. Spencer, "Twenty Years of Life," 309.

73. David Cort, "Once upon a Time, Inc.: Mr. Luce's Fact Machine," *Nation*, February 18, 1956, 135.

74. Swanberg, *Luce and His Empire*, 258.

75. John Kobler, *Luce: His Time, Life, and Fortune* (Garden City, NY: Doubleday, 1968), 202–3.

76. Ibid., 204.

77. Champlin, *A Life in Writing*, 128–29.

78. White, *In Search of History*, 207.

79. David Cort, *The Sin of Henry R. Luce* (Fort Lee, NJ: Lyle Stuart, 1974), 86.

80. Swanberg, *Luce and His Empire*, 259.

81. Ibid., 257.

82. Ibid., 258.

83. TR, 285.

84. Ibid., 287.

85. Ibid., 295.

86. Wainwright, *Great American Magazine*, 239.

87. Ibid.; Hamblin, *That Was the Life*, 117.

88. Champlin, *A Life in Writing*, 161.

89. Ibid.

90. Hamblin, *That Was the Life*, 117.

91. Wainwright, *Great American Magazine*, 240.

92. Ibid.

93. TR, 239.

94. "True Crime Inspires Tense Play," *Life*, February 28, 1955, 75.

95. TR, 240.

96. "True Crime Inspires Tense Play," 75.

97. Ibid.

98. TR, 288.

99. Ibid., 251.

100. "True Crime Inspires Tense Play," 75.

101. Ibid.

102. Ibid.

103. Ibid., 76.

104. Ibid., 78.

105. TR, 62.

106. Ibid.

Chapter 4

1. Transcript of Record (TR), Hill v. Hayes, 15 N.Y.2d 986 (1965), 65.

2. David Engel, "Perception and Decision at the Threshold of Tort Law: Explaining the Infrequency of Claims," *DePaul Law Review* 62 (2013): 293–94.

3. Frank Thayer, "The Changing Libel Scene," *Wisconsin Law Review* 1943 (1943): 341.

4. Clifford G. Christians, John P. Ferré, and P. Mark Fackler, *Good News: Social Ethics and the Press* (New York: Oxford University Press, 1993), 74 ("Angered by the way that the media treated them, [libel plaintiffs] decide to sue in order to punish the media and to restore their reputations, not to win large settlements or awards"). Randall P. Bezanson, Gilbert Cranberg, and John Soloski, *Libel Law and the Press: Myth and Reality* (New York: Free Press, 1987), 94. ("The objectives of restoring reputation and punishing the media were largely served by the very act of commencing the libel suit itself.")

5. Kenneth S. Abraham, *The Liability Century: Insurance and Tort Law from the Progressive Era to 9/11* (Cambridge, MA: Harvard University Press, 2008), 83–85.

6. C. Wright Mills, *White Collar: The American Middle Classes* (New York: Oxford University Press, 1951), 123. On the history of Mudge, Rose, see Thomas W. Evans, "Mudge Rose Guthrie Alexander & Ferdon" (unpublished manuscript, n.d.). Courtesy of Jeffrey Frank.

7. Ibid., 123. See also *Martindale-Hubbell Law Directory* (New Providence, NJ: Martindale-Hubbell Law Directory, 1954).

8. Ibid., 124; "Law Firm Rents Large New Space," *New York Times*, March 22, 1955, 50.

9. Paul Hoffman, *Lions in the Street: The Inside Story of the Great Wall Street Law Firms* (New York: New American Library, 1973), 108.

10. Ibid.

11. Jonathan Aitken, *Nixon: A Life* (Washington, D.C.: Regnery, 1996), 363.

12. Paul Hoffman, "Mudge, Rose & Alexander: The Firm to See?" *New York Magazine*, April 26, 1971, 37, 40.

13. *Martindale-Hubbell Law Directory*.

14. Leonard Garment, *Crazy Rhythm: From Brooklyn and Jazz to Nixon's White House, Watergate, and Beyond* (Cambridge, MA: Da Capo Press, 1997), 61.

15. Aitken, *Nixon*, 363.

16. Garment, *Crazy Rhythm*, 61.

17. Ibid.

18. Aitken, *Nixon*, 310; James Fallows, "Remembering Leonard Garment," *Atlantic*, July 15, 2013.

19. Garment, *Crazy Rhythm*, 103. Leonard Garment passed away in 2013. For a sampling of tributes to Garment, see Eric Lichtblau, "Leonard Garment, Lawyer and Nixon Adviser during Watergate, Dies at 89," *New York Times*, July 15, 2013; James Fallows, "Remembering Leonard Garment," *Atlantic*, July 15, 2013; Emily Langer, "Leonard Garment, Lawyer to President Nixon during Watergate Scandal, Dies at 89," *Washington Post*, July 16, 2013; "Leonard Garment Dies at 89; Advised President Nixon during Watergate," *Los Angeles Times*, July 15, 2013.

20. Garment, *Crazy Rhythm*, 22.

21. Ibid., 41–42.

22. "Adhere to Legal Ethics, Jurist Tells Law School Grads," *Brooklyn Daily Eagle*, June 10, 1949, 9; "To Address Fellow Law School Grads," *Brooklyn Daily Eagle*, February 17, 1959, 15.

23. Erwin Orson Smigel, *The Wall Street Lawyer: Professional Organization Man?* (Bloomington: Indiana University Press, 1969), 44–45, 65. According to one sociologist who conducted an extensive study of law firms in the 1950s and 1960s, "The firms probably feel they must consider a man's religion because, as one hiring partner puts it, 'prejudice is very strong among many clients. . . . There are clients to whom you can't take a Jewish lawyer; sometimes Catholic lawyers present problems, too, but not as often.'"

24. In 1942, a recent law graduate, Helen Silving, found herself on Wall Street, "behind a desk in one of the many rooms occupied by the venerable law firm of Mudge, Stern, Williams, and Tucker. The atmosphere of the office was anything but reassuring to a timid

soul such as myself." She had the feeling that every minute of the working day she was "on trial," even though she knew there was nothing she could expect if she passed the test—women would be fired at war's end to make room for returning veterans. Helen Silving, *Helen Silving: Memoirs* (New York: Vantage Press, 1988), 310.

25. Lincoln Caplan, *Skadden: Power, Money, and the Rise of a Legal Empire* (New York: Farrar, Straus and Giroux, 1994), 154.

26. Garment, *Crazy Rhythm*, 61.

27. Ibid., 62.

28. Ibid., 61; Wright v. Carter Products, Inc., 244 F.2d 53 (2d Cir. 1957).

29. Douglas Parker interview, February 2015.

30. Garment, *Crazy Rhythm*, 53.

31. Ibid., 80–82.

32. Clarence Morris, "Inadvertent Newspaper Libel and Retraction," *Illinois Law Review* 32 (1937): 38. "Ordinary newspaper practice is to follow inadvertent libel by offer to retract as soon as the newspaper discovers its mistake."

33. Eustace Cullinan, "The Rights of Newspapers: May They Print Whatever They Choose?" *American Bar Association Journal* 41 (1955): 1023.

34. Lee Hills, "Libel—Woe of the Weak," *Bulletin of the American Society of Newspaper Editors*, February 19, 1962, 6.

35. "Developments in the Law: Defamation," *Harvard Law Review* 69 (1956): 907; Thayer, "The Changing Libel Scene," 342. ("If . . . a retraction is made in good faith, and is used promptly, damages may be mitigated, although the publisher will not necessarily be exonerated from his original carelessness, or recklessness, in publishing the libel.") On retraction statutes, see 344–46.

36. *Libel Law and the Press*, 43; William G. Flanagan, "Gerald Levin: When in Doubt, Merge," in *Dirty Rotten CEOs: How Business Leaders Are Fleecing America*, ed. William G. Flanagan (New York: Citadel Press, 2004), 167.

37. Richard Clurman, *Beyond Malice: The Media's Years of Reckoning* (New York: Transaction Publishers, 2011), 162.

38. Untitled, November 28, 1935, Arthur Hays Sulzberger Papers, Box 196, Folder 17, Manuscripts and Archives Division, New York Public Library.

39. Hills, "Libel," 5.

40. John Kobler, *Luce; His Time, Life, and Fortune* (St. Louis: MacDonald, 1968), 158.

41. Hewitt Griggs Robertson, "Letters to the Editor," *Life*, August 12, 1946, 2.

42. "Letters to the Editors," *Life*, February 21, 1938, 2.

43. "Letters to the Editors," *Life*, August 26, 1940, 2, 4.

44. Garment, *Crazy Rhythm*, 90.

45. On the pre-twentieth-century history of defamation, especially the law of libel, see Norman Rosenberg, *Protecting the Best Men: An Interpretive History of the Law of Libel* (Chapel Hill: University of North Carolina Press, 1990); Randall Bezanson, "The Libel Tort Today," *Washington and Lee Law Review* 45 (1988): 536–39; Robert Post, "The Social Foundations of Defamation Law: Reputation and the Constitution," *California Law Review* 74 (1986): 693–707; William Prosser, "Libel Per Quod," *Virginia Law Review* 46 (1960):

841–43; Stanley Ingber, "Defamation: A Conflict between Reason and Decency," *Virginia Law Review* 65 (1979): 796–801; Van Vechten Veeder, "The History and Theory of the Law of Defamation," *Columbia Law Review* 4 (1904); Roger Shuy, *The Language of Defamation Cases* (New York: Oxford University Press, 2010), 16–22.

46. "Developments in the Law: Defamation," *Harvard Law Review* 69 (1956): 945–46.

47. Rosenberg, *Protecting the Best Men*, chap. 1.

48. William Blake Odgers, *A Digest of the Law of Libel and Slander*, ed. James Bromley Eames (London, 1911), 32.

49. "Developments in the Law: Defamation," 906.

50. Ibid., 905.

51. Martin Newell, *The Law of Libel and Slander in Civil and Criminal Cases* (Chicago: Callaghan and Company, 1898), 564.

52. Stanley Walker, *City Editor* (Baltimore, MD: Johns Hopkins University Press, 1999), 186. "The law of libel is the newspaper man's most constant nightmare." Robert Miller Neal, *Newspaper Desk Work* (New York: Appleton, 1933), 289.

53. "Detecting Libel before It Appears," *Editor and Publisher*, May 29, 1937, 7.

54. Burton Rascoe, "Libel's Lawyer," *Esquire*, August 1938, 103.

55. Odgers, *A Digest of the Law*, 18.

Chapter 5

1. Leverton v. Curtis Publishing Co., 97 F. Supp. 181, 182 (E.D. Pa. 1951).

2. Don R. Pember, *Privacy and the Press: The Law, the Mass Media, and the First Amendment* (Seattle: University of Washington Press, 1972), 10.

3. Michael Winship, "The Rise of a National Book Trade System in the United States," in *A History of the Book in America*, vol. 4, ed. Carl F. Kaestle and Janice A. Radway (Chapel Hill: University of North Carolina Press, 2009), 57, 60–61; David Sumner, *The Magazine Century* (New York: Peter Lang, 2010), 16; Carl F. Kaestle and Janice A. Radway, "A Framework for the History of Publishing and Reading in the United States, 1880–1940," *A History of the Book in America*, 10.

4. John D. Stevens, *Sensationalism and the New York Press* (New York: Columbia University Press, 1991), 65.

5. Leonard Teel, *The Public Press, 1900–1945* (Westport, CT: Praeger, 2006), 7.

6. Joseph B. Bishop, "Newspaper Espionage," *Forum*, August 1886, 534.

7. "The Right to Privacy," *Youth's Companion*, December 10, 1891, 641.

8. "The Right of Privacy," *New York Times*, July 19, 1896, 11.

9. "Newspaper Brutality," *Christian Union*, December 5, 1889, 708.

10. "The Right of Privacy," *New York Times*, August 23, 1902, 8.

11. "Sensational Newspaper Sins," *Evening Telegram*, June 22, 1896, 3.

12. Elbridge Adams, "The Right of Privacy and Its Relation to the Law of Libel," *Journal of Social Science* 41 (1903): 104.

13. Pember, *Privacy and the Press*, 21; Dorothy J. Glancy, "The Invention of the Right to Privacy," *Arizona Law Review* 21 (1979): 5.

14. Glancy, "Invention," 5; Amy Gajda, "What If Samuel D. Warren Hadn't Mar-

ried a Senator's Daughter? Uncovering the Press Coverage That Led to 'The Right to Privacy,'" *Michigan State Law Review* 1 (2008): 37. See also James H. Barron, "Warren and Brandeis, The Right to Privacy: Demystifying a Landmark Citation," *Suffolk University Law Review* 13 (1979): 892–93; William Prosser, "Privacy," *California Law Review* 48 (1960): 383; Alpheus Thomas Mason, *Brandeis: A Free Man's Life* (New York: Viking Press, 1956), 70.

15. Samuel D. Warren and Louis D. Brandeis, "The Right to Privacy," *Harvard Law Review* 4 (1890): 193.

16. Ibid., 214.

17. Ibid.

18. On the concept of dignity in the nineteenth-century United States, see Lawrence Friedman, *The Republic of Choice: Law, Authority, and Culture* (Cambridge: Harvard University Press, 1998), 41. See also Edward Ayers, *Vengeance and Justice: Crime and Punishment in the 19th Century American South* (New York: Oxford University Press, 1984), 19.

19. See William Prosser, "Intentional Infliction of Mental Suffering: A New Tort," *Michigan Law Review* 37 (1939): 880.

20. Quoted in Alpheus Thomas Mason, *Brandeis: A Free Man's Life* (New York: Viking Press, 1946), 366.

21. Ken Gormley, "One Hundred Years of Privacy," *Wisconsin Law Review* 1992 (1992): 1335, 1343.

22. John W. Johnson, *Griswold v. Connecticut: Birth Control and the Constitutional Right of Privacy* (Lawrence: University Press of Kansas, 2005), 56–57.

23. Alan F. Westin, *Privacy and Freedom* (New York: Atheneum Books, 1967), 333.

24. Union Pac. Ry. Co. v. Botsford, 141 U.S. 250 (1891); Thomas M. Cooley, *A Treatise on the Law of Torts, or the Wrongs Which Arise Independent of Contract* (Chicago: Callaghan, 1880), 29.

25. Boyd v. U.S., 116 U.S. 616, 630 (1886).

26. Ibid., 633–34.

27. Johnson, *Griswold v. Connecticut*, 55.

28. Westin, *Privacy and Freedom*, 331.

29. Henry Billings Brown, "The Liberty of the Press," *American Law Review* 24 (1900): 321, 329.

30. Archibald McClean, "The Right of Privacy," *Green Bag* 15 (1903): 497.

31. "St. Louis, January 23, 1891, Additional Material," *Central Law Journal*, January 23, 1891, 69.

32. N.Y. Civ. Rights Law § 50, 51 (1903).

33. Roberson v. Rochester Folding Box Co., 64 N.E. 442, 443 (N.Y. 1902).

34. "The Right of Privacy," *Los Angeles Times*, July 28, 1905, 4.

35. Thompson v. Tillford, 137 N.Y.S. 523, 523 (App. Div. 1912).

36. Moser v. Press Publishing Co., 59 Misc. 78, 81 (N.Y. Sup. Ct. 1908).

37. Samantha Barbas, "From Privacy to Publicity: The Tort of Appropriation in the Age of Mass Consumption," *Buffalo Law Review* 61 (2013): 1142–43.

38. Louis Nizer, "The Right of Privacy: A Half Century's Developments," *Michigan*

Law Review 39 (1940): 536. See also Basil Kacedan, "The Right of Privacy," *Boston University Law Review* 12 (1932); Gerald Dicklcr, "Right of Privacy—A Proposed Redefinition," *United States Law Review* 70 (1936); Roy Moreland, "Right of Privacy Today," *Kentucky Law Journal* 19 (1931); L. S. Clemons, "Right of Privacy in Relation to the Publication of Photographs," *Marquette Law Review* 14 (1930); Edward Doan, "The Newspaper and the Right of Privacy," *Journal of the Bar Association of Kansas* 5 (1937): 203–61.

39. *Restatement (First) of Torts* § 867 (1939).

40. "Recent Developments in the Right of Privacy," *University of Chicago Law Review* 15 (1948): 926.

41. Ibid.

42. David E. Kyvig, *Daily Life in the United States, 1920–1940* (Chicago: Ivan R. Dee, 2004), 190–91.

43. Charles Sprague, "Our Free Press. How Free?" *Nieman Reports* (January 1953): 3.

44. Sean Cashman, *America in the Twenties and Thirties: The Olympian Age of Franklin Delano Roosevelt* (New York: New York University Press, 1989), 326.

45. Newman Levy, "The Right to Be Let Alone," *American Mercury* (June 1935): 197.

46. Harry Shaw, "Pocket and Pictorial Journalism," *North American Review* 243 (1937): 303.

47. H. L. Smith, "The News Camera on Trial," *Forum and Century* 5 (1937): 267–69.

48. Leon R. Yankwich, "The Right of Privacy," *Notre Dame Lawyer* 27 (1951): 525.

49. George Seldes, "The Press and the Individual," in *Killing the Messenger: 100 Years of Media Criticism*, ed. Tom Goldstein (New York: Columbia University Press, 1989), 31.

50. Lewis Nichols, "Our Sacred Privacy Becomes a Memory: No Longer Can We Sit and Think Alone in Peace, or Even Just Sit," *New York Times*, October 11, 1931, 8.

51. Ibid., 16.

52. Mitchell Dawson, "Law and the Right of Privacy," *American Mercury* (October 1948): 397.

53. Mitchell Dawson, "Paul Pry and Privacy," *Atlantic Monthly* (October 1932): 385; Meyer Berger, "Surrender of Privacy," *Scribner's*, April 1939, 16.

54. J. A. Thalheimer and J. R. Gerberick, "Reader Attitudes toward Questions of Newspaper Policy and Practice," *Journalism Quarterly* 12 (1935): 268, 270.

55. Charles E. Swanson, "The Midcity Daily," *Journalism Quarterly* 26 (1949): 24.

56. Marlin Pew, "The Press and Personal Privacy," *Chino Champion*, April 26, 1935, 2.

57. "Judge Discusses Privacy Right in Baltimore Damage Suit," *Editor and Publisher*, December 24, 1932, 14.

58. Peed v. Washington Times, 55 Wash. L. Rep 182–183 (D.C. 1927).

59. Melvin v. Reid, 112 Cal. App. 285, 292–293 (Cal. Dist. Ct. App. 1931).

60. Peay v. Curtis, 78 F. Supp. 305, 306 (D.D.C. 1948).

61. Ibid., 309.

62. "Canons of Journalism," *Annals of the American Academy of Political and Social Science* 109 (September 1923): 305–6.

63. Stanley Walker, *City Editor* (Baltimore: Johns Hopkins University Press, 1999), 171.

64. Silas Bent, *Ballyhoo: The Voice of the Press* (New York: Boni & Liveright, 1927), 68.

65. Nancy Mavity, *The Modern Newspaper* (New York: Holt, 1930), 36.

66. "Right of Privacy Undetermined," *Editor and Publisher*, April 25, 1936, 113, 122.

Chapter 6

1. U.S. Const. Amend. I § 2

2. Paul Murphy, "*Near v. Minnesota* in the Context of Historical Developments," *Minnesota Law Review* 66 (1981): 106–9.

3. James Magee, *Mr. Justice Black: Absolutist on the Court* (Charlottesville: University Press of Virginia, 1980), 50–51; Zechariah Chafee, "Book Review," *Harvard Law Review* 71 (1962): 898, reprinted in Robert G. McCloskey, ed., *Essays in Constitutional Law* (New York: Random House, 1957), 281, 290.

4. See, e.g., Edward S. Corwin, "Freedom of Speech and Press under the First Amendment: A Résumé," *Yale Law Journal* 30 (1920): 48 ; W. R. Vance, "Freedom of Speech and of the Press," *Minnesota Law Review* 2 (1918); Leonard W. Levy, *Legacy of Suppression: Freedom of Speech and Press in Early American History* (Cambridge: Belknap Press, 1960); David Lange, "The Speech and Press Clauses," *UCLA Law Review* 23 (1975): 97; David Anderson, "The Origins of the Press Clause," *UCLA Law Review* 30 (1982): 487–88; Leonard Levy, "On the Origins of the Free Press Clause," *UCLA Law Review* 32 (1984): 202–3.

5. See David Anderson, "Freedom of the Press," *Texas Law Review* 80 (2002); C. Edwin Baker, "The Independent Significance of the Press Clause under Existing Law," *Hofstra Law Review* 35 (2007): 956.

6. David Rabban, *Free Speech in Its Forgotten Years, 1870–1920* (Cambridge: Cambridge University Press, 1997), 132; Levy, "Origins," 204.

7. Paul Murphy, "*Near v. Minnesota* in the Context of Historical Developments," *Minnesota Law Review* 66 (1981): 114, quoting State ex rel. Olson v. Guilford, 174 Minn. 457, 460 (1928).

8. Rabban, *Forgotten Years*, 142.

9. Ibid.

10. Ibid., 144.

11. Patterson v. Colorado, 205 U.S. 454, 462 (1907).

12. Rabban, *Forgotten Years*,175.

13. "Notes of Cases," *Virginia Law Register* 11 (1905–1906): 63.

14. John Gilmer Speed, "The Right of Privacy," *North American Review* 163 (1896): 74.

15. "Rights in a Portrait," *Case and Comment* 9 (1902): 15.

16. Corliss v. E. W. Walker Co., 57 F. 434 (C.C.D. Mass. 1893).

17. Ibid. See also Atkinson v. John E. Doherty & Co., 121 Mich. 372, 377, 80 N.W. 285, 287 (Mich. 1899).

18. Harry Kalven Jr., *A Worthy Tradition: Freedom of Speech in America*, ed. Jamie Kalven (New York: Harper & Row, 1988), 167.

19. Frederick Siebert, "Legal Developments Affecting the Press," *Annals of the American Academy of Political and Social Science* 219 (1942): 93.

20. Gitlow v. People of State of New York, 268 U.S. 652, 666 (1925).

21. Schenck v. United States, 249 U.S. 47, 52 (1919).

22. Murphy, "*Near v. Minnesota*," 138.

23. Whitney v. California, 274 U.S. 357, 374–75 (1927) (Brandeis, J., concurring).

24. Michael Kent Curtis, *Free Speech: The People's Darling Privilege* (Durham, NC: Duke University Press, 2000), 398.

25. Palko v. State of Connecticut, 302 U.S. 319, 327 (1937).

26. See, e.g., Wallace Mendelson, "Clear and Present Danger—From *Schenck* to *Dennis*," *Columbia Law Review* 52 (1952): 313–33.

27. Magee, *Justice Black*, 81.

28. Thornhill v. State of Alabama, 310 U.S. 88, 102 (1940).

29. Grosjean v. American Press Co., 297 U.S. 233, 243 (1936).

30. Siebert, "Legal Developments," 94.

31. See Eric Easton, "The Colonel's Finest Campaign: Robert R. McCormick and *Near v. Minnesota*," *Federal Communications Law Journal* 60 (2008): 184.

32. Frank Thayer, "The Changing Libel Scene," *Wisconsin Law Review* 1943 (1943): 331.

33. Samuel Walker, *In Defense of American Liberties: A History of the ACLU* (New York: Oxford University Press, 1999), 19.

34. Near v. Minnesota, 283 U.S. 697 (1931).

35. Edward Deutsch, "Freedom of the Press and of the Mails," *Michigan Law Review* 36 (1938): 749; Easton, "Colonel's Finest Campaign," 184.

36. Bridges v. State of Cal., 314 U.S. 252, 270 (1946).

37. Winters v. New York, 333 U.S. 507, 510 (1948).

38. See Thomas Emerson, "Towards a General Theory of the First Amendment," *Yale Law Journal* 72 (1963): 877–955.

39. Chaplinsky v. New Hampshire, 315 U.S. 568, 572 (1942). See also Beauharnais v. Illinois, 343 U.S. 250, 266 (1952) ("Libelous utterances not being within the area of constitutionally protected speech, it is unnecessary, either for us or for the State courts, to consider the issues behind the phrase 'clear and present danger.' Certainly no one would contend that obscene speech, for example, may be punished only upon a showing of such circumstances. Libel, as we have seen, is in the same class.").

40. See Samuel D. Warren and Louis D. Brandeis, "The Right to Privacy," *Harvard Law Review* 4 (1890): 214–15.

41. *Restatement (First) of Torts* § 867 comment c. (1939).

42. Chaplin v. National Broadcasting Co., 15 F.R.D. 134, 139 (S.D.N.Y. 1953).

43. Cohen v. Marx, 94 Cal. App.2d 704, 705 (1949).

44. *Restatement (First) of Torts* § 867 comment c. (1939).

45. Ibid., comment d. "One who unwillingly comes into the public eye because of his own fault, as in the case of a criminal, is subject to . . . limitations upon his right to be let alone. Community custom achieves the same result with reference to one unjustly charged with crime or the subject of a striking catastrophe. Both groups of persons are the objects of legitimate public interest during a period of time after their conduct or misfortune has brought them to public attention." Ibid., comment c.

46. Jones v. Herald Post Co., 18 S.W.2d 972, 972–73 (Ky. Ct. App. 1929).

47. See Chaplinsky v. New Hampshire, 315 U.S. 568 (1942); Beauharnais v. Illinois, 343 U.S. 250 (1952).

48. Lahiri v. Daily Mirror, Inc., 294 N.Y.S. 382, 388 (N.Y. Sup. Ct. 1937).

49. Kapellas v. Kofman, 459 P.2d 912, 923–24 (Cal. 1969); Blount v. T. D. Publishing, 423 P.2d 421 (N.M. 1966).

50. Moser v. Press Publishing, 109 N.Y.S. 963 (Sup. Ct. 1908).

51. Colyer v. Richard K. Fox Publishing Co., 162 A.D. 297, 298–99 (2d Dep't 1914).

52. Sweenek v. Pathe News, Inc., 16 F. Supp. 746, 747 (E.D.N.Y. 1936).

53. D'Altomonte v. New York Herald Co., 154 A.D. 453 (1st Dep't 1913).

54. Sutton v. Hearst Corp., 277 A.D. 155, 157 (1st Dep't 1950).

55. Ibid., 161, 164 (Peck, J., dissenting).

56. Ettore v. Philco Television Broadcasting Corp., 229 F.2d 481, 485 (3d Cir. 1956).

57. Complaint, Hill v. Hayes, 155 N.Y.S.2d 234 (N.Y. Sup. Ct. 1956), 434. The complaint is part of the Transcript of Record (TR) on appeal (Hill v. Hayes, 15 N.Y.2d 986).

58. Leonard Garment, *Crazy Rhythm: From Brooklyn and Jazz to Nixon's White House, Watergate, and Beyond* (Cambridge, MA: Da Capo Press, 1997), 93.

59. Complaint, Hill v. Hayes, 434.

60. Ibid., 426–27.

61. Ibid., 429.

62. Ibid., 431.

63. Ibid., 436.

64. An amended complaint and second amended complaint, in March 1956 and July 1956, asked for a total of $500,000 for James and Elizabeth, from all of the defendants. See Second Amended Complaint, TR, 481.

Chapter 7

1. John Kobler, *Luce: His Time, Life and Fortune* (New York: Doubleday, 1968), 158.

2. Charles Champlin, *A Life in Writing: The Story of an American Journalist* (Syracuse: Syracuse University Press, 2006), 132.

3. "John F. Dowd Dead; Ex-Time Aide Was 60: A Lawyer, He Was Chief Editorial Counsel for 28 Years Prior to 1973 Retirement," *New York Times*, February 17, 1977, 42.

4. "E. Gabriel Perle," *Greenwich Time*, August 10, 2014.

5. "John F. Dowd Dead"; Richard M. Clurman, *Beyond Malice: The Media's Years of Reckoning* (New York: Transaction Publishing, 1988), 164.

6. Champlin, *A Life in Writing*, 131.

7. Ibid., 132.

8. M. Marvin Berger, "Detecting Libel before It Appears," *Editor and Publisher*, May 29, 1937.

9. "Publishers' Corner," *Saturday Review of Literature*, July 15, 1950, 26.

10. Alan Hruska interview, May 2014.

11. Clurman, *Beyond Malice*, 164.

12. Ed Thompson, *A Love Affair with Life and Smithsonian* (Columbia: University of Missouri Press, 1995), 142.

13. Dora Jane Hamblin, *That Was the Life* (New York: Norton, 1977), 148.

14. Adolph Ochs to Alfred A. Cook, May 9, 1922, Adolph Ochs Papers, Box 86, Folder 6, Manuscripts and Archives Division, New York Public Library.

15. Kathy Roberts Forde, *Literary Journalism on Trial: Masson v. New Yorker and the First Amendment* (Amherst: University of Massachusetts Press, 2008), 93–97.

16. On the *New Yorker's* refusal to settle, see Kathy Roberts Forde, "Libel, Freedom of the Press, and the *New Yorker*," *American Journalism* 23 (2006): 76

17. Hamblin, *That Was the Life*, 147.

18. Ibid., 148–49.

19. Robert T. Swaine, *The Cravath Firm and Its Predecessors*, vol. 2 (New York: Ad Press, 1948).

20. On Lord, Day & Lord, see Kermit L. Hall and Melvin Urofsky, *New York Times v. Sullivan: Civil Rights, Libel Law and the Free Press* (Lawrence: University Press of Kansas, 2011); on Kirkland and Ellis and the *Chicago Tribune*, see Eric B. Easton, "The Colonel's Finest Campaign: Robert R. McCormick and Near v. Minnesota," *Federal Communications Law Journal* 60 (2008): 183.

21. On Greenbaum, Wolff, and Ernst, see David M. Margolick, "Law Firm That Won Battle to Publish Ulysses Is Closing Its Doors," *New York Times*, March 19, 1982, B4.

22. Glenn Fowler, "Ephraim London, A Lawyer Who Fought Censorship, Is Dead," *New York Times*, June 14, 1990, B13.

23. See, for example, Winters v. New York, 333 U.S. 507 (1948); Hannegan v. Esquire, Inc., 327 U.S. 146 (1946); Near v. Minnesota, 283 U.S. 697 (1931)

24. Swaine, *The Cravath Firm*, 3.

25. Charles Reich, "The Way We Were," *American Lawyer*, December 1, 2007.

26. Swaine, *The Cravath Firm*, 612.

27. Ibid.

28. "$3 Million Libel Suit Is Filed by Dempsey," *New York Times*, April 2, 1964, 38; "Long Sues Time, Inc., in 6 Million Action," *New York Times*, July 25, 1959, 15; "Hope Sues for $2,010,000: He Charges Life Said He Stole Jokes from Fred Allen," *New York Times*, November 17, 1950, 43.

29. Alan Hruska interview, May 2014.

30. "Some Idiots Afloat," *Life*, December 21, 1962, 63–64.

31. Cowan v. Time, Inc., 245 N.Y.S.2d 723, 725–26 (N.Y. Sup. Ct. 1963).

32. "Publishers' Corner," *Saturday Review of Literature*, July 15, 1950, 26.

33. George Norris to Godfrey Nelson, October 28, 1948, Arthur Hays Sulzberger Papers, Box 196, Folder 17, Manuscripts and Archives Division, New York Public Library.

34. Van Arsdale v. Time, 35 N.Y.S.2d 951, 953 (N.Y. Sup. Ct. 1942).

35. Kobler, *Luce*, 159.

36. "Two Eagles Claim Libel: Kilroy and Robinson of Pro Eleven Sue Life Magazine," *New York Times*, October 29, 1955, 14.

37. Thompson, *A Love Affair with Life and Smithsonian*, 142.

38. Timothy W. Gleason, *The Watchdog Concept: The Press and the Courts in Nineteenth Century America* (Ames: Iowa State University, 1990), 12.

39. Margaret A. Blanchard, "The Institutional Press and Its First Amendment Privileges," *Supreme Court Review* 1978 (1978): 227–28, 228 n.12

40. Margaret A. Blanchard, *Revolutionary Sparks: Freedom of Expression in Modern America* (New York: Oxford University Press, 1992), 174.

41. Associated Press v. United States, 326 U.S. 1, 7 (1945).

42. See Commission on Freedom of the Press, *A Free and Responsible Press: A General Report on Mass Communication, Newspapers, Radio, Motion Pictures, Magazines, and Books* (Chicago: University of Chicago Press, 1947).

43. See Henry R. Luce, "Responsibility of the Press in the Cold War," *Vital Speeches of the Day* 19 (April 1953): 368–72.

44. Loudon Wainwright, *The Great American Magazine: An Inside History of Life* (New York: Knopf, 1986), 97.

45. People v. Larsen, 5 N.Y.S.2d 55, 56 (Ct. of Special Sessions 1938).

46. Ibid., 57.

47. Ibid., 56.

48. Wainwright, *The Great American Magazine*, 98; Jill Lepore, *Mansion of Happiness: A History of Life and Death* (New York: Knopf, 2012), 46–48.

49. Petition for Certiorari, Caldwell v. Crowell-Collier Publishing Company, 332 U.S. 336 (1947), 17–18.

50. Petition for Certiorari, Readers Digest Association v. Grant, 326 U.S. 797 (1946), 7–8; see also Time, Inc. v. Hartmann, 334 U.S. 838 (1948).

51. Schenectady Union Publishing v. Sweeney, 316 U.S. 642 (1942). See also Barr v. Matteo, 360 U.S. 564 (1959); Beauharnais v. Illinois, 343 U.S. 250 (1952) (involving Illinois "group libel" statute).

52. Frederick Seaton Siebert, *The Rights and Privileges of the Press* (New York: D. Appleton-Century, 1934), 33–32; Snively v. Record Publishing Co., 185 Cal. 565 (Cal. 1921); Van Vechten Veeder, "Freedom of Public Discussion," *Harvard Law Review* 23 (1910): 416–17.

53. Coleman v. MacLennan, 98 P. 281, 286 (Kan. 1908).

54. Alan Hruska interview, May 2014.

55. Hartmann v. Time, 64 F. Supp. 671, 676 (E.D. Pa. 1946); see Itai Maytal, "Libel Lessons from across the Pond: What British Courts Can Learn from the United States' Chilling Experience with the 'Multiple Publication Rule' in Traditional Media and the Internet," *Journal of International Media and Entertainment Law* 3 (2010): 122–24.

56. Hartmann v. American News, 171 F.2d 581, 582 (7th Cir. 1948).

57. Ibid., 583.

58. Petitioner's Brief, Hartmann v. Time, Inc., 334 U.S. 838 (1948).

59. Hartmann v. Time, Inc., 166 F.2d 127, 134 (3rd Cir. 1947).

60. Fraser Bond, *An Introduction to Journalism* (New York: Macmillan, 1954), 64.

61. Chilton Rowlette Bush, *Newspaper Reporting of Public Affairs: An Advanced Course in Newspaper Reporting and a Manual for Professional Newspaper Men* (New York: D. Appleton, 1940). See also Sidis v. F-R Publishing Corp., 113 F.2d 806, 809 (2d Cir. 1940).

62. "Starving Glutton," *Time*, March 13, 1939, 31.

63. Appellant's Statement, Brief, and Argument, Barber v. Time, Inc., 159 S.W.2d 291 (1942).

64. Respondent's Supplemental Statement, Points, and Authorities, Barber v. Time, Inc., 159 S.W.2d 291 (1942).

65. Barber v. Time, Inc., 159 S.W.2d 291, 294–96 (Mo. 1942).

66. Ibid.

Chapter 8

1. James Hill deposition, September 1956, 72, Box 15, Joseph Hayes Papers, Lilly Library, Indiana University.

2. Ibid., 73.

3. Ibid.

4. Ibid., 39, 43.

5. Ibid., 38.

6. Letter from Stanley Dean, Transcript of Record (TR), U.S. Supreme Court, Time, Inc. v. Hill, 385 U.S. 374 (1967), 569.

7. Ibid., 490.

8. Ibid., 481.

9. Elizabeth Hill deposition, October 30, 1958, 63, Box 15, Joseph Hayes Papers, Lilly Library, Indiana University.

10. TR, 382.

11. "Play Opens Wednesday," *Amarillo Globe Times,* March 18, 1958, 19.

12. Elizabeth Hill deposition, 76.

13. TR, 569.

14. Hill v. Hayes, et al., 14 Misc.2d 249, 155 N.Y.S.2d 234 (Sup. Ct. NY County 1956).

15. Born in 1921, Biddle attended Harvard University and Columbia Law School, served in the Navy after World War II, and was the nephew of Francis Biddle, one-time U.S. Attorney. "Mrs. Kerstein, Oliver C. Biddle Wed in Redding," *New York Times,* April 1, 1960, 30.

16. "Jerome E. Malino, at 83; Lawyer at Gilbert Firm," *New York Times,* December 10, 1977, 24.

17. Letter from Malino to Hayes, November 23, 1956, Box 10, Folder 6, Joseph Hayes Papers, Lilly Library, Indiana University.

18. James Hill deposition, 72.

19. Letter from Malino to Hayes, November 23, 1956.

20. Ibid.

21. Joseph Hayes deposition, July 30, 1957, Box 15, Joseph Hayes Papers.

22. Hayes deposition, 15–16.

23. Tom Prideaux deposition, June 18, 1957, 66, Box 15, Joseph Hayes Papers.

24. Ibid., 111.

25. TR, 335.

26. Ibid., 180.

27. Ibid., 240.

28. Third Amended Complaint, March 1958.

29. Ibid., 11.

30. Ibid., 12.

31. Berman to Hayes, May 8, 1958, Box 10, Folder 6, Joseph Hayes Papers.

32. Nathan Blumberg, "The Press and Its Ineffective Critics," *Nieman Reports* (July 1961): 31.

33. Theodore Peterson, "A Criticism of Press Criticism," *Christian Century*, September 16, 1959, 1048.

34. William Albig, "Good and Evil from the Press," *Annals of the American Academy of Political and Social Science* 280 (March 1952): 113.

35. David E. Sumner, *The Magazine Century: American Magazines since 1900* (New York: Peter Lang, 2010), 117.

36. William H. Young, *The 1950s* (Westport, CT: Greenwood Press, 2004), 153.

37. Lee Burress, *Battle of the Books: Literary Censorship in the Public Schools, 1950–1985* (Metuchen, NJ: Scarecrow Press, 1989), 73.

38. Melvin DeFleur, "How Massive Are the Mass Media? Implications for Communications Education and Research," *Syracuse Scholar* 10 (1990): 24.

39. Bill Sloan, *I Watched a Wild Hog Eat My Baby: A Colorful History of Tabloids and Their Cultural Impact* (Amherst, NY: Prometheus Books, 2001).

40. Vance Packard, *The Status Seekers* (New York: David McKay, 1959), 217.

41. Anthony Harrigan, "The Surrender of Privacy," *Nieman Reports* (July 1958): 8.

42. Ibid.

43. William Allen White, quoted in Tom Goldstein, *Killing the Messenger: 100 Years of Media Criticism* (New York: Columbia University Press, 2007), 25.

44. Goldstein, *Killing the Messenger,* 118. On one paper's "taboo list" were the words *nude, naked, rape, gossip,* and *scandal.* See Max Hall, "The Role of the Press," in *Reporting the News: Selections from Nieman Reports,* ed. Louis Lyons (Cambridge: Belknap Press, 1965).

45. Neil MacNeil, *Without Fear or Favor* (New York: Harcourt, Brace, 1940), 345.

46. Louis B. Seltzer, "The Press Looks at the Bar and at Itself," *Journal of the Cleveland Bar Association* 22 (November 1950): 28; Louis B. Seltzer, "The Bar and the Public Trust: A Newspaperman Speaks Frankly to Lawyers," *American Bar Association Journal* 37 (1951): 744.

47. Ignaz Rothenberg, "Newspaper Sins against Privacy," *Nieman Reports* (January 1957): 43.

48. *Ace in the Hole* (1951).

49. Curtis MacDougall, *The Press and Its Problems* (Dubuque, IA: W. C. Brown, 1964), 338.

50. Commission on Freedom of the Press, *A Free and Responsible Press: A General Report on Mass Communication: Newspapers, Radio, Motion Pictures, Magazines, and Books* (Chicago: University of Chicago Press, 1947), 53, 56–60.

51. Bernard A. Weisberger, "Keeping the Free Press Free: Who Watches the Watchmen?" *Antioch Review* 13 (Autumn 1953): 333.

52. Morris Ernst, *The First Freedom* (New York: Macmillan, 1946), 53.

53. Weisberger, "Keeping the Free Press Free," 329–30.

54. Ibid., 331–33.

55. "Criticism of Press Seen in Survey," *New York Times*, May 14, 1952, 23.

56. Warren Breed, "Mass Communication and Socio Cultural Integration," *Social Forces* 37 (December 1958): 114.

57. Leslie Mueller, "How Free Is the Press," *Vital Speeches of the Day* 23 (October 1957): 751.

58. Ibid.

59. Ibid.

60. Rothenberg, "Newspaper Sins against Privacy," 43.

61. Eustace Cullinan, "The Rights of Newspapers: May They Print Whatever They Choose?" *American Bar Association Journal* 41 (1955): 1022.

62. "Bill Sent to Florida Aims at Ruling Press," *New York Times*, April 8, 1951, 46.

63. "Georgia Libel Bill on Press Is Passed," *New York Times*, February 2, 1956, 17.

64. Samuel Krislov, "Mr. Justice Black Reopens the Free Speech Debate," *UCLA Law Review* 11 (1964): 210.

65. Don R. Pember, *Privacy and the Press: The Law, the Mass Media, and the First Amendment* (Seattle: University of Washington Press, 1972), 147.

66. Francis Murnaghan, "From Figment to Fiction to Philosophy—the Requirement of Proof of Damages in Libel Actions," *Catholic University Law Review* 22 (1972): 4.

67. Melvin Belli, *Ready for the Plaintiff* (New York: Grosset & Dunlap, 1956), 160.

68. Rosenberg, *Protecting the Best Men*, 247.

69. Harry Kalven Jr., "Privacy in Tort Law—Were Warren and Brandeis Wrong?" *Law and Contemporary Problems* 31 (1966): 327. One journalist described privacy law as a "Pandora's box," resulting in an "endless tide of litigation." Marcus Gleisser, "Newspaper Libel," *Cleveland-Marshall Law Review* 1955 (1955): 144.

70. Gill v. Hearst Publishing Co., 239 P.2d 636, 638 (Cal. 1952). The decision was later reversed on the grounds that the photo was not offensive and was "public" since it was taken in a public place. 253 P.2d 441, 444–45 (Cal. 1953).

71. Metzger v. Dell Publishing Co., 136 N.Y.S.2d 888, 889–91 (N.Y. Sup. Ct. 1955).

72. Strickler v. National Broadcasting Co., 167 F. Supp. 68, 71 (S.D. Cal. 1958).

73. William L. Prosser, "Privacy," *California Law Review* 48 (1960): 389.

74. Spahn v. Julian Messner, Inc., 250 N.Y.S.2d 529 (N.Y. Sup. Ct. 1964).

75. Geoffrey R. Stone, "Justice Brennan and the Freedom of Speech: A First Amendment Odyssey," *University of Pennsylvania Law Review* 139 (1991): 1336.

76. Margaret Blanchard, *Revolutionary Sparks: Freedom of Expression in Modern America* (New York: Oxford University Press, 1992), 274.

77. "Censorship Curb on Books Is Seen," *New York Times*, May 10, 1951, 7.

78. Murray Schumach, "Censorship Fight Waged on a Nation-Wide Front," *New York Times*, November 1, 1953, E7.

79. "Censorship Called Threat," *New York Times*, March 15, 1953, 54.

80. Joseph Burstyn, Inc. v. Wilson, 343 U.S. 495, 505–506 (1952).

81. Yates v. United States, 354 U.S. 298 (1957).

82. Speiser v. Randall, 357 U.S. 513, 514–15, 528–29 (1958).

83. In *Sweeney v. Patterson* (1942) involving political criticism of a U.S. senator in the

Washington Times-Herald, the U.S. Court of Appeals for the District of Columbia adopted the conditional privilege for "matters of public concern" and affirmed a ruling in favor of the publisher, declaring that strict "liability for erroneous reports of the political conduct of officials reflect[s] the obsolete doctrine that the governed must not criticize their governors." Under a strict liability regime, "information and discussion will be discouraged, and the public interest in public knowledge of important facts will be poorly defended." Sweeney v. Patterson, 128 F.2d. 457, 458 (D.C. Cir., 1942).

Strict liability in libel cases was "not justified by the realities of the present day," a Washington State judge observed in 1955. The rule resulted in the "public's being deprived of information concerning the public acts of public officials because newspapers cannot afford to assume the risk of being unable to prove . . . the truth of every fact stated in such publication." Owens v. Scott Publishing Co., 284 P.2d 296, 313 (Wash. 1955) (en banc).

84. Prosser, "Privacy," 394.

85. Waters v. Fleetwood, 91 S.E.2d 344, 348 (Ga. 1956). See also Smith v. Doss, 37 So.2d 118, 120 (Ala. 1948); Jacova v. Southern Radio & Television Co., 83 So.2d 34, 35–36, 40 (Fla. 1955).

86. Samuel v. Curtis Publishing Co., 122 F. Supp. 327, 328–29 (N.D. Cal. 1954).

87. Kelley v. Post Publishing, 98 N.E.2d 286, 287 (Mass. 1951).

88. Answer of Defendant Time, Inc., TR 21.

89. Ibid., 22.

90. Ibid., 21.

91. Ibid., 35.

92. Hill v. Hayes, 207 N.Y.S.2d 901 (N.Y. Sup. 1960).

93. Hill v. Hayes, 216 N.Y.S.2d 497, 497 (N.Y. App. Div. 1961).

Chapter 9

1. Leonard Garment, *Crazy Rhythm: From Brooklyn and Jazz to Nixon's White House, Watergate, and Beyond* (Cambridge, MA: Da Capo Press, 1997), 81.

2. Trial memorandum, Wilderness Years Collection, Series VI, Legal Papers, Time, Inc. v. Hill, Nixon Presidential Library.

3. Ibid., 16.

4. Transcript of Record, Hill v. Hayes, 18 A.D.2d 485 (N.Y. App. Div. 1963), 350.

5. Ibid., 473.

6. Kurt F. Stone, *The Jews of Capitol Hill: A Compendium of Jewish Congressional Members* (Lanham, MD: Scarecrow Press, 2010), 155–56.

7. Larkin v. G. P. Putnam's Sons, 242 N.Y.S.2d 746, 753 (N.Y. Sup. Ct. 1963).

8. Glenn Fowler, "H.R. Medina Jr., 78, Lawyer and Expert in Libel and Privacy," *New York Times*, February 20, 1991, D23; "Harold Medina, U.S. Judge, Dies at 102," *New York Times*, March 16, 1990, B7; Daniel Hawthorne, *Judge Medina, A Biography* (New York: W. Funk, 1952), 165–66.

9. Alan Hruska interview, May 2014.

10. Examples are Time, Inc. v. Hartmann, 334 U.S. 838 (1948); Curtis v. Time, Inc., 251 F.2d 389 (D.C. Cir. 1958); Green v. Time, Inc., 3 N.Y.2d 732 (1957); Booth v. Curtis

Publishing Co., 15 A.D.2d 343 (N.Y. App. Div. 1962); Fugazy v. Time, Inc., 17 A.D.2d 618 (N.Y. App. Div. 1962); Berkson v. Time, Inc., 8 A.D.2d 352 (N.Y. Sup. Ct. 1959).

11. See Lewis Harshorn, *Alger Hiss, Whittaker Chambers, and the Case That Ignited McCarthyism* (Jefferson, MO: McFarland, 2010), 123.

12. Opening Address for Plaintiffs, April 5, 1962, Transcript of Record, U.S. Supreme Court, Time, Inc. v. Hill, 385 U.S. 374 (1967), 461–62.

13. Ibid.

14. Ibid., 463.

15. Ibid., 467.

16. Ibid., 470, 479.

17. Ibid., 464, 469–70.

18. Ibid., 472.

19. Ibid., 476.

20. Ibid., 500.

21. Don Zoeller Interview, February 20, 2015.

22. Transcript of Record (TR), U.S. Supreme Court, Time, Inc. v. Hill, 554

23. Zoeller interview.

24. Transcript of Record (TR), Hill v. Hayes, 15 N.Y.2d 986 (1965), 81.

25. Transcript of Record, Hill v. Hayes, 18 A.D.2d 485 (N.Y. App. Div. 1963), 36.

26. "The Final Days," Box 45, Folder 6, Leonard Garment Papers, Library of Congress.

27. Ibid.

28. Ibid.

29. TR, 102.

30. Ibid., 113.

31. Ibid., 201.

32. Ibid., 197.

33. Ibid., 260–61.

34. Ibid., 277.

35. Garment, *Crazy Rhythm*, 82.

36. TR, 200.

37. Transcript of Record, U.S. Supreme Court, Time, Inc. v. Hill, 515.

38. Ibid., 528–29.

39. Ibid., 555.

40. Ibid., 539.

41. Ibid., 544.

42. Ibid.

43. Ibid., 549.

44. Ibid., 559–60.

45. Ibid., 558.

46. Ibid., 560.

47. Ibid., 564.

48. Ibid.

49. Charge of the Court to the Jury, April 17, 1962, TR, 317.

50. TR, 326.

51. Ibid.

52. Transcript of Record, U.S. Supreme Court, Time, Inc. v. Hill, 566.

53. TR, 332.

54. Ibid., 333–34.

55. Ibid., 334.

56. Zoeller interview.

57. TR, 335–36.

58. Ibid., 349.

59. Ibid., 350.

Chapter 10

1. David Seipp, "The Right to Privacy in American History" (PhD diss., Harvard University, 1978), 3–8; Robert Ellis Smith, *Ben Franklin's Website: Privacy and Curiosity from Plymouth Rock to the Internet* (Providence, RI: Privacy Journal, 2004), 8, 21.

2. Seipp, "The Right to Privacy in American History," 95.

3. Smith, *Ben Franklin's Website,* 25–49; Frederick S. Lane, *American Privacy: The 400–Year History of Our Most Contested Right* (Boston: Beacon Press, 2009), 2.

4. Smith, *Ben Franklin's Website,* 58–63; Lane, *American Privacy,* chap. 3; Seipp, "The Right to Privacy in American History," chap. 2.

5. In this era, technologies for hidden cameras were being developed. One popular magazine of the 1890s advertised a bowler hat with a built-in camera that could be used to take pictures of people surreptitiously. In 1870, the microphone was invented, and in 1890, the dictograph recorder. "Bugging," or microphone eavesdropping of private conversations, was reportedly used in the late nineteenth century by private detectives and city police forces. See Alan F. Westin, *Privacy and Freedom* (New York: Atheneum, 1967), 442.

6. "The Right of Privacy," *New York Times,* August 23, 1902, 8.

7. Lane, *American Privacy,* 78.

8. Ibid.

9. Rupert Hughes, "The Music of the Streets," *Godey's Magazine* 135 (1897): 467–72.

10. "Electric Lights Will Annoy Them," *New York Times,* June 29, 1894, 9.

11. Burton Bledstein, *The Culture of Professionalism: The Middle Class and the Development of Higher Education in America* (New York: Norton, 1976), 61.

12. Meyer Berger, "Surrender of Privacy," *Scribner's,* April 1939, 16–21.

13. Mark Sullivan, "The Right to Privacy," *Washington Post,* March 2, 1940.

14. Berger, "Surrender of Privacy," 18.

15. Robert Benchley, "The Questionnaire Craze," *Chicago Tribune,* February 9, 1930.

16. Berger, "Surrender of Privacy," 16.

17. Lewis Nichols, "Our Sacred Privacy Becomes a Memory," *New York Times,* October 11, 1931, 8.

18. Deborah Nelson, *Pursuing Privacy in Cold War America* (New York: Columbia University Press, 2002), 9.

19. "Gadgets with Big Ears: An End to Privacy," *U.S. News and World Report*, April 22, 1955, 46.

20. Westin, *Privacy and Freedom*, 71.

21. "Invaders," *Newsweek*, March 9, 1964, 80–81.

22. See Anthony Lewis, "Tangled Issue of Wiretapping," *New York Times*, August 21, 1960, SM18, 116.

23. Westin, *Privacy and Freedom*, 118–32.

24. Ibid., 173.

25. Ibid., 159–60.

26. Richard H. Rovere, "The Invasion of Privacy," *American Scholar* 27 (1957): 413.

27. Lewis, "Tangled Issue of Wiretapping," 116.

28. Bernard B. Spindel with Bill Davidson, "Who Else Is Listening?" *Collier's*, June 1955, 25.

29. Myron Brenton, *The Privacy Invaders* (New York: Coward & McCann, 1964), 157.

30. Westin, *Privacy and Freedom*, 90.

31. Gay Talese, "Union Protests Hidden Camera," *New York Times*, September 25, 1963, 44.

32. Vance Packard, "The Walls Do Have Ears," *New York Times*, September 20, 1964, SM23.

33. Brenton, *The Privacy Invaders*, 179.

34. John Brooks, "There's Somebody Watching You," *New York Times*, March 15, 1964, BR1.

35. Packard, "The Walls Do Have Ears," SM23.

36. Walter Goodman, "Lie Detectors Don't Lie, But," *New York Times*, January 24, 1965, SM12.

37. Westin, *Privacy and Freedom*, 134.

38. Ibid., 136.

39. "Psychological Testing Grows," *New York Times*, December 11, 1960, E7.

40. Brenton, *The Privacy Invaders*, 228.

41. Edward Shils, "Privacy: Its Constitution and Vicissitudes," *Law and Contemporary Problems* 31 (Spring 1966): 179–81.

42. Westin, *Privacy and Freedom*, 158–59.

43. Vance Packard, "The Right to Privacy," *Atlantic Monthly*, March 1964, 55–61.

44. Kenneth L. Karst, "'The Files': Legal Controls over the Accuracy and Accessibility of Stored Personal Data," *Law and Contemporary Problems* 31 (1966): 342.

45. Theodore Irwin, "About: Mailing Lists," *New York Times*, March 22, 1964, SM96.

46. Ibid.

47. Martin Gross, "How Many Secrets Do You Have Left?" *Cosmopolitan* (November 1955): 27.

48. Ibid., 26.

49. Westin, *Privacy and Freedom*, 158–68, 298–326.

50. Ibid., 161–62.

51. Ibid., 299.

52. Ashley Montagu, "The Annihilation of Privacy," *Saturday Review,* March 31, 1956, 10.

53. "In Defense of Privacy," *Time,* July 15, 1966, 38.

54. Lynn Spigel, *Make Room for TV: Television and the Family Ideal in Postwar America* (Chicago: University of Chicago Press, 1992), 101.

55. Quoted in ibid.

56. Edmond J. Bartnett, "Darien House Carries Out Idea of 'Privazone' to Fullest Extent," *New York Times,* August 7, 1960, R1.

57. "Individual Privacy as Must," *Hartford Courant,* June 11, 1961, 12D; "Lack of Privacy Blamed for Family Breakdowns," *Hartford Courant,* May 22, 1950, 7.

58. See Cotton Seiler, *Republic of Drivers: A Cultural History of Automobility in America* (Chicago: University of Chicago Press, 2008), 57.

59. See Elaine Tyler May, *Homeward Bound: American Families in the Cold War Era* (New York: Basic Books, 1990), 155.

60. August Heckscher, "The Invasion of Privacy (II): The Reshaping of Privacy," *American Scholar* 28 (1959): 19.

61. Shils, "Privacy: Its Constitution and Vicissitudes," 305.

62. Philip Rieff, *Triumph of the Therapeutic: Uses of Faith after Freud* (Chicago: University of Chicago Press, 1966); Deborah Weinstein, *The Pathological Family: Postwar America and the Rise of Family Therapy* (Ithaca, NY: Cornell University Press, 2013), 3–4.

63. Jesse Battan, "'The New Narcissism' in 20th Century America: The Shadow and Substance of Social Change," *Journal of Social History* 17 (1983): 207.

64. Westin, *Privacy and Freedom,* 11, citing the work of anthropologist Dorothy Lee in her work *Freedom and Culture* (Prospect Heights, IL: Waveland Press, 1959).

65. Ibid., 11.

66. Lawrence Meir Friedman, *The Republic of Choice: Law, Authority, and Culture* (Cambridge: Harvard University Press, 1990), 3.

67. Hamilton Cravens, ed., *The Social Sciences Go to Washington: The Politics of Knowledge in the Postmodern Age* (New Brunswick, NJ: Rutgers University Press, 2004), 131.

68. "A New Year, a New Hope," *New York Times,* December 31, 1962, 6.

69. "In Defense of Privacy," *Time,* July 15, 1966, 39.

70. William Faulkner, "On Privacy, the American Dream: What Happened to It," *Harper's,* July 1955, 33.

71. "Let Me Alone!" *Christian Century,* September 21, 1966, 1135.

72. Margaret Mead, "Our Right to Privacy," *Redbook,* April 1, 1965, 15.

73. Brenton, *The Privacy Invaders,* 18–9.

74. Shils, "Privacy: Its Constitution and Vicissitudes," 305.

75. Westin, *Privacy and Freedom,* 322.

Chapter 11

1. "Couple Wins Suit against Magazine," *Hartford Courant,* April 19, 1962, 1.

2. Leonard Garment, *Crazy Rhythm: From Brooklyn and Jazz to Nixon's White House, Watergate, and Beyond* (Cambridge, MA: Da Capo Press, 1997), 83.

3. "Critical Question: What Is Legitimate News?" *Newsweek,* April 30, 1962, 60.

4. Right after the verdict, Medina filed a motion to set aside the verdict. The argument was that Mrs. Hill was not called to testify. Judge Klein held that Medina's contention was without merit because Time, Inc. "could have obtained a physical examination of Mrs. Hill by its doctor or a court appointed physician and could have called such doctor as a witness, if his opinion indicated this plaintiff was well enough to testify. This it did not do." *New York Law Journal,* May 10, 1962.

5. Brief of Appellant, Hill v. Hayes, 18 A.D.2d 485 (N.Y. App. Div. 1963), 118.

6. Time, Inc. v. Hill, 385 U.S. 374, 395 (1967).

7. Brief of Appellant, Hill v. Hayes, 118.

8. Ibid., 54.

9. Ibid., 118.

10. Hill v. Hayes, 18 A.D.2d 485, 489 (N.Y. App. Div. 1963).

11. Ibid., 489–90.

12. On Rabin, see Kurt F. Stone, *The Jews of Capitol Hill: A Compendium of Jewish Congressional Members* (Lanham, MD: Scarecrow Press, 2010), 156; "Benjamin Rabin Justice, 72, Dead: Was in Appellate Division—Ex-Bronx Congressman," *New York Times,* February 24, 1969, 37.

13. Hill v. Hayes, 491.

14. On Botein, see Bernard Botein, "The People's Right to Know," *Harvard Law Review* 67 (1954): 920; Bernard Botein, *Trial Judge: The Candid Behind-the-Bench Story of Justice Botein* (New York: Simon & Schuster, 1952); "Innovator on the Bench: Bernard Botein," *New York Times,* March 26, 1966, 12; "Presiding Justice Botein," *New York Times,* October 2, 1957, 32; "Bernard Botein Dies," *New York Times,* February 4, 1974, 61.

15. Hill v. Hayes, 492–93.

16. See John W. Wade, "Defamation and the Right of Privacy," *Vanderbilt Law Review* 15 (1962): 1117; Edward J. Bloustein, "Privacy as an Aspect of Human Dignity: An Answer to Dean Prosser," *New York University Law Review* 39 (1964): 988; Marc A. Franklin, "A Constitutional Problem in Privacy Protection: Legal Inhibitions on Reporting of Fact," *Stanford Law Review* 16 (1963): 110. The *Hastings Law Review* devoted an entire article to the case. Presaging the later reaction of the U.S. Supreme Court, the author was troubled by the Rabin concurrence, noting that the "dictum of the concurring opinion proposes a basis of liability which reaches beyond the scope of the statute." John W. Warnock, "Publisher's Treatment of Newsworthy Event Held Violation of Privacy Statute: *Hill v. Hayes,* Note," *Hastings Law Journal* 17 (1965): 383.

17. Given the assaults to the press that were being issued "under the rubrics of libel and privacy," she suggested that the courts adopt "a new approach to cases involving limitations on the press." In addition to the "applicable technical rules," she suggested "a special overall rule as to burden and quantum of proof—that whoever seeks to restrict freedom of expression must prove beyond a reasonable doubt that the good which will be accomplished by the restriction will outweigh the evil necessarily involved in muzzling or punishing expression." Harriet Pilpel, "The Right of Privacy: An Approach Worth Considering," *Publishers' Weekly,* August 26, 1963, 244.

18. Memorandum from LG to RN, May 28, 1967, Wilderness Years Collection, Series VI, Legal Papers, Time, Inc. v. Hill, Nixon Presidential Library.

19. Ibid.

20. On the civil rights movement, see Robert Weisbrot, *Freedom Bound: A History of America's Civil Rights Movement* (New York: Norton, 1990); Taylor Branch, *Parting the Waters: America in the King Years, 1954–1963* (New York: Simon & Schuster, 1988).

21. New York Times Co. v. Sullivan, 376 U.S. 254, 256–57 (1964); Kermit L. Hall, "Dignity, Honor, and Civility: New York Times *v. Sullivan*," *OAH Magazine of History* 9 (1995): 33–34. On the *Sullivan* case, see Kermit L. Hall and Melvin I. Urofsky, *New York Times v. Sullivan: Civil Rights, Libel Law, and the Free Press* (Lawrence: University Press of Kansas, 2011); Anthony Lewis, *Make No Law: The Sullivan Case and the First Amendment* (New York: Random House, 1991); W. Wat Hopkins, *Actual Malice: Twenty-Five Years after Times v. Sullivan* (New York: Praeger, 1989).

22. New York Times Co. v. Sullivan, 256–57.

23. Ibid., 257–58, 289.

24. Ibid., 256–58.

25. Christopher W. Schmidt, "*New York Times v. Sullivan* and the Legal Attack on the Civil Rights Movement," *Alabama Law Review* 66 (2014): 305.

26. New York Times Co. v. Sullivan, 256.

27. Elena Kagan, "A Libel Story: *Sullivan* Then and Now," *Law and Social Inquiry* 18 (1993): 200.

28. AHS to Dryfoos, February 19, 1960, Arthur Hays Sulzberger Papers, Manuscripts and Archives Division, New York Public Library.

29. "Blackjacking the Press," *Nation*, November 26, 1960, 407.

30. Hall and Urofsky, *New York Times v. Sullivan*, 46, 100–102.

31. Brief of Petitioner, New York Times Co. v. Sullivan, 376 U.S. 254 (1964), 29.

32. Ibid.

33. Petition for Writ of Certiorari, New York Times Co. v. Sullivan, 376 U.S. 254 (1964), 15.

34. Ibid., 13. The *Chicago Tribune* filed an amicus brief in which it emphasized that the judgment of the Alabama courts was "an unconstitutional attempt to reincarnate the long-buried doctrine of seditious libel." "We submit that no one could read the seditious libel cases and not be struck by the ominous parallel between these actions and what has now occurred in Alabama." Brief for the *Chicago Tribune* as Amicus Curiae Supporting Petitioner, New York Times Co. v. Sullivan, 376 U.S. 254 (1964), 11.

35. Brief for ACLU as Amicus Curiae Supporting Petitioner, New York Times Co. v. Sullivan, 376 U.S. 254 (1964), 31–32.

36. Ibid., 17.

37. Ibid., 27, citing Coleman v. MacLennan, 98 P. 281, 285 (Kan. 1908).

38. Alan Hruska interview, May 2014.

39. Petition for Writ of Certiorari, New York Times Co. v. Sullivan, 376 U.S. 254 (1964), 20.

40. Brief for ACLU as Amicus Curiae Supporting Petitioner, New York Times Co. v. Sullivan, 376 U.S. 254 (1964), 18.

41. Brief of Respondent, New York Times Co. v. Sullivan, 376 U.S. 254 (1964), 29–30, 33.

42. Schenectady Union Publishing v. Sweeney, 316 U.S. 642 (1942); Barr v. Matteo, 360 U.S. 564 (1959); Beauharnais v. Illinois, 343 U.S. 250 (1952).

43. Norman Dorsen, "Libel and the Free Press," *Nation*, 1964, 93, 95.

44. New York Times Co. v. Sullivan, 268.

45. Ibid., 279.

46. Ibid.

47. Ibid., 280; Coleman v. MacLennan, 78 Kan. 711 (Kan. 1908).

48. New York Times Co. v. Sullivan., 271–72.

49. Ibid., 279.

50. Ibid., 298.

51. Ibid.

52. Harry Kalven Jr., "The New York Times Case: A Note on 'The Central Meaning of the First Amendment,'" *Supreme Court Review* 1964 (1964): 193–94.

53. "Libel Landmark," *Newsweek*, March 23, 1964, 74.

54. "Free Press and Free People," *New York Times*, March 10, 1964, 36.

55. Richard L. Tobin, "The New York Times' Vital Victory," *Saturday Review*, April 1964, 69.

56. Melvin Urofsky, *The Warren Court: Justices, Rulings, and Legacy* (Santa Barbara, CA: ABC-CLIO, 2001), 62.

57. Kim Isaac Eisler, *The Last Liberal: Justice William J. Brennan, Jr. and the Decisions that Transformed America* (New York: Simon & Schuster, 1993), 189.

58. "A Fine Judge Ready for His Biggest Job," *Life*, October 29, 1956, 116. See also Francis P. McQuade and Alexander T. Kardos, "Mr. Justice Brennan and His Legal Philosophy," *Notre Dame Lawyer* 33 (May 1958): 324; Jack Alexander, "Mr. Justice from New Jersey," *Saturday Evening Post*, September 28, 1957, 25.

59. Ibid., 115–16. For biographies of Brennan, see Seth Stern and Stephen Wermiel, *Justice Brennan: Liberal Champion* (Boston: Houghton Mifflin Harcourt, 2010); Frank I. Michelman, *Brennan and Democracy* (Princeton, NJ: Princeton University Press, 1999); David E. Marion, *The Jurisprudence of Justice William J. Brennan, Jr.: The Law and Politics of "Libertarian Dignity"* (Lanham, MD: Rowman & Littlefield, 1997); W. Wat Hopkins, *Mr. Justice Brennan and Freedom of Expression* (New York: Praeger, 1991).

60. Daniel M. Berman, "Mr. Justice Brennan: A Preliminary Appraisal," *Catholic University Law Review* 7 (1958): 11, 14–15.

61. Geoffrey Stone, "Justice Brennan and the Freedom of Speech: A First Amendment Odyssey," *University of Pennsylvania Law Review* 139 (1991): 1333. Law professor Geoffrey Stone describes Brennan as "one of the staunchest defenders of the freedom of speech the Court has ever known." Of the 252 free speech decisions in which Brennan participated, the Court accepted the free speech claim in 59 percent of cases. Brennan accepted the claim in 88 percent of cases.

62. Speiser v. Randall, 357 U.S. 513, 526 (1958).

63. Smith v. California, 361 U.S. 147, 153 (1959).

64. NAACP v. Button, 371 U.S. 415, 433 (1963).

65. Horwitz, *The Warren Court*, 5. For biographies of Black, see Howard Ball, *Hugo L. Black: Cold Steel Warrior* (New York: Oxford University Press, 1996); Roger K. Newman, *Hugo Black: A Biography* (New York: Pantheon Books, 1994); Tony Allan Freyer, *Hugo L. Black and the Dilemma of American Liberalism* (Glenview, IL: Little, Brown Higher Education, 1990); Tinsley E. Yarbrough, *Mr. Justice Black and His Critics* (Durham, NC: Duke University Press, 1988).

66. Sylvia Snowiss, "The Legacy of Justice Black," *Supreme Court Review* 1973 (1973): 196.

67. Horwitz, *The Warren Court*, 5.

68. Anthony Lewis, "Justice Black at 75: Still the Dissenter," *New York Times Magazine*, February 26, 1961, SM3.

69. John P. Frank, "Mr. Justice Black, a Biographical Appreciation," *Yale Law Journal* 65 (1956): 454.

70. Howard Ball and Phillip Cooper, "Fighting Justices: Hugo L. Black and William O. Douglas and Supreme Court Conflict," *American Journal of Legal History* 38 (1994): 20–21; Walter F. Murphy, "Marshaling the Court: Leadership, Bargaining, and the Judicial Process," *University of Chicago Law Review* 29 (1962): 642.

71. Jeffrey Rosen, *The Supreme Court: The Personalities and Rivalries that Defined America* (New York: Holt, 2007), 133.

72. Ibid., 132.

73. "Warren Court: Fateful Decade," *Newsweek*, May 11, 1964, 25. For biographies of Warren, see Jim Newton, *Justice for All: Earl Warren and the Nation He Made* (New York: Riverhead Books, 2006); Ed Cray, *Chief Justice: A Biography of Earl Warren* (New York: Simon & Schuster, 1997); G. Edward White, *Earl Warren: A Public Life* (New York: Oxford University Press, 1982); Jack Harrison Pollack, *Earl Warren, The Judge Who Changed America* (Englewood Cliffs, NJ: Prentice Hall, 1979); Earl Warren, *The Memoirs of Earl Warren* (Garden City, NY: Doubleday, 1977); Leo Katcher, *Earl Warren: A Political Biography* (New York: McGraw-Hill, 1967).

74. "Warren Court: Fateful Decade"; Lucas A. Powe, *The Warren Court and American Politics* (Cambridge: Harvard University Press, 2009), 303.

75. Francis X. Beytagh, "Address," in "In Memoriam: Earl Warren Chief Justice of the United States," *California Law Review* 64 (January 1976): 11.

76. Gary Hoenig, "Earl Warren, of the 'People's Court,'" *New York Times,* July 14, 1974, 177.

77. Powe, *The Warren Court*; Mark Tushnet, ed., *The Warren Court in Historical and Political Perspective* (Charlottesville: University of Virginia, 1993); Bernard Schwartz, *The Warren Court: A Retrospective* (New York: Oxford University Press, 1996).

78. Fred Rodell, "The Warren Court Stands Its Ground," *New York Times,* September 27, 1964, 23, 120.

79. "Chief Justice of a Court under Fire," *U.S. News and World Report*, September 12, 1958, 38.

80. Ibid.

81. Newton, *Justice for All,* 386.

82. Horwitz, *Warren Court,* 56.

83. G. Edward White, "The First Amendment Comes of Age: The Emergence of Free Speech in Twentieth-Century America," *Michigan Law Review* 95 (November 1996): 340.

84. Thomas Emerson, "Towards a General Theory of the First Amendment," *Yale Law Journal* 72 (1963): 912.

85. Dennis v. United States, 341 U.S. 494, 508–9 (1951).

86. Laurent B. Frantz, "The First Amendment in the Balance," *Yale Law Journal* 71 (1962): 1442.

87. See, e.g., Wallace Mendelson, "On the Meaning of the First Amendment: Absolutes in the Balance," *California Law Review* 50 (December 1962): 313–33; Frantz, "The First Amendment in the Balance."

88. Emerson, "Toward a General Theory," 877.

89. Alexander Meiklejohn, *Free Speech and Its Relation to Self-Government* (New York: Harper & Brothers, 1948), 1–2.

90. Alexander Meiklejohn, "The First Amendment Is an Absolute," *Supreme Court Review* 1961 (1961): 255; White, "The First Amendment Comes of Age," 359.

91. Meiklejohn, "Absolute," 259.

92. See William J. Brennan Jr., "The Supreme Court and the Meiklejohn Interpretation of the First Amendment," *Harvard Law Review* 79 (1965): 1–20.

93. New York Times Co. v. Sullivan, 256.

94. Lee Levine and Stephen Wermiel, *The Progeny: Justice William J. Brennan's Fight to Preserve the Legacy of New York Times v. Sullivan* (Chicago: American Bar Association Publishing, 2014), 19.

95. See Brennan's opinion in *Garrison v. Louisiana*: "That speech is used as a tool for political ends does not automatically bring it under the protective mantle of the Constitution. For the use of the known lie as a tool is at once at odds with the premises of democratic government and with the orderly manner in which economic, social, or political change is to be effected. Calculated falsehood falls into that class of utterances which 'are no essential part of any exposition of ideas, and are of such slight social value as a step to truth that any benefit that may be derived from them is clearly outweighed by the social interest in order and morality'" (citing Chaplinsky v. New Hampshire, 315 U.S. 568, 572 (1942)). Garrison v. State of La., 379 U.S. 64, 75 (1964).

96. Hugo L. Black, "The Bill of Rights," *New York University Law Review* 35 (1960): 880. See also Charles Black, "Mr. Justice Black, the Supreme Court, and the Bill of Rights," *Harper's* (February 1961): 63; Charles Reich, "Mr. Justice Black and the Living Constitution," *Harvard Law Review* 76 (1963); James J. Magee, *Mr. Justice Black: Absolutist on the Court* (Charlotte: University of Virginia Press, 1980).

97. "Justice Black and First Amendment 'Absolutes': A Public Interview," *New York University Law Review* 37 (1962): 563. In his early years on the Court, the doctrine of absolutism was "alien to his jurisprudence," writes one legal historian. "Black believed that the First Amendment was designed to ensure that people would be allowed maximum

freedom to discuss public affairs, but that in an 'orderly society' there were implicit limits to that freedom, and such limits were to be ascertained by applying the clear and present danger test." But the Court's seeming distortions of "clear and present danger" in the red scare cases, and its adoption of the "ad hoc balancing" doctrine, led Black to denounce all balancing tests when it came to the First Amendment. Magee, *Mr. Justice Black*, 97.

98. Charles Black, "Mr. Justice Black, the Supreme Court, and the Bill of Rights," *Harper's* (February 1961): 63.

99. Hugo Black, "The Bill of Rights," *New York University Law Review* 35 (1960): 874–75.

100. Hugo Black and Edmond Cahn, "Mr. Justice Black and First Amendment Absolutes: A Public Interview," *New York University Law Review* 37 (1962): 553, 557.

101. "Minority Opinion," *Time,* June 22, 1962, 55.

102. Brief of Appellant, Hill v. Hayes, 15 N.Y.2d. 986 (1965), 34.

103. Ibid., 77.

104. Ibid.

105. Section 50 of the law made a violation a misdemeanor; Section 51 granted the right to sue for an injunction and damages for emotional distress. N.Y. Civil Rights Law § 50, 51 (1903). Brief of Appellant, Hill v. Hayes, 15 N.Y.2d. 986 (1965), 25.

106. Respondent's Brief, Hill v. Hayes, 15 N.Y.2d. 986 (1965), 36.

107. Ibid., 23.

108. Ibid., 29.

109. Hill v. Hayes, 15 N.Y.2d. 986 (1965). Time, Inc. asked the court for permission to file a motion to revise the damage award; the court granted the motion and issued the following statement with it: "Upon the appeal herein there was presented and necessarily passed upon a question under the Constitution of the United States. . . . The Court of Appeals held that sections 50 and 51 of the Civil Rights Law of the State of New York, as so applied, were valid." Jurisdictional Statement, 7, Time, Inc. v. Hill, 385 U.S. 374 (1967), filed September 13, 1965. The court's acknowledgment of a federal constitutional question allowed Time, Inc. to appeal directly to the U.S. Supreme Court.

110. Ibid., 987.

111. Ronald Sullivan, "Court Says Life Invaded Privacy," *New York Times*, April 16, 1965, 31.

112. Harriet Pilpel, "The Desperate Hours and the Right of Privacy," *Publishers' Weekly*, November 1, 1965, 32.

113. Harriet Pilpel, "Laws of Libel and Privacy Opposite on the See Saw," *Publishers' Weekly*, August 31, 1964, 295.

114. Ibid.

Chapter 12

1. Alan Westin, *Privacy and Freedom* (New York: Atheneum, 1967); Edward J. Bloustein, "Privacy as an Aspect of Human Dignity: An Answer to Dean Prosser," *New York Law Review* 39 (1964); Harry Kalven Jr., "Privacy in Tort Law—Were Warren and Brandeis Wrong?" *Law and Contemporary Problems* 31 (1966): 251–335.

2. Myron Brenton, *The Privacy Invaders* (New York: Coward & McCann, 1964); Vance Packard, *The Naked Society* (New York: David McKay, 1964); Lewis Nichols, "Still Naked: The Privacy Invaders," *New York Times*, April 26, 1964, BR45. Privacy scholar Priscilla Regan describes the wave of popular writings on privacy in this era as a "literature of alarm." Priscilla M. Regan, *Legislating Privacy: Technology, Social Values, and Public Policy* (Chapel Hill: University of North Carolina Press, 1995), 13.

3. One, headed by Edward Long of Missouri, probed wiretapping and bugging conducted by the government's own agencies. Another was headed by Sam Ervin of North Carolina, who was concerned with psychological testing. The third, under the chairmanship of Cornelius Gallagher, looked at the growing use of polygraphs, as well as proposals for a comprehensive federal databank, a "National Data Center." Westin, *Privacy and Freedom*, 50.

4. Packard, *Naked Society*, 5

5. "Let Me Alone!" *Christian Century*, September 21, 1966, 1135.

6. Westin, *Privacy and Freedom*, 196.

7. Paul Crowell, "Bar Unit Studies Privacy Threat," *New York Times*, February 17, 1964, 53

8. "To Preserve Privacy," *New York Times*, August 9, 1966, 36.

9. Jack Gould, "Exploiting Sorrow: A Review of TV-Radio Disaster Coverage," *New York Times*, December 25, 1960; Jack Gould, "TV: Questions of Taste and Restraint," *New York Times*, September 5, 1963, 63.

10. Westin, *Privacy and Freedom*, 110.

11. "Revenue Service Is Building Data Center in Philadelphia," *New York Times*, November 4, 1962, 83.

12. "Big Board Will Help Set Up Data Center," *New York Times*, January 15, 1965, 33.

13. Kenneth L. Karst, "'The Files': Legal Controls over the Accuracy and Accessibility of Stored Personal Data," *Law and Contemporary Problems* 31 (1966): 360.

14. Ibid.

15. Barry Schweid, "Court Battle over Sale of Public Names," *Hope Star*, May 9, 1968, 1.

16. Nan Robertson, "Data Center Held Peril to Privacy," *New York Times*, July 27, 1966, 41.

17. "A Government Watch on 200 Million Americans," *U.S. News & World Report*, May 16, 1966, 57.

18. Robertson, "Data Center," 41.

19. "A Government Watch on 200 Million Americans," 58.

20. Nan Robertson, "Data Center Aims Scored in Inquiry," *New York Times*, July 28, 1966, 24.

21. "To Preserve Privacy," *New York Times*, August 9, 1966, 36.

22. "A Government Watch on 200 Million Americans," 59.

23. In 1967 and 1968, both the House and the Senate again held hearings on the data center and rejected the proposal due to concerns that the center would not adequately protect the privacy of personal records. Regan, *Legislating Privacy*, 72.

24. Westin, *Privacy and Freedom*, 367.

25. There was a "'minimum position' in support of privacy" that "unite[d] both liberals and conservatives." Ibid.

26. McCandlish Phillips, "City Schools Bar Sex Habits Test," *New York Times,* February 10, 1966, 44.

27. Arthur R. Miller, "Personal Privacy in the Computer Age: The Challenge of a New Technology in an Information Oriented Society," *Michigan Law Review* 67 (1969): 1125.

28. Mrs. H. Turner Hodgdon Jr., "Letters to the Editor," *New York Times*, July 24, 1966, 138.

29. "Coast Personal Dossier Plan Stirs Fear of Privacy Invasion," *New York Times*, August 1, 1966, 27.

30. "Continuing Assault on Privacy," *National Review*, November 1966, 608–9.

31. "In Defense of Privacy," *Time,* July 15, 1966, 38–39.

32. Martin Gross, "How Many Secrets Do You Have Left?" *Cosmopolitan*, November 1955, 30.

33. "Invaders," *Newsweek*, March 9, 1964, 82.

34. "In Defense of Privacy," 39.

35. See Hamberger v. Eastman, 206 A.2d 239, 241–42 (N.H. 1964).

36. Westin, *Privacy and Freedom*, 360.

37. Theodore Irwin, "About: Mailing Lists," *New York Times,* March 22, 1964, SM96–SM97.

38. Daily Times Democrat v. Graham, 276 Ala. 380, 383 (Ala. 1964).

39. Harms v. Miami Daily News, Inc., 127 So.2d 715, 716–17 (Fla. Dist. Ct. App. 1961).

40. Olmstead v. U.S., 277 U.S. 438, 466 (1928).

41. West Virginia Board of Education v. Barnette, 319 U.S. 624 (1943).

42. Kovacs v. Cooper, 336 U.S. 77, 87–89 (1949).

43. Breard v. Alexandria, 341 U.S. 622, 640 (1951).

44. Prince v. Massachusetts, 321 U.S. 158, 166 (1944); Richard F. Storrow, "The Policy of Family Privacy: Uncovering the Bias in Favor of Nuclear Families in American Constitutional Law and Policy Reform," *Missouri Law Review* 66 (2001): 536. See also Pierce v. Society of Sisters, 268 U.S. 510, 534–35 (1925); Meyer v. Nebraska, 262 U.S. 390, 400 (1923).

45. Kovacs v. Cooper, 77, 87–88 (1949).

46. Breard v. Alexandria, 622, 640, 644–45 (1951).

47. See Ken Gormley, "One Hundred Years of Privacy," *Wisconsin Law Review* 1992 (1992): 1335.

48. Lane, *American Privacy*, 153.

49. Public Utility Commission of District of Columbia v. Pollak, 343 U.S. 451, 468–69 (1952).

50. Ibid., 467–69. See also William O. Douglas, *The Right of the People* (New York: Doubleday, 1958); Sheldon S. Adler, "Toward a Constitutional Theory of Individuality: The Privacy Jurisprudence of Justice Douglas," *Yale Law Journal* 87 (1978): 1579.

51. "This Court has recognized the vital relationship between freedom to associate and privacy in one's associations. Inviolability of privacy in group association may in many circumstances be indispensable to freedom of association." NAACP v. Alabama, 357 U.S.

449 (1958). See also Shelton v. Tucker, 364 U.S. 479 (1960); Talley v. California, 362 U.S. 60 (1960); Bates v. Little Rock, 361 U.S. 516 (1960); Gibson v. Florida Legislative Comm., 372 U.S. 539 (1963); Uphaus v. Wyman, 360 U.S. 72 (1959).

52. Sweezy v. New Hampshire, 354 U.S. 234, 249–50 (1957).

53. Silverman v. U.S., 365 U.S. 505, 511–12 (1961).

54. Mapp v. Ohio, 367 U.S. 643, 656 (1961).

55. Poe v. Ullman, 367 U.S. 497, 521 (1961).

56. Ibid., 549 (Harlan, J., dissenting).

57. Draft, Griswold v. Connecticut, April 1965, Box 1347, William O. Douglas Papers, Library of Congress.

58. Ibid.

59. Notes on Griswold, April 24, 1965, I:126, Folder 13, William J. Brennan Papers, Library of Congress.

60. Griswold v. Connecticut, 381 U.S. 479, 484 (1965).

61. Chase Sanders, "Ninth Life: An Interpretive Theory of the Ninth Amendment," *Indiana Law Journal* 69 (1994): 769; Thomas McAffee, "A Critical Guide to the Ninth Amendment," *Temple Law Review* 69 (1996): 61–94; R. H. Clark, "Constitutional Sources of the Penumbral Right to Privacy," *Villanova Law Review* 19 (1974): 835, 837–40. See also Ryan C. Williams, "The Paths to *Griswold*," *Notre Dame Law Review* 89 (2014): 2172–76.

62. Griswold v. Connecticut, 498; John Johnson, *Griswold v. Connecticut: Birth Control and the Constitutional Right of Privacy* (Lawrence: University Press of Kansas, 2005); William Beaney, "The Griswold Case and the Expanding Right to Privacy," *Wisconsin Law Review* 64 (1965): 976–95.

63. Griswold v. Connecticut, 479, 502 (White, J., concurring).

64. Ibid., 492.

65. Ibid., 496 (Goldberg, J., concurring).

66. See Adamson v. California, 332 U.S. 46, 69 (1947).

67. Griswold v. Connecticut, 479, 509–10 (1965).

68. Ibid., 509–10, fn. 1.

69. Robert G. Dixon, "The Griswold Penumbra: Constitutional Charter for an Expanded Law of Privacy?" *Michigan Law Review* 64 (1965): 197.

70. Westin, *Privacy and Freedom*, 355.

71. Griswold v. Connecticut, 511–12 (Black, J., dissenting); James Kilpatrick, "Shift of Power to Courts Denounced by Justice Black," *Morning Herald* (Hagerstown, MD), June 16, 1965, 4.

72. "Opinion, at Home and Abroad," *New York Times*, June 13, 1965, E13. See also Paul G. Kauper, "Penumbras, Peripheries, Emanations, Things Fundamental and Things Forgotten: The *Griswold* Case," *Michigan Law Review* 64 (1965): 244, describing the decision as "ambiguous and uncertain in its use of the specifics of the Bill of Rights." See also Williams, "Paths to Griswold," 2178 ("Justice Douglas's explanation for how he derived a right to privacy from the specific guarantees in the Bill of Rights was so 'convoluted,' 'confusing,' and 'opaque' that a small cottage industry of scholarship has grown up around the project of trying to figure out exactly what he was trying to say").

73. Kilpatrick, "Shift of Power to Courts Denounced by Justice Black."

74. Fred Graham, "The Law: Picketing vs. Privacy," *New York Times*, May 15, 1966, E6.

75. Sidney E. Zion, "Wiretap v. Privacy: Court's Recent Ruling on Birth Control Seen as Wedge against Eavesdropping," *New York Times*, June 15, 1965, 25.

76. Robert B. McKay, "The Right of Privacy: Emanations and Intimations," *Michigan Law Review* 64 (1965): 278.

77. "Life, Liberty, and Privacy," *Life*, July 2, 1965, 4.

78. Thomas I. Emerson, "Nine Justices in Search of a Doctrine," *Michigan Law Review* 64 (1965): 232–33.

79. "New Life for a Forgotten Amendment," *U.S. News & World Report*, July 5, 1965, 14.

80. Isidore Silver, "Privacy and the First Amendment," *Fordham Law Review* 34 (1966): 565.

81. Under the law the time, it had a statutory right of appeal. 28 U.S.C. § 1257.

82. Jurisdictional Statement, 2–3, 16–17, Time, Inc. v. Hill, 385 U.S. 374 (1967), filed September 13, 1965.

83. Ibid., 20.

84. Ibid.

85. Ibid., 8, 11. This argument had actually been presaged by Stanford Law professor Marc Franklin. See "A Constitutional Problem in Privacy Protection: Legal Inhibition on Reporting of Fact," *Stanford Law Review* 16 (1963) 138–40.

86. Ibid., 13.

87. Ibid., 15.

88. Ibid., 23.

89. Ibid., 21. "Since its enactment, the statute has been consistently construed by the New York state courts so as to effectuate the legislative intention to preserve the 'news privilege.' . . . New York, guided by constitutional principles, has . . . carved out an extremely limited right of action." Appellee's Motion to Dismiss or Affirm, Time, Inc. v. Hill, October 13, 1965, 15, 17.

90. Ibid., 20.

91. Time, Inc. v. Hill, 385 U.S. 374, 380 (1967).

Chapter 13

1. For biographies of Nixon, see Jonathan Aitken, *Nixon: A Life* (Washington D.C.: Regnery Publishing, 1994); Stephen E. Ambrose, *Nixon* (New York: Simon & Schuster, 1987), 3 vols.; Fawn M. Brodie, *Richard Nixon: The Shaping of His Character* (New York: Norton, 1981); Rick Perlstein, *Nixonland: The Rise of a President and the Fracturing of America* (New York: Scribner, 2009).

2. John Aloysius Farrell, "When Nixon Met the Press," Politico.com, August 6, 2014.

3. Richard Nixon, *Speeches, Writings, Documents*, ed. Rick Perlstein (Princeton: Princeton University Press, 2008).

4. Ibid., xxxvi.

5. Aitken, *Nixon,* 308.

6. Thomas W. Evans, "Mudge Rose Guthrie Alexander & Ferdon" (unpublished manuscript, n.d.). Courtesy of Jeffrey Frank.

7. Paul Hoffman, *Lions in the Street: The Inside Story of the Great Wall Street Law Firms* (New York: Saturday Review Press, 1973), 106, 108.

8. Aitken, *Nixon*, 309.

9. Peter Kihss, "Nixon's Law Firm Changes Its Name," *New York Times*, December 22, 1963, 25.

10. Jeffrey Frank, *Ike and Dick: Portrait of a Strange Political Marriage* (New York: Simon & Schuster, 2013), 242.

11. "Nixon Says He May Move to New York," *Los Angeles Times*, May 2, 1963, 2; Raymond Moley, "Nixon's Move to NY—the Personal Motives," *Los Angeles Times*, May 13, 1963, A4.

12. "Nixon Denies His NY Move Is Political," *Los Angeles Times*, May 5, 1963, B.

13. "Nixon Is Reported Joining Firm Here," *New York Times*, May 2, 1963, 1; "Nixon Says He May Move to New York," *Los Angeles Times*, May 2, 1963, 2.

14. Thomas P. Ronan, "Nixon Will Move to City on June 1: Will Join Law Firm—Plan Raises Political Questions," *New York Times*, May 3, 1963, 1, 17.

15. Earl Mazo and Stephen Hess, *Nixon: A Political Portrait* (New York: Popular Library, 1968), 286–87.

16. "Nixon Buys $135,000 Flat," *Hartford Courant*, May 7, 1963, 26A.

17. Mazo and Hess, *Nixon*, 291.

18. Aitken, *Nixon*, 364; Peter Kihss, "Nixon, Happy as New Yorker, Says Job Is Law, Not Politics," *New York Times*, December 29, 1963, 1, 18.

19. Ambrose, *Nixon*, 24.

20. Ibid., 320.

21. Ibid., 309.

22. Hoffman, *Lions in the Street*, 110.

23. Evans, *Mudge Rose Guthrie Alexander & Ferdon*.

24. Aitken, *Nixon*, 311.

25. Ambrose, *Nixon*, 24.

26. Aitken, *Nixon*, 307.

27. Frank, *Ike and Dick*, 270.

28. Eric Lichtblau, "Leonard Garment, Lawyer and Nixon Adviser during Watergate, Dies at 89," *New York Times*, July 16, 2013, A21.

29. Aitken, *Nixon*, 311.

30. Ibid., 310.

31. Leonard Garment, *Crazy Rhythm: From Brooklyn and Jazz to Nixon's White House, Watergate, and Beyond* (Cambridge, MA: Da Capo Press, 1997), 83.

32. Ibid.

33. Bernard Schwartz, *Super Chief: Earl Warren and His Supreme Court: A Judicial Biography* (New York: New York University Press, 1984), 21.

34. Aitken, *Nixon*, 313.

35. Garment, *Crazy Rhythm*, 83.

36. Aitken, *Nixon*, 313.

37. "Time, Inc. v. Hill, Notes," March 15, 1966, Wilderness Years Collection, Series VI, Legal Papers, Time, Inc. v. Hill, Nixon Presidential Library.

38. Cyrus Abbe, "Public Issues and Public Figures," Wilderness Years Collection.

39. Ibid.

40. Garment to Nixon, n.d., Wilderness Years Collection.

41. "Time, Inc. v. Hill, Notes."

42. Untitled, March 16, 1966, Wilderness Years Collection.

43. "Time, Inc. v. Hill, Notes."

44. Untitled, n.d., Wilderness Years Collection.

45. Untitled, n.d., Wilderness Years Collection.

46. Memo, n.d., Wilderness Years Collection.

47. Douglas Parker interview, February 6, 2015.

48. Ibid.

49. Untitled, n.d., Wilderness Years Collection.

50. On Stewart, see Lewis F. Powell, Jr., "Justice Stewart," *Harvard Law Review* 95 (1981): 1–5; Terrance Sandalow, "Potter Stewart," *Harvard Law Review* 95 (1981): 6–10. On Clark, see Mimi Clark Gronlund, *Supreme Court Justice Tom C. Clark: A Life of Service* (Austin: University of Texas Press, 2010); Evan A. Young, *Lone Star Justice: A Biography of Justice Tom C. Clark* (Houston: Hendrick Long Pub. Co., 1998).

51. "Warren Court, Fateful Decade," *Newsweek*, May 11, 1964, 65. On Harlan, see Tinsley E. Yarbrough, *John Marshall Harlan: Great Dissenter of the Warren Court* (New York: Oxford University Press, 1992).

52. See Konigsberg v. State Bar, 366 U.S. 36 (1961); Barenblatt v. United States, 360 U.S. 109 (1959).

53. Yates v. United States, 354 U.S. 298 (1957); Daniel Farber and John Nowak, "Justice Harlan and the First Amendment," *Constitutional Commentary* 2 (1985): 425.

54. "Warren Court, Fateful Decade." On White, see Dennis J. Hutchinson, *The Man Who Once Was Whizzer White: A Portrait of Justice Byron R. White* (New York: Free Press, 1998); David M. Ebel, "Justice Byron R. White: The Legend and the Man," *Stanford Law Review* 55 (2002): 5–9; John Paul Stevens, "A Tribute to Justice Byron R. White," *Yale Law Journal* 112 (2003): 969–72; Linda Greenhouse, "Byron R. White, Supreme Court Justice for 31 Years, Dies at 84," *New York Times*, April 15, 2002.

55. Untitled, n.d., Wilderness Years Collection.

56. Bernard W. Bell, "Judging in Interesting Times: The Free Speech Clause Jurisprudence of Justice Byron R. White," *Catholic University Law Review* 52 (2003): 901.

57. Seth Stern and Stephen Wermiel, *Justice Brennan: Liberal Champion* (Boston: Houghton Mifflin Harcourt, 2010), 223.

58. Durham v. United States, 214 F.2d 862 (D.C. Cir. 1954); Gideon v. Wainwright, 372 U.S. 335 (1963).

59. Kalman, *Abe Fortas*, 146.

60. Fred Rodell, "The Complexities of Mr. Justice Fortas," *New York Times*, July 28, 1968, 12.

61. Ibid.

62. Untitled, n.d., Wilderness Years Collection.

63. Parker, "Memories of Len," in author's possession.

64. "92 Year Old Nixon Friend Is Night Owl," *Omaha World Herald*, November 11, 1968.

65. Untitled, n.d., Wilderness Years Collection.

66. Dorr to Neier, January 20, 1966, Wilderness Years Collection.

67. Dorr to Angell, January 26, 1966, Wilderness Years Collection.

68. Angell to Dorr, February 1, 1966, Wilderness Years Collection.

69. According to a memo from Don Zoeller, Victor Earle of Cravath "stated that he had heard that the ACLU had planned to come in on Cravath's side but had not finished its brief and therefore would not be in." Memorandum, n.d., Wilderness Years Collection.

70. Parker, "Memories of Len."

71. Garment, *Crazy Rhythm*, 83–84.

72. Leonard Garment, "The Hill Case," *New Yorker*, April 17, 1989, 94.

73. Fred Graham, "Time, Inc. v. Hill," in *A Good Quarrel: America's Top Legal Reporters Share Stories from Inside the Supreme Court*, ed. Timothy Johnson and Jerry Goldman (Ann Arbor: University of Michigan Press, 2009), 171.

74. Mazo and Hess, *Nixon*, 289.

75. Stephen Hess and David Broder, "What Keeps Nixon Running," *Harper's*, August 1, 1967, 57.

76. Pat Buchanan, *The Greatest Comeback: How Richard Nixon Rose from Defeat to Create the New Majority* (New York: Crown, 2015), 35–36.

77. Garment, "The Hill Case," 111.

78. Hess and Broder, "What Keeps Nixon Running," 58.

79. Untitled, n.d., Wilderness Years Collection.

80. Ibid.

81. Ibid.

82. Untitled, March 14, 1966, Wilderness Years Collection.

83. Untitled, n.d., Wilderness Years Collection.

84. Douglas Parker interview, February 6, 2015.

85. See William Safire, "To Be Let Alone," *New York Times*, May 21, 1973, 33. "Mr. Nixon, a genuinely private person, chose to represent this client in this case out of his personal conviction that Justice Brandeis was right—that there was a 'right to be let alone,' and that it must be vigorously asserted."

86. Perlstein, *Nixonland*, 68.

87. Jules Witcover, *The Resurrection of Richard Nixon* (New York: Putnam, 1970), 128.

88. Douglas Brinkley and Luke Nichter, *The Nixon Tapes 1973* (Boston: Houghton Mifflin Harcourt, 2015), 4.

89. Garment, "The Hill Case," 98.

Chapter 14

1. Fred Graham, "The Law: Free Press vs. Privacy—An Issue for the Court," *New York Times*, December 12, 1965, E8.

2. Ibid.

3. Kermit L. Hall and Melvin I. Urofsky, *New York Times v. Sullivan: Civil Rights, Libel Law, and the Free Press* (Lawrence: University Press of Kansas, 2011), 33.

4. Rosenblatt v. Baer, 383 U.S. 75, 85 (1966).

5. Curtis Publishing Co. v. Butts, 388 U.S. 130, 134 (1967); Associated Press v. Walker, 388 U.S. 130, 134 (1967).

6. New York Times Co. v. Sullivan, 376 U.S. 254, 270 (1964).

7. Harry Kalven Jr., "The New York Times Case: A Note on 'The Central Meaning of the First Amendment,'" *Supreme Court Review* 1964 (1964): 221.

8. Memo from MES to Earl Warren, November 18, 1965, Box 293, Earl Warren Papers, Library of Congress.

9. Ibid.

10. October Term 1966 History, William J. Brennan Papers, Library of Congress.

11. Brief for the Appellant, Time, Inc. v. Hill, 385 U.S. 374 (1967), 18.

12. Ibid., 32.

13. Ibid., 25.

14. Brief for the Appellant on Reargument, Time, Inc. v. Hill, 385 U.S. 374 (1967), 29. "We submit that the publication here had considerably more than slight redeeming social importance, that it described a public event involving public issues, and that it was an attempt to engage in free public discussion."

15. Ibid., 31–32.

16. Ibid., 35, 37.

17. Brief for the Appellant, Time, Inc. v. Hill, 385 U.S. 374 (1967), 39.

18. Ibid., 39–40.

19. Brief for the Appellee, Time, Inc. v. Hill, 385 U.S. 374 (1967), 19.

20. Ibid., 20.

21. Ibid., 39.

22. The New York privacy law "protects the individual from 'commercialization of his personality' at the pleasure of a mass communications industry and thus stands as a significant safeguard of individual dignity." See Brief for Appellee on Reargument, Time, Inc. v. Hill, 385 U.S. 374 (1967), 29.

23. Ibid., 21–22.

24. Ibid., 22.

25. Brief for the Appellee on Reargument, Time, Inc. v. Hill, 385 U.S. 374 (1967), 33.

26. Brief for the Appellee, Time, Inc. v. Hill, 385 U.S. 374 (1967), 20.

27. Ibid., 24. The New York State attorney general's office filed an amicus brief on behalf of the Hills, arguing that "Time, Inc.'s reliance upon *New York Times Co. v. Sullivan* . . . for the proposition that its false depiction of the Hills' relationship to *The Desperate Hours* is protected by the First Amendment is wholly misplaced. The decision in the *Times* case emphasized the strong interest in open debate on public issues, and limited the protection to statements about the official conduct of public officials. In the present case . . . the plaintiff was not a public official, the conduct which was the subject of the publication was not in any manner official conduct, and the use of the plaintiff's name cannot be said to have made

any contribution to the interchange of ideas." Brief for the Attorney General of the State of New York, as Amicus Curiae, on Reargument, Time, Inc. v. Hill, 385 U.S. 374 (1967), 18–19.

28. Fred Graham, "*Time Inc. v. Hill*: A Future President Makes His Case," in *A Good Quarrel: America's Top Legal Reporters Share Stories from Inside the Supreme Court*, ed. Timothy R. Johnson and Jerry Goldman (Ann Arbor: University of Michigan Press, 2009), 171.

29. Leonard Garment, "The Hill Case," *New Yorker*, April 17, 1989, 96.

30. Graham, "A Future President," 171.

31. Garment, "The Hill Case," 96.

32. Jim Newton, *Justice for All: Earl Warren and the Nation He Made* (New York: Riverhead Books, 2006), 474.

33. James Hill to Nixon, April 19, 1966, Wilderness Years Collection, Series VI, Legal Papers, Time, Inc. v. Hill, Nixon Presidential Library.

34. See "High Court Hears Argument by Nixon, His First before It," *New York Times*, April 28, 1966, 20; "Nixon to Argue First Supreme Court Case," *Los Angeles Times*, April 28, 1966, 17 (describing Nixon as "a smooth and deferential advocate"); Ronald Ostrow, "Restrictions of Press, or Defense of Privacy," *Los Angeles Times*, April 21, 1966.

35. "Nixon Holds Center Stage in High Court Debut," *Miami Herald*, April 28, 1966, 6.

36. "Nixon to Argue First Supreme Court Case," 17.

37. Oral argument, Time, Inc. v. Hill, April 27, 1966, accessed on Oyez.org.

38. Ibid.

39. "Nixon Defends Damage Award," *Philadelphia Inquirer*, April 28, 1966.

40. "High Court Hears Argument," 20.

41. Oral argument, Time, Inc. v. Hill.

42. "Nixon Charges Life with Lie about Clients," *Washington Post*, October 19, 1966, A2.

43. Oral argument, Time, Inc. v. Hill.

44. Notes, Abe Fortas Papers, Box 31, Folder 699, Yale University Manuscripts and Archives.

45. Oral argument, Time, Inc. v. Hill.

46. Garment, "The Hill Case," 97.

47. Ibid.

48. "Nixon Makes Debut before Supreme Court," *Washington Evening Star*, April 28, 1966.

49. "Nixon Holds Center Stage in High Court Debut," *Miami Herald*, April 28, 1966.

50. "Nixon Makes Debut before Supreme Court."

51. Graham, "A Future President," 175.

52. Melvin v. Reid, 297 P.91 (Cal. Dist. Ct. App. 1931), in which a California appeals court held that a reformed prostitute had a privacy right under the state constitution to recover damages for the depiction of her criminal past in a motion picture.

53. "Nixon Makes Debut before Supreme Court."

54. Stanley Reed to Richard Nixon, April 30, 1966, Wilderness Years Collection, Series VI, Legal Papers, Time, Inc. v. Hill, Nixon Presidential Library.

55. Interview with Stephen M. Goodman, former clerk for Justice William Brennan, December 3, 2014.

56. Garment, "The Hill Case," 97. But see Bernard Schwartz, *Super Chief: Earl Warren and His Supreme Court—A Judicial Biography* (New York: New York University Press, 1983), 643 (claiming that Fortas deemed Nixon's performance "mediocre").

57. Memo, Nixon to Garment, April 28, 1966, Wilderness Years Collection, Series VI, Legal Papers, Time, Inc. v. Hill, Nixon Presidential Library.

58. Ibid.

59. Ibid.

60. Ibid.

61. Ibid. This position was adopted in the Nixon, Mudge brief to the Court on reargument: "Privacy should be seen for what it is—a limited but useful tool, akin to private libel, which the states have developed under the Ninth and Tenth Amendments to redress injury to the personality and sensibilities of an individual." Brief for the Appellee on Reargument, Time, Inc. v. Hill, 385 U.S. 374 (1967), 2–3.

62. As Garment later observed, Nixon regretted his failure to give "more precise expression to his intuition that Justice Douglas's weak reasoning in *Griswold* was going to get the Court into deep and dangerous constitutional waters." Nixon believed that the Court had a looming problem on its hands because of *Griswold*'s vague privacy right and believed that it should not compound the problem by using *Griswold* to encroach on state libel and privacy laws. Nixon knew that by making this argument, he "would demote the concept of privacy from the high status that *Griswold* had given it—an ironic task for James Hill's lawyer. He thought, though, that if he had laid greater stress on this point the Court might have been more hesitant to impair the vitality of the New York state privacy law governing the *Hill* case." Garment, "The Hill Case," 90.

63. Memo, Nixon to Garment, April 28, 1966.

64. Ibid.

65. Eric Lichtblau, "Leonard Garment, Lawyer and Nixon Adviser during Watergate, Dies at 89," *New York Times,* July 15, 2013.

Chapter 15

1. Nina Totenberg, "Behind the Marble, beneath the Robes," *New York Times*, March 16, 1975, SM14.

2. Notes on Conference, April 29, 1966, Box 1375, William O. Douglas Papers, Library of Congress.

3. Jim Newton, *Justice for All: Earl Warren and the Nation He Made* (New York: Riverhead Books, 2006), 476.

4. Notes on Conference, April 29, 1966.

5. Note, n.d., Box I: 141, Folder 7, William J. Brennan Papers, Library of Congress.

6. Notes on Conference, April 29, 1966.

7. Fortas draft opinion, 7, Time, Inc. v. Hill, June 8, 1966, Box 31, Folder 700, Abe Fortas Papers, Yale University Manuscripts and Archives.

8. Ibid., 4–5.

9. Ibid.

10. Ibid., 7.

11. Ibid.

12. Laura Kalman, *Abe Fortas: A Biography* (New Haven, CT: Yale University Press, 1990), 254–5.

13. Fortas draft opinion, 9–11.

14. Ibid., 9

15. Ibid, 11. Kovacs v. Cooper, 336 U.S. 77, 87–88 (1949); Breard v. Alexandria, 341 U.S. 622, 640 (1951).

16. Ibid.

17. Ibid., 12

18. Ibid., 14.

19. Ibid., 16.

20. Kalman, *Abe Fortas*, 264–65.

21. Fred Rodell, "The Complexities of Mr. Justice Fortas," *New York Times*, July 28, 1968, 12.

22. Bruce Allen Murphy, *Fortas: The Rise and Ruin of a Supreme Court Justice* (New York: Morrow, 1988), 230.

23. Kalman, *Abe Fortas*, 262.

24. Leonard Garment, *Crazy Rhythm: From Brooklyn and Jazz to Nixon's White House, Watergate, and Beyond* (Cambridge, MA: Da Capo Press, 1997), 93.

25. Rodell, "Complexities of Mr. Justice Fortas," 12.

26. Lucas A. Powe Jr., *The Warren Court and American Politics* (Cambridge: Harvard University Press, 2002), 304.

27. Tom Clark to Fortas, June 9, 1966, Box A199, Folder 9, Tom Clark Papers, Tarlton Law Library, University of Texas School of Law.

28. See notes on Fortas draft opinion in Box 1: 141, William J. Brennan Papers.

29. October Term 1966 History, William J. Brennan Papers.

30. Douglas draft dissent, June 9, 1966, 1, Box 545, Earl Warren Papers, Library of Congress.

31. Black to Douglas, June 9, 1966, Box 1387, William O. Douglas Papers.

32. Harlan concurrence, June 20, 1966, Box 545, Earl Warren Papers. See also draft concurrence, John Marshall Harlan Papers, Box 261, Folder 22, Seeley G. Mudd Manuscript Library, Princeton University.

33. White to Brennan, June 8, 1966, Box 1:141, Folder 7, William J. Brennan Papers.

34. White draft dissent, June 9, 1966, 5, Box 545, Earl Warren Papers.

35. Ibid., 6–7.

36. "One who publishes the news and facts behind it has a constitutional right to do so, even if those he writes about would rather he had not written at all. The same result should obtain when he uses ordinary care to report the news but falls short of the truth in some respects." Ibid., 8–9.

37. Notes, Box 1:141, Folder 7, William J. Brennan Papers.

38. October Term 1966 History, William J. Brennan Papers.

39. Untitled, Abe Fortas, June 14, 1966, Box 545, Earl Warren Papers.

40. Fortas draft opinion, 17.

41. Ibid.

42. Ibid., 16.

43. Ibid., 15.

44. Referencing the opinion upholding the group libel statute in Beauharnais v. Illinois, 343 U.S. 250 (1952).

45. This habit began when Black joined the Court in 1937. Howard Ball, *The Supreme Court in the Intimate Lives of Americans: Birth, Sex, Marriage, Childrearing, and Death* (New York: NYU Press, 2004), 84.

46. Fortas draft opinion, June 14, 1966, Box 396, Folder 7, Hugo Black Papers, Library of Congress.

47. Ibid., 5, 6.

48. Ibid.

49. Murphy, *Rise and Ruin*, 231.

50. Garment, "The Hill Case," *New Yorker,* April 17, 1989, 106; Murphy, *Rise and Ruin*, 231.

51. Memo, Abe Fortas, June 16, 1966, Box 545, Earl Warren Papers.

52. Garment, "The Hill Case," 100.

53. Hugo L. Black and Elizabeth Black, *Mr. Justice and Mrs. Black: The Memoirs of Hugo L. Black and Elizabeth Black* (New York: Random House, 1988), 151.

54. Howard Ball, *Hugo L. Black: Cold Steel Warrior* (New York: Oxford University Press, 1996), 155.

55. Ibid.

56. Ibid., 154; Fred Graham, "The Many Sided Justice Fortas," *New York Times*, June 4, 1967.

57. Ball, *Hugo L. Black*, 155–56.

58. Kalman, *Abe Fortas*, 260; Brown v. Louisiana, 383 U.S. 131 (1966).

59. Memorandum, August 24, 1966, Box 396, Hugo Black Papers.

60. Schwartz, *The Unpublished Opinions of the Warren Court*, 299.

61. Memorandum, October 17, 1966, 7, Box 545, Earl Warren Papers.

62. Ibid., 1–2.

63. Ibid., 3.

64. Ibid., 4.

65. Ibid., 4–5.

66. Ibid., 5.

67. Ibid., 6.

68. Ibid., 8.

69. Ibid., 13.

70. Ibid., 8.

71. Ibid., 7.

72. Ibid., 15. Personally, Justice Black detested the press, having suffered at the hands of journalists on several occasions. Most notably, shortly after his confirmation, a series of articles exposed that Black had been a member of the Ku Klux Klan but had concealed that fact. Anthony Lewis, "Justice Black and the First Amendment," *Alabama Law Review* 38

(1987): 301–2. Despite his decision in *Griswold*, Black felt strongly about privacy, according to the *New York Times*'s Anthony Lewis. Black was an intensely private man and would have resented *Life*'s article as much as James Hill. But for Black, when it came to the First Amendment, "principle came ahead of personal feelings." Ibid., 303.

73. Roger K. Newman, *Hugo Black: A Biography* (New York: Pantheon, 1994), 590.

74. Black and Black, *Mr. Justice and Mrs. Black*, 153.

75. Garment, "The Hill Case," 100.

76. Fred Graham, "*Time Inc. v. Hill*: A Future President Makes His Case," in *A Good Quarrel: America's Top Legal Reporters Share Stories from inside the Supreme Court*, ed. Timothy R. Johnson and Jerry Goldman (Ann Arbor: University of Michigan Press, 2009), 177.

77. Garment, "The Hill Case," 100.

78. John P. Mackenzie, "Nixon Charges Life with Lie about Clients," *Washington Post*, October 19, 1966, A2.

79. See Brief for the Appellant on Reargument, 385 U.S. 374 (1967), 23; Reply Brief for the Appellant on Reargument, 3–4, 11–12.

80. Transcript of Reargument, Time, Inc. v. Hill, 385 U.S. 374 (1967), 89, contained in Leonard Garment Papers, Box 40, Folder 2, Library of Congress.

81. Ibid., 34.

82. Ibid., 10.

83. Ibid., 89.

84. Ibid., 89–90.

85. Lee Levine and Stephen Wermiel, *The Progeny: Justice William J. Brennan's Fight to Preserve the Legacy of New York Times v. Sullivan* (Chicago: ABA Publishing, 2014), 60.

86. Ibid., 41.

87. See also Brief for the Appellee on Reargument, 7 ("the statute is a limited and reasonable regulation which does not, in any application, abridge freedom of speech").

88. Transcript of Reargument, 42.

89. Ibid., 53; Levine and Wermiel, *The Progeny*, 60.

90. Ibid., 67–69.

91. Ibid., 50. See also Brief for the Appellee on Reargument, 29: "False words which invade privacy and cause harm to an individual's sensibilities and feelings should be subject to the same degree of state regulation as false words which injure private reputation. Statutory and case law developments in the law of privacy, as in other areas of the law, reflect the growing recognition that injury to personality and feelings is as tangible as injury to body or reputation."

92. Notes, Abe Fortas Papers, Box 31, Folder 699, Yale University Manuscripts and Archives.

93. Stephen Hess and David Broder, "What Keeps Nixon Running," *Harper's*, August 1, 1967, 57.

94. "Nixon Juggles Two Hats," *Christian Science Monitor*, October 21, 1966, 3.

95. Garment, "The Hill Case," 106.

96. Notes on Conference, October 21, 1966, Box 1375, William O. Douglas Papers.

97. Ibid.

98. Spahn v. Julian Messner, Inc., 18 N.Y.2d 324, 328 (N.Y. 1966).

99. Ibid., 329.

100. Ibid.

101. Black and Black, *Mr. Justice and Mrs. Black*, 153.

102. Interview, Stephen M. Goodman, December 3, 2014.

103. Fortas to Brennan, December 1, 1966, Box 149, Folder 2, William J. Brennan Papers.

104. "The appellant argues that the statute should be declared unconstitutional on its face if construed by the New York courts to impose liability without proof of knowing or reckless falsity. Such a declaration would not be warranted even if it were entirely clear that this had previously been the view of the New York courts. The New York Court of Appeals, as the Spahn opinion demonstrates, has been assiduous in construing the statute to avoid invasion of the constitutional protections of speech and press. We, therefore, confidently except that the New York courts will apply the statute consistently with the constitutional command." Time, Inc. v. Hill, 385 U.S. 374, 397 (1967).

105. Ibid., 394–95.

106. White to Brennan, December 1, 1966, Box 149, Folder 2, William J. Brennan Papers.

107. On December 1, 1966, Fortas sent a letter to the justices indicating that he intended to "circulate a dissenting opinion in this case as soon as it is prepared." Box 545, Earl Warren Papers.

108. Fortas to Brennan, December 22, 1966, Box 149, Folder 2, William J. Brennan Papers.

109. Clark to Fortas, January 2, 1967, Box A 199, Folder 9, Tom Clark Papers.

110. Harlan opinion, January 3, 1967, Box 545, Earl Warren Papers; see also Harlan's recirculated opinion, January 1, 1967.

111. Douglas concurrence, December 1, 1966, Box 396, Hugo Black Papers.

112. See Black to Douglas, December 30, 1966, Box 396, Hugo Black Papers. "I have stricken out all of the language to which you objected in the case."

113 See Rosenblatt v. Baer, 383 U.S. 75, 91–94 (1966) (Stewart, J., concurring).

114. Stewart to Brennan, January 5, 1967, Box 149, Folder 2, William J. Brennan Papers.

Chapter 16

1. Justice John Marshall Harlan wrote a partially concurring, partially dissenting opinion.

2. Time, Inc. v. Hill, 385 U.S. 374, 388 (1967).

3. Ibid., 394–98.

4. Ibid., 388.

5. John D. O'Reilly, Jr., "Constitutional Law," *1971 Annual Survey of Massachusetts Law* § 16.10, 1970–1971: 446.

6 Interview with Stephen Wermiel, November 25, 2014.

7. Time, Inc. v. Hill, 385 U.S. 374, 388 (1967).

8. Thornhill v. Alabama, 310 U.S. 88, 102 (1941).

9. "What is one man's amusement teaches another's doctrine. Though we can see nothing of any possible value to society in these magazines, they are as much entitled to

the protection of free speech as the best of literature." Winters v. New York, 333 U.S. 507, 510 (1948).

10. Time, Inc. v. Hill, 385 U.S. 374, 388 (1967).

11. Ibid.

12. Ibid., 389.

13. Ibid. (quoting Speiser v. Randall, 357 U.S. 513, 526 (1958)).

14. Ibid., 394.

15. Ibid., 388.

16. Ibid., 398.

17. Ibid, 400.

18. Ibid, 401.

19. Ibid., 406.

20. Time, Inc. v. Hill, 385 U.S. 374, 405–7 (Harlan, J., concurring in part, dissenting in part),

21. Ibid., 408-409.

22. Ibid., 408.

23. Ibid., 410.

24. Ibid., 411.

25. Ibid., 412 (quoting N.A.A.C.P. v. Button, 371 U.S. 415, 433 (1963)).

26. Ibid., 412.

27. Fortas draft opinion, 9, Time, Inc. v. Hill, June 8, 1966, Box 31, Folder 700, Abe Fortas Papers, Yale University Manuscripts and Archives.

28. Ibid

29. Ibid.

30. Time, Inc. v. Hill, 385 U.S. 374, 412–14 (1967).

31. Ibid., 416, 418, 419–20.

32. Ibid., 420.

33. Ibid., 411.

34. Garment to Nixon, May 18, 1967, Box 3, Wilderness Years Collection, Series VI, Legal Papers, Nixon Presidential Library.

35. Leonard Garment, "The Hill Case," *New Yorker,* April 17, 1989, 96.

Chapter 17

1. Harry Kalven Jr., "The Reasonable Man and the First Amendment: Hill, Butts, and Walker," *Supreme Court Review* 1967 (1967): 283.

2. Alexander Meiklejohn, "The First Amendment Is an Absolute," *Supreme Court Review* (1961): 257; G. Edward White, "The First Amendment Comes of Age: The Emergence of Free Speech in Twentieth-Century America," *Michigan Law Review* 95 (1996): 359.

3. Donald Smith, "Privacy: The Right That Failed," *Columbia Journalism Review* 8 (Spring 1969): 21.

4. William O. Bertelsman, "The First Amendment and Protection of Reputation and Privacy—New York Times Co. v. Sullivan and How It Grew," *Kentucky Law Journal* 56 (1967–1968): 748.

5. Kalven, "The Reasonable Man and the First Amendment," 286.

6. Katz v. U.S., 389 U.S. 347 (1967).

7. Eisenstadt v. Baird, 405 U.S. 438, 453 (1972).

8. Roe v. Wade, 410 U.S. 113, 129 (1973).

9. Whalen v. Roe, 429 U.S. 589, 598–600 (1977).

10. Privacy Act of 1974, 5 U.S.C. § 552(a) (2014).

11. See, e.g., Family Educational Rights and Privacy Act of 1974, 20 U.S.C. § 1232(g) (1974); Foreign Intelligence Surveillance Act of 1978, 50 U.S.C. § 1801–71 (1978); Fair Credit Reporting Act of 1970, 15 U.S.C. § 1681 (1970); Video Privacy Protection Act of 1988, 18 U.S.C. § 2710 (1988); Electronic Communications Privacy Act of 1986, 18 U.S.C. § 2510 (1986).

12. "Constitutional Law," *Texas Law Review* 45 (1967): 758, 765.

13. "Constitutional Law—State Cannot Award Damages for Invasion of Privacy without Proof of Actual Malice," *North Carolina Law Review* 45 (1967): 747.

14. Arthur R. Miller, "Personal Privacy in the Computer Age: The Challenge of a New Technology in an Information-Oriented Society," *Michigan Law Review* 67 (1968): 1163.

15. Arthur Miller, *The Assault on Privacy* (New York: Penguin, 1972), 190.

16. John P. Mackenzie, "Court Restricts Newsworthy People in Damage Suits over False Reports," *Washington Post*, January 10, 1967, A1.

17. "Invasion of Privacy," *Editor and Publisher*, January 14, 1967, 6.

18. "The press does not seek the privilege of prying inordinately. But it does cherish the responsibility of being able to inform. Today more and more attempts are being made to hedge that responsibility roundabout. It is healthy and helpful not only to the press but the public, when the Supreme Court clarifies issues well as it did in this instance." "Privacy and Press," *Hartford Courant*, January 12, 1967, 14.

19. "The Right to Be Informed," *Des Moines Register*, January 28, 1967, 8.

20. Fred P. Graham, "Supreme Court Supports Press on a Privacy Issue," *New York Times*, January 10, 1967, 1.

21. "Extending Press Freedom," *New York Times*, January 11, 1967, 24.

22. "A Vote for the Press over Privacy," *Time*, January 20, 1967, 64.

23. Graham, "Supreme Court Supports Press on a Privacy Issue," 1.

24. Leonard Garment, *Crazy Rhythm: From Brooklyn and Jazz to Nixon's White House, Watergate, and Beyond* (Cambridge, MA: Da Capo Press, 1997), 95.

25. See John Tebbel, "Journalism: Public Enlightenment or Private Interest?" *Annals of the American Academy of Political and Social Science* (January 1966): 79–88; A. H. Raskin, "What's Wrong with American Newspapers," *New York Times*, June 11, 1967, 249.

26. Smith, "Privacy: The Right That Failed," 20.

27. Marshall Shapo, "Media Injuries to Personality: An Essay on Legal Regulation of Public Communication," *Texas Law Review* 46 (1968): 662.

28. Willard H. Pedrick, "Publicity and Privacy: Is It Any of Our Business?" *University of Toronto Law Journal* 20 (1970): 402–3.

29. Melville Nimmer, "The Right to Speak from Times to Time: First Amendment Theory Applied to Libel and Misapplied to Privacy," *California Law Review* 56 (1968): 966.

30. Shapo, "Media Injuries to Personality," 659.

31. Philip L. Kellogg, "Note, Time, Inc. v. Hill," *North Carolina Law Review* 45 (1967): 744.

32. "The Supreme Court 1966 Term, Time, Inc. v. Hill," *Harvard Law Review* 81 (1967): 164.

33. Edward J. Bloustein, *Individual and Group Privacy* (New Brunswick, NJ: Transaction Publishers, 2003), 120.

34. Edward Bloustein, "Privacy, Tort Law, and the Constitution: Is Warren and Brandeis' Tort Petty and Unconstitutional as Well?" *Texas Law Review* 46 (1968): 626.

35. See "Comment, Time, Inc. v. Hill," *Texas Law Review* 45 (1966–1967): 758, 765; "Comment, Time, Inc. v. Hill," *Chicago-Kent Law Review* 44 (Spring 1967): 58–63; "Comment, Time, Inc. v. Hill," *North Carolina Law Review* 45 (1967): 747; "Supreme Court 1966 Term," *Harvard Law Review* 81 (1967): 164; "Privacy, Defamation, and the First Amendment: The Implications of Time, Inc. v. Hill," *Columbia Law Review* 67 (1967): 929–52; Dwayne L. Oglesby, "Freedom of the Press v. the Rights of the Individual—A Continuing Controversy," *Oregon Law Review* 47 (1968): 132–45, 137 ("On balance, the arguments of Justice Fortas and Justice Harlan seem more cogent than those of the majority"); "Right to Privacy: Social Interest and Legal Right," *Minnesota Law Review* 51 (1966–1967): 547 ("It is submitted that Fortas' position is the more accurate view of the necessary balance"); Melville Nimmer, "The Right to Speak from Times to Time: First Amendment Theory Applied to Libel and Misapplied to Privacy," *California Law Review* 56 (1968): 967; "Privacy, Property, Public Use, and Just Compensation," *Southern California Law Review* 41 (1968): 915–16; John P. Burton Jr., "Privacy and the Press," *Harvard Legal Commentary* 4 (1967): 89–98.

For law review commentary praising the Brennan opinion, see Eugene N. Aleinikoff, "Privacy in Broadcasting," *Indiana Law Journal* 42 (1967): 373–85; M. C. Slough, "Privacy, Freedom, and Responsibility," *University of Kansas Law Review* 16 (1968): 331; Arthur B. Hanson, "The Right to Know: Fair Comment—Twentieth Century," *Villanova Law Review* 12 (1967): 751–63; "Privacy, Defamation, and the First Amendment: The Implications of Time, Inc. v. Hill," *Columbia Law Review* 67 (1967): 926.

36. Jerome Lawrence Merin, "Libel and the Supreme Court," *William and Mary Law Review* 11 (1969): 402–3.

37. "The Supreme Court 1966 Term, Time, Inc. v. Hill," 163.

38. Miller, "Personal Privacy in the Computer Age," 1166.

39. Kalven, "The Reasonable Man and the First Amendment," 284.

40. Don Pember and Dwight Teeter, "Privacy and the Press since Time, Inc. v. Hill," *Washington Law Review* 50 (1974): 65.

41. Lucas A. Powe Jr., *The Warren Court and American Politics* (Cambridge: Belknap Press, 2000), 320 ("*Hill* was quite an opinion . . . it pointed towards protecting the press in a true privacy case as well, given the newsworthy nature of any information").

42. See Diane L. Zimmerman, "Requiem for a Heavyweight: A Farewell to Warren and Brandeis's Privacy Tort," *Cornell Law Review* 68 (1983): 291; Jonathan Mintz, "The Remains of Privacy's Disclosure Tort: An Exploration of the Private Domain," *Maryland Law Review* 55 (1996): 425, 426; Samantha Barbas, "The Death of the Public Disclosure Tort: A Historical Perspective," *Yale Journal of Law and Humanities* 22 (2010): 171.

43. Varnish v. Best Medium Publishing Co., 405 F.2d 608, 612–13 (2d Cir. 1968).

44. Costlow v. Cusimano, 311 N.Y.S.2d 92, 94 (N.Y. App. Div. 1970).

45. Howard v. Des Moines Register & Tribune Co., 283 N.W.2d 301, 303 (Iowa 1979) (quoting Thornhill v. Alabama, 210 U.S. 88, 102 (1940)).

46. Sipple v. Chronicle Publishing Co., 201 Cal. Rptr. 665, 668 (Cal. Ct. App. 1984).

47. McNamara v. Freedom Newspapers, Inc., 802 S.W.2d 901, 904 (Tex. Ct. App. 1991).

48. Ibid. (quoting Time, Inc. v. Hill, 385 U.S. 374, 388 (1967)).

49. Smith v. Daily Mail Publishing Co., 443 U.S. 97, 103 (1979). See also Cox Broadcasting Corp. v. Cohn, 420 U.S. 469 (1975); Florida Star v. B.J.F., 491 U.S. 524 (1989); Bartnicki v. Vopper, 532 U.S. 514 (2001).

50. Cantrell v. Forest City Publishing Co., 419 U.S. 245, 246–48, 254 (1974).

51. United Medical Laboratories, Inc. v. Columbia Broadcasting System, 404 F. 2d 706, 710–11 (9th Cir. 1968); All Diet Food Distributors v. Time, Inc., 290 N.Y.S.2d 445, 447–48 (N.Y. Sup. Ct. 1967); Altoona Clay Products, Inc. v. Dun & Bradstreet, Inc., 286 F. Supp. 899, 913 (W.D. Pa. 1968); Bon Air Hotel, Inc. v. Time, Inc., 295 F. Supp. 704, 707–8 (S.D. Ga. 1969).

52. Curtis Publishing Co. v. Butts, 388 U.S. 130, 153–55 (1967); Associated Press v. Walker, 388 U.S. 130, 153–55 (1967).

53. Rosenbloom v. Metromedia, Inc., 403 U.S. 29, 43 (1971). Brennan's *Rosenbloom* opinion emphasized the broad scope of his category of "public or general interest": "The constitutional protection was not intended to be limited to matters bearing broadly on issues of responsible government," he wrote, citing *Hill.*

54. Gertz v. Robert Welch, Inc., 418 U.S. 323, 345 (1974).

55. Ibid., 361 (Brennan, J., dissenting).

56. On the uncertainty around this issue, see Justice Powell's concurring opinion in Cox Broadcasting Corp. v. Cohn, 420 U.S. 497–98, and Justice Stewart's remarks in Cantrell v. Forest City Publishing Co., 419 U.S. 250–51. Section 652E of the Restatement (Second) of Torts retains the *Hill* "false light" approach. Restatement (Second) of Torts § 652E (1977). See also Dresbach v. Doubleday & Co., Inc., 518 F. Supp. 1285, 1288 (D.D.C. 1981); Crump v. Beckley Newspapers, Inc., 320 S.E.2d 70, 77 (W. Va. 1983); Fils-Aime v. Enlightenment Press, Inc., 507 N.Y.S.2d 947, 949–50 (N.Y. App. Term 1986); Rinsley v. Brandt, 700 F.2d 1304, 1307 (10th Cir. 1983); Fitzgerald v. Penthouse International, Ltd., 776 F.2d 1236, 1243 (4th Cir. 1985); Dodrill v. Arkansas Democrat Co., 590 S.W.2d 840, 845 (Ark. 1979) (en banc); McCall v. Courier-Journal & Louisville Times Co., 623 S.W.2d 882, 886 (Ky. 1981).

57. Pickering v. Board of Education , 391 U.S. 563, 574 (1968).

58. Connick v. Myers, 461 U.S. 138, 143 n.5, 152–54 (1983).

59. City of San Diego v. Roe, 543 U.S. 77, 83–84 (2004).

60. Connick v. Myers, 461 U.S. 163, 165 n. 5 (Brennan, J., dissenting).

61. Snyder v. Phelps, 562 U.S. 443, 453–54, 458 (2011).

62. See William P. Marshall and Susan Gilles, "The Supreme Court, the First Amendment, and Bad Journalism," *Supreme Court Review* (1994): 207 ("The Court has created a jurisprudence that too often encourages a trivial, lax, and sensationalistic press over a press that is devoted to the thorough and accurate investigation and reporting of matters of

public import"); Gerald Ashdown, "Journalism Police," *Marquette Law Review* 89 (2008), 739–60; James L. Aucoin, *The Evolution of American Investigative Journalism* (Columbia: University of Missouri Press, 2006). But see Russell L. Weaver and Geoffrey Bennett, "Is The *New York Times* 'Actual Malice' Standard Really Necessary? A Comparative Perspective," *Louisiana Law Review* 53 (1993): 1182–85 (suggesting that editors' and reporters' decisions are governed more by journalistic ethics rather than laws and legal standards).

63. Garment, "The Hill Case," 109.

64. Robert Ellis Smith, *Ben Franklin's Web Site: Privacy and Curiosity from Plymouth Rock to the Internet* (Providence, RI: Privacy Journal, 2004), 252.

65. See David Kamp, "The Tabloid Decade," *Vanity Fair* (February 1999): 64.

66. See Deirdre Carmody, "Campaigns Raising Debates on Privacy," *New York Times,* November 18, 1979, 31. "Perhaps the most common tabloid characteristic adopted by the mainstream media during the 1990s was the aggressive intrusion on the private lives of public figures." Herbert N. Foerstel, *From Watergate to Monicagate: Ten Controversies in Modern Journalism and Media* (Westport, CT: Greenwood Publishing, 2001).

67. Rodney A. Smolla, "Will Tabloid Journalism Ruin the First Amendment for the Rest of Us?" *DePaul-LCA Journal of Art and Entertainment Law* 9 (1998): 2, 6.

68. Alex S. Jones, "News Media Torn Two Ways in Debate on Privacy," *New York Times,* April 30, 1992.

69. "Midwinter Meeting 2008," *American Libraries* 39 (2008): 63. See also Anthony Lewis, "Journalistic Freedom and Privacy: A Case of Relative Compatibility," *Suffolk Law Review* 43 (2010): 79–88; Anthony Lewis, *Make No Law: The Sullivan Case and the First Amendment* (New York: Random House, 1991), 184–85 (distinguishing *Hill* from *Sullivan*).

70. Anthony Lewis, "The Sullivan Decision," *Tennessee Journal of Law and Policy* 1 (2004), 135, 148.

71. Anthony Lewis, "Privacy and Civilization: An Essay," *Nova Law Review* 27 (2002): 235.

72. Ibid., 241–42.

73. Anthony Lewis, "The Press: Free But Not Exceptional," in *Reason and Passion: Justice Brennan's Enduring Influence,* ed. Joshua Rosencrantz and Bernard Schwartz (New York: Norton, 1997), 58.

74. Kalven, "The Reasonable Man and the First Amendment," 301.

75. Jim Newton, *Justice for All: Earl Warren and the Nation He Made* (New York: Penguin Books, 2006), 477.

76. Leonard Garment, "The Hill Case," *New Yorker,* April 17, 1989, 109.

77. See letters in Box 31, Folder 701, Abe Fortas Papers, Yale University Manuscripts and Archives.

78. Garment, "The Hill Case," 107.

79. Ibid.

80. See Bob Woodward and Scott Armstrong, *The Brethren: Inside the Supreme Court* (New York: Simon & Schuster, 2005), 5–7.

81. William Lambert, "Fortas of the Supreme Court," *Life,* May 9, 1969, 32–33.

82. Bruce Allen Murphy, *Fortas: The Rise and Ruin of a Supreme Court Justice* (New York: Morrow, 1988), 362.

83. Ibid.

84. Doug Parker, "Memories of Len" (in author's possession).

85. Laura Kalman, *Abe Fortas* (New Haven, CT: Yale University Press, 1990), 370.

86. Jonathan Aitken, *Nixon: A Life* (Washington, D.C.: Regnery Publishing, 1993), 314.

87. Thomas W. Evans, "Mudge Rose Guthrie Alexander and Ferdon" (unpublished manuscript, n.d.).

88. Aitken, *Nixon*, 314.

89. Michal R. Belknap, *The Supreme Court under Earl Warren, 1953–1969* (Columbia: University of South Carolina Press, 2005), 256.

90. Untitled, June 23, 1969, John Marshall Harlan Papers, Box 261, Folder 22, Mudd Library, Princeton University; Fred Graham, "Time v. Hill: A Future President Makes His Case," in A *Good Quarrel: America's Top Legal Reporters Share Stories from Inside the Supreme Court, ed. Timothy R. Johnson and Jerry* Goldman (Ann Arbor: University of Michigan Press, 2009), 178.

91. Ronald Ostrow, "High Court Backs Press in False Report Cases," *Los Angeles Times*, January 10, 1967, 7.

92. Garment, "The Hill Case," 104.

93. Lewis, *Make No Law*, 188.

94. Douglas Brinkley and Luke A. Nichter, *The Nixon Tapes: 1973* (New York: Houghton Mifflin Harcourt, 2015), 4.

95. Bernard Schwartz, *The Unpublished Opinions of the Warren Court* (New York: Oxford University Press, 1985).

96. Anthony Lewis, "The Arguments That Mattered Most," *New York Times,* December 29, 1985, BR20.

97. Garment, "The Hill Case," 104.

98. Fawn Brodie, *Richard Nixon: The Shaping of His Character* (New York: Norton, 1981), 454.

99. R. V. Denenberg, "Privacy: Wanted But Vague," *New York Times*, February 3, 1974, 181; John Herbers, "Nixon Weighs New Plan to Shield Citizens' Privacy," *New York Times,* November 18, 1973, 61.

100. Stanley I. Kutler, *The Wars of Watergate: The Last Crisis of Richard Nixon* (New York: Norton, 1992), 589.

101. Nixon v. Administrator of General Services, 433 U.S. 425, 465 (1977).

102. Jerome M. Balsam, "Cover Up and Privacy in Nixon v. ABC," *New York Times*, October 6, 1989, A30.

103. Kalven, "The Reasonable Man and the First Amendment," 286.

104. Garment, "The Hill Case," 109. The *Washington Post*'s Dana Bullen concluded that *Hill*, following on the heels of *Sullivan*, may have been an "unintended victim of the civil rights struggle." Dana Bullen, "When Two Sides of Law Collide," *Washington Post*, contained in John Marshall Harlan Papers, Box 261, Folder 22.

105. Ibid.

Bibliography

Manuscript Collections

Abe Fortas Papers, Manuscripts & Archives, Yale University.

John Marshall Harlan Papers, Seeley G. Mudd Manuscript Library, Princeton University.

William J. Brennan Papers, Manuscript Division, Library of Congress.

William O. Douglas Papers, Manuscript Division, Library of Congress.

Byron R. White Papers, Manuscript Division, Library of Congress.

Potter Stewart Papers, Manuscripts & Archives, Yale University.

Wilderness Years (1962–1968) Collection, Richard Nixon Presidential Library and Museum.

Tom C. Clark Papers, Tarlton Law Library, Jamail Center for Legal Research, University of Texas School of Law.

Earl Warren Papers, Manuscript Division, Library of Congress.

Hugo LaFayette Black Papers, Manuscript Division, Library of Congress.

Leonard Garment Papers, Manuscript Division, Library of Congress.

Joseph Arnold Hayes Papers, Lilly Library Manuscript Collections, Indiana University.

Adolph Ochs Papers, Manuscripts and Archives Division, New York Public Library.

Arthur Hays Sulzberger Papers, Manuscripts and Archives Division, New York Public Library.

Books and Articles

Abraham, Kenneth S. *The Liability Century: Insurance and Tort Law from the Progressive Era to 9/11.* Cambridge: Harvard University Press, 2008.

Adams, Elbridge. "The Right of Privacy and Its Relation to the Law of Libel." *American Law Review* 39 (1905): 37–58.

Adler, Sheldon S. "Toward a Constitutional Theory of Individuality: The Privacy Jurisprudence of Justice Douglas." *Yale Law Journal* 87 (1978): 1579–1600.

Aitken, Jonathan. *Nixon: A Life.* Washington, D.C.: Regnery Publishing, 1996.

Albig, William. "Good and Evil from the Press." *Annals of the American Academy of Political and Social Science* 280 (March 1952): 113.

Alexander, George J. "Free Expression and the Law of Torts." *Syracuse Law Review* 19 (1967): 457–77.

Alfred Politz Research. *A Study of Four Media.* New York: Time, Inc., 1953.

Ambrose, Stephen E. *Nixon.* 3 vols. New York: Simon & Schuster, 1987.

Anderson, David. "Freedom of the Press." *Texas Law Review* 80 (2002): 429–530.

———. "The Origins of the Press Clause." *UCLA Law Review* 30 (1982): 455–541.

Ashdown, Gerald. "Journalism Police." *Marquette Law Review* 89 (2008): 739–60.

Aucoin, James L. *The Evolution of American Investigative Journalism.* Columbia: University of Missouri Press, 2006.

Baker, C. Edwin. "The Independent Significance of the Press Clause under Existing Law." *Hofstra Law Review* 35 (2007): 955–1026.

Ball, Howard. *Hugo L. Black: Cold Steel Warrior.* New York: Oxford University Press, 1996.

———. *The Supreme Court in the Intimate Lives of Americans: Birth, Sex, Marriage, Child-rearing, and Death.* New York: New York University Press, 2004.

Banta, Ray. *Indiana's Laughmakers: The Story of over 400 Hoosiers: Actors, Cartoonists, Writers, and Others.* Indianapolis: PennUltimate Press, 1990.

Barbas, Samantha. "The Death of the Public Disclosure Tort: A Historical Perspective." *Yale Journal of Law and Humanities* 22 (2010): 171–215.

———. "From Privacy to Publicity: The Tort of Appropriation in the Age of Mass Consumption." *Buffalo Law Review* 61 (2013): 1119–90.

Barron, James H. "Warren and Brandeis, *The Right to Privacy*, 4. Harv. L. Rev. 193 (1890): Demystifying a Landmark Citation." *Suffolk University Law Review* 13 (1979): 875–922.

Battan, Jesse. "'The New Narcissism' in 20th Century America: The Shadow and Substance of Social Change." *Journal of Social History* 17 (1983): 199–220.

Baughman, James. *Henry Luce and the Rise of the American News Media.* Baltimore: Johns Hopkins University Press, 2001.

———. "Who Reads *Life*?" In *Looking at Life Magazine,* edited by Erika Doss. Washington, D.C.: Smithsonian, 2001.

Beaney, William. "The Griswold Case and the Expanding Right to Privacy." *Wisconsin Law Review* 64 (1965): 976–95.

Bell, Bernard W. "Judging in Interesting Times: The Free Speech Clause Jurisprudence of Justice Byron R. White." *Catholic University Law Review* 52 (2003): 893–914.

Belli, Melvin. *Ready for the Plaintiff.* New York: Grosset & Dunlap, 1956.

Belknap, Michal R. *The Supreme Court under Earl Warren, 1953–1969.* Columbia: University of South Carolina Press, 2005.

Bent, Silas. *Ballyhoo: The Voice of the Press.* New York: Boni & Liveright, 1927.

Berman, Daniel M. "Mr. Justice Brennan: A Preliminary Appraisal." *Catholic University Law Review* 7 (1958): 1–15.

Bertelsman, William O. "The First Amendment and Protection of Reputation and Privacy— New York Times Co. v. Sullivan and How It Grew." *Kentucky Law Journal* 56 (1967–1968): 718–56.

Bezanson, Randall. "The Libel Tort Today." *Washington and Lee Law Review* 45 (1988): 535–56.

Bezanson, Randall P., Gilbert Cranberg, and John Soloski. *Libel Law and the Press: Myth and Reality.* New York: Free Press, 1987.

Bird, George, and Frederic Merwin, eds. *The Newspaper and Society.* New York: Prentice Hall, 1942.

Black, Hugo L. "The Bill of Rights." *New York University Law Review* 35 (1960): 865–81.

Black, Hugo L., and Elizabeth Black. *Mr. Justice and Mrs. Black: The Memoirs of Hugo L. Black and Elizabeth Black.* New York: Random House, 1988.

Black, Hugo, and Edmond Cahn. "Mr. Justice Black and First Amendment Absolutes: A Public Interview." *New York University Law Review* 37 (1962): 549–63.

Blanchard, Margaret A. "The Institutional Press and Its First Amendment Privileges." *Supreme Court Review* 1978 (1978): 227–28.

———. *Revolutionary Sparks: Freedom of Expression in Modern America.* New York: Oxford University Press, 1992.

Bledstein, Burton. *The Culture of Professionalism: The Middle Class and the Development of Higher Education in America.* New York: Norton, 1976.

Bloustein, Edward J. "Privacy as an Aspect of Human Dignity: An Answer to Dean Prosser." *New York Law Review* 39 (1964): 156–202.

Bloustein, Edward. "Privacy, Tort Law, and the Constitution: Is Warren and Brandeis' Tort Petty and Unconstitutional as Well?" *Texas Law Review* 46 (1968): 611–29.

Bond, Fraser. *An Introduction to Journalism.* New York: Macmillan, 1954.

Botein, Bernard. "The People's Right to Know." *Harvard Law Review* 67 (1954): 920–22.

———. *Trial Judge: The Candid Behind-the-Bench Story of Justice Botein.* New York: Simon and Schuster, 1952.

Breed, Warren. "Mass Communication and Socio Cultural Integration." *Social Forces* 37 (1958): 109–16.

Breines, Wini. *Young, White, and Miserable: Growing up Female in the Fifties.* Chicago: University of Chicago Press, 1992.

Brennan, William J. Jr. "The Supreme Court and the Meiklejohn Interpretation of the First Amendment." *Harvard Law Review* 79 (1965): 1–20.

Brenton, Myron. *The Privacy Invaders.* New York: Coward & McCann, 1964.

Brinkley, Alan. *The Publisher: Henry Luce and His American Century.* New York: Vintage Books, 2011.

Brinkley, Douglas, and Luke Nichter. *The Nixon Tapes 1973.* New York: Houghton Mifflin Harcourt, 2015.

Brinkley, William. *The Fun House.* New York: Random House, 1961.

Brodie, Fawn M. *Richard Nixon: The Shaping of His Character.* New York: Norton, 1981.

Brown, Henry Billings. "The Liberty of the Press." *American Law Review* 34 (1900): 321–41.

Bruggemier, Gert, Aurelia Colombi Ciacchi, and Patrick O'Callaghan, eds. *Personality Rights in European Tort Law.* Cambridge: Cambridge University Press, 2010.

Buchanan, Pat. *The Greatest Comeback: How Richard Nixon Rose From Defeat to Create the New Majority.* New York: Crown Publishing 2015.

Burress, Lee. *Battle of the Books: Literary Censorship in the Public Schools, 1950–1985.* Metuchen, NJ: Scarecrow Press, 1989.

Burton, John P. Jr. "Privacy and the Press." *Harvard Legal Commentary* 4 (1967): 89–98.

Bush, Chilton Rowlette. *Newspaper Reporting of Public Affairs: An Advanced Course in Newspaper Reporting and a Manual for Professional Newspaper Men.* New York: D. Appleton, 1940.

Caplan, Lincoln. *Skadden: Power, Money, and the Rise of a Legal Empire.* New York: Farrar, Straus and Giroux, 1994.

Carlson, Allan C. "Luce, Life, and the American Way." *This World* (Winter 1986): 56–74.

Cashman, Sean. *America in the Twenties and Thirties: The Olympian Age of Franklin Delano Roosevelt.* New York: New York University Press, 1989.

Chafee, Zechariah. "Book Review." In *Essays in Constitutional* Law, edited by Robert G. McCloskey. New York: Random House, 1957.

Champlin, Charles. *A Life in Writing: The Story of an American Journalist.* Syracuse, NY: Syracuse University Press, 2006.

Channing, Carol. *Just Lucky I Guess.* New York: Simon & Schuster, 2002.

Christians, Clifford G., John P. Ferré, and P. Mark Fackler, *Good News: Social Ethics and the Press.* New York: Oxford University Press, 1993.

Clemons, L. S. "Right of Privacy in Relation to the Publication of Photographs." *Marquette Law Review* 14 (1930): 193–98.

Clurman, Richard. *Beyond Malice: The Media's Years of Reckoning.* New York: Transaction Books, 1988.

"Comment, Privacy, Defamation, and the First Amendment: The Implications of Time, Inc. v. Hill." *Columbia Law Review* 67 (May 1967): 926–52.

"Comment, Time, Inc. v. Hill." *Chicago-Kent Law Review* 44 (1967): 58-63.

"Constitutional Law." *Texas Law Review* 45 (1966–1967): 758–65.

"Constitutional Law–State Cannot Award Damages for Invasion of Privacy without Proof of Actual Malice." *North Carolina Law Review* 45 (1967): 740–47.

Commission on Freedom of the Press. *A Free and Responsible Press: A General Report on Mass Communication: Newspapers, Radio, Motion Pictures, Magazines and Books.* Chicago: University of Chicago Press, 1947.

Cooley, Thomas M. *A Treatise on the Law of Torts, or the Wrongs Which Arise Independent of Contract.* Chicago: Callaghan, 1880.

Corwin, Edward S. "Freedom of Speech and Press under the First Amendment: A Résumé." *Yale Law Journal* 30 (1920): 48–55.

Cort, David. *The Sin of Henry Luce: An Anatomy of Journalism.* New York: Lyle Stuart, 1974.

Cravens, Hamilton, ed. *The Social Sciences Go to Washington: The Politics of Knowledge in the Postmodern Age.* New Brunswick, NJ: Rutgers University Press, 2004.

Cray, Ed. *Chief Justice: A Biography of Earl Warren.* New York: Simon & Schuster, 1997.

Cullinan, Eustace. "The Rights of Newspapers: May They Print Whatever They Choose?" *ABA Journal* 41 (1955): 1020–23.

Curtis, Michael Kent. *Free Speech: The People's Darling Privilege.* Raleigh, NC: Duke University Press, 2000.

DeFleur, Melvin. "How Massive Are the Mass Media? Implications for Communications Education and Research." *Syracuse Scholar* 10 (1990): 1–21.

Deutsch, Eberhard P. "Freedom of the Press and of the Mails." *Michigan Law Review* 36 (1938): 703–51.

"Developments in the Law: Defamation." *Harvard Law Review* 69 (1956): 875–959.

Dickler, Gerald. "Right of Privacy—A Proposed Redefinition." *United States Law Review* 70 (1936): 435–56.

Dixon, Robert G. "The Griswold Penumbra: Constitutional Charter for an Expanded Law of Privacy?" *Michigan Law Review* 64 (1965): 197–218.

Doan, Edward. "The Newspaper and the Right of Privacy." *Journal of the Bar Association of Kansas* 5 (1937): 203–61.

Donovan, Hedley. *Right Places, Right Times*. New York: Touchstone, 1991.

Douglas, William. *The Right of the People*. New York: Doubleday, 1958.

Easton, Eric. "The Colonel's Finest Campaign: Robert R. McCormick and *Near v. Minnesota*." *Federal Communications Law Journal* 60 (2008): 183–228.

Eisler, Kim Isaac. *The Last Liberal: Justice William J. Brennan, Jr. and the Decisions That Transformed America*. New York: Simon & Schuster, 1993.

Elson, Robert. *Time, Inc.: The Intimate History of a Publishing Enterprise*, vol. 2. New York: Atheneum, 1968.

Emerson, Thomas I. "Nine Justices in Search of a Doctrine." *Michigan Law Review* 64 (1965): 219–34.

———. "Towards a General Theory of the First Amendment." *Yale Law Journal* 72 (1963): 877–956.

Engel, David. "Perception and Decision at the Threshold of Tort Law: Explaining the Infrequency of Claims." *DePaul Law Review* 62 (2013): 293–94.

Ernst, Morris. *The First Freedom*. New York: Macmillan, 1946.

Evans, Thomas W. "Mudge Rose Guthrie Alexander & Ferdon." Unpublished manuscript, n.d.

Farber, David. *The Age of Great Dreams: America in the 1960s*. New York: Hill and Wang, 1994.

Fielding, Raymond. "Time Flickers Out: Notes on the Passing of the March of Time." *Quarterly of Film, Radio, and Television* 11 (1957): 354–61.

Frank, Jeffrey. *Ike and Dick: Portrait of a Strange Political Marriage*. New York: Simon & Schuster, 2013.

Frank, John P. "Mr. Justice Black, a Biographical Appreciation." *Yale Law Journal* 65 (1956): 454–63.

Franklin, Marc. "A Constitutional Problem in Privacy Protection: Legal Inhibition on Reporting of Fact." *Stanford Law Review* 107 (1963): 107–48.

Forde, Kathy Roberts. "Libel, Freedom of the Press, and the *New Yorker*." *American Journalism* 23 (2006): 61–91.

Forde, Kathy Roberts. *Literary Journalism on Trial: Masson v. New Yorker and the First Amendment*. Amherst: University of Massachusetts Press, 2008.

Friedman, Lawrence. *The Republic of Choice: Law, Authority, and Culture*. Cambridge: Harvard University Press, 1998.

Gajda, Amy. *The First Amendment Bubble: How Privacy and Paparazzi Threaten a Free Press*. Cambridge: Harvard University Press, 2015.

———. "What If Samuel D. Warren Hadn't Married a Senator's Daughter? Uncovering the Press Coverage That Led to 'the Right to Privacy.'" *Michigan State Law Review* 2008 (2008): 35–60.

Garment, Leonard. *Crazy Rhythm: From Brooklyn and Jazz to Nixon's White House, Watergate, and Beyond*. Cambridge, MA: Da Capo Press, 1997.

———. "The Hill Case." *New Yorker*, April 17, 1989.

Gillmor, Donald, and Jerome Barron. *Mass Communications Law: Cases and Comment*. Eagen, MN: West Publishing, 1969.

Glancy, Dorothy J. "The Invention of the Right to Privacy." *Arizona Law Review* 21 (1979): 1–40.

Gleason, Timothy W. *The Watchdog Concept: The Press and the Courts in Nineteenth Century America*. Ames: Iowa State University, 1990.

Goldstein, Tom. *Killing the Messenger: 100 Years of Media Criticism*. New York: Columbia University Press, 2007.

Gormley, Ken. "One Hundred Years of Privacy." *Wisconsin Law Review* 1992 (1992): 1335–1442.

Graham, Fred. "*Time Inc. v. Hill*: A Future President Makes His Case." In *A Good Quarrel: America's Top Legal Reporters Share Stories from Inside the Supreme Court*, edited by Timothy R. Johnson and Jerry Goldman. Ann Arbor: University of Michigan Press, 2009.

Halasz, Piri. *A Memoir of Creativity: Abstract Painting, Politics and the Media, 1956–2008*. Bloomington: iUniverse Publishing, 2009.

Hall, Kermit, and Melvin Urofsky. *New York Times v. Sullivan: Civil Rights, Libel Law and the Free Press*. Lawrence: University Press of Kansas, 2011.

Hall, Max. "The Role of the Press." In *Reporting the News: Selections from Nieman Reports*, edited by Louis Lyons. Cambridge: Belknap Press, 1965.

Hamblin, Dora Jean. *That Was the Life*. New York: Norton, 1977.

Harshorn, Lewis. *Alger Hiss, Whittaker Chambers, and the Case That Ignited McCarthyism*. Jefferson: McFarland, 2010.

Hauch, Jeanne. "Protecting Private Facts in France: The Warren and Brandeis Tort Is Alive and Well and Flourishing in Paris." *Tulane Law Review* 68 (1994): 1219–1302.

Hawthorne, Daniel. *Judge Medina, a Biography*. New York: W. Funk, 1952.

Hayes, Arthur. *Press Critics are the Fifth Estate: Media Watchdogs in America*. Westport, CT: Praeger, 2008.

Hayes, Joseph. *The Desperate Hours*. New York: Random House, 1954.

Heckscher, August. "The Invasion of Privacy (II): The Reshaping of Privacy." *American Scholar* 28 (1959): 11–20.

Hoffman, Paul. *Lions in the Street: The Inside Story of the Great Wall Street Law Firms*. New York: New American Library, 1973.

Horwitz, Morton J. *The Warren Court and the Pursuit of Justice*. New York: Hill and Wang, 1999.

Hopkins, W. Wat. *Actual Malice: Twenty-Five Years after Times v. Sullivan*. New York: Praeger, 1989.

Ides, Allan. "The Jurisprudence of Justice Byron White." *Yale Law Journal* 103 (1993): 419–61.

Ingber, Stanley. "Defamation: A Conflict between Reason and Decency." *Virginia Law Review* 65 (1979): 796–801.

Jessup, John J., ed. *The Ideas of Henry Luce*. New York: Atheneum, 1969.

Johnson, John W. *Griswold v. Connecticut: Birth Control and the Constitutional Right of Privacy.* Lawrence: University Press of Kansas, 2005.

Kabatchnik, Amnon. *Blood on the Stage, 1950–1975: Milestone Plays of Crime, Mystery, and Detection.* Lanham, MD: Scarecrow Press, 2011.

Kacedan, Basil. "The Right of Privacy." *Boston University Law Review* 12 (1932): 353–95.

Kaestle, Carl F., and Janice A. Radway. "A Framework for the History of Publishing and Reading in the United States, 1880–1940." In *A History of the Book in America*, vol. 4, edited by Carl F. Kaestle and Janice A. Radway. Chapel Hill: University of North Carolina Press, 2009.

Kalman, Laura. *Abe Fortas: A Biography.* New Haven, CT: Yale University Press, 1990.

Kalven, Harry Jr. "The New York Times Case: A Note on 'The Central Meaning of the First Amendment.'" *Supreme Court Review* 64 (1964): 191–221.

———. "Privacy in Tort Law—Were Warren and Brandeis Wrong?" *Law and Contemporary Problems* 31 (1966): 326–41.

———. "The Reasonable Man and the First Amendment: Hill, Butts, and Walker." *Supreme Court Review* 1967 (1967): 267–310.

———. *A Worthy Tradition: Freedom of Speech in America*, edited by Jamie Kalven. New York: Harper & Row, 1988.

Kanfer, Stefan. *Tough without a Gun.* New York: Knopf, 2011.

Karst, Kenneth L. "'The Files': Legal Controls over the Accuracy and Accessibility of Stored Personal Data." *Law and Contemporary Problems* 31 (1966): 342–76.

Kauper, Paul G. "Penumbras, Peripheries, Emanations, Things Fundamental and Things Forgotten: The *Griswold* Case." *Michigan Law Review* 64 (1965): 235–58.

Kobler, John. *Luce: His Time, Life, and Fortune.* Garden City, NY: Doubleday, 1968.

Kozol, Wendy. *Life's America: Family and Nation in Postwar Photojournalism.* Philadelphia: Temple University Press, 1994.

Krislov, Samuel. "Mr. Justice Black Reopens the Free Speech Debate." *UCLA Law Review* 11 (1964): 189–211.

Krotoszynski, Ronald J. "Reconciling Privacy and Speech in the Era of Big Data: A Comparative Legal Analysis." *William and Mary Law Review* 56 (2015): 1289–90, 1298–1309.

Kutler, Stanley I. *The Wars of Watergate: The Last Crisis of Richard Nixon.* New York: Norton, 1992.

Kyvig, David E. *Daily Life in the United States, 1920–1940.* Chicago: Ivan R. Dee, 2004.

Lane, Frederick S. *American Privacy: The 400-Year History of Our Most Contested Right.* Boston: Beacon Books, 2009.

Lange, David. "The Speech and Press Clauses." *UCLA Law Review* 23 (1975): 77–119.

Leigh, Robert D., ed. *A Free and Responsible Press: A General Report on Mass Communication: Newspapers, Radio, Motion Pictures, Magazines, and Books.* Chicago: University of Chicago Press, 1947.

Lepore, Jill. *Mansion of Happiness: A History of Life and Death.* New York: Knopf, 2012.

Levine, Lee, and Stephen Wermiel. *The Progeny: Justice William J. Brennan's Fight to Preserve the Legacy of New York Times v. Sullivan.* Chicago: American Bar Association Publishing, 2014.

Levy, Leonard W. *Legacy of Suppression: Freedom of Speech and Press in Early American History*. Cambridge: Belknap Press, 1960.

————. "On the Origins of the Free Press Clause." *UCLA Law Review* 32 (1984): 177–218.

Levy, Shawn. *Paul Newman: A Life*. New York: Crown, 2009.

Lewis, Anthony. "Journalistic Freedom and Privacy: A Case of Relative Compatibility." *Suffolk Law Review* 43 (2010): 79–88.

————. "Justice Black and the First Amendment." *Alabama Law Review* 38 (1986): 289–306.

————. *Make No Law: The Sullivan Case and the First Amendment*. New York: Random House, 1991.

————. "Privacy and Civilization: An Essay." *Nova Law Review* 27 (2002): 225–42.

————. "The Press: Free But Not Exceptional." In *Reason and Passion: Justice Brennan's Enduring Influence,* edited by Joshua Rosencrantz and Bernard Schwartz. New York: Norton, 1997.

————. "The Sullivan Decision." *Tennessee Journal of Law and Policy* 1 (2004): 135–52.

Luce, Henry R. "Responsibility of the Press in the Cold War." *Vital Speeches of the Day* 19 (April 1953): 368–72.

MacDougall, Curtis. *The Press and Its Problems*. Dubuque, IA: W. C. Brown, 1964.

MacNeil, Neil. *Without Fear or Favor*. New York: Harcourt, Brace, 1940.

Magee, James. *Mr. Justice Black: Absolutist on the Court*. Charlottesville: University Press of Virginia, 1980.

Maisel, Louise Sandy, Ira N. Forman, and Donald Altschiller. *Jews in American Politics*. Lanham, MD: Rowman & Littlefield, 2001.

Marshall, William P., and Susan Gilles. "The Supreme Court, the First Amendment, and Bad Journalism." *Supreme Court Review* 169 (1994): 169–208.

Mason, Alpheus Thomas. *Brandeis: A Free Man's Life*. New York: Viking Press, 1956.

Mavity, Nancy. *The Modern Newspaper*. New York: Holt, 1930.

May, Elaine Tyler. *Homeward Bound: American Families in the Cold War Era*. New York: Basic Books, 1990.

Maytal, Itai. "Libel Lessons from across the Pond: What British Courts Can Learn from the United States' Chilling Experience with the 'Multiple Publication Rule' in Traditional Media and the Internet." *Journal of International Media and Entertainment Law* 3 (2010): 122–24.

Mazo, Earl, and Stephen Hess. *Nixon: A Political Portrait*. New York: Popular Library, 1968.

McClean, Archibald. "The Right of Privacy." *Green Bag* 15 (1903): 494–97.

McDonald, Barbara. "Privacy, Princesses, and Paparazzi." *New York Law School Law Review* (2005): 205–36.

McKay, Robert B. "Congressional Investigations and the Supreme Court." *California Law Review* 51 (May 1963): 267–95.

————. "The Right of Privacy: Emanations and Intimations." *Michigan Law Review* 64 (1965): 259–82.

Meiklejohn, Alexander. "The First Amendment Is an Absolute." *Supreme Court Review* 1961 (1961): 245–66.

———. *Free Speech and Its Relation to Self-Government*. New York: Harper & Brothers, 1948.

Mendelson, Wallace. "Clear and Present Danger—From *Schenck* to *Dennis*." *Columbia Law Review* 52 (1952): 449–56.

———. "On the Meaning of the First Amendment: Absolutes in the Balance." *California Law Review* 50 (December 1962): 821–28.

Meyerowitz, Joanne. "Beyond the Feminine Mystique: A Reassessment of Postwar Mass Culture, 1946–1958." *Journal of American History* 79 (1993): 1455, 1460.

Miller, Arthur. *The Assault on Privacy*. New York: Penguin, 1972.

———. "Privacy in the Computer Age: The Challenge of a New Technology in an Information Oriented Society." *Michigan Law Review* 67 (1969): 1089–1246.

Miller, Douglas, and Marion Nowak. *The Fifties: The Way We Really Were*. Garden City, NY: Doubleday, 1977.

Miller, Fredrick, Morris Vogel, and Allen Davis. *Philadelphia Stories: A Photographic History, 1920–1960*. Philadelphia: Temple University Press, 1988.

Miller, Gabriel. *William Wyler: The Life and Films of Hollywood's Most Celebrated Director*. Louisville: University Press of Kentucky, 2013.

Mills, C. Wright. *White Collar: The American Middle Classes*. Oxford: Oxford University Press, 1951.

Mintz, Jonathan. "The Remains of Privacy's Disclosure Tort: An Exploration of the Private Domain." *Maryland Law Review* 55 (1996): 425–66.

Moreland, Roy. "Right of Privacy Today." *Kentucky Law Journal* 19 (1931): 101–36.

Morris, Clarence. "Inadvertent Newspaper Libel and Retraction." *Illinois Law Review* 32 (1937): 36–49.

Mott, Frank Luther. *A History of American Magazines, 1741–1850*. Cambridge: Harvard University Press, 1930.

Mueller, Gerhard. "Problems Posed by Publicity to Crime and Criminal Proceedings." *University of Pennsylvania Law Review* 110 (1961): 1–26.

Murnaghan, Francis. "From Figment to Fiction to Philosophy—the Requirement of Proof of Damages in Libel Actions." *Catholic University Law Review* 22 (1972): 1–38.

Murphy, Bruce Allen. *Fortas: The Rise and Ruin of a Supreme Court Justice*. New York: Morrow, 1988.

Murphy, Paul. "*Near v. Minnesota* in the Context of Historical Developments." *Minnesota Law Review* 66 (1981): 95–160.

Neal, Robert Miller. *Newspaper Desk Work*. New York: D. Appleton, 1933.

Nelson, Deborah. *Pursuing Privacy in Cold War America*. New York: Columbia University Press, 2002.

Newell, Martin. *The Law of Libel and Slander in Civil and Criminal Cases*. Chicago: Callaghan and Company, 1898.

Newman, Roger K. *Hugo Black: A Biography*. New York: Pantheon Books, 1994.

Newton, Jim. *Justice for All: Earl Warren and the Nation He Made*. New York: Riverhead Books, 2006.

Nimmer, Melville. "The Right to Speak from Times to Time: First Amendment Theory Applied to Libel and Misapplied to Privacy." *California Law Review* 56 (1968): 935–67.

Nixon, Richard. *Speeches, Writings, Documents*, edited by Rick Perlstein. Princeton, NJ: Princeton University Press, 2008.

Nizer, Louis. "The Right of Privacy: A Half Century's Developments." *Michigan Law Review* 39 (1940): 526–96.

"Notes of Cases." *Virginia Law Register* 11 (1905): 58–65.

Odgers, William Blake. *A Digest of the Law of Libel and Slander*. London: Bradbury, Agnew & Co., 1911.

Oglesby, Dwayne L. "Freedom of the Press v. The Rights of the Individual: A Continuing Controversy." *Oregon Law Review* 47 (1968): 132–45.

Packard, Vance. *The Naked Society*. New York: David McKay, 1964.

———. *The Status Seekers*. New York: David McKay, 1959.

Pedrick, Willard. "Privacy and Publicity: Is It Any of Our Business?" *University of Toronto Law Review* 20 (1970): 391–411.

Pember, Don R. *Privacy and the Press: The Law, the Mass Media, and the First Amendment*. Seattle: University of Washington Press, 1972.

Pember, Don, and Dwight Teeter. "Privacy and the Press since Time, Inc. v. Hill." *Washington Law Review* 50 (1974): 57–92.

Perlstein, Rick. *Nixonland: The Rise of a President and the Fracturing of America*. New York: Scribner, 2009.

Post, Robert. "The Social Foundations of Defamation Law: Reputation and the Constitution." *California Law Review* 74 (1986): 691–742.

Powe, Lucas A. *The Warren Court and American Politics*. Cambridge: Harvard University Press, 2009.

"Privacy, Defamation, and the First Amendment: The Implications of Time, Inc. v. Hill." *Columbia Law Review* 67 (1967): 926–52.

Prosser, William. "Intentional Infliction of Mental Suffering: A New Tort." *Michigan Law Review* 37 (1939): 391–400.

———. "Libel Per Quod." *Virginia Law Review* 46 (1960): 839–55.

———. "Privacy." *California Law Review* 48 (1960): 383–423.

Rabban, David. *Free Speech in Its Forgotten Years, 1870–1920*. Cambridge: Cambridge University Press, 1997.

Rayfield, Stanley. *How Life Gets the Story: Behind the Scenes in Photojournalism*. New York: Doubleday, 1955.

Regan, Priscilla M. *Legislating Privacy: Technology, Social Values, and Public Policy*. Chapel Hill: University of North Carolina Press, 1995.

Reich, Charles. "Mr. Justice Black and the Living Constitution." *Harvard Law Review* 76 (1963): 673–754.

Rieff, Philip. *Triumph of the Therapeutic: Uses of Faith after Freud*. Chicago: University of Chicago Press, 1966.

Riesman, David, *The Lonely Crowd: A Study of the Changing American Character*, with Nathan Glazer and Reuel Denney. New Haven, CT: Yale University Press, 1950.

Rosen, Jeffrey. *The Supreme Court: The Personalities and Rivalries That Defined America*. New York: Holt, 2007.

Rosenberg, Norman. *Protecting the Best Men: An Interpretive History of the Law of Libel.* Chapel Hill: University of North Carolina Press, 1990.

Schmidt, Christopher W. "*New York Times v. Sullivan* and the Legal Attack on the Civil Rights Movement." *Alabama Law Review* 66 (2014): 292–335.

Schwartz, Bernard. *The Warren Court: A Retrospective.* New York: Oxford University Press, 1996.

Seiler, Cotton. *Republic of Drivers: A Cultural History of Automobility in America.* Chicago: University of Chicago Press, 2008.

Seipp, David. "The Right to Privacy in American History." PhD dissertation, Harvard University, 1978.

Seldes, George. "The Press and the Individual." In *Killing the Messenger: 100 Years of Media Criticism,* edited by Tom Goldstein. New York: Columbia University Press, 1989.

Shapo, Marshall. "Media Injuries to Personality: An Essay on Legal Regulation of Public Communication." *Texas Law Review* 46 (1968): 650–57.

Shils, Edward. "Privacy: Its Constitution and Vicissitudes." *Law and Contemporary Problems* 31 (1966): 281–306.

Schwartz, Bernard. *Super Chief: Earl Warren and His Supreme Court: A Judicial Biography.* New York: New York University Press, 1984.

———. *The Unpublished Opinions of the Warren Court.* New York: Oxford University Press, 1985.

Seltzer, Louis. "The Press Looks at the Bar and at Itself." *Journal of the Cleveland Bar Association* 22 (1950): 19, 28–32.

Siebert, Frederick. "Legal Developments Affecting the Press." *Annals of the American Academy of Political and Social Science* 219 (1942): 93–99.

———. *The Rights and Privileges of the Press.* New York: D. Appleton-Century, 1934.

Silver, Isidore. "Privacy and the First Amendment." *Fordham Law Review* 34 (May 1966): 553–68.

Silving, Helen. *Helen Silving: Memoirs.* New York: Vantage Press, 1988.

Sloan, Bill. *I Watched a Wild Hog Eat My Baby: A Colorful History of Tabloids and Their Cultural Impact.* Amherst, NY: Prometheus Books, 2001.

Smigel, Erwin. *The Wall Street Lawyer: Professional Organization Man?* Bloomington: Indiana University Press, 1969.

Smith, Donald. "Privacy: The Right That Failed." *Columbia Journalism Review* 8 (Spring 1969): 18–22.

Smith, Robert Ellis. *Ben Franklin's Website: Privacy and Curiosity from Plymouth Rock to the Internet.* Providence, RI: Privacy Journal, 2004.

Smolla, Rodney. "Will Tabloid Journalism Ruin the First Amendment for the Rest of Us?" *DePaul Journal of Arts and Entertainment Law* (Fall 1998): 1–34.

Snowiss, Sylvia. "The Legacy of Justice Black." *Supreme Court Review* 1973 (1973): 187–252.

Speed, John Gilmer. "The Right of Privacy." *North American Review* 163 (1896): 64–74.

Spencer, Otha C. "Twenty Years of Life." PhD dissertation, University of Missouri, 1958.

Spigel, Lynn. *Make Room For TV: Television and the Family Ideal in Postwar America.* Chicago: University of Chicago Press, 1992.

Stern, Seth, and Stephen Wermiel. *Justice Brennan: Liberal Champion.* Boston: Houghton Mifflin Harcourt, 2010.

Stevens, John D. *Sensationalism and the New York Press.* New York: Columbia University Press, 1991.

Stole, Inger L. *Advertising at War: Business, Consumers, and Government in the 1940s.* Urbana: University of Illinois Press, 2012.

Stone, Geoffrey. "Justice Brennan and the Freedom of Speech: A First Amendment Odyssey." *University of Pennsylvania Law Review* 139 (1991): 1333–55.

Stone, Kurt F. *The Jews of Capitol Hill: A Compendium of Jewish Congressional Members.* Lanham, MD: Scarecrow Press, 2010.

Storrow, Richard F. "The Policy of Family Privacy: Uncovering the Bias in Favor of Nuclear Families in American Constitutional Law and Policy Reform." *Missouri Law Review* 66 (2001): 527–622.

Sumner, David. *The Magazine Century: American Magazines since 1900.* New York: Peter Lang, 2010.

"Supreme Court 1966 Term." *Harvard Law Review* 81 (1967): 69–109.

Swaine, Robert T. *The Cravath Firm and Its Predecessors,* vol. 2. New York: Ad Press, 1948.

Swanberg, W. A. *Luce and His Empire.* New York: Scribner, 1972.

Swanson, Charles E. "The Midcity Daily." *Journalism Quarterly* 26 (1949): 20–28.

Teel, Leonard *The Public Press, 1900–1945.* Westport, CT: Praeger, 2006.

Thalheimer, J. A., and J. R. Gerberick. "Reader Attitudes toward Questions of Newspaper Policy and Practice." *Journalism Quarterly* 12 (1935): 268, 270.

Thayer, Frank. "The Changing Libel Scene." *Wisconsin Law Review* 1943 (1943): 331–51.

Thompson, Edward K. *A Love Affair with Life and Smithsonian.* Columbia: University of Missouri Press, 1995.

Urofsky, Melvin. *The Warren Court: Justices, Rulings, and Legacy.* Santa Barbara, CA: ABC-CLIO, 2001.

Vance, W. R. "Freedom of Speech and of the Press." *Minnesota Law Review* 2 (1918): 239–60.

Vanderlan, Robert. *Intellectuals Incorporated: Politics, Art and Ideas in Henry Luce's Media Empire.* Philadelphia: University of Pennsylvania Press, 2011.

Veeder, Van Vechten. "The History and Theory of the Law of Defamation." *Columbia Law Review* 4 (1904): 1093–1126.

Wade, John W. "Defamation and the Right of Privacy." *Vanderbilt Law Review* 15 (1962): 1093–1126.

Wainwright, Loudon. *The Great American Magazine: An Inside History of Life.* New York: Knopf, 1986.

Walker, Stanley. *City Editor.* Baltimore, MD: Johns Hopkins University Press, 1999.

———. *In Defense of American Liberties: A History of the ACLU.* New York: Oxford University Press, 1999.

Warnock, John W. "Publisher's Treatment of Newsworthy Event Held Violation of Privacy Statute: *Hill v. Hayes.*" *Hastings Law Journal* 17 (1965): 383.

Warren, Earl. *The Memoirs of Earl Warren.* Garden City, NY: Doubleday, 1977.

Warren, Samuel D., and Louis D. Brandeis. "The Right to Privacy." *Harvard Law Review* 4 (1890): 193–220.

Weaver, Russell, and Geoffrey Bennett. "Is the New York Times Actual Malice Standard Really Necessary." *Louisiana Law Review* 4 (1993): 1–64.

Weinstein, Deborah. *The Pathological Family: Postwar America and the Rise of Family Therapy.* Ithaca, NY: Cornell University Press, 2013.

Weisberger, Bernard A. "Keeping the Free Press Free: Who Watches the Watchmen?" *Antioch Review* 13 (Autumn 1953): 329–40.

Welky, David. *Everything Was Better in America: Print Culture in the Great Depression.* Champaign: University of Illinois Press, 2008.

Westin, Alan F. *Privacy and Freedom.* New York: Atheneum, 1967.

White, G. Edward. *Earl Warren: A Public Life.* New York: Oxford University Press, 1982.

White, G. Edward. "The First Amendment Comes of Age: The Emergence of Free Speech in Twentieth-Century America." *Michigan Law Review* 95 (1996): 299–392.

White, Theodore. *In Search of History: A Personal Adventure.* New York: HarperCollins, 1979.

Whitman, James Q. "The Two Western Cultures of Privacy: Dignity Versus Liberty." *Yale Law Journal* 113 (2004): 1151–1222.

Williams, Ryan. "The Paths to *Griswold.*" *Notre Dame Law Review* 89 (2014): 2172–76.

Wilson, Sloan. *The Man in the Gray Flannel Suit.* New York: Simon & Schuster, 1955.

Winship, Michael. "The Rise of a National Book Trade System in the United States." In *A History of the Book in America*, vol. 4, edited by Carl F. Kaestle and Janice A. Radway. Chapel Hill: University of North Carolina Press, 2009.

Witcover, Jules. *The Resurrection of Richard Nixon.* New York: Putnam, 1970.

Whyte, William. *The Organization Man.* New York: Simon & Schuster, 1956.

Woodward, Bob, and Scott Armstrong. *The Brethren: Inside the Supreme Court.* New York: Simon & Schuster, 2005.

Young, William H. *The 1950s.* Westport, CT: Greenwood Press, 2004.

Zimmerman, Diane L. "Requiem for a Heavyweight: A Farewell to Warren and Brandeis's Privacy Tort." *Cornell Law Review* 68 (1983): 291–367.

Index